A GUIDE TO
THE HISTORY OF
CALIFORNIA

A GUIDE TO THE HISTORY OF CALIFORNIA

Edited by Doyce B. Nunis, Jr., *and* Gloria Ricci Lothrop

REFERENCE GUIDES TO STATE HISTORY AND RESEARCH

Light T. Cummins and Glen Jeansonne, Series Editors

GREENWOOD PRESS
NEW YORK • WESTPORT, CONNECTICUT • LONDON

Library of Congress Cataloging-in-Publication Data

A Guide to the history of California / edited by Doyce B. Nunis, Jr.,
  and Gloria Ricci Lothrop.
    p. cm.— (Reference guides to state history and research)
    Includes index.
    ISBN 0-313-24970-9 (lib. bdg. : alk. paper)
    1. California—History—Sources—Bibliography. 2. California—
Historiography. 3. Archives—California—Directories.
4. Historical libraries—California—Directories. I. Nunis, Doyce
Blackman. II. Lothrop, Gloria Ricci. III. Series.
Z1261.G85 1989
[F861]
016.9794—dc19   88-15488

British Library Cataloguing in Publication Data is available.

Library of Congress Catalog Card Number: 88-15488
ISBN: 0-313-24970-9

First published in 1989

Greenwood Press, Inc.
88 Post Road West, Westport, Connecticut 06881

Printed in the United States of America

∞™

The paper used in this book complies with the
Permanent Paper Standard issued by the National
Information Standards Organization (Z39.48-1984).

10 9 8 7 6 5 4 3 2 1

CONTENTS

INTRODUCTION

THE PHENOMENAL GROWTH of California is one of the spectacular aspects of its history. Founded as imperial Spain's last colonial venture in 1769, it hardly prospered, let alone grew under Spanish rule. With Mexico's independence from Spain, 1821, California witnessed important changes, not least of which was the arrival of foreign immigrants with Anglo surnames. This Anglo population contributed to broadening the base of the province's economic life. Agriculture, commerce, lumbering, and trade were greatly stimulated. On the eve of the United States' war with Mexico in 1846, one objective of which was to obtain California, the non-Indian population was probably less than 15,000, with the heaviest concentration in and around Los Angeles. On July 7, 1846, American naval forces officially occupied California, a conquest sanctioned by purchase in the Treaty of Guadalupe Hidalgo, February 2, 1848.

With American acquisition, few dreamed that the former Mexican province would be ready for territorial status, let alone statehood, for decades to come. Fate decreed otherwise. Ten days before the purchase of the Mexican Cession, a lowly New Jersey-born mechanic, James W. Marshall, working in partnership with John A. Sutter, discovered gold in a millrace at Coloma on the American River. What ensued was the modern world's first great gold rush. Less than two years later, pastoral California became the thirty-first state in the Union, admitted on September 9, 1850. A century and a decade later California became the most populous state in the nation. It remains so today.

It would appear a safe assumption to declare that beginning with the Mexican War California has received continuing national attention. Not that the state has always held center stage, to be sure, but it has received more than passing notice, especially in the large number of published diaries, travel accounts, journals, letters, reports, and commentaries. California has also been ably served by an enormous outpouring and growing body of published literature detailing its history from pre-European contact down to the present. In addition, archival materials have been collected and preserved from the outset: first by Spain, then Mexico, then provincial California, finally through statehood and on down through the decades that have followed. Fortunately, much of these archival materials are located in the state.

Thus, one of the objectives of this guide is to open this world of published and archival materials to individuals who wish to undertake investigations and research into the myriad facets of California's rich history. The guide does not pretend to be definitive, but it does strive to provide a basic footing for research to novice and scholar alike. The richness of the materials available is eloquently attested to by the essays that follow.

The guide has been conveniently broken into two parts. Part I presents both a chronological and topical approach to the essential elements that have shaped California's history. This includes particular attention to its varied ethnicity as well as to specific topics that have played a major role in shaping the state's development. Part II is focused on source materials with particular attention to archival depositories and the respective holdings, as well as the state's major and/or important manuscript collections. Each of the essays that elaborates specific periods, topics, or holdings has been written by experts in their respective field or institution. Their credentials are detailed in the concluding pages of the book, "About the Contributors." As editors of the guide we wish to express our appreciation to all the contributors for their individual contribution. Without these valued colleagues' cooperation, the completion of the guide would not have been possible.

Wherever possible and pertinent, essays contain references to printed sources, as well as documentary sources. The latter includes attention to photographic holdings, for photographs are an essential ingredient in the study of history. To shorten citations for periodicals and institutions, a list of abbreviations has been created and the reader should refer to it for complete titles.

It is the editors' hope that this guide will stimulate interest and research into the Golden State's history, hopefully resulting in new insights that will find their way to publications. Although a large body of published materials is available, there remain many facets and topics yet to be explored and plumbed by eager scholars, young and old.

Users of this guide should be aware that California's history has been made more accessible by a growing number of bibliographies, both specialized and topical. Reader attention is called to several particularly valuable bibliographical aids, notably Margaret M. Rocq, ed., *California Local History: A Bibliography and Union List of Library Holdings* (2nd rev. ed., Stanford, 1970) and *The Supplement* (Stanford, 1976). The classic work by Robert E. Cowan and Robert G. Cowan, *A Bibliography of the History of California, 1510-1930* (San Francisco, 1933), remains highly useful. Researchers should also take note that all the past and current single-volume state histories have bibliographies usually at the end of each chapter or at the end of the text. The more current state histories have been authored by John W. Caughey and Norris Hundley, Jr.; Walton Bean and James J. Rawls; Andrew F. Rolle; and W. H. Hutchinson—all of which have gone through several or more editions. The reader should seek out the latest edition. Also useful is *The Golden State Series* under the editorship of John A. Schutz and Norris Hundley, Jr. (San Francisco, 1980-present), which centers on topical subjects relating to California history. Each of these succinct overviews contains a bibliographical essay relating to each book's individual subject.

Another bibliography which is especially helpful is Francis J. Weber, comp., "A Bibliography of California Bibliographies," *SCQ*, 50 (March 1968). Though dated, it is presently under revision, and an updated version will be published in the same quarterly in 1989 or 1990.

Since graduate theses and doctoral dissertations are omitted from the chapters devoted herein to "The Historical Literature," the reader should be made aware that there is a rich body of such studies in the state's institutions of higher learning. A helpful, though dated bibliography is Pamela A. Bleich, "A Study of Graduate Research in California History in California Colleges and Universities," published in six parts in *CHSQ*, 43 (September/December 1964); 44 (March/June/September/December 1965). Entries are alphabetical by institution, then by author, and each entry is annotated. Since the list is dated, it should be noted that most institutions' reference libraries maintain a current special card catalogue of their theses and dissertations. Other disciplines other than history should also be consulted where appropriate to the researcher's interest. Unfortunately, it is more difficult to locate out-of-state graduate studies. The best reference tool would be to consult *Dissertations on Microfilm*, an annual publication. Most institutions will send graduate studies on interlibrary loan, while microprint copies may be purchased for studies on microfilm at fairly reasonable costs. Consult a reference librarian when such need arises.

Lastly, researchers should know that the state's two oldest historical periodicals, *California History* and *Southern California Quarterly*, both published under previous varying titles, have cumulative indexes. In addition, there exist several excellent card indexes to California newspapers. The most important are the California Section, State Library, which has indexes of San Francisco, San Jose, Sacramento, and Fresno newspapers and the San Diego Public Library, which maintains a card index to its city's newspapers. Los Angeles is served poorly. The University of California, Los Angeles, Department of Special Collections has an index to the Los Angeles *Star*, 1850-1868, and the Los Angeles *Times* has been printing an ongoing index beginning in 1970, but there are no aids for the century in between these two files. Since many California newspapers are on microfilm and are available on interlibrary loan, consult *Newspaper Holdings of the California State Library*, comp. by Marianne Leach (Sacramento, 1986). For statewide holdings and locations, see *Newspapers in California* (Sacramento, 1985).

Finally, a word to those interested in working in local history. The American Association for State and Local History has sponsored a series of publications relating to such research. The first was *Nearby History: Exploring the Past Around You* (Nashville, 1982) by David E. Kyvig and Myron A. Marty, the series editors. This invaluable book shows how to find and use published, unpublished, visual, and material records; collect information through interviews; use photographs, documents, and objects; and connect individual investigations with broader historical issues. A second title, *On Doing Local History* (Nashville, 1986) by Carol Kammen, offers a new way for local historians to think about their work and question the sources they use and the subjects they investigate. A third, *Local Schools: Exploring Their History* (Nashville, 1986) by Ronald F. Butchart, indicates that future titles in this series will be devoted to specific research topics.

Also useful for the serious researcher is Barbara Allen and Lynwood Montell, *From Memory to History: Using Oral Sources in Local Historical Research* (Nashville, 1981) and Willa K. Baum, *Transcribing and Editing Oral History* (Nashville, 1977), both of which are indispensable if one wishes to record the immediate past from individuals who played roles in various walks of life that touch our lives. With the advent of video tapes, Brad Jolly, *Videotaping Local History* (Nashville, 1982) offers basic instruction in using equipment, coupled with techniques on oral interviews with video recordings. This new dimension of research is aided by William Fletcher's *Talking Your Roots: A Family Guide to Tape Recording and Videotaping Oral History* (New York, 1986).

Finally, those who wish to pursue the more established tradition of working toward a published study will find immensely useful the American Association for State and Local History's important book, Thomas E. Felt, *Researching, Writing, and Publishing Local History* (2nd ed.; Nashville, 1981).

In bringing this guide to publication, the editors wish to acknowledge the help afforded by their respective institutions for aid and assistance. In particular they wish to express their gratitude to departmental secretarial staff who did yeoman service in preparing the final copy: at the University of Southern California, hats off to Brenda R. Johnson and Martha Rothermel as well as several work-study students who prepared Xerox copies and research assistant Lori Lisowski who helped with the task of proofreading; at California State Polytechnic University, Pomona, thanks to Sandra Sharp, who accomplished much with efficiency and dispatch.

Every effort has been made to render a correct text. Should users discover an inadvertent error or serious omission, the editors would appreciate receiving such information, for the ultimate responsibility for the book's content is ours alone.

ABBREVIATIONS

The following abbreviations are used in citations for the following periodicals and institutions:

AAAPSS	Annals of the American Academy of Political and Social Sciences
AH	Agricultural History
AHR	American Historical Review
AJ	Amerasia Journal
APHSSC	Annual Publication Historical Society of Southern California
AW	American West
A&W	Arizona & the West
CH	California History
CHQ	California Historical Quarterly
CHSQ	California Historical Society Quarterly
HLQ	Huntington Library Quarterly
JAH	Journal of American History
JES	Journal of Ethnic Studies
JMAH	Journal of Mexican American History
JNH	Journal of Negro History
JSDH	Journal of San Diego History
JW	Journal of the West
LH	Labor History

MVHR	*Mississippi Valley Historical Review*
NMHR	*New Mexico Historical Review*
NPQ	*Northwest Pacific Quarterly*
PH	*Pacific Historian*
PHR	*Pacific Historical Review*
PNQ	*Pacific Northwest Quarterly*
QHSSC	*Quarterly Historical Society Southern California*
SCQ	*Southern California Quarterly*
SHQ	*Southwestern Historical Quarterly*
WHQ	*Western Historical Quarterly*
WPQ	*Western Political Quarterly*
WSJHQ	*Western States Jewish Historical Quarterly*

PART ONE

THE HISTORICAL LITERATURE

1

HISPANIC CALIFORNIA, 1542–1848

IRIS H.W. ENGSTRAND AND DANIEL TYLER

HISPANIC CALIFORNIA, which encompassed the period from 1533 to 1821 under Spanish rule and to 1846 as a Mexican province, included both Baja and Alta California. For a time these were considered a political as well as a geographic unit. Early contemporary histories of the southern peninsula were mostly authored by Jesuits, and many have been translated, edited, and published in the *Baja California Travel Series* (48 vols. to date; Los Angeles, 1965–1987). A good one-volume treatment of the peninsula is Pablo L. Martínez, *History of Baja California* (México, 1956). Indispensable is Ellen C. Barrett, *Baja California, 1535–1956* (Los Angeles, 1957) and *Baja California II, 1535–1964* (Los Angeles, 1967), the major bibliography.

After expulsion of the Jesuits in 1767, Franciscans were assigned to continue missionary activity among the native population; under military direction, they assisted in Spain's expansion northward. Fray Francisco Palóu, student and companion of Fray Junípero Serra, chronicled the history of this early era in *Noticias de la Nueva California*, completed in 1783 (trans. and published as *Historical Memoirs of New California* by Herbert E. Bolton, 4 vols., Berkeley, 1926), and in his biographical study *Vida del Padre Serra*, ed. and trans. by C. S. Williams (Pasadena, 1913) and a more recent edition by Maynard Geiger (Washington, D.C., 1955).

At the time that Mexico gained independence from Spain in 1821, California was sparsely populated with four presidios, three pueblos, twenty Franciscan missions, and about twenty private ranchos. During this time changes in the governorship occurred regularly and the missions, after several attempts, were secularized by 1836. Good contemporary accounts begin with Alfred Robinson's *Life in California* (New York, 1846). Robinson, a native of Massachusetts and

California resident, 1829-1842, wrote a short history of the area, the first by an American. Richard Henry Dana, Jr., described his impressions of the Mexican province during a sixteen-month visit, 1834-1836, in his best-selling *Two Years Before the Mast*, first published in New York in 1840 and reprinted numerous times. Given to greater imagination was James Ohio Pattie, who wrote of his fur trader and captive experiences in San Diego, 1829-1830, in *The Personal Narrative of a Voyage to the Pacific and Mexico, June 20, 1824-August 30, 1830*, ed. by Timothy Flint (Cincinnati, 1831). The Mexican period also produced a descriptive British account, Alexander Forbes, *California: a History of Upper and Lower California* (London, 1839).

Other narratives and journals produced by foreign travelers and American visitors have been reprinted in the *Early California Travel Series* (50 vols.; Los Angeles, 1951-1961). Also useful are Thomas Farnham's *Travels in the Californias and Scenes in the Pacific Ocean* (New York, 1844) and Henry Thomes' *On Land & Sea, or California in the Years 1843-44-45* (Chicago, 1888).

It was not until the 1870s that a new generation of historians, or chroniclers, began to show an interest in preserving the state's Hispanic past. Fortunately, these individuals gathered a tremendous amount of information which contributed to three multivolume state histories. First, and best known, is the thirty-nine-volume series published by San Francisco book-seller Hubert H. Bancroft (1884-1890). Seven volumes are devoted specifically to Alta California, 1542-1848, and made more accessible by *The Zamorano Index to History of California by . . . Bancroft* (2 vols.; Los Angeles, 1985). The series also includes *History of the North Mexican States* (1531-1889); *History of the Northwest Coast* (1543-1846); and *California Pastoral, 1769-1848* (San Francisco, 1888), which offers a romanticized story of life on the ranchos.

Bancroft's thick, heavily footnoted volumes (about 700 pages each) were partially written by himself, but the majority were produced by an able staff of paid assistants. He was also helped by the native-born and well-educated Mariano Guadalupe Vallejo, who prepared his own extensive manuscript history. The most valuable contribution of the series is the extensive footnoting to primary sources, including Spanish and Mexican government documents, letters and diaries of early residents, interviews of first generation pioneers, maps, and other memorabilia, most of which form the core of the Bancroft Library collections, University of California, Berkeley. Volumes 2-5 include a "Pioneer Register" listing nearly every person living in California during the Hispanic period, also separately published (Los Angeles, 1964).

Another writer, Theodore H. Hittell, made use of autobiographical accounts and California Hispanic archives to produce a highly detailed *History of California* (4 vols.; San Francisco, 1885-1897). The first two volumes are devoted to the period before 1850 and emphasize activities of the military governors. Josiah Royce, *California* (Cambridge, Mass., 1886), though dated, is of interest because of his views on the Mexican War.

After the turn of the twentieth century, another amateur historian, Zoeth S.

Eldredge, edited many first-generation accounts in his *History of California* (5 vols.; New York, 1915). A lengthy and highly detailed history of the Franciscan missions was written by Zephyrin Engelhardt, OFM, entitled *The Missions and Missionaries in California* (4 vols.; San Francisco, 1908-1915), which utilized the personal correspondence of the missionaries and other primary documents of the period. He also prepared individual histories of sixteen of the twenty-one Franciscan missions. Francis J. Weber's twenty-three-volume *Documentary History of the California Missions* (Los Angeles, 1975-1987) is also useful.

Although the early works must be used with some caution, they utilized archival materials that were later lost in the San Francisco fire of 1906; numerous documents cited in volumes written before 1906 no longer exist. Many of the manuscripts in what is called the California Archives today are copies or summaries made by Bancroft's assistants during the preparation of his series. An excellent description and evaluation of these materials is J. N. Bowman, "History of the Provincial Archives of California," *SCQ*, 64 (Spring 1982).

It was during the early twentieth century that university-trained historians began to produce scholarly works on California. One of the first, and still of great value, is Irving B. Richman, *California Under Spain and Mexico, 1535-1857* (Boston, 1911). Herbert E. Bolton edited important documents for his *Spanish Exploration in the Southwest, 1542-1706* (New York, 1916) and prepared a *Guide to Materials for the History of the United States in the Principal Archives of Mexico* (Washington, D.C., 1913). He also translated and edited several primary documents: Francisco Eusebio Kino's *Historical Memoir of Pimeria Alta* (2 vols.; Berkeley, 1919); Crespi's narrative account of the expedition to California in 1769, *Fray Juan Crespi: Missionary Explorer on the Pacific Coast* (Berkeley, 1927); and *Anza's California Expeditions* (5 vols.; Berkeley, 1930), which documented the opening of a trail from Sonora to Monterey.

Charles E. Chapman produced *The Founding of Spanish California: The Northwestward Expansion of New Spain, 1687-1783* (New York, 1916) and *A History of California: The Spanish Period* (New York, 1921). Chapman, who researched in Spain, prepared a *Catalogue of Materials in the Archivo General de Indias for the History of the Pacific Coast and the American Southwest* (Berkeley, 1919). George Davidson published *The Discovery of San Francisco Bay* (San Francisco, 1907) and wrote widely on Spanish voyages of discovery along the Pacific coast, as well as on Francis Drake and the origin and meaning of the name California.

One of the most productive scholars on the history of Spanish Pacific exploration was Henry R. Wagner, a retired mining engineer. His *California Voyages, 1539-1541* (San Francisco, 1925) and *Sir Francis Drake's Voyage Around the World: Its Aims and Achievements* (San Francisco, 1926) led to further study into the primary logs and other materials of naval exploration. He wrote *Spanish Voyages to the Northwest Coast of America in the Sixteenth Century* (San Francisco, 1929), *Apocryphal Voyages to the Northwest Coast of America* (Worcester, 1931), *Spanish Exploration in the Strait of Juan de Fuca* (Santa Ana, 1933),

Cartography of the Northwest Coast of America to the Year 1800 (2 vols.; Berkeley, 1937); and *The Spanish Southwest, 1542-1794: An Annotated Bibliography* (Albuquerque, 1937).

On the subject of exploration and travel in the Spanish period, books and articles generally cover the initial period of sixteenth-century discovery or the later eighteenth-century colonization phase. Those who have written on the early years include Maurice G. Holmes, *From New Spain by Sea to the Californias, 1519-1668* (Glendale, 1963) and Peter Gerhard, *Pirates on the West Coast of New Spain, 1575-1742* (Glendale, 1960). Harry Kelsey has answered some long-standing questions in his biography, *Juan Rodriguez Cabrillo* (San Marino, 1986) and in his "Mapping the California Coast: The Voyages of Discovery, 1533-1543," *A&W*, 26 (Winter 1984). W. Michael Mathes, who has produced a number of works on Baja California, has traced some "Apocryphal Tales of the Island of California and Straits of Anian," *CH*, 62 (Spring 1983) and given new dimension to Sebastián Vizcaíno in *Vizcaíno and Spanish Expansion in the Pacific Ocean* (San Francisco, 1968); "Sebastián Vizcaíno and San Diego Bay," *JSDH*, 18 (Spring 1972); and "California's First Explorer," *PH*, 25 (Fall 1981). A pioneer work on the Philippine trade is William L. Schurz, *The Manila Galleon* (New York, 1939).

Works on Sir Francis Drake's voyage to California abound. Since the location of Drake's Pacific Coast landing has not been confirmed by archeological findings, except for the controversial Plate of Brass, there is little agreement on the site. A good introduction is *The World Encompassed by Sir Francis Drake* (London, 1628; Cleveland, 1966). The Fall 1974 *CHQ* issue, "The Francis Drake Controversy: His California Anchorage, June 17–July 23, 1579," has articles by Robert Power, V. Aubrey Neasham, and Raymond Aker, while Warren L. Hanna has written *Lost Harbor: The Controversy over Drake's California Anchorage* (Berkeley, 1979), the best summary to date.

Donald C. Cutter, who has worked extensively in Spanish and Mexican archives, edited *The California Coast: A Bilingual Edition of Documents from the Sutro Collection* (Norman, 1969), which covers the period from 1584 through 1774. A specialist in eighteenth-century Spanish expeditions, he has also written *Malaspina in California* (San Francisco, 1960). Works by students of Cutter, on related fields, include: Michael Thurman, *The Naval Department of San Blas: New Spain's Bastion for Alta California and Nootka, 1767-1798* (Glendale, 1967) and Iris H.W. Engstrand, *Spanish Scientists in the New World: The Eighteenth Century Expeditions* (Seattle, 1981). David J. Weber, *New Spain's Far Northern Frontier: Essays on Spain in the American West, 1540-1821* (Albuquerque, 1979), contains articles pertaining to Pacific exploration and related areas of the Spanish Borderlands, a subject treated by John F. Bannon in *The Spanish Borderlands Frontier, 1713-1821* (New York, 1970).

Additional works concerning visits to the Pacific coast include a number of translations of original Spanish journals: John Galvin, ed., *The First Spanish Entry into San Francisco Bay 1775* (San Francisco, 1971); Iris H. Wilson

[Engstrand], ed., *Noticias de Nutka: An Account of Nootka Sound in 1792* (Seattle, 1970); and Lesley B. Simpson, ed., *California in 1792: The Expedition of José Longinos Martínez* (San Marino, 1938; San Francisco, 1961). Related works are Theodore E. Treutlein, *San Francisco Bay: Discovery and Colonization, 1769-1776* (San Francisco, 1968) and Frank M. Stanger and Alan K. Brown, *Who Discovered the Golden Gate? The Explorers' Own Accounts—How They Discovered a Hidden Harbor and at Last Found its Entrance* (San Mateo, 1969), for specifics on San Francisco; and Warren L. Cook, *Flood Tide of Empire: Spain and the Pacific Northwest, 1543-1819* (New Haven, 1973), for general coverage.

Overland exploration, with the exception of Jesuit activity in Baja California and the expedition of Francisco Vásquez de Coronado into the interior of the continent, begins with the arrival of the Portolá-Serra colonizing expedition of 1769. In addition to the original diaries mentioned above, a popular and well-illustrated summary is Richard Pourade, *Call to California* (San Diego, 1968). Bolton's five-volume work on Anza has been supplemented by Richard Pourade, *Anza Conquers the Desert* (San Diego, 1971) and John Galvin, ed., *A Record of Travels [of Garcés] in Arizona and California, 1775-1776* (San Francisco, 1965). Harlan Hague gives an excellent overall summary of southwestern travel in *The Road to California: The Search for a Southern Overland Route, 1540-1848* (Glendale, 1978).

The period following Vizcaíno's 1602 expedition to Alta California has been little considered except in terms of Jesuit missionary activities in Baja California and northwestern frontier areas of New Spain. Exceptions have been W. Michael Mathes, "Don Pedro Porter y Casanate: Admiral of the South Sea, 1611-1662," *SCQ*, 54 (Spring 1972) and Donald C. Cutter, "Plans for the Occupation of Upper California: A New Look at the 'Dark Age' from 1602 to 1769," *JSDH*, 24 (Winter 1978). The bulk of eighteenth-century treatment begins with the plans of José de Gálvez to occupy Alta California following shortly after the 1767 expulsion of the Jesuits, although more work needs to be done on the military and civilian aspects of the period.

A basic knowledge of Spanish viceregal government, frontier military procedures, and the office of commandant general of the interior provinces is necessary to the study of Hispanic California. Well-documented studies in these areas include: Bernard E. Bobb, *The Viceregency of Antonio María Bucareli in New Spain, 1771-1779* (Austin, 1962); Alfred B. Thomas, *Teodoro de Croix and the Northern Frontier of New Spain, 1776-1783* (Norman, 1941); Janet R. Fireman, *The Spanish Royal Corps of Engineers in the Western Borderlands* (Glendale, 1977); John Galvin, ed., *The Coming of Justice to California* (San Francisco, 1963); and Sidney B. Brinckerhoff and Odie B. Faulk, *Lancers for the King: A Study of the Frontier Military System of Northern New Spain, with a Translation of the Royal Regulations of 1772* (Phoenix, 1965).

Douglas S. Watson, ed., *The Spanish Occupation of California* (San Francisco, 1963), includes journals and diaries of the major participants in California colonization. Military participants in the exploration and settlement of the Californias are emphasized in Ernest J. Burrus, "Rivera y Moncada, Explorer and Military Commander of Both Californias, in the Light of His Diary and Other Contemporary Documents," *Hispanic American Historical Review*, 50 (November 1970) and Donald A. Nuttall, "The Gobernantes of Spanish Upper California: A Profile," *CHQ*, 51 (Fall 1972), which gives a sketch of all governors during the Spanish era. Nuttall's "Gaspar de Portolá: Disenchanted Conquistador of Spanish Upper California," *SCQ*, 53 (September 1971) and "Light Cast upon Shadows: The Non-California Years of Don Pedro Fages," *CHQ*, 56 (Fall 1977), contain further insights. Manuel Servín, in "The Quest for the Governorship of Spanish California," *CHQ*, 43 (March 1964), looks at the applicants for the position obtained by Diego de Borica in 1794. The only governor rendered a biography is *Felipe de Neve: First Governor of California* (San Francisco, 1971), by Edwin A. Beilharz.

Presidial life is discussed in Paige W. Christiansen, "The Presidio and the Borderlands: A Case Study," *JW*, 8 (January 1969); Bill Mason, "The Garrisons of San Diego Presidio: 1770-1794," *JSDH*, 24 (Fall 1978); John P. Langellier and Katherine M. Peterson, "Lances and Leather Jackets: Presidial Forces in Spanish Alta California, 1769-1821," *JW*, 20 (October 1981); Leon G. Campbell, "The Spanish Presidio in Alta California during the Mission Period, 1769-1784," *JW*, 16 (October 1977); and Richard S. Whitehead, "Alta California's Four Fortresses," *SCQ*, 65 (Spring 1983), which discusses recently discovered maps of the four presidios. Finally, David Langum, in "The Caring Colony: Alta California's Participation in Spain's Foreign Affairs," *SCQ*, 62 (Fall 1980), talks about the contributions of Californians to the Spanish wars, including the American Revolution.

Civilian life in the Spanish period is covered generally in Oakah L. Jones, Jr., *Los Paisanos: Spanish Settlers on the Northern Frontier of New Spain* (Norman, 1979); Dora P. Crouch, Daniel J. Garr, and Axel I. Mundigo, *Spanish City Planning in North America* (Cambridge, Mass., 1982), which includes a good study of the city planning ordinances under Spain's Laws of the Indies; and in the older, but useful standard work of Frank W. Blackmar, *Spanish Institutions of the Southwest* (Baltimore, 1891). Works covering specific topics include: Francis F. Guest, "Municipal Institutions in Spanish California," *CHQ*, 46 (December 1967); Oscar O. Winther, "The Story of San José, 1777-1869, California's First Pueblo," *CHSQ*, 14 (March/June 1935); Harry Kelsey, "A New Look at the Founding of Old Los Angeles," *CHQ*, 55 (Winter 1976); and Howard J. Nelson, "The Two Pueblos of Los Angeles: Agricultural Village and Embryo Town," *SCQ*, 59 (Spring 1977).

Additional specialized studies are Francis F. Guest, "The Establishment of the Villa de Branciforte," *CHQ*, 41 (March 1962); Daniel Garr, "Villa de Branciforte: Innovation and Adaptation on the Frontier," *The Americas*, 55 (Summer 1978) and "Power and Priorities: Church-State Boundary Disputes in Spanish California," *CH*, 57 (Winter 1978); Benjamin F. Gilbert, "Spain's Port of San

Francisco, 1755-1822," *JW*, 20 (July 1981); and John B. McGloin, "William A. Richardson, Founder and First Resident of Yerba Buena," *JW*, 5 (October 1966). Augusta Fink, "Old Monterey: The Romance of California's First Capital as Revealed through its Historic Adobes," *AW*, 16 (November/December 1979) and James Culleton, *Indians and Pioneers of Old Monterey* (Fresno, 1950) cover Monterey's development into the Mexican period. Richard Pourade's *History of San Diego: The Explorers* (San Diego, 1960) and *Time of the Bells* (San Diego, 1961) give good overviews of San Diego's Hispanic past.

Mission and missionary history in California begins with the 1697 founding of the first Jesuit mission at Loreto, Baja California. In addition to Bolton, *Rim of Christendom* (New York, 1936) and the pertinent volumes of the *Baja California Travel Series*, there are the classic general works by Peter M. Dunne, *Pioneer Black Robes on the West Coast of New Spain* (Berkeley, 1940), *Pioneer Jesuits in Northern Mexico* (Berkeley, 1944), and *Black Robes in Lower California* (Berkeley, 1952). The transition period between the eras of the Jesuits and Franciscans is presented in Kieran McCarty, *A Spanish Frontier in the Enlightened Age: Franciscan Beginnings in Sonora and Arizona, 1767-1770* (Washington, D.C., 1981). On the Dominicans, who replaced the Franciscans in 1772, Peveril Meigs, *The Dominican Mission Frontier of Lower California* (Berkeley, 1935), provides details.

There is abundant information on Franciscan activities in Upper California due in large part to the work of the American Academy of Franciscan History. A good beginning is Maynard Geiger, *Franciscan Missionaries in Hispanic California, 1769-1848: A Biographical Dictionary* (San Marino, 1969), which gives short sketches on every missionary. Philosophical backgrounds are found in Iris Engstrand, "The Enlightenment in Spain: Influences on New World Policy," *The Americas*, 61 (April 1985) and Francis F. Guest, "Mission Colonization and Political Control in Spanish California," with a commentary by David Piñera Ramírez, *JSDH*, 24 (Winter 1978).

The life of Serra is detailed in Geiger's *The Life and Times of Fray Junípero Serra* (2 vols.; Washington, D.C., 1959) and Antonine Tibesar, trans. and ed., *The Writings of Fray Junípero Serra* (4 vols.; Washington, D.C., 1955-1966). The most recent popular biography is Don DeNevi and Noel F. Moholy, *Junípero Serra* (San Francisco, 1985), based on Geiger's definitive treatment. Francis J. Weber has given a good summary of writings in "California's Serrana Literature," *SCQ*, 51 (December 1969) and *Some Fugitive Glimpses at Fray Junípero Serra* (Los Angeles, 1983). The September/October 1984 issue of *The Californians* was devoted to Serra. Fermín Francisco de Lasuén, second Father President of the California missions, can be studied in Finbar Kenneally, ed. and trans., *Writings of Lasuén* (Washington, D.C., 1965) and Francis F. Guest, *Fermín Francisco de Lasuén: A Biography* (Washington, D.C., 1973).

Life at the missions from an economic standpoint is covered in Robert Archibald, *Economic Aspects of the California Missions* (Washington, D.C., 1978), whereas Kurt Baer discusses the physical structures in *Architecture of the*

California Missions (Berkeley, 1958). Various aspects of mission life are included in Edith B. Webb, *Indian Life at the Old Missions* (Reprint ed.; Lincoln, 1982). Francis F. Guest, "Cultural Perspectives on California Mission Life," *SCQ*, 65 (Spring 1983) and "Junípero Serra and His Approach to the Indians," *SCQ*, 67 (Fall 1985) are illuminating. Other useful studies are Lesley B. Simpson, ed., and Paul Nathan, trans., *Letters of José Señan* (San Francisco, 1962); Patricia M. Bauer, "The Beginnings of Tanning in California," *CHQ*, 23 (March 1954); and George W. Hendry, "The Adobe Brick as an Historical Source," *AH*, 5 (July 1931). Francis J. Weber has written about non-mission chapels in Spanish California in "California's *Caminito Real*," *CHQ*, 54 (Spring 1975).

Some works taking the description of missions through the process of restoration include: Robert S. Smilie, *The Sonoma Mission, San Francisco Solano de Sonoma* ... (Fresno, 1975); Gerald McKevitt, "From Franciscan Mission to Jesuit College: A Troubled Transition at Mission Santa Clara," *SCQ*, 58 (Summer 1976); Nicholas M. Magalousis and Paul M. Martin, "Mission San Juan Capistrano: Preservation and Excavation of a Spanish Colonial Landmark," *Archaeology*, 36 (May/June 1981); Robert S. Aiken, "The Spanish Missions of Alta California: Rise, Decline, and Restoration," *Pioneer America*, 15 (March 1983); and Fred C. Hageman and Russell C. Ewing, *An Archeological and Restoration Study of Mission La Purísima Concepción*, ed. by Richard S. Whitehead (Santa Barbara, 1980). Norman Neuerburg discusses mission decoration in "The Function of Prints in California Missions," *SCQ*, 67 (Fall 1985) and *The Decoration of the California Missions* (Santa Barbara, 1987).

Pioneer anthropologist Alfred E. Kroeber worked at the University of California, Berkeley, during the Bolton years in the closely related field of California Indian studies. He produced his monumental *Handbook of the Indians of California* (Washington, D.C., 1925), numerous monographs, and trained many anthropologists. His wife Theodora worked with him and wrote several books, including *Ishi in Two Worlds: A Biography of the Last Wild Indian in North America* (Berkeley, 1961), a study of a California native.

Some general works on Indians include *Handbook of North American Indians: California*, vol. 8, ed. by Robert F. Heizer (Washington, D.C., 1978) and C. Hart Merriam, *Studies of California Indians* (Berkeley, 1955), which attempts to measure the effect of white contact. More recently James J. Rawls, *Indians and California: The Changing Image* (Norman, 1984), surveyed Indian life from pre-Columbian times to the late nineteenth century.

Indians played an important role in influencing the structure of Hispanic society in California and considerable literature is available on individual Indian groups. Sherburne F. Cook, *The Conflict Between the California Indian and White Civilization, I, The Indian Versus the Spanish Mission* (Berkeley, 1943), asked some difficult questions about the effects of mission life on California Indians to 1834. In Part II, *The Physical and Demographic Reaction of the Nonmission Indians in Colonial and Provincial California* (Berkeley, 1943), he compared the non-Mission and Mission Indians, concluding that the former were better prepared to adapt to challenges presented by Spaniards and Mexicans than were the latter. Both of these volumes were later published under the title *The Conflict Between the California Indian and White Civilization* (Berkeley, 1976). Cook and Woodrow Borah collaborated on *Essays in Population History: Mexico and California*, vol. 3 (Berkeley, 1979), which contains information on vital statistics of California's northern missions, data on the non-Indian population, and suggestions for research on related matters. Francis F. Guest challenges Cook's analysis in "An Examination of the Thesis of S. F. Cook on the Forced Conversion of Indians in the California Missions," *SCQ*, 61 (Spring 1979), as does Clement Meighan in "Indians and California Missions," *SCQ*, 69 (Summer 1987), while Harry Kelsey questions Cook's population statistics in "European Impact on the California Indians, 1530-1830," *The Americas*, 41 (April 1985).

Robert F. Heizer wrote and edited a number of Indian studies, including the new *Handbook of North American Indians: California*. Other studies include *The California Indians: A Source Book*, with M. A. Whipple (Berkeley, 1951); *Languages, Territories, and Names of California Indian Tribes* (Berkeley, 1966); *Almost Ancestors: The First Californians*, with Theodora Kroeber (San Francisco, 1968); *The Destruction of California Indians: A Collection of Documents from the Period 1847 to 1865* (Santa Barbara, 1974); *The Other Californians: Prejudice and Discrimination under Spain, Mexico and the United States to 1920*, with Alan F. Almquist (Berkeley, 1971); and *The Indians of California: A Critical Bibliography* (Bloomington, Ind., 1976). Heizer's *The California Indians vs. The United States of America* (Socorro, N.M., 1978) gives a description of Indian claims.

Several articles have focused on the inability, or unwillingness, of the Indians to adapt to mission life. George H. Phillips, for example, noted that many Indians withdrew en masse and willingly from the mission social system in his "Indians and the Breakdown of the Spanish Mission System in California," *Ethnohistory*, 21 (Fall 1974). Linda Sizelove, "Indian Adaptation to the Spanish Missions," *PH*, 22 (Winter 1978), focuses on the fundamental conflict between Indian and white cultures and the ravages brought about by white diseases.

Daniel Garr, "Planning, Politics and Plunder: The Missions and Indian Pueblos of Hispanic California," *SCQ*, 54 (Winter 1972), relates the failure of the mission system and the acquisitiveness of the non-Indian population, while James A. Sandos, "Levantamiento!: The 1824 Chumash Uprising Reconsidered," *SCQ*, 67 (Summer 1985), recounts a major native uprising at Santa Barbara. Jack D. Forbes, in *Warriors of the Colorado: The Yumas of the Quechan Nation and Their Neighbors* (Norman, 1965), discusses Mexican failure to assimilate or control the Yuman peoples. Jack Holtman's two articles in *Indian Historian*, "The Revolt of Estanislao" 3 (Spring 1970) and "The Revolt of Yozcolo: Indian Warrior in the Fight for Freedom" 3 (Winter 1970), portray the situation at Santa Clara where Indians were conducting guerrilla raids, 1829-1839. "Conflict at Monterey: Indian Horse Raiding, 1820-1850," *Journal of California*

Anthropology, 1 (Spring 1974) by Sylvia M. Broadbent, discusses how Indians stole horses from white settlements. George H. Phillips examines the plight of Indians who lost employment and turned to crime, while the topic of Indian resistance is incorporated into his *Chiefs and Challengers: Indian Resistance and Cooperation in Southern California* (Berkeley, 1975).

In regard to secularization of the missions, C. Alan Hutchinson, "The Mexican Government and the Mission Indians of Upper California," *The Americas*, 21 (April 1965), is a good place to begin. Hutchinson discusses the evolution of the secularization policy against the broader background of Mexican politics and thought. Manuel P. Servín has argued in "The Secularization of the California Missions: A Reappraisal," *SCQ*, 47 (June 1965), that the Franciscans were far too zealous and inflexible and that they contributed to their own demise. A useful synthesis of the secularization controversy is Gerald J. Geary, *The Secularization of the California Missions (1810–1846)* (Washington, D.C., 1934). David J. Weber discusses the role of organized religion after secularization in "Failure of a Frontier Institution: The Secular Church in the Borderlands under Independent Mexico, 1821–1846," *WHQ*, 12 (April 1981).

David J. Weber summed up the historiography of Mexican California in an article entitled, "Mexico's Far Northern Frontier, 1821–1854: Historiography Askew," *WHQ*, 7 (July 1976), which surveyed the status of Mexican Borderlands historical scholarship up to that year, noting that California had received by far the lion's share of attention. Much of the literature, moreover, has concentrated on American visitors to California and has neglected important Mexican figures. In comparison to the output by Americans about Americans, too little has been written by Mexican historians.

Another problem with Mexican period historiography is that too little has been written from Spanish language source materials. This is understandable owing to the fragmentary nature of document collections and the immense difficulty of reading the handwriting of unlettered officials whose records were often affected by inclement weather and untutored vermin. David J. Weber has used Mexican materials to produce a singular view of the Mexican Borderlands, *The Mexican Frontier, 1821–1846* (Albuquerque, 1982). It is a pioneering effort to synthesize information about the northern frontier from the perspective of Mexico's internal and international problems.

There are no book-length biographies of Mexican California governors. Good articles are Raymond K. Morrison, "Luis Antonio Argüello: First Mexican Governor of California," *JW*, 2 (April/July 1963) and Katherine Sheehey, "The Last Governor of Mexican California," *Desert*, 41 (November 1978), which concerns Pío Pico. A few chronicles of Mexican frontiersmen have been published: Joseph A. Thompson, *El Gran Capitán: José de la Guerra* (Los Angeles, 1961); Myrtle M. McKittrick, *Vallejo: Son of California* (Porland, Oreg., 1944); George Tays, "Mariano Guadalupe Vallejo and Sonoma," *CHSQ*, 16–17 (run serially 1937/1938); George R. Harding, *Don Agustín V. Zamorano: Statesman, Soldier,*

Craftsman, and California's First Printer (Los Angeles, 1934); and Terry E Stephenson, *Don Bernardo Yorba* (Los Angeles, 1941).

In his "Mexico's Far Northern Frontier, 1821-1845: A Critical Bibliography," *A&W*, 19 (Autumn 1977), David J. Weber separates the Mexican Borderlands into four areas and lists the most significant works dealing with California up through 1976. Because California has been the state most capable of supplying financial support to historians, presses, journals, and archives, and because its Hispanic history was notably shorter than that of New Mexico and progressed smoothly into the American period without the same sort of bitterness experienced in Texas, the volume of literature on Mexican California is relatively large, even though it is somewhat unbalanced, ethnocentric, and lacking in comparative studies.

One of the broadest categories of historical inquiry has been non-Mexican interest in California. British policies are discussed in Ephraim D. Adams, "English Interests in the Annexation of California," *AHR*, 14 (October 1908) and in Russell M. Posner, "A British Consular Agent in California: The Reports of James A. Forbes, 1843-1846," *SCQ*, 52 (June 1971). Lester G. Engelson, in "Proposals for the Annexation of California by England: In Connection with the Mexican Debt to British Bondholders, 1837-1846," *CHSQ*, 18 (June 1939), discusses how Mexico considered paying off its debt to the British by issuing land warrants to public lands in the Mexican Borderlands. Sheldon G. Jackson focused on Forbes in "Two Pro-British Plots in Alta California," *SCQ*, 55 (Summer 1973) and in "The British and the California Dream: Rumors, Myths, and Legends," *SCQ*, 57 (Fall 1975). For French interest, one should consult Abraham Nasatir, ed., *French Activities in California: An Archival Calendar Guide* (Stanford, 1945) and Rufus K. Wyllys, "French Imperialists in California," *CHSQ*, 7 (June 1929).

The Russian American Company's Fort Ross is described in detail by E. O. Essig, "The Russian Settlement at Ross," *CHSQ*, 12 (September 1933). Included in the article is a seven-page bibliography dealing generally with Russians in California. Another view of Ft. Ross and the Russian American Company can be found in Harvey Schwartz, "Fort Ross, California: Imperial Russian Outpost on America's Western Frontier, 1812-1841," *JW*, 18 (April 1979).

American infiltration into California has been the subject of extensive writing. John A. Hawgood, "The Pattern of Yankee Infiltration in Mexican California, 1821-1846," *PHR*, 27 (February 1958), is a brief overview of the Americans who came to California. Robert G. Cleland, "The Early Sentiment for the Annexation of California, 1835-1846," *SHQ*, 18 (July/October 1914/January 1915), is another general survey concentrating on President James K. Polk's preoccupation with British activities in California. Mexican officials were aware of United States interest in California and were bothered by the role of North American immigrants in local uprisings of 1836 and 1844 against the central government. But, as pointed out by Frank A. Knapp, Jr., "The Mexican Fear of

Manifest Destiny in California," in Thomas E. Cotner and Carlos E. Castañeda, eds., *Essays in American History* (Austin, 1958), Mexicans made no attempt to block further immigration of United States citizens into California, although a more determined posture in Texas might have been related to these events.

Perceptions of California's vulnerability also resulted from Commodore Thomas Ap Catesby Jones' seizure of Monterey in 1842. This incident is clearly described by Frank A. Knapp, Jr., "Preludios de la perdida de California," *Historia Mexicana*, 4 (October-December 1954). Written in Spanish and well documented, the article notes that Californians reacted only mildly to the incident, but in Mexico City it provoked cries of outrage. Articles focusing on military aspects include: George M. Brooke, Jr., "The Vest Pocket War of Commodore Jones," *PHR*, 31 (August 1962); Lou Ann Garrett, "The Commodore's Decision," *QHSSC*, 40 (December 1958); James High, "Jones at Monterey, 1842," *JW*, 5 (April 1966); and Lawrence C. Allin, "Log of Conquest," *PHR*, 37 (May 1968).

American immigration to California by way of the overland trails provides additional information on Mexican California. The *Old Spanish Trail: Santa Fe to Los Angeles* (Glendale, 1954) by LeRoy R. and Ann W. Hafen is a thorough study based on both primary and secondary sources. Other works on land routes include: George W. Beattie, "Reopening the Anza Road," *PHR*, 2 (March 1933); John Lowell Bean and William M. Mason, ed., *Diaries and Accounts of the Romero Expeditions in Arizona and California, 1823-1826* (Palm Springs, 1962); Harlan H. Hague, "The Search for a Southern Overland Route to California," *CHQ*, 55 (Summer 1976); Odie Faulk, *Destiny Road: The Gila Trail and the Opening of the Southwest* (New York, 1973); and Dennis G. Casebier, *The Mojave Road* (Norco, Calif., 1975).

Works abound on maritime routes to California and the overland California Trail. Several of the more significant volumes are: A. H. Clark, *The Clipper Ship Era, 1843-1869* (New York, 1910); Richard Henry Dana, Jr., *Two Years Before the Mast*—especially the two-volume edition ed. by John H. Kemble (Los Angeles, 1964), which can be used along with Robert F. Lucid, ed., *The Journal of Richard Henry Dana, Jr.* (Cambridge, Mass., 1968). The studies of Adele Ogden, in particular, *The California Sea Otter Trade, 1784-1848* (Berkeley, 1941), utilize Spanish and Mexican sources.

Works on exploration by land can begin with John C. Frémont, *Memoirs of My Life* (New York, 1956), ed. by Allan Nevins. Nevins also authored *Frémont, Pathmarker of the West* (2 vols.; New York, 1955). George R. Stewart, *The California Trail* (New York, 1962) is a good general survey of the principal immigrant route to California. Stewart also wrote *Ordeal by Hunger: The Story of the Donner Party* (Boston, 1960).

Mexican California, ed. by Carlos E. Cortes (New York, 1976), is a collection of essays which includes descriptions of California in 1828 and 1832 plus several other articles on the Mexican period. For revealing impressions of Mexican California by Americans, one should look at the narratives of William Heath Davis,

Sixty Years in California (San Francisco, 1889) and *Seventy-Five Years in California* (San Francisco, 1929; reprint, 1967); as well as Andrew F. Rolle's biography of Davis, *An American in California . . .* (San Marino, 1956; reprint, 1981). Absolutely indispensable are the voluminous papers of the U.S. consul, Thomas O. Larkin, *The Larkin Papers* (10 vols.; Berkeley and Los Angeles, 1951-1968), ed. by George P. Hammond.

The economic history of Mexican California touches on land ownership and speculation. Warren A. Beck and Ynez Haase's *Historical Atlas of California* (Norman, 1974) is a good point of departure because it contains a dozen maps devoted to Mexican period land grants. Richard R. Powell, *Compromises of Conflicting Claims: A Century of California Law in the Period 1760-1860* (Dobbs Ferry, N.Y., 1977), is a major contribution to California land grant history. David Langum, *The Anglo-American Legal Experience in Mexican California* (Norman, 1987), provides much needed information on Mexican law.

Studies of rancho life include: William H. Ellison and Francis Price, eds., *The Life and Adventures in California of Don Agustin Janssens, 1834-1856* (San Marino, 1953); Robert C. Gillingham, *Rancho San Pedro*, ed. by Judson Grenier (Rev. ed.; Los Angeles, 1983); Walter A. Tompkins, *Santa Barbara's Royal Rancho* (Berkeley, 1960); Sheldon G. Jackson, *A British Ranchero in Old California: the Life and Times of Henry Dalton and the Rancho Azusa* (Glendale, 1977); Wallace E. Smith, *This Land Was Ours: The Del Valles and Camulos* (Ventura, 1978); and Virginia L. Carpenter, *The Ranchos of Don Pacífico Ontiveros* (Fullerton, 1982). Robert G. Cowan, *Ranchos of California* (Fresno, 1956) lists all of the land grants from 1775 to 1846; W. W. Robinson, *Ranchos Become Cities* (Pasadena, 1939) concerns the Los Angeles area; and Cecil Moyer, *Historic Ranchos of San Diego* (San Diego, 1969) gives a brief history of those ranchos.

There are numerous works concerning ranching activities. Books concerning the lives of additional ranchero families include Albert Shumate, *Francisco Pacheco of Pacheco Pass* (Stockton, 1977); Susanna B. Dakin, *The Lives of William Hartnell* (Stanford, 1949) and *A Scotch Paisano: Hugo Reid's Life in California, 1832-1852* (Berkeley, 1939); Jane R. McClosky, *6 Horses and 10 Head: Two Hundred Years of the Rancho San Pascual, 1770-1970* (Pasadena, 1971); Doris M. Wright, *A Yankee in Mexican California: Abel Stearns, 1798-1848* (Santa Barbara, 1977); Joseph J. Hill, *The History of Warner's Ranch* (Los Angeles, 1927); and Sister Mary Therese Wittenburg, *The Machados and Rancho La Ballona* (Los Angeles, 1973).

Various aspects of trade are covered in Eleanor Lawrence, "Mexican Trade Between Santa Fe and Los Angeles, 1830-1848," *CHQ*, 10 (March 1931); Adele Ogden, "Captain Henry Fitch, San Diego Merchant, 1825-1849," *JSDH*, 27 (Fall 1981); and Mary H. Haggland, "Don José Antonio Aguirre: Spanish Merchant and Ranchero," *JSDH*, 29 (Winter 1983). Duncan and Dorothy Gleason, eds., *Beloved Sister: The Letters of James Henry Gleason, 1841-1859* (Glendale, 1978), illustrates the importance of a trader's life in Mexican California.

Historians have also looked for evidence that Mexicans were extracting precious metals prior to the Gold Rush. James M. Guinn addressed this question in his "Early Gold Discoveries in Southern California," *APHSSC*, III, Pt. 1 (1893). The trail was followed by J. N. Bowman, who contributed "The First Authentic Placer Mine in California," *QHSSC*, 31 (September 1949). Francis J. Weber added his views in "California's Gold Discovery: The Record Set Straight," *PH*, 18 (Fall 1974), singling out several gold prospecting activities in the Mission San Fernando district. Duane K. Hale, "California's First Mining Frontier and Its Influence on the Settlement of that Area," *JW*, 18 (January 1979), discusses early placer gold mining near San Luis Obispo and Los Angeles.

Agriculture has concerned only a few historians. Iris A. Wilson [Engstrand] wrote "Early Southern California Viniculture, 1830–1865," in *SCQ*, 39 (September 1957) and *William Wolfskill: Frontier Trapper to California Ranchero* (Glendale, 1965). Francis J. Weber discussed wine making in "The Mission Grape," *PH*, 23 (Fall 1979). Russian agricultural activities can be found in James R. Gibson, "Two New Chernykh Letters," *PH*, 12 (Summer 1968).

Readers will also find useful Woodrow J. Hansen, *The Search for Authority in California* (Oakland, 1960) and John A. Hawgood, ed., *First and Last Consul: Thomas Oliver Larkin and the Americanization of California* (Rev. ed.; Palo Alto, 1970). A good summation of the Mexican period of one area is Richard Pourade, *History of San Diego: The Silver Dons* (San Diego, 1963).

A brief glimpse of an active politician's life in California can be found in Arthur P. Botello, trans., *Don Pío Pico's Historical Narrative* (Glendale, 1973), ed. by Martin Cole. The statement of José Figueroa, published in *A Manifesto to the Mexican Republic*, trans. and ed. by C. Alan Hutchinson (Berkeley, 1978), can be used to show how Figueroa and the leaders of the Hijar-Padrés colony fell into difficulties as a result of ill-defined parameters of political responsibility. Two essays on the role of California alcaldes reveal the significance of this post in the Mexican period: Theodore Grivas, "Alcalde Rule: The Nature of Local Government in Spanish and Mexican California," *CHSQ*, 40 (March 1961) and Benjamin F. Gilbert, "Mexican Alcaldes of San Francisco, 1835-1846," *JW*, 2 (July 1963) are useful.

Works which treat urbanization, as well as the earlier stages of colonization, concentrate on individual communities. A pioneer study, John W. Dwinelle, *The Colonial History of California* (San Francisco, 1863), includes translations of numerous Spanish and Mexican documents. On Los Angeles are John W. Caughey, "The Distant Pawn of Empire," *CHQ*, 60 (Spring 1981); Neal Harlow, *Maps and Surveys of the Pueblo Lands of Los Angeles* (Los Angeles, 1976) and *Maps of the Pueblo Lands of San Diego, 1602-1874* (Los Angeles, 1988); Daniel J. Garr, "Los Angeles and the Challenge of Growth, 1836-1849," *SCQ*, 61 (Summer 1979); and Howard J. Nelson, "The Two Pueblos of Los Angeles: Agricultural Village and Embryo Town," *SCQ*, 59 (Spring 1977).

Monterey has long attracted historical curiosity, as in Augusta Fink, *Monterey: The Presence of the Past* (San Francisco, 1972); James Culleton, *Indians and Pioneers of Old Monterey* (Fresno, 1950); and David Hornbeck and Mary

Tucey, "Anglo Immigration and the Hispanic Town: A Study of Urban Change in Monterey, California, 1835-1860," *Social Science Journal*, 13 (April 1976).

Several Mexican colony ventures have attracted scholarly interest. By far the most extensive and illuminating study is that of C. Alan Hutchinson in *Frontier Settlement in Mexican California: The Hijar-Padrés Colony and Its Origins, 1769-1835* (New Haven, 1969). In a later article, "An Official List of the Members of the Hijar-Padrés Colony for Mexican California 1834," *PHR*, 42 (August 1973), Hutchinson notes that twice as many people were in the expedition as previously believed. Joyce C. Vickery discussed the settlement of San Salvador north of Riverside in *Defending Eden: New Mexican Pioneers in Southern California, 1830-1890* (Riverside, 1977). Also useful is John R. Bumgardt and William D. Putney, "San Salvador: New Mexican Settlement in California," *SCQ*, 59 (Winter 1977).

The social history of the Mexican period could be expanded in several areas. Perhaps the greatest attention has been directed at the medical profession. Studies include George D. Lyman, "The Scalpel Under Three Flags in California," *CHSQ*, 5 (June 1925); Sherburne F. Cook, "Smallpox in Spanish and Mexican California, 1770-1845," *Bulletin of the History of Medicine*, 7 (February 1939) and "The Epidemic of 1830-1833 in California and Oregon," University of California *Publications in American Archaeology and Ethnology*, 48 (May 1955); Rosemary K. Valle, "The Caesarean Operation in Alta California during the Franciscan Mission Period (1769-1833)," *Bulletin of the History of Medicine*, 48 (Summer 1974); and Robert J. Moes, "Smallpox Immunization in Alta California: A Story Based on José Estrada's 1821 Postscript," *SCQ*, 61 (Summer 1979).

Something of an historical debate on the true nature of the *Californio*, and how he was perceived by Americans, has surfaced in current historical literature. Leonard Pitt, in *The Decline of the Californios, 1846-1890* (Berkeley, 1966), portrayed them as badly beaten by Americans, while Cecil Robinson maintained that the first American visitors to the Mexican Borderlands formed their opinions of Mexicans from what they encountered on the frontier in *With the Ears of Strangers: The Mexican in American Literature* (Tucson, 1963), revised as *Mexico and the American Southwest in American Literature* (Tucson, 1977). The latter emphasized the impact of northern Mexican communities on Anglo-American prejudices.

David J. Weber, "Stereotyping of Mexico's Far Northern Frontier," in Manuel P. Servín, ed., *An Awakened Minority: The Mexican-Americans* (Los Angeles, 1974), reasoned that Americans brought their own prejudices in regard to miscegenation, racial inferiority, and the indolent Hispano to the Borderlands. David Langum in "Californios and the Image of Indolence," *WHQ*, 9 (April 1978) pointed out that the prejudices of Americans were similar to those of other Europeans, even of Spanish writers. Weber criticized this argument in "Here Rests Juan Espinosa: Towards a Clearer Look at the Image of the 'Indolent' Californios," *WHQ*, 10 (January 1979). Langum also studied American views in "Californio Women and the Image of Virtue," *SCQ*, 59 (Fall 1977) and concluded that the impressions of observers depended to a great extent on the class of women observed.

For a study of church activities in Mexican California, one might begin with Francis J. Weber, "Sources for Catholic History of California: A Biblio-Archival Survey," *SCQ*, 57 (Fall 1975). Weber's *California Catholicity* (Los Angeles, 1979) deals with the life of the church taken from articles published in various Catholic newspapers. The views of one notable priest have been analyzed by Michael C. Neri in "González Rubio and California Catholicism, 1846-1850," *SCQ*, 58 (Winter 1976). Since Hispanic California was essentially Catholic, no other non-Indian religions were practiced.

Basic data for family history appears in Marie E. Northrop, *Spanish-Mexican Families of Early California: 1769-1850* (2 vols.; New Orleans, 1976; Burbank, 1984). Very little has been done to explore the lives of California women, but an excellent overview is Joan M. Jensen and Gloria R. Lothrop, *California Women* (San Francisco, 1987). Gloria E. Miranda, "Hispano-Mexican Child-rearing Practices in Pre-American Santa Barbara," *SCQ*, 65 (Winter 1983), provides some interesting glimpses of their status in the Mexican period. Family ties are considered by John E. Baur, *Growing Up with California: A History of California's Children* (Los Angeles, 1978).

Further study of education, literacy, and language will prove useful in better understanding the Californians. Frank M. Woolley's "The Three Rs in Spanish California," *High Country*, 23 (Winter 1972), looks at education; Daniel Tyler's "The Mexican Teacher," *Red River Valley Historical Review*, 1 (Autumn 1974), compares education in California with the Mexican Borderlands; and Doyce B. Nunis, Jr., *Books in Their Sea Chests: Reading Along the Early California Coast* (Berkeley, 1964), notes how secular literature entered during the Mexican period. Sister Julie Bellefeuille's "Printing in California, 1831-1930," *PH*, 19 (Fall 1975), traces the development of printing from the first recorded line of type to the time when printing first won international recognition for California.

A variety of additional subjects have been considered by social historians. Dance was the subject of Anthony Shay in "Fandangos and Bailes: Dancing and Dance Events in Early California," *SCQ*, 64 (Summer 1982). Jeanne Van Nostrand studied California artists in *The First Hundred Years of Painting in California, 1775-1885* (San Francisco, 1980), with one chapter devoted to "Painting in Hispanic California, 1775-1845." *Adobes in the Sun: Portraits of a Tranquil Era* (San Francisco, 1972), with photographs by Morley Baer and text by Augusta Fink and Amelia Elkington, depicts pioneer living in nineteenth-century California. Very useful for the Mexican period is J. N. Bowman's "Weights and Measures of Provincial California," *CHSQ*, 30 (December 1951), which shows that standards varied according to time and place, even though official efforts were made to enforce a single system.

The Mexican War in California began in July 1846, although it can be linked with the Bear Flag Revolt that had just occurred in mid-June. Two good articles on this subject are John A. Hussey, "New Light on the Original Bear Flag," *CHQ*, 31 (September 1952) and John A. Hawgood, "John C. Frémont and the Bear Flag Revolution," *SCQ*, 44 (June 1962).

A significant work on the conduct of the war in California is Neal Harlow, *California Conquered: War and Peace on the Pacific, 1846–1850* (Berkeley, 1982). Another important work is Donald C. Biggs, *Conquer and Colonize: Stevenson's Regiment and California* (San Rafael, 1977). One study specifically concerning Indians is Albert L. Hurtado, "Controlling California's Indian Labor Force: Federal Administration of California Indian Affairs during the Mexican War," *SCQ*, 61 (Fall 1979). For those who wish to raise questions about the role of Mexicans and Indians during the war, economic conditions, family ties and loyalties, and a host of other issues which remain to be investigated, Norman E. Tutorow, ed., *The Mexican-American War: An Annotated Bibliography* (Westport, 1981), is a good place to look for primary sources, periodical literature, and some Mexican archival materials.

2

EARLY AMERICAN CALIFORNIA, 1848–1880

JOHN E. BAUR

THE GOLD RUSH has been recognized as one of the great American historical events, an episode that became a worldwide phenomenon. Its unexpected occurrence, the sudden and dramatic changes wrought, produced a vast and varied body of published literature. It still attracts the attention of outstanding historians, casual scholars, and dedicated amateurs.

Historians are divided on the issue as to whether California's history, particularly from 1849–1880, was unique. Theodore H. Hittell, Gertrude Atherton, and Robert G. Cleland would say yes, while Josiah Royce and Kevin Starr would see it as western and American experiences in microcosm. Paradoxically, it can be argued that both sides are right. Kevin Starr, *Americans and the California Dream, 1850–1915* (New York, 1973), sees the rush as the noble and inspiring hopes of the *Odyssey* and the pettiness and miseries of the *Iliad*.

Usually centennials lead to production of hurried, pedestrian writings rushed to meet artificial deadlines. However, this was untrue when, in 1949, the California Gold Rush Centennial and the following year the Statehood Centennial occurred. New works and reprints of rare, unavailable classics appeared in abundance. Many have concluded that little more could be written on the gold rush, but J. S. Holliday's *The World Rushed In* (New York, 1981) stirred considerable comment immediately and went through several printings.

That rush, America's first great encounter with "gold fever," followed James W. Marshall's discovery of placer gold in the lumber mill tailrace at Coloma on the South Fork of the American River east of John A. Sutter's fort, on January 24, 1848; Marshall remained little known until Theressa Gay's biography, *James Marshall* (Georgetown, Calif., 1967). A useful compilation of discovery writings is *The California Gold Discovery* (Georgetown, Calif., 1966), ed. by

Rodman W. Paul. His excellent analysis of the technology, economics, and legal practices of the rush are detailed in *California Gold* (Reprint ed.; Lincoln, Nebr., 1947). For a sound treatment emphasizing cultural, social, and economic results, see John W. Caughey, *Gold Is the Cornerstone* (Berkeley, 1948).

Reminiscences of the rush are so valuable and extensive that no perfect list of best works is possible. Reminiscences may have begun with J. H. Carson, *Early Recollections of the Mines* (Stockton, Calif., 1852). *In Pursuit of the Golden Dream . . .* (Stoughton, Mass., 1970), ed. by Dale L. Morgan, lists in its introduction ninety-four known memoirs. Carl I. Wheat, *Books of the California Gold Rush* (San Francisco, 1948), mentions 239 titles of printed works and eighty-two titles of varying importance.

Among the best contemporary guidebooks to the gold fields, especially useful for their knowledge—or error—is Joseph E. Ware, *The Emigrant's Guide to California* (St. Louis, 1849; ed. by John W. Caughey, Princeton, 1932).

Routes to gold rush California were worldwide. Those from the United States have been traced and interpreted both by participants and recent historians. Among these writers are: John H. Kemble, *The Panama Route, 1848–1869* (Berkeley, 1943) and Oscar Lewis, *Sea Routes to the Goldfields* (New York, 1949). For the Nicaragua journey, David I. Folkman, Jr., *The Nicaragua Route* (Salt Lake City, 1972), is useful. An excellent discourse on the Cape Horn passage stressing first-hand accounts is Raymond A. Rydell, *Cape Horn to the Pacific* (Berkeley, 1952); data on sea routes are also in John W. Caughey, ed., *Rushing for Gold* (Berkeley, 1949).

Most Americans are familiar with the land routes to California. Hundreds of diaries have been written, and scores published. American humorist Alonzo Delano ("Old Block") wrote *Life on the Plains and Among the Diggings* (Auburn, N.Y., 1854). J. Goldsborough Bruff was as interesting as any adventurer, as seen in Georgia W. Read and Ruth Gaines, eds., *Gold Rush: The Journals, Drawings and Other Papers of J. Goldsborough Bruff* (2 vols.; New York, 1944). A myriad of personal letters reveal much; fortunately social historians have harvested them. Walker D. Wyman searched the era's newspaper letters—the result, the invaluable *California Emigrant Letters* (New York, 1952). Two excellent 1849 overland diaries are: David M. Potter, ed., *Trail to California: The Overland Journal of Vincent Geiger and Wakeman Bryarly* (New Haven, 1945) and Dale L. Morgan, ed., *The Overland Diary of James A. Pritchard . . .* (Denver, 1959), the latter containing an appendix of all known diarists *via* South Pass. Of special interest is the account of overland women, Sandra L. Myers, ed., *Ho for California! Women's Overland Diaries from the Huntington Library* (San Marino, 1980), a pioneer group not studied until recently. (Also see Chapter 9, *post*.)

The dean of overland routes, Irene D. Paden, covered main trails and detours, using little-known or neglected materials. The impressive results were *In the Wake of the Prairie Schooner* (New York, 1943) and *Prairie Schooner Detours* (New York, 1949). An earlier work is Owen C. Coy, *The Great Trek* (Los Angeles, 1932).

In the 1960s and later, specialists have delved deeply into the social and political aspects of early overland travel. John P. Reid, *Law for the Elephant: Property and Social Behavior on the Overland Trail* (San Marino, 1980), reveals how four-months or longer journeys were socially managed. Stephen Fender, *Plotting the Golden West: American Literature and the Rhetoric of the California Trail* (New York, 1981), treats the images of the West, and discusses much that was written at the time about the frontier.

Acclaimed by most reviewers, John D. Unruh, Jr., *The Plains Across: The Overland Emigrants and the Trans-Mississippi West, 1840-60* (Urbana, 1979), dealing with a wider scope of time and space than the rush, is a thoughtful study of California migrations. George R. Stewart, *The California Trail: An Epic of Many Heroes* (New York, 1962), is equally valuable.

Many eyewitnesses recorded their personal accounts, among them Buffum and Delano. A collection of several sound narrative accounts of the rush is ingeniously woven together in Archer B. Hulbert's *Forty-Niners* (Boston, 1931), and one can profit from consulting it. The literary Briton, Frank Marryat, published *Mountain and Molehills* (London, 1855), and a similar account, J. D. Borthwick, *Three Years in California* (London, 1857), contains rich material.

Written by a second-generation Californian who analyzed skillfully the government and politics of gold rush mining camps, Charles H. Shinn's *Mining Camps: A Study of American Frontier Government* (New York, 1885), pioneered in presenting more than contemporary descriptions of mining. *Prentice Mulford's Story: Life By Land and Sea* (New York, 1889) is a humorous account, true to human nature, of recollections of the diggings by one of California's cleverest wits.

In 1846, the Mexican province of Alta California was conquered by Americans and governed by the military until 1849. Only brief political accounts of this transition appeared until Theodore Grivas, *Military Governments of California, 1846-1850* (Glendale, 1963), which praised the records of California's military governors. Two older works of this period are William H. Ellison, *A Self-Governing Dominion: California, 1849-1860* (Berkeley, 1950) and Cardinal L. Goodwin, *The Establishment of State Government in California, 1846-1850* (New York, 1914). Joseph Ellison, *California and the Nation, 1850-1869* (Berkeley, 1927), shows with clarity California's important political relations with the United States.

Adequate coverage of admission to the Union is found in J. Ross Browne, ed., *Report of the Debates in the Convention of California, on the Formation of the State Constitution* (Washington, D.C., 1850), the official record. The Rev. Walter Colton wrote extensively of these changing times in *Three Years in California* (Cincinnati, 1850). Bayard Still, "California's First Constitution, A Reflection of the Political Philosophy of the Frontier," *PHR*, 4 (February 1935), is thought-provoking, as is James A. B. Scherer, *Thirty-First Star* (New York, 1942).

While California was revealing that it could function as a state, vigilantism put a question mark to whether it was fully a democracy. In the pioneer historian

Hubert H. Bancroft's, *Popular Tribunals* (2 vols.; San Francisco, 1887), he sought the roots of do-it-yourself government in camps, towns, and cities. San Francisco's famous vigilance committee of 1851 was recreated in a pioneer work by Mary F. Williams, *History of the San Francisco Committee of Vigilance* (Berkeley, 1921). She also edited the committee's papers (Berkeley, 1919). Stanton A. Coblenz, *Villains and Vigilantes; The Story of James King of William and Pioneer Justice in California* (New York, 1936), claimed that King, whose murder in San Francisco led to the city's second vigilance committee in 1856, had remained obscure to historians. Though its "necessity" has been regretted, vigilantism was generally approved by nineteenth-century historians and well into the twentieth century, except for William H. Ellison, *A Self-Governing Dominion* and Josiah Royce, *California*. In recent years John W. Caughey, *Their Majesties the Mob* (Chicago, 1960), viewed it as a setback, as did Leonard Pitt, "The Beginnings of Nativism in California," *PHR*, 30 (February 1961). California had more of such groups than has any other western state or territory, though vigilantism had begun in the East. For a description of a leading vigilante, see James A. B. Scherer, *"The Lion of the Vigilantes," William T. Coleman . . .* (Indianapolis, 1939), which lauds Coleman, and Doyce B. Nunis, Jr., ed., *The San Francisco Vigilance Committee of 1856: Three Views* (Los Angeles, 1971), which includes worthy analyses by James O'Meara, William T. Sherman, and Coleman. Robert M. Sankewicz, SJ, *Vigilantes in Gold Rush San Francisco* (Stanford, 1985), is the latest monograph.

California writers fed on Western legends of badmen. Joaquín Murieta, probably most controversial, yet least known, had his biographer. John Rollin Ridge ("Yellow Bird"), gold-rush author and himself heir to injustices to the Cherokees, empathized with Mexican Americans and helped portray Murieta as early California's "Robinhood." In *The Real Joaquin Murieta: Robinhood Hero or Gold Rush Gangster?* (Corona del Mar, 1974), Remi Nadeau gives a wide compilation of writings on Murieta, from Ridge to mid-twentieth century literati. Nadeau denied what recent writers have averred, that Murieta was mostly legend and an outlaw. Frank F. Latta, *Joaquin Murieta and His Horse Gangs* (Santa Cruz, 1980), holds the view that California Rangers in 1854 did not kill Murieta.

Tiburcio Vásquez, whose robberies and killings came at the end of the violent age in the early 1870s, is more easily documented. Major Ben C. Truman, pioneer Angeleno, wrote a brief account, *Tiburcio Vásquez* (Los Angeles, 1941). Charles H. Shinn, *Graphic Description of Pacific Coast Outlaws* (San Francisco, 1887), ed. by J. E. Reynolds (Los Angeles, 1958), gives exciting and fair coverage. (See also Chapter 6, *post*.)

Despite the overall image of violence, Roger D. McGrath discovered through in-depth examination of Bodie's and Aurora's wayward years that violence was more limited than formerly thought in these two infamous "wild" mining towns, and mostly employed against criminals by criminals in *Gunfights, Highwaymen, and Vigilantes: Violence on the Frontier* (Berkeley, 1984). For a dramatic coverage of urban violence see George R. Stewart, *Committee of Vigilance: Revolution in San Francisco* (Boston, 1964).

Transformer of all things Californian, the gold rush inevitably brought an economic revolution far beyond the mere value of gold. Over more than a century historians have enriched our understanding of it. Three excellent contemporary economic surveys of California's potentials and early developments are important: John S. Hittell, *The Resources of California* (San Francisco, 1863); J. Ross Brown, *Resources of the Pacific Slope* (San Francisco, 1869); and Titus F. Cronise, *The Natural Wealth of California* (San Francisco, 1868).

The problems of clearing land titles after the Mexican War were complicated and resulted in the breaking up of large estates, the decline of native owners, and long confusion over ownership. Most historians, including H. H. Bancroft, Theodore H. Hittell, John S. Hittell, Josiah Royce, and Henry George, strongly criticized federal government policy toward Mexican grants. The dean of land grant experts was William W. Robinson. His *Land in California* (Berkeley, 1948) used archival records extensively and showed the results of change in land use. More recently Paul W. Gates covered the issue in "The Adjudication of Spanish-Mexican Land Grants in California," *HLQ*, 12 (May 1958); in his excellent "California's Embattled Settlers," *CHSQ*, 41 (June 1962), he modified earlier conclusions through his argument that settlers rather than grantees were most unfairly treated. He noted that the United States only did what it had done in earlier decisions in the West. A contemporary document which offers insight is Ogden Hoffman, *Reports of Land Cases, Determined in the United States District Court for the Northern District of California* (San Francisco, 1862). The famous single-tax advocate, San Franciscan Henry George, presented his views in *Land and Our Land Policy, National and State* (San Francisco, 1871).

Commercially in this period, agriculture underwent a renaissance, a metamorphosis from the limited prewar barter system to a flourishing modern production system. A good overview is Lawrence J. Jelinek's *Harvest Empire* (2nd ed.; San Francisco, 1982). The overall story of California banking still seeks a great chronicler, but a beginning was made in Ira B. Cross, *Financing an Empire: History of Banking in California* (4 vols.; Chicago, 1927).

When gold was discovered, the world beat a path to California's door. Ever since, historians have constructed interpretive studies in transportation history. The early twentieth century produced a wealth of monographs. Ernest A. Wiltsee, *The Pioneer Miner and the Pack Mule Express* (New York, 1931), covered a primitive method, while William and George Banning's *Six Horses* (New York, 1930), dealt with stagecoach lines. Lewis B. Lesley, *Uncle Sam's Camels* (Cambridge, Mass., 1929) and Harlan D. Fowler, *Camels to California* (Palo Alto, 1950), depict the federal government's unusual experiment in using Middle Eastern camels and their drivers in Far Western "desert" lands in the 1850s. LeRoy R. Hafen produced the excellent *The Overland Mail, 1849–1869* (Cleveland, 1926). For the famous Butterfield overland, Roscoe P. and

Margaret B. Conkling, *The Butterfield Overland Mail, 1857–1869* (3 vols.; Glendale, 1947), is a sound, dramatic narration. More dramatic, if not financially successful, was the privately financed Pony Express, which carried mail from Missouri to Sacramento in ten days. The story is related in Arthur Chapman, *The Pony Express* (New York and London, 1932); Roy S. Bloss, *Pony Express: The Great Gamble* (Berkeley, 1959); and Waddell Smith, *The Story of the Pony Express* (San Rafael, 1969).

Ben Holladay, developer of overland stage lines, is introduced in J. V. Frederick, *Ben Holladay the Stagecoach King* (Glendale, 1940) and in Ellis Lucia, *The Saga of Ben Holladay* (New York, 1959). See also William Tallack, *The California Overland Express* (Los Angeles, 1935), a fine reminiscence. Raymond and Mary L. Settle dedicated much of their careers to studies of early California transportation in *Empire on Wheels* (Stanford, 1949); *Saddles and Spurs* (Harrisburg, 1955), on the Pony Express; and *War Drums and Wagon Wheels: The Story of Russell, Majors and Waddell* (Lincoln, 1966), on the overland freighters. W. Turrentine Jackson, *Wagon Roads West* (Berkeley, 1952) chronicles early road building on the Pacific Slope.

The rush also brought improved water transportation. A. H. Clark, *The Clipper Ship Era, 1843–1869* (New York, 1910), covers voyages to California. Jerry MacMullen, *Paddlewheel Days in California* (Stanford, 1944), deals with river traffic of the times. MacMullen also wrote, with Jack McNairn, *Ships of the Redwood Coast* (Stanford, 1945).

The transcontinental railroad, long predicted, transformed California into a postfrontier state in 1869. The drama still receives historical attention. The voluminous *Pacific Railroad Records* (13 vols.; Washington, D.C., 1855) is a rare treasure trove on federal attempts to find the optimum routes, while John D. Galloway, *The First Transcontinental Railroad* (New York, 1950), and a more engineering-centered book, Wesley S. Griswold, *A Work of Giants: Building the First Transcontinental Railway* (New York, 1963), clarified readers' understanding of construction. The engineering and lobbying genius of the Central Pacific, Theodore D. Judah, was given long overdue praise in Carl I. Wheat, "A Sketch of the Life of Theodore D. Judah," *CHSQ*, 4 (September 1925). Oscar Lewis' monumental work, *The Big Four* (New York, 1938), presents fine delineations of the Central's builders, Collis P. Huntington, Leland Stanford, Mark Hopkins, and Charles Crocker, critically exposing their methods and explaining their achievements. Many railroad documents were purposely destroyed and others were consumed in the San Francisco fire of 1906. David S. Lavender, *The Great Persuader* (New York, 1970), renders a convincing biography of C. P. Huntington, as does Norman E. Tutorow, *Leland Stanford: Man of Many Careers* (Menlo Park, 1971).

Virtual colony of early California, Nevada was produced by the discovery of the Comstock Lode of silver at Virginia City. The history of California's economic growth to the 1880s is tied to the Nevada story. This, America's first silver rush, was fueled by California labor, money, and administration. George D.

Lyman, *The Saga of the Comstock* (New York, 1934) and Charles H. Shinn, *The Story of the Mine* (New York, 1896), are both useful secondary accounts. Oscar Lewis continued to recount fortune building in *The Silver Kings* (New York, 1947). Probably the best account is Grant H. Smith, *A History of the Comstock Lode, 1858-1920* (Reno, 1943). Most Nevada historians have been bitter toward California imperialism in the exploitation of their state, a view expressed in Gilman M. Ostrander, *The Great Rotten Borough* (New York, 1966). Comstock influence on San Francisco is detailed in David Lavender, *Nothing Seemed Impossible: William C. Ralston and Early San Francisco* (Palo Alto, 1975).

While Nevada felt victimized by California, California Indians, already degenerated under Spanish and Mexican rule, had even more reason to feel so. Sherburne F. Cook, *The Conflict Between the California Indian and White Civilization: Part III; The American Invasion, 1848-1870* (Berkeley, 1943), explains and documents their decline, while George H. Phillips' *Chiefs and Challengers* and James J. Rawls, "Gold Diggers: Indian Miners in the California Gold Rush," *CHQ*, 55 (Spring 1976), give further evidence. Even in the gold rush era many Anglo-Californians were interested in and sympathetic toward local Indians. Benjamin D. Wilson showed this in his report, *The Indians of Southern California*, ed. by John W. Caughey (San Marino, 1952); as did John Ross Browne, much earlier, in *The Indians of California* (New York, 1864; reprint, San Francisco, 1944). An innovator in the reservation system of California, Edward F. Beale, has been treated by Gerald Thompson, *Edward F. Beale and the American West* (Albuquerque, 1984).

The Modoc War of 1873 in northeasternmost California's lava beds was the bloodiest in California history. It was chronicled extensively by the San Francisco press, and its controversial course has since been interpreted by Clio's penmen. Most notable is Keith A. Murray, *The Modocs and Their War* (Norman, 1959). The Modocs' impressive resistance against a well-armed force is detailed in Erwin N. Thompson, *Modoc War: Its Military History and Topography* (Sacramento, 1971).

Until 1849 the typical American frontier that was moving westward was semi-isolated, poor, underdeveloped, and possessing few amenities of eastern culture. Immediately, California broke the stereotype. As diaries, autobiographies, letters, and memoirs long suggested, the 49ers were cross-sections of American life, and indeed, represented much of the world. Franklin Walker, *San Francisco's Literary Frontier* (New York, 1939), reveals that the gold rush Bay Area had a high percentage of college and professional men, more newspapers by 1860 than London, and a wealth and appreciation of culture which produced a renaissance (or naissance) unique in America's western frontiers, a point well made in Roger W. Lotchin, *San Francisco, 1846-1856* (New York, 1974).

California's public education began with the gold rush. Despite few children in its interior towns and camps, the new state developed some of the latest methods and principles of schooling. William W. Ferrier saw this in his two perceptive works, *Ninety Years of Education in California* (Berkeley, 1937) and

Origin and Development of the University of California (Berkeley, 1930), founded in 1868. Educational giant of the period, John Swett, is the subject of two admiring biographies, William G. Carr, *John Swett: The Biography of an Educational Pioneer* (Santa Ana, 1933) and Nicholas C. Poles, *John Swett: California Frontier Schoolmaster* (Washington, D.C., 1978). Standing next to Swett was Judge John G. Marvin, well described in David F. Ferris, *Judge Marvin and the Founding of the California School System* (Berkeley, 1962). For abundant first-hand data consult the *Annual Reports of the Superintendent of Public Instruction* (Sacramento, 1851; yearly thereafter) and the revealing periodical *California Teacher* (San Francisco, 1863-1876). Irving G. Hendrick's survey, *California Education: A Brief History* (San Francisco, 1980), is a good general study. Also see Hendrick's *The Education of Nonwhites in California, 1849-1970* (San Francisco, 1977), a perceptive study of minorities.

An outstanding literature and press early served an eager California public. A useful reference is Joseph Gaer, ed., *Bibliography of California Literature* (n.p., 1935). California's most famous early-day author, Samuel L. Clemens, is well treated in Justin Kaplan, *Mr. Clemens and Mark Twain: A Biography* (New York, 1966). One of the best biographies of Mark Twain's contemporary and associate is George R. Stewart, *Bret Harte: Argonaut and Exile* (Boston, 1931). The dramatic career of another able communicator is found in David Goodman, *A Western Panorama, 1849-1875: The Travels, Writings and Influence of J. Ross Browne* (Glendale, 1966), as well as in the aforementioned work by Walker. For Joaquin Miller, see especially M. A. Mayberry, *Splendid Poseur* (New York, 1953). Of comparable interest is Ray E. Held, *Public Libraries in California, 1849-1878* (Berkeley, 1963).

Few of the dozens of newspapers that gold rush California offered have had their worthwhile histories, but most useful is the pioneer teenage journalist, Edward C. Kemble, *A History of California Newspapers, 1846-1858* (San Francisco, 1858; reprint, New York, 1927) and ed. by Helen M. Bretnor (Los Gatos, 1962).

Theatrical model for the whole West for many years, San Francisco drama has been treated in Edmond M. Gagey's classic, *The San Francisco Stage* (New York, 1950) and in George R. MacMinn, *The Theater of the Golden Era in California* (Caldwell, Idaho, 1941). Constance M. Rourke produced the pleasant work, *Troupers of the Gold Coast* (New York, 1928), on gold rush actors.

An eminent modern historian, Andrew F. Rolle, has said that no first-rate art history of the state has yet appeared, but there are many monographic writings on the painters of the gold rush, particularly on Albert Bierstadt, German-born landscapist. The best is probably the shortest and latest, Matthew Baigell, *Albert Bierstadt* (New York, 1981). Eugen Neuhaus, *William Keith: The Man and the Artist* (Berkeley, 1938), is a capable account of a Scottish-born landscapist of Yosemite; see also Brother Fidelis Cornelius, *Keith, Old Master of California* (2 vols.; New York, 1941-1945). The paintings and engravings of Charles Christian Nahl captured the genre of gold rush California where he gained fame.

Useful is Moreland L. Stevens, *Charles Christian Nahl: Artist of the Gold Rush* (Sacramento, 1976). A highly informative and richly illustrated analysis of California painting from earliest times through the rush was produced by Jeanne Van Nostrand and Edith M. Coulter, *California Pictorial, 1786-1859* (Berkeley, 1948).

The history of architecture, music, and sculpture in early California needs more attention. A pioneer in the field was Harold Kirker, *California's Architectural Frontier: Style and Tradition in the Nineteenth Century* (San Marino, 1960).

Although Alta California began as a religious frontier of imperial Spain, by the end of Mexican era, 1848, secularization had virtually denied the province its Catholic clergy and Protestantism had not yet been established. Thus the 1849-1880 era saw the rebirth of religion in California. There is no overall history of religion in this period, but much has been published on individual clergymen and various denominations after 1849.

Not until the 1940s was serious attention given to the history of early Protestantism, especially in a number of USC dissertations (see Pamela A. Bleich bibliography). Well done is Arnold Crompton, *Unitarianism on the Pacific Coast: The First Sixty Years* (Boston, 1957). The Catholic Church is the focus of Henry L. Walsh, *Hallowed Were the Gold Rush Trails* (Santa Clara, 1946), which details the history of pioneer priests in northern California, and John B. McGloin, *California's First Archbishop: The Life of Joseph Sadoc Alemany, O.P., 1814-1888* (New York, 1966). On Jews see Rudolf Glantz, *The Jews of California* (New York, 1961) and many articles pertinent to Judaism in *The Western States Jewish Historical Quarterly* since 1968.

Ethnic studies of the gold rush and the immediately succeeding years have received extensive attention since minority works became well recognized after the 1950s. (See Chapters 6-8, *post*.) Covering several non-Anglo groups, Robert F. Heizer and A. F. Almquist, *The Other Californians* (Berkeley, 1971), is an excellent overview. For information on Australians, see Charles Bateson, *Gold Fleet to California: Forty Niners from Australia and New Zealand* (East Lansing, 1964).

Despite their small numbers, Chileños made an imprint upon the rush and suffered and survived prejudice. The works on them are numerous, including Enrique Bunster, *Chileños en California* (Santiago, Chile, 1954); George E. Flaugsted, *The Chileños in the California Gold Rush* (San Francisco, 1973); Stephen Giacobbi, *Chile and Her Argonauts in the Gold Rush* (Palo Alto, 1974); and *We Were 49ers: Chilean Accounts of the California Gold Rush*, ed. and trans. by Edwin A. Beilharz and Carlos U. Lopez (Pasadena, 1976).

Andrew F. Rolle has led the advance guard on the study of Italians in "Success in the Sun: The Italians in California," *Westerners' Brand Book* (Los Angeles, 1962) and in his more extensive *The Immigrant Upraised: Italian Adventurers and Colonists in an Expanding America* (Norman, 1968). Erwin G. Gudde has given us *German Pioneers in Early California* (Hoboken, 1927) and Hallock F. Raup's incisive study of *The German Colonization of Anaheim* (Berkeley, 1932) in the 1850s is worth attention. For the French, Gilbert Chinard edited and translated the original 1850 reprint, *When the French Came to California* (San Francisco, 1944). Daniel Levy, *Les François en Californie* (San Francisco, 1889), is a little-known work of value. It is not surprising that so active a group as the Irish should be well documented in politics, society, and economics. Thomas F. Prendergast, *Forgotten Pioneers: Irish Leaders in Early California* (San Francisco, 1942), is appreciative. More recently R. A. Burchell produced a detailed study, *The San Francisco Irish, 1848-1880* (Berkeley, 1980).

In the colorful and significant pre-Civil War politics the historic duel between Judge Terry and Senator Broderick must be noted. A. Russell Buchanan, *David S. Terry of California: Dueling Judge* (San Marino, 1959), introduces the fiery, brilliant supreme court justice who symbolized Southern interests. David A. Williams, *David C. Broderick: A Political Portrait* (San Marino, 1970), gives a more sympathetic and useful account of Terry's ill-fated adversary than did Jeremiah Lynch, *A Senator of the Fifties: David C. Broderick* (San Francisco, 1911). Another fiery issue of the 1850s was state division, a matter that has recurred at least once a generation ever since. See William H. Ellison, "The Movement for State Division in California, 1849-1860," *Southwestern Historical Quarterly*, 17 (October 1913).

Much error and concocted myth have surrounded California's role in the Civil War. Loyalty to the Union was debated before the war, during its occurrence, and ever since. Bancroft, Hittell, and Eldredge erred in their overly favorable assessments of California's role in the war, while Elijah R. Kennedy, *The Contest for California in 1861* (Boston, 1912), insisted that Republican Senator Edward D. Baker of Oregon, Lincoln's friend, a 49er and spellbinding orator, "saved" the Pacific coast. With equal zest and zeal other writers have given credit to the San Francisco Universalist minister, Thomas Starr King, but such claims are simplistic. No one had to save California. After Fort Sumter was attacked, April 12, 1861, Californians quickly demonstrated great Union sentiment. Contemporary writers and their next generation thought pro-Confederate sentiment was strong. This was true in southern California, but not so clear elsewhere. Those boosting the image of Starr King thought that 60 percent of Californians were from slave states, while Charles W. Wendte, *Thomas Starr King* (Boston, 1921), put it at 40 percent. Actually, only seven percent came from secession states, according to Benjamin F. Gilbert, who found that Republicans had exaggerated this for campaign purposes and that the 1860 census soundly showed otherwise. Although boosters of a "Pacific Republic" were noisy in the California press in their advocacy of a sort of "third world" neutral Far Western nation, little happened, and there was no plot, either, by Col. Albert S. Johnston, then stationed in California, nor by anyone else to take California. James A. B. Scherer, *Thirty-First Star* (New York, 1942), corrected Elijah R. Kennedy on his attacks upon Johnston, as did Benjamin F. Gilbert later. See Avery C. Moore, *Destiny's Soldier* (San Francisco, 1958) on Johnston, and Benjamin F. Gilbert, "California and the Civil War: A Bibliographical Essay," *CHSQ*, 40 (December 1961).

Few Californians went east to participate actively in the theater of war. The draft was not extended to the Far West, where local men were primarily needed to fight Indians and guard overland routes. See Fred B. Rogers, *Soldiers of the Overland* (San Francisco, 1938), for an excellent detailed work on the military in California. Long outstanding has been Aurora Hunt, *The Army of the Pacific* (Glendale, 1951). Her excellent research is also evident in a biography of *Major-General John Henry Carlton* (Glendale, 1948), who commanded the California Column in Arizona, the latter detailed in Darlis A. Miller, *The California Column in New Mexico* (Albuquerque, 1982).

Equally engrossing are Ronald C. Woolsey, "Disunion or Dissent? A New Look at an Old Problem in Southern California Attitudes Toward the Civil War," *SCQ*, 66 (Fall 1984) and John W. Robinson, *Los Angeles in Civil War Days, 1860–1865* (Los Angeles, 1977). Dealing with a key economic contribution of the state is James F. Carson, "California Gold to Help Finance the War," *JW*, 16 (January 1975). The December 1961 issue of *CHQ*, dedicated to the war and California, offers new light on the period.

In the middle and late 1870s California for the first time felt the deep pangs of a major national depression, the Panic of 1873. Two groups were blamed for the decline of employment, rise of monopoly, and increase in taxes along with decrease of prices—the Central Pacific Railroad and Chinese immigrants. Note particularly Stuart Daggett, *Chapters of the History of the Southern Pacific* (New York, 1922). Defending the Central Pacific's (later Southern Pacific) role are Creed Hammond, *The Central Pacific Railroad Company: Its Relation to the Government* (Washington, D.C., 1888) and Neill C. Wilson and Frank J. Taylor, *The Roaring Story of a Fighting Railroad* (New York, 1952). Lloyd J. Mercer, "Land Grants to American Railroads: Social Cost or Social Benefits?" *Business History Review*, 43 (Summer 1969) saw good in government land grants. One of the worst roles of the Southern Pacific as a land settler is told in James L. Brown, *The Mussel Slough Tragedy* (2nd ed.; Hanford, Calif., 1980).

Any study of the depression-ridden and violent seventies is impossible without perusing major works on anti-Oriental sentiment. (This subject is treated fully in Chapter 8, *post*.) Gladys C. Hansen and William F. Heintz, *The Chinese in California: A Bibliographic History* (Portland, Oreg., 1970), list and discuss the wealth of monographic studies recently issued on little-known topics of labor and culture.

The radical labor movement of the 1870s and its antirailroad and anti-Chinese issues have an extensive literature. Ralph Kauer, "The Workingmen's Party in California," *PHR*, 13 (September 1944) is excellent, while J. C. Stedman and R. A. Leonard, *The Workingmen's Party in California* (San Francisco, 1878), was a contemporary work that praised Denis Kearney and his efforts. Gerald D. Nash, "The Influence of Labor on State Policy, 1860-1920: The Experience of California," *CHSQ*, 42 (September 1963), might well be read beside Spencer C. Olin, *California Politics, 1846-1920: The Emerging Corporate State* (San Francisco, 1981).

The still functioning and usually controversial second California Constitution has a growing literature. Carl B. Swisher, *Motivation and Political Technique in the California Constitutional Convention, 1878-1879* (Claremont, 1930), is still a fine study of the constitution's genesis. Dudley T. Moorehead, "Sectionalism and the California Constitution of 1879," *PHR*, 12 (September 1943), deals with the vast differences in state, rural, and urban society, north and south. See for first-hand references the *Debates and Proceedings of the Constitutional Convention of the State of California* (3 vols.; Sacramento, 1880). Filled with useful references for political history is Winfield J. Davis, *History of Political Conventions in California* (Sacramento, 1893).

One may find much on local California history of those years through county histories, though these are hardly objective. California's "mugbooks" began in 1875 when Thomas H. Thompson and Albert A. West formed a partnership to print county maps and atlases. The first firm actually to publish regularly county histories was Smith & Elliott, Oakland, with their *Butte County* in 1877 by W. T. Sexton. Each of the county volumes was supported by successful pioneers. Mugbooks remained a local history phenomenon in California through the 1920s. Some of the data, though obviously slanted as success stories, are of some interest today as evidence of the attributes of local achievement. A good summary of the more reliable ones for southern California is found in Doyce B. Nunis, Jr., "The Historians of Los Angeles," *SCQ*, 66 (Spring 1984).

Representative southern Californians of the time have received biographical treatment: John W. Caughey, "Don Benito Wilson: An Average Southern Californian," *HLQ*, 2 (1939); *Port Admiral: Phineas Banning, 1830-1885* (San Francisco, 1957), by Maymie Krythe; *L. J. Rose of Sunny Slope, 1827-1899* (San Marino, 1959), by L. J. Rose, Jr.; and Midge Sherwood, *Days of Vintage, Years of Vision* (2 vols.; San Marino, 1982, 1987), a biography of James de Barth Shorb.

San Diego history has been best explained in the multivolumed work of Richard F. Pourade. *The Glory Years* (San Diego, 1964) is especially appropriate for this period. Santa Barbara's Anglo beginnings are traced in James C. Williams, "Cultural Tension: The Origins of American Santa Barbara," *SCQ*, 60 (Winter 1973). Donald Pflueger has chronicled the beginnings of agricultural communities of the south in *Covina* (Claremont, 1964) and *Glendora* (Claremont, 1951). He showed convincingly that local history could be significant, exciting, and not primarily provincial.

Franklin Walker, *A Literary History of Southern California* (Berkeley, 1950), continued his inquiry into California writers and indicated that at least by 1880 the region was no longer completely a wasteland and changeless. See Gerald T. White, *Baptism in Oil: Stephen F. Peckham in Southern California, 1865-66* (San Francisco, 1984) and S. T. Harding, *Water in California* (Palo Alto, 1960), on the beginnings of two vital developments.

Another study which reinforces the view that southern California was not wholly a wasteland in the gold rush and its aftermath is William B. Rice, *The Los Angeles Star, 1851-1864* (Berkeley, 1947), ed. by John W. Caughey, which details the city's first newspaper and its influence. In addition, there are numerous articles found in the publications of the Historical Society of Southern California, made accessible by an annotated bibliography and two indices compiled by Anna Marie and Everett C. Hager (Los Angeles, 1958, 1977) and in the *Journal of San Diego History*, which touches on all facets of southern California history.

Most of the newspapers, travel accounts, and memoirs of southern California, 1869-1880, describe briefly some aspects of the rush of invalids to the sunny region. See Oscar O. Winther, "The Use of Climate as a Means of Promoting Migration to Southern California," *MVHR*, 33 (Fall 1946) and George W. Groh, *Gold Fever* (New York, 1966), which covers California health seekers from the gold rush to the postfrontier era. John E. Baur, *The Health Seekers of Southern California, 1870-1900* (San Marino, 1959), offers a comprehensive treatment of this southern California phenomenon.

The historical literature of this most colorful and in many ways most moving period of California history will predictably continue to grow, and its earlier authors will again be analyzed in the historiographical studies of the future, for, although its particular factors may have not been indispensable for California, as once thought, it was surely the crossroads epoch of the state's future greatness and of its future problems.

3

THE GILDED AGE AND PROGRESSIVISM, 1880–1930

JACKSON K. PUTNAM

THE HALF CENTURY that encompasses 1880–1930 was a period of impressive growth in California. General trends are discussed in Warren S. Thompson, *Growth and Changes in California Population* (Los Angeles, 1955) and in Commonwealth Club of California, *The Population of California* (San Francisco, 1946). On migration aspects see J. Donald Fisher, *A Historical Study of the Migrant in California* (San Francisco, 1973) and Charles Reynolds and Sara Miles, *Statistical Memorandum No. 6, Series: Growth of Population, No. 3, Migration* (Berkeley, 1944). On a related subject see Margaret Gordon, *Employment Expansion and Population Growth, 1900–1950* (Berkeley, 1954).

From the outset of the founding of California, the state has had a cosmopolitan population. Useful is California Institute of Public Affairs, *Ethnic Groups in California: A Guide to Organization and Information Sources* (Claremont, 1981). General studies include Anne Loftis, *California: Where the Twain Did Meet* (New York, 1973). On specific ethnic groups, a large, though "spotty" literature exists. A sizeable number of graduate theses and dissertations at USC from the Department of Sociology focus on sociohistorical treatments, with a considerable ethnic range. Too numerous to list here, a card index is available in Doheny Memorial Library. There are numerous articles and monographs devoted to various ethnic groups listed in Margaret M. Rocq, ed., *California Local History*.

California social history of the modern type is so undeveloped that it is scarcely in its infancy. Even social mobility is largely unexplored, with one exception: Peter Decker, *Fortunes and Failures: White Collar Mobility in Nineteenth Century California* (Cambridge, Mass., 1978). On another kind of mobility, the impact of the automobile on California society ("automobility"), a substantial literature exists. A portion of it includes Mark S. Foster, "The

Model-T, the Hard Sell and Los Angeles's Urban Growth," *PHR*, 44 (November 1975); Ashleigh Brilliant, "Some Aspects of Mass Motorization in Southern California, 1919-1929," *SCQ*, 67 (June 1965); and Richard R. Mathisin, *Three Cars in Every Garage: A Motorist's History of the Automobile and the Automobile Club in Southern California* (Garden City, N.Y., 1968).

On California's notorious capacity for generating cults and utopian movements generally, see Robert V. Hine, *California's Utopian Colonies* (New York, 1953; 1966) and *California Utopianism* (San Francisco, 1981), and Carey McWilliams, *Southern California Country: An Island on the Land* (New York, 1946). An important study is Paul Conkin, *Two Paths to Utopia: The Hutterites and the Llano Colony* (Lincoln, 1964). On Kaweah, see Ruth R. Lewis, "Kaweah, An Experiment in Cooperative Colonization," *PHR*, 17 (November 1948). Much of the voluminous literature on the Point Loma theosophical colony is summarized in Lauren R. Brown, *The Point Loma Theosophical Society: A List of Publications, 1898-1942* (San Diego, 1977). See also Emmett Greenwalt, *The Point Loma Community in California, 1897-1942: A Theosophical Experiment* (Berkeley, 1955).

A good general economic history of California is yet to be written. The major theme for this period would be massive and uncontrolled economic growth. Some good introductory treatments are Frank L. Kidner, *California Business Cycles* (Berkeley, 1946); Gerald D. Nash, "Stages of California Economic Growth, 1870-1970: An Interpretation," *CHSQ*, 51 (Winter 1972); and Glenn Dumke, *The Prosperous Decade: California During the 1920's* (Sonoma, Calif., 1956).

A general account of business and industry is Robert G. Cleland and Osgood Hardy, *The March of Industry* (Los Angeles, 1929). Selected treatments of specific industries follow.

Aviation and aircraft: David Hatfield, *Los Angeles Aeronautics, 1920-1929* (Los Angeles, 1973); William A. Schoeneberger, *California Wings: A History of Aviation in the Golden State* (Northridge, 1984); and John B. Rae, *Climb to Greatness: The American Aircraft Industry, 1920-1960* (Cambridge, Mass., 1968).

Banking and bankers: Ira B. Cross, *Financing an Empire* (4 vols.; Chicago, 1927); Julian Dana, *A. P. Giannini, Giant in the West* (New York, 1947); Marquis James, *The Biography of a Bank: The Story of the Bank of America* (New York, 1954); and Robert G. Cleland and Frank B. Putnam, *Isaias W. Hellman and the Farmers and Merchants Bank* (San Marino, 1965).

Electric power: Charles M. Coleman, *P. G. and E. of California: The Centennial Story of Pacific Gas and Electric Company, 1852-1952* (San Francisco, 1952), and Patricia G. Sikes, "George Roe and California's Centennial of Light," *CH* 58 (Fall 1979).

Lumbering and forest products: C. Raymond Clar, *California Government and Forestry From Spanish Days . . . [to] 1927* (Sacramento, 1959); Lynwood Carranco, *Redwood Lumber Industry* (San Marino, 1982); W. H. Hutchinson,

California Heritage: A History of Northern California Lumbering (Rev. ed., Santa Cruz, 1974); Hank Johnston, *The Whistles Blow No More: Railroad Logging in the Sierra Nevada, 1874-1942* (Glendale, 1984); and Stuart Nixon, *Redwood Empire* (New York, 1966).

Maritime activities: Giles T. Brown, *Ships that Sail No More: Marine Transportation from San Diego to Puget Sound, 1910-1940* (Lexington, Ky., 1966); Wallace E. Martin, comp., *Sail and Steam on the Northern California Coast, 1850-1900* (San Francisco, 1985); Robert J. Schwendinger, *International Port of Call: An Illustrated History of the Golden Gate* (Woodland Hills, 1984); and Nicholas P. Hardeman, *Harbor of the Heartlands: A History of The Inland Seaport of Stockton . . . from the Gold Rush to 1985* (Stockton, 1986).

Mining: Gary L. Shumway, et al., *Desert Fever: An Overview of Mining in the California Desert* (Canoga Park, 1981); George H. Hildebrand, *Borax Pioneer: Francis Marion Smith* (La Jolla, 1982); Ruth C. Woodman, *The Story of the Pacific Coast Borax Company* (Los Angeles, 1951); and Robert L. Kelley, *Gold vs. Grain, The Hydraulic Mining Controversy in California's Central Valley* (Glendale, 1960).

Oil: Indispensable are "The Petroleum Industry," entire *PHR* issue, 39 (May 1970) and two books by Gerald T. White, *Scientists in Conflict: The Beginnings of the Oil Industry in California* (New York, 1968) and *Formative Years in the Far West: A History of the Standard Oil Company of California and Predecessors through 1919* (San Marino, 1968). Other good treatments of corporate founders and leaders are William H. Hutchinson, *Oil Land and Politics: The California Career of Thomas Robert Bard* (2 vols.; Norman, 1965) and Frank J. Taylor and Earl M. Welty, *The Black Bonanza* (2nd ed.; New York, 1958).

The basic sourcebook on labor in California is Mitchell Slobodek, *A Selective Bibliography of California Labor History* (Los Angeles, 1964). (Works cited hereafter are *not* in Slobodek.) Two recent general histories have been written by David F. Selvin: *Sky Full of Storm: A Brief History of California Labor* (San Francisco, 1975) and *A Place in the Sun: A History of California Labor* (San Francisco, 1981). On labor politics see Gerald D. Nash, "The Influence of Labor on State Policy, 1860-1920," *CHQ*, 42 (September 1963) and Philip Taft, *Labor Politics, American Style: The California State Federation of Labor* (Cambridge, Mass., 1968).

On the IWW in specific places and incidents see Cletus Daniel, "In Defense of the Wheatland Wobblies: A Critical Analysis of the I.W.W. in California," *LH*, 19 (Fall 1978); Grace L. Miller, "The I.W.W. Free Speech Fight: San Diego, 1912," *SCQ*, 54 (Fall 1972); Ronald Genini, "Industrial Workers of the World and Their Fresno Free Speech Fight, 1910-1911," *CHQ*, 53 (Summer 1974); Charles P. Le Warne, "On the Wobbly Train to Fresno," *LH*, 14 (Spring 1973); Nelson Van Valen, "'Cleaning up the Harbor': The Suppression of the I.W.W. at San Pedro, 1922-1925," *SCQ*, 66 (Summer 1984); and Elizabeth Reis, "Cannery Row: The AFL, the IWW and the Bay Area Cannery Workers," *CH*, 64 (Summer 1985).

An overriding and continuous California issue is water. A basic work on the subject is Lawrence B. Lee, *Reclaiming the American West: An Historiography and Guide* (Santa Barbara, 1980). (Works cited in Lee are not listed here.) General studies include Barney Hope and Michael Sheehan, "The Political Economy of Centralized Water Supply in California," *Social Science Journal*, 20 (April 1983); William L. Kahrl, ed., *California Water Atlas* (Sacramento, 1979); Donald J. Pisani, *From Family Farm to Agribusiness: The Irrigation Crusade in California and the West, 1850-1931* (Berkeley, 1984); "Water in California," entire *PH* issue, 26 (Spring 1983); and Albert N. Williams, *The Water and the Power: Development of the Five Great River Systems of the West* (New York, 1951). On the central region see W. Turrentine Jackson and Alan M. Paterson, *The Sacramento-San Joaquin Delta and the Evolution and Implementation of a Water Policy: An Historical Perspective* (Davis, 1977); W. T. Jackson and S. D. Mikesell, *The Stanislaus River Drainage Basin and the New Melones Dam: Historical Evolution of Water Use Priorities* (Davis, 1979); Tim Palmer, *Stanislaus: The Struggle for a River* (Berkeley, 1982); and Richard A. Walker and Matthew J. Williams, "Water from Power: Water Supply and Regional Growth in the Santa Clara Valley," *Economic Geography*, 58 (April 1982). On San Francisco and the Hetch Hetchy controversy, studies include Kendrick A. Clements, "Politics and the Park: San Francisco's Fight for Hetch Hetchy, 1908-1913," *PHR*, 48 (May 1979); J. S. Holliday, "The Politics of John Muir," *CH*, 63 (Spring 1984); Elmo R. Richardson, "The Struggle for the Valley: California's Hetchy Controversy," *CHSQ*, 38 (September 1959); Eric Seaborg, "The Battle for Hetch Hetchy," *Sierra*, 66 (November/December 1981); Ted Wurm, *Hetch Hetchy and Its Dam Railroad* (Berkeley, 1973); and John W. Noble, *Its Name was M.U.D.* (San Francisco, 1970).

There is a voluminous literature on southern California water. On the subject in general, still useful is J. A. Alexander, *The Life of George Chaffey* (Melbourne, Australia, 1928), as is Anthony F. Turhollow, *A History of the Los Angeles District, U.S. Army Corps of Engineers, 1898-1965* (Los Angeles, 1975). On the Colorado River and Boulder Dam see Paul L. Kleinsorge, *The Boulder Canyon Project: Historical and Legal Aspects* (Stanford, 1941) and Beverly B. Moeller, *Phil Swing and Boulder Dam* (Berkeley, 1971). On Imperial Valley see Alton Duke, *When the Colorado River Quit the Ocean* (Yuma, 1974); Robert L. Sperry, "When the Imperial Valley Fought for Its Life," *JSDH*, 21 (Winter 1975); and Paul S. Taylor, "Water, Land, and Environment in Imperial Valley: Law Caught in the Wind of Politics," *Natural Resources Journal*, 13 (January 1973).

On the notorious Owens Valley controversy all of the voluminous earlier writings have been superseded by two superb recent works: Abraham Hoffman, *Vision or Villainy: Origins of the Owens Valley-Los Angeles Water Controversy* (College Station, Tex., 1981) and William L. Kahrl, *Water and Power: The Conflict Over Los Angeles' Water Supply in the Owens Valley* (Berkeley, 1982).

The phenomenal growth of southern California, 1880-1930, most historians agree, was a part of the general economic boom wrought chiefly by railroad expansion. An overall treatment is found in Doyce B. Nunis, Jr., ed., *A Southern California Historical Anthology* (Los Angeles, 1985) and in McWilliams, *Southern California Country*. Very useful are W. W. Robinson, *Panorama: A Picture History of Southern California* (Los Angeles, 1953) and Remi A. Nadeau, *City Makers* (Garden City, N.Y., 1948). On other southern California cities see the numerous pamphlet histories by W. W. Robinson. Richard Pourade's *History of San Diego* is helpful. On the great real estate boom the basic study is Glenn S. Dumke, *The Boom of the Eighties in Southern California* (San Marino, 1944), which has a good bibliography of earlier studies. An extended study is Michael F. Sheehan, "Land Speculation in Southern California: The Roles of Railroads, Trolley Lines, and Autos," *American Journal of Economics and Sociology*, 40 (April 1982).

On "boosters" promoting such booms see Donald P. Culton, "Los Angeles' 'Citizen Fixit': Charles Dwight Willard, City Booster and Progressive Reformer," *CH*, 57 (Summer 1978); Tom Zimmerman, "Paradise Promoted—Boosterism and the Los Angeles Chamber of Commerce," *CH*, 64 (Winter 1985); and John E. Baur, "California's Nineteenth Century Futurists," *SCQ*, 53 (March 1971).

On Los Angeles' famous "free harbor" fight Charles A. Matson, *Building a World Gateway: The Story of Los Angeles Harbor* (Los Angeles, 1945), is still useful as a general study. The roles of political leaders in the fight are portrayed in Edith Dobie's and Curtis Grassman's works on Stephen Mallory White, Culton's article on Willard, and Don A. Shotliff, "San Pedro Harbor or Los Angeles Harbor? Senator W. H. Savage and the Home Rule Advocates Fail to Stem the Tide of Consolidationism, 1906-1909," *SCQ*, 44 (Summer 1972). On the role of the railroads in the movement see Ernest Marquez, *Port of Los Angeles: A Phenomenon of the Railroad Era* (San Marino, 1976).

On the seemingly crucial role played by railroads generally in southern California's development, the major lines are treated in Edna M. Parker, "The Southern Pacific Railroad and Settlement in Southern California," *PHR*, 6 (June 1937); Lewis B. Lesley, "The Entrance of the Santa Fe Railroad into California," *PHR*, 8 (March 1939); and Keith Bryant, *History of the Atchison, Topeka, and Santa Fe Railway* (New York, 1975). On smaller lines and interurbans see Spencer Crump, *Ride the Big Red Cars: How Trolleys Helped Build Southern California* (Los Angeles, 1962); Eli Bail, *From Railway to Freeway: Pacific Electric and the Motor Coach* (Glendale, 1984); William A. Myers and Ira L. Swett, *Trolleys to the Surf: The Story of the Los Angeles Pacific Railway* (Glendale, 1976); and Patrick W. O'Bannon, "Railroad Construction in the Early Twentieth Century: The San Diego and Arizona Railway," *SCQ*, 61 (Fall 1979).

California experienced a cultural as well as an economic boom in the Gilded Age/Progressive era. The outstanding general works, with extensive bibliographies, are Kevin Starr, *Americans and the California Dream, 1850-1915* (New York, 1973) and *Inventing the Dream: California Through the Progressive Era* (New York, 1985).

Useful surveys on the arts include Thomas Albright, *Twentieth Century Art in the San Francisco Bay Region: An Illustrated History* (Berkeley, 1984) and Henry W. Splitter, "Art in Los Angeles Before 1900," *SCQ*, 41 (January 1959). Nancy D. W. Moure, *The Dictionary of Art and Artists in Southern California Before 1900* (La Jolla, 1974) is a useful introduction, and Edan M. Hughes, *Artists in California, 1786-1940* (San Francisco, 1986) is basic. The art of photography has long been an important element in California culture. General treatments of this gigantic subject are Joseph A. Baird, Jr., ed., *Images of El Dorado: A History of California Photography, 1850-1975* (Davis, 1975) and Terry Mangan and Laverne Dicker, *California Photographers, 1852-1920* (San Francisco, 1977).

The enormous literature on the motion picture industry inevitably defeats efforts of bibliographers to be comprehensive. Useful guides, however, are Frances M. Christenson, *A Guide to the Literature of the Motion Picture* (Los Angeles, 1938) and Theatre Arts Library, UCLA, *Motion Pictures: A Catalog of Books, Periodicals, Screen Plays, and Production Stills* (Los Angeles, 1972). A few of the comprehensive histories are Jack C. Ellis, *A History of Film* (Englewood Cliffs, N.J., 1979); Albert R. Fulton, *Motion Pictures: The Development of an Art from Silent Films to the Age of Television* (Norman, 1960); Richard Griffith and Arthur Mayer, *The Movies: A Sixty-Year Story of the World of Hollywood and Its Effect on America from the Pre-Nickelodeon Days to the Present* (Rev. ed.; New York, 1981); Lewis Jacobs, *The Rise of the American Film: A Critical History* (Rev. ed.; New York, 1968); Arthur Knight, *The Liveliest Art* (Rev. ed.; New York, 1978); and Gerald Mast, *A Short History of the Movies* (Indianapolis, 1976).

A plethora of good writing on California architecture and architects exists. On the subject in general see Geoffrey E. Bangs, *Portals West: A Folio of Late Nineteenth Century Architecture in California* (San Francisco, 1960) and two works by Harold Kirker, *California's Architectural Frontier: Style and Tradition in the Nineteenth Century* (Rev. ed.; Santa Barbara, 1973) and "California Architecture and Its Relation to Contemporary Trends in Europe and America," *CHQ*, 51 (Winter 1972). On San Francisco and northern California, see Joseph A. Baird, *Time's Wondrous Changes: San Francisco Architecture, 1776-1915* (San Francisco, 1963); David Gebhard, et al., *A Guide to Architecture in San Francisco and Northern California* (Santa Barbara, 1973); and Roger Olmsted, T. H. Watkins, and Morley Baer, *Here Today: San Francisco's Architectural Heritage* (San Francisco, 1979). On Los Angeles and the south, see David Gebhard and Robert Winter, *A Guide to Architecture in Los Angeles and Southern California* (Layton, 1980) and Frank Harris, ed., *A Guide to Contemporary Architecture in Southern California* (Los Angeles, 1951).

For the urban theatre, 1880-1930, see Edmond M. Gagey, *The San Francisco Stage, A History* (New York, 1950). On music, see Howard Swan, *History of Music in the Southwest, 1825-1950* (San Marino, 1952); John Sanders, "Los Angeles Grand Opera Association: The Formative Years, 1924-1926," *SCQ*,

55 (Fall 1973); and Caroline E. Smith, *The Philharmonic Orchestra of Los Angeles: "The First Decade," 1919-1929* (Los Angeles, ca.1930).

A standard introduction to literary California, a huge subject, is Edgar J. Hinkel, ed., *A Bibliography of California Fiction, Poetry, Drama* (3 vols.; Oakland, 1938). Selective use can be made of two excellent recent works: Richard W. Etulain, *A Bibliographic Guide to Western Literature* (Lincoln, 1982) and J. Golden Taylor and Thomas J. Lyon, et al., eds. *A Literary History of the American West* (Fort Worth, 1986). Among general studies two books by Ella S. Mighels, *The Story of the Files: A Review of California Writers and Literature* (San Francisco, 1893) and *Literary California: Poetry, Prose and Portraits* (San Francisco, 1918) are still useful. Excellent recent studies are Stoddard Martin, *California Writers* (New York, 1984) and Charles Crow, ed., *Itinerary: Criticism, Essays on California Writers* (Bowling Green, Ohio, 1978), and among several books by Lawrence C. Powell his *California Classics: The Creative Literature of the Golden State* (Los Angeles, 1971) is indispensable. Useful regional studies include Marvin R. Nathan, "San Francisco's *Fin de Siecle* Bohemian Renaissance," *CH*, 61 (Fall 1982); Lawrence Ferlinghetti and Nancy J. Peters, *Literary San Francisco* (San Francisco and New York, 1980); Lionel Rolfe, *Literary Los Angeles* (San Francisco, 1981); Henry W. Splitter, "Literature in Los Angeles Before 1900," *JW*, 5 (January 1966); Franklin Walker, *The Seacoast of Bohemia* (2nd ed.; Salt Lake City, 1972); and his volumes on San Francisco and Los Angeles.

California has been premier in the art of fine printing. Succinct and useful is Julie Bellefeuille, "Printing in California, 1831-1930," *PH*, 19 (Fall 1975); James D. Hart, *Fine Printing in California* (Berkeley, 1960); Ward Ritchie, "Fine Printing in Southern California," in *A Bookman's View of Los Angeles* (Los Angeles, 1961); and the latter two authors' joint essays in *Influence on California Printing* (Los Angeles, 1970). An excellent work is Louise F. Barr, *Presses of Northern California and Their Books, 1900-1933* (Berkeley, 1934). *The Book Club of California Quarterly News-Letter* has a number of biographical and bibliographical essays, as does *The Kemble Occasional*, published by the California Historical Society.

Journalism has flourished in California since 1846. The basic guide is California State Library Foundation, *Newspapers in California* (Sacramento, 1985). Still useful is John P. Young, *Journalism in California* (San Francisco, 1915). On San Francisco journalism, John R. Bruce, *Gaudy Century: The Story of San Francisco's Hundred Years of Robust Journalism* (New York, 1948) is stimulating. Informative is Jerome Hart, *In Our Second Century, From an Editor's Notebook* (San Francisco, 1931). Noteworthy is M. Suzanne Donovan, *San Francisco Neighborhood and Ethnic Newspapers* (San Francisco, 1980).

On publishers and editors the literature tends to be dominated by the presence of William Randolph Hearst. Probably the best biography is W. A. Swanberg, *Citizen Hearst: A Biography of William Randolph Hearst* (New York, 1961).

On other commanding figures see Evelyn Wells, *Fremont Older* (New York, 1916) and Fremont Older, *My Own Story* (New York, 1926). Also useful is Marshall Berges, *The Life and Times of Los Angeles: A Newspaper, A Family, and a City* (New York, 1982).

California has been a leader in education and academe. On the public school system consult Nicolas C. Polos, *John Swett* and "The Educational Philosophy of John Swett and John Muir," *PH*, 26 (Spring 1982); and Solomon P. Jaeckel, "Edward Hyatt, 1858-1919: California Educator," *SCQ*, 52 (March/June/September 1970), are also excellent on education leaders.

Public education in California has been the subject of numerous masters theses and doctoral dissertations, most completed in schools of education. Too numerous to list, these graduate studies range across the entire spectrum, from histories of local school districts and individual schools, to outstanding educational leaders. In addition, there are a considerable number of articles on the history of California education in the *CHSQ, PH, APHSSC, QHSSC, SCQ*, and the *JSDH*.

In the field of higher education the scholarship is somewhat spotty. John R. Thelin, "California and the Colleges," *CHQ*, 56 (Summer/Fall 1977), is very useful. On the University of California, Berkeley, are Verne A. Stadtman, *The University of California, 1868-1968* (New York, 1970) and Alberta G. Pickerell and May Dornin, *The University of California: A Pictorial History* (Berkeley, 1968). See also Thomas Barnes, *Hastings College of the Law: The First Century* (San Francisco, 1978). On the sister campus, see Andrew Hamilton and John B. Jackson, *UCLA On the Move During Fifty Golden Years, 1919-1969* (Los Angeles, 1969). The oldest member of the State University system (formerly State College system) is treated capably in Benjamin F. Gilbert, *Washington Square, 1857-1979: The History of San Jose State University* (San Jose, 1980).

Private colleges and universities have been treated in histories by Mark D. McNamee, *Light in the Valley: The Story of California's College of Notre Dame* (San Diego, 1967); Andrew F. Rolle, *Occidental College: The First Century* (Los Angeles, 1987); E. Wilson Lyon, *The History of Pomona College, 1877-1969* (Claremont, 1977); Gerald McKevitt, *The University of Santa Clara: A History, 1851-1977* (Stanford, 1979); Peter C. Allen, *Stanford: From the Foothills to the Bay* (Stanford, 1980); Charles B. Burdick, *Ralph H. Lutz and the Hoover Institution* (Stanford, 1974); Manuel Servin and Iris H. Wilson, *Southern California and Its University: A History of USC, 1880-1964* (Los Angeles, 1969); and Charles W. Cooper, *Whittier: Independent College in California, Founded by Quakers, 1887* (Los Angeles, 1967).

The history of the medical profession in California, which has its ancestral roots in the Spanish colonial period, has been treated in Henry Harris, *California's Medical Story* (San Francisco, 1932); George H. Kress, *History of the Medical Profession of Southern California* (Los Angeles, 1910); and J. Roy Jones, *History of the Medical Society of the State of California* (Sacramento, 1964).

Individual histories exist for the medical associations in San Francisco, Sacramento, and Los Angeles, as well as in the counties of Alameda and Orange.

The religious landscape in California is varied. Most studies of California Protestantism focus on the southland. Two recent exceptions are Douglas F. Anderson, "San Francisco Evangelicalism, Regional Religious Identity and the Revivalism of D. L. Moody," *Fides et Historia*, 15 (1983) and Mike Foster, "Franklin Rhoda and Bay Area Presbyterianism, 1880–1916," *Journal of Presbyterian History*, 62 (Summer 1984).

On California Catholicism all students are indebted to superbibliographer and historian Francis J. Weber. A few of his most useful contributions are *A Select Guide to California Catholic History* (Los Angeles, 1966); *A Select Bibliography to California Catholic Literature, 1856–1974* (Los Angeles, 1974); *A Select Bibliographical Guide to California Catholic Periodical Literature* (Los Angeles, 1973); *A Select Bibliography of the California Missions* (Los Angeles, 1972); *California Catholicism* (Los Angeles, 1974); and his edited work, *The Religious Heritage of Southern California* (Los Angeles, 1976). Weber's mentioned books are a veritable gold mine of historical information on the Catholic Church in California's history.

Important general treatments of California politics during the Gilded Age, 1880–1900, and beyond are Royce D. Delmatier, Clarence F. McIntosh, and Earl G. Waters, eds., *The Rumble of California Politics, 1848–1970* (New York, 1970); H. Brett Melendy and Benjamin F. Gilbert, *The Governors of California: Peter Burnett to Edmund G. Brown* (Georgetown, 1965); Michael P. Rogin and John L. Shover, *Political Change in California: Critical Elections and Social Movements* (Westport, 1970); Robert G. Cleland, *From Wilderness to Empire* (New York, 1959) and *California in Our Time, 1900–1940* (New York, 1947); Herbert L. Phillips, *Big Wayward Girl: An Informal Political History of California* (Garden City, N.Y., 1968); and Carey McWilliams, *California: The Great Exception* (New York, 1949).

General treatments of California's governmental and administrative systems and certain aspects of public policy are Elizabeth Cappell, *Constitutional Officers, Agencies, Boards and Commissions in California State Government, 1849–1975* (Berkeley, 1977); Greg King, *Deliver Us From Evil: A Public History of the California Civil Service System* (Sacramento, 1979); William C. Frankhouser, *A Financial History of California: Public Revenues and Expenditures* (Berkeley, 1913); Frances Cahn and Valeska Bary, *Welfare Activities of Federal, State and Local Governments in California, 1850–1934* (Berkeley, 1936); and Richard W. Fox, *So Far Disordered in Mind: Insanity in California, 1870–1930* (Berkeley, 1978).

Studies arguing that a large amount of cooperation and coordination existed between California government and the business community both in the Gilded Age and Progressive Era following it are Mansel G. Blackford, *The Politics of Business in California, 1890–1920* (Columbus, Ohio, 1977) and Gerald D. Nash,

State Government and Economic Development: A History of Administrative Policies in California, 1849-1933 (Berkeley, 1964). Agreeing somewhat with this contention, but more inclined to deplore it and to emphasize progressive efforts to curb some business behavior is Spencer C. Olin, *California Politics, 1846-1920: The Emerging Corporate State* (San Francisco, 1981).

The most important, or at least the most controversial, business remained the railroads, and previously mentioned books by Daggett, Lavender, Lewis, Taylor, and Tutorow are also useful for this period. The traditional view that the railroads, especially the Southern Pacific, dominated California political life and defeated all attempts at governmental regulation at that time, e.g., S. E. Moffett, "The Railroad Commission of California, A Study in Irresponsible Government," *AAAPSS*, 6 (November 1895), is challenged by Nash in his book (above) and in "The California Railroad Commission, 1876-1911," *SCQ*, 44 (December 1962). Nash in turn is challenged by Ward McAfee in "A Constitutional History of Railroad Rate Regulation in California, 1879-1911," *PHR*, 37 (August 1968) and at greater length and with qualifications in his *California's Railroad Era, 1850-1911* (San Marino, 1973). Nash's view is supported by W. H. Hutchinson, "Southern Pacific: Myth and Reality," *CHSQ*, 48 (December 1969) and by R. Hal Williams, *The Democratic Party and California Politics, 1880-1896* (Stanford, 1973).

On the question of the railroads and land monopoly Richard J. Orsi has an interesting revisionist article, "The *Octopus* Reconsidered: The Southern Pacific and Agricultural Modernization in California, 1865-1915," *CHQ*, 54 (Fall 1975). On the notorious Mussel Slough affair, the best authority is James L. Brown, *The Mussel Slough Tragedy* (2nd ed.; Hanford, Calif., 1980) and "More Fictional Memorials to Mussel Slough," *PHR*, 26 (November 1957), the latter, a sequel to Irving McKee, "Notable Memorials to Mussel Slough," *PHR*, 17 (March 1948). See also Wallace Smith, *Garden of the Sun* (3rd ed., Fresno, 1956).

The 1880s and early 1890s are usually characterized as a period of conservatism and corruption. Both Delmatier, et al., Melendy and Gilbert (above) are useful here. So is George H. Tinkham, *California Men and Events: 1769-1890* (Stockton, 1915). On the notorious political corruption of the time, especially associated with "Boss Buckley," see William A. Bullough, *The Blind Boss and His City: Christopher Augustine Buckley and Nineteenth Century San Francisco* (Berkeley, 1979).

Trends toward xenophobic bigotry other than racism are well treated in John Higham, "The American Party, 1886-1891," *PHR*, 19 (February 1950) and Roger Daniels and Eric F. Petersen, "California's Grandfather Clause: The 'Literacy in English' Amendment of 1894," *SCQ*, 50 (March 1968). One of the leading opponents of nativism, directed against his fellow Irish Catholics, was Father Peter C. Yorke, about whom a substantial literature exists. See James P. Walsh, *Ethnic Militancy* (San Francisco, 1972) and Joseph Brusher, *Consecrated Thunderbolt* (Hawthorne, N.J., 1973).

The subject of radicalism in California is ably treated in David B. Griffiths,

"Anti-Monopoly Movements in California, 1873-1898," *SCQ*, 52 (June 1970), and Howard Quint, "Gaylord Wilshire and Socialism's First Congressional Campaign," *PHR*, 26 (November 1957), is enlightening on the "Nationalist" movement.

Despite the alleged conservatism of the period, it is widely recognized that California virtually rained reform movements at this time. Their degree of success or failure, however, is a matter of some disagreement. Agrarian reform movements of all kinds are described in Clarke A. Chambers, *California Farm Organizations* (Berkeley, 1951).

For labor-led reform movements Gerald Nash shows convincingly that unions were quite successful in securing passage of labor legislation during this era in "The Influence of Labor on State Policy, 1860-1920: The Experience of California," *CHSQ*, 42 (September 1963). On the Workingmen's Party and its decline, see Ralph Kauer, "The Workingmen's Party of California," *PHR*, 13 (September 1944). On specific labor disputes, see William R. Ray, "Crusade or Civil War? The Pullman Strike in California," *CH*, 58 (September 1979) and Henry W. Splitter, "Concerning Vinette's Los Angeles Regiment of Coxey's Army," *PHR*, 17 (February 1948).

On the subject of urban reform and reform leaders a number of good studies exist. An excellent summation is Curtis E. Grassman, "Prologue to California Reform: The Democratic Impulse, 1886-1898," *PHR*, 42 (November 1973). A good study on an outstanding Los Angeles civic leader is Kenneth Johnson, *Stephen Mallory White* (Los Angeles, 1980). An outstanding modern study on the San Francisco scene is William Issel and Robert W. Cherny, *San Francisco, 1865-1932: Politics, Power, and Urban Development* (Berkeley, 1986). Two good studies of reform achievements during this period are Eric F. Peterson, "The Struggle for the Australian Ballot in California," *CH*, 51 (Fall 1972) and Martha Chickering, "An Early Experiment in State Aid to the Aged, 1883-1895," *Social Service Review*, 12 (March 1938).

The California conservation and preservation movements also have their roots in the era. Basic general studies are Gordon B. Dodds, "Conservation and Reclamation: A Critical Bibliography," *A&W*, 13 (Summer 1971); Samuel P. Hays, *Conservation and the Gospel of Efficiency: The Progressive Conservation Movement* (Cambridge, Mass., 1959); and Roderick Nash, *Wilderness and the American Mind* (3rd ed.; New Haven, 1982).

Efforts to reform the state by splitting it in two continued in this era, as discussed in two articles by Roberta McDow, "To Divide or Not to Divide?" *PH*, 10 (Autumn 1966) and "State Separation Schemes, 1907-1921," *CHSQ*, 49 (March 1970). See also Michael Di Leo and Eleanor Smith, *Two Californias: The Truth about the Split-State Movement* (Covelo, Calif., 1983).

The effects of these various reform upheavals on party politics and party realignment are handled skillfully by at least three able scholars. R. Hal Williams' book (above) is very informative. Eric F. Petersen, "The End of an Era: California's Gubernatorial Election of 1894," *PHR*, 38 (May 1969), is indispensable.

Three articles by Harold F. Taggart are also very enlightening: "The Senatorial Election in California in 1893," *CHSQ*, 19 (March 1940); "The Party Realignment of 1896 in California," *PHR*, 8 (December 1939); and "The Election of 1898 in California," *PHR*, 19 (December 1950). Winfield F. Davis, *History of Political Conventions in California* (Sacramento, 1893) is useful as far as it goes.

Although the heyday of California progressivism came after the election of 1910, several scholars have shown that a considerable amount of piecemeal progressivism occurred during the preceding decade. An excellent summary of many advances is Gerald D. Nash, "Bureaucracy and Economic Reform: The Experience of California, 1899-1911," *WPQ*, 13 (September 1960). Various aspects of reform politics are discussed in Petersen, "Prelude to Progressivism" and W. H. Hutchinson, *Oil, Land, and Politics*. Hutchinson's "Prologue to Reform: The California Anti-Railroad Republicans, 1899-1905," *SCQ*, 44 (September 1962), is also highly relevant.

The effort to reform the cities during this decade was an important prelude to progressivism. Good general accounts of the San Francisco situation can be found in Issel and Cherny, *San Francisco* and in John B. McGloin, *San Francisco: The Story of a City* (San Rafael, 1978). On the famed Ruef-Schmitz machine, Walton Bean, *Boss Ruef's San Francisco* (Berkeley, 1952), is a classic study, and James P. Walsh, "Abe Ruef Was No Boss," *CHQ*, 51 (Spring 1972), is an important revisionist study. On Los Angeles see Martin J. Schiesl, "Progressive Reform in Los Angeles under Mayor Alexander, 1909-1913," *CHQ*, 44 (Spring 1975).

On the role of the Lincoln-Roosevelt League in bringing about the Progressive triumph in 1910, the best modern study is Spencer C. Olin, "Hiram Johnson, the Lincoln-Roosevelt League, and the Election of 1910," *CHSQ*, 45 (September 1966).

The outstanding studies of the California progressive movement in general (which also cover much of the background data discussed above) are George Mowry, *The California Progressives* (Berkeley, 1951) and Spencer C. Olin, *California's Prodigal Sons: Hiram Johnson and the Progressives, 1911-1917* (Berkeley, 1968). Franklin Hichborn published several separate histories of the legislative sessions of 1909, 1911, 1913, 1915, and 1921, each entitled *The Story of the California Legislature* . . . (San Francisco, 1913-1922), which are very partisan but also full of useful information.

On progressive leaders Mowry wrote an interesting profile, "The California Progressive and His Rationale: A Study in Middle Class Politics," *MVHR*, 26 (September 1949). Much has been written about Hiram Johnson's early political and gubernatorial career (his career in the U.S. Senate is dealt with below under foreign policy), but surprisingly he still lacks a full-length, published, scholarly biography. Irving McKee provides vital background information in "The Background and Early Career of Hiram Johnson," *PHR*, 19 (February 1950).

Studies of other progressive leaders, perhaps some questionable as to their progressive credentials, are Schiesl's article on Mayor Alexander; Keith W. Olson, *Biography of a Progressive: Franklin K. Lane, 1864-1921* (Westport, 1979); Marshall Stimson, "A Los Angeles Jeremiah: Homer Lea, Military Genius and Prophet," *QHSSC*, 24 (March 1942); Charles K. McClatchy, *Private Thinks by C.K.* (New York, 1936); Roger W. Lotchin, "John Francis Neylan: San Francisco Irish Progressive," in James P. Walsh, ed., *San Francisco Irish, 1850-1976* (San Francisco, 1978); Cornelia S. Parker, *An American Idyll: The Life of Carleton H. Parker* (Boston, 1919); Moses Rischin, "Sunny Jim Rolph: The First Mayor of all the People," *CHQ*, 53 (Summer 1974); Donald R. Culton, "Los Angeles' 'Citizen Fixit': Charles Dwight Willard, City Booster and Progressive Reformer," *CH*, 57 (Summer 1978); and Grace H. Larsen, "A Progressive in Agriculture: Harris Weinstock," *AH*, 32 (July 1958).

Most historians see the progressives as moderates disassociating themselves from both right-wing and left-wing extremism that troubled the state in this era. An interesting sidelight on this frame of mind is Gerald S. Henig, "'He Did Not Have a Fair Trial'—California Progressives React to the Leo Frank Case," *CH*, 58 (Summer 1979). On left-wing extremism and violence, both Graham Adams, Jr., *The Age of Industrial Violence, 1910-1915* (New York, 1966) and Louis Adamic, *Dynamite* (New York, 1935), have chapters on California. On the famous Los Angeles *Times* bombing case surprisingly little good scholarship exists. A good beginning is W. W. Robinson, *Bombs and Bribery* (Los Angeles, 1969) and Herbert Shapiro, "The McNamara Case: A Crisis of the Progressive Era," *SCQ*, 59 (Fall 1977). On the Mooney case, however, an extensive and largely partisan literature exists. It is nicely summarized in Albert F. Gunns, "The Mooney-Billings Case: An Essay Review," *PNQ*, 60 (October 1969). The outstanding scholarly work is Richard H. Frost, *The Mooney Case* (Stanford, 1968); Estolv E. Ward, *The Gentle Dynamiter: A Biography of Tom Mooney* (Palo Alto, 1983) makes some interesting if unverified assertions. On the nonviolent left, see Ira B. Cross, "Socialism in California Municipalities," *National Municipal Review*, 1 (October 1912). On right-wing extremism, see Stephen C. Levi's, "The Trial of William McDevitt," *SCQ*, 59 (Fall 1977) and *Committee of Vigilance: The San Francisco Chamber of Commerce Law and Order Committee* (Jefferson, N.C., 1983).

Progressive socioeconomic reform includes labor legislation and policies. These are capably handled in Nash, "Influence of Labor on State Policy." Norris Hundley, Jr., "Katherine Phillips Edson and the Fight for the California Minimum Wage, 1912-1915," *PHR*, 29 (August 1960), is excellent. On agricultural labor, see Carleton Parker, *The Casual Laborer and Other Essays* (New York, 1920). Spencer C. Olin, Jr., "European Immigrant and Oriental Alien: Acceptance and Rejection by the California Legislature of 1913," *PHR*, 35 (August 1966), shows adeptly how progressive sympathy for white immigrants and laborers was offset by hostile prejudice toward Orientals. (See Chapter 8, *post*.) Another reform is treated in Gene and Helen Caite, *Police Reform in the United States: The Era of August Vollmer, 1905-1932* (Berkeley, 1975). On business regulation Mansel G. Blackford, "Businessmen and the Regulation of Railroads and Public Utilities in California During the Progressive Era," *Business History Review*, 44 (August 1970), is very sound.

On conservation and the environment during this crucial era general studies such as Richard White, "American Environmental History: The Development of a New Historical Field," *PHR*, 54 (August 1985) and Elmo R. Richardson, *The Politics of Conservation: Crusades and Controversies, 1897-1913* (Berkeley, 1963), are very relevant to California. On specific conservation projects of the era, see Susan R. Schrepfer's excellent *The Fight to Save the Redwoods: A History of Environmental Reform* (Madison, 1983); Ronald F. Lockman, *Guarding the Forests of Southern California: Evolving Attitudes Toward Conservation of Watershed, Woodlands, and Wilderness* (Glendale, 1981); and Diana Lindsay, "The Creation of the Anza Borrego Desert State Park," *JSDH*, 19 (Fall 1973).

That progressivism wrought fundamental changes in California's political system, practically all historians and political scientists agree. A good general description is Dean McHenry, "The Pattern of California Politics," *WPQ*, 1 (March 1948). The reapportionment issue is capably treated in Francis N. Ahl, "Reapportionment in California," *American Political Science Review*, 22 (November 1928) and Thomas S. Barclay, "Reapportionment in California," *PHR*, 5 (June 1936).

Voting patterns in the era are revealingly disclosed in three articles by Charles H. Titus in *Southwestern Political and Social Science Quarterly*: "Voting in California Cities, 1900-1925," 8 (March 1928); "Rural Voting in California, 1900-1926," 9 (September 1928); and "Voting in California, 1900-1926," 10 (June 1929). The success of the progressives in securing the support of organized labor is convincingly shown in Michael Rogin, "Progressivism and the California Electorate," *JAH*, 55 (September 1968). See also Mary Ann M. Burki, "The California Progressives: Labor's Point of View," *LH*, 17 (Winter 1976). (See Chapter 9, *post*, for woman suffrage movement.)

The direct primary, a progressive reform which actually preceded the main Progressive Era, is capably dealt with in Eric F. Petersen, "The Adoption of the Direct Primary in California," *SCQ*, 54 (Winter 1972); Arthur Harris and Carl Uhr, *Direct Primary Elections: Bureau of Public Administration, 1941 Legislative Problems, No. 3* (Berkeley, 1941); Victor J. West, "The California Direct Primary," *AAAPSS*, 106 (March 1923); and E. C. Campbell, "Party Nominations in California," *Southwestern Social Science Quarterly*, 12 (December 1931). On direct legislation, see Winston W. Crouch, *The Initiative and Referendum in California* (Los Angeles, 1950) and Frederick L. Bird and Frances M. Ryan, *The Recall of Public Officers: A Study of the Operation of the Recall in California* (New York, 1930).

Probably the most radical of the progressive political innovations was the cross-filing system, which reputedly played a major role in weakening political parties in the state. See James C. Findley, "Cross Filing and the Progressive Movement in California Politics," *WPQ*, 12 (September 1959); Dean McHenry, "Cross

Filing of Political Candidates in California," *AAAPSS*, 248 (November 1946); Franklin Hichborn, "The Party, the Machine, and the Vote: The Story of Cross-filing in California Politics," *CHSQ*, 38 (December 1959) and 39 (March 1960); H. Brett Melendy, "California's Cross-Filing Nightmare: The 1918 Gubernatorial Election," *PHR*, 33 (August 1964); and Robert Pitchell, "The Electoral System and Voting Behavior: The Case of California's Cross-Filing," *WPQ*, 12 (June 1959). On the weakening and fragmenting of political parties, see Stanley D. Hopper, "Fragmentation of the Republican Party in the One Party Era, 1893–1932," *WPQ*, 28 (July 1975).

On the decline of the Democratic party during the progressive era, see Robert E. Hennings, "California Democratic Politics in the Period of Republican Ascendancy," *PHR*, 31 (August 1962). On the controversial election of 1916 and Hiram Johnson's role in the Democrats' victory for Woodrow Wilson, the earlier literature is largely summarized and superseded by Spencer C. Olin, Jr., "Hiram Johnson, the California Progressives and the Hughes Campaign of 1916," *PHR*, 31 (November 1962).

Because of the times in which they lived, the California progressives had a considerable impact on American foreign policy. See Thomas G. Patterson, "California Progressives and Foreign Policy," *CHSQ*, 47 (December 1968). Of course their main impact was through the long and largely negative influence of Hiram Johnson in the U.S. Senate. Johnson's personal papers for this period are expertly edited and arranged by Robert E. Burke in *The Diary Letters of Hiram Johnson* (7 vols.; New York, 1983). General studies of the positions taken by Johnson are Selig Adler, *The Isolationist Impulse* (New York, 1957) and Ralph A. Stone, *The Irreconcilables: The Fight Against the League of Nations* (Lexington, Ky., 1970). A well-done study is Richard C. Lower, "Hiram Johnson: The Making of an Irreconcilable," *PHR*, 41 (November 1972). Howard De Witt has three pertinent articles on the subject: "Hiram Johnson and World War I: A Progressive in Transition," *SCQ*, 56 (Fall 1974); "Hiram W. Johnson and Economic Opposition to Wilsonian Diplomacy: A Note," *PH*, 19 (Spring 1975); and "The 'New' Harding and American Foreign Policy: Warren G. Harding, Hiram W. Johnson, and Pragmatic Diplomacy," *Ohio History*, 86 (Spring 1977). Johnson's continuing relationship with "Teddy" is seen in A. Lincoln, "My Dear Senator— Letters Between Theodore Roosevelt and Hiram Johnson in 1917," *CHSQ*, 42 (September 1963) and "My Dear Friend and Champion: Letters Between Theodore Roosevelt and Hiram Johnson in 1918," *CHSQ*, 48 (March 1969). Senator Johnson's various bids for the presidency of the United States are dealt with in Ralph Arnold, "Laying Foundation Stones," *QHSSC*, 37 (June/September/ December 1955) and Robert E. Hennings, "Harold Ickes and Hiram Johnson in the Presidential Primary of 1924," in Donald L. Tingley, ed., *Essays in Illinois History: In Honor of Glen Huron Seymour* (Carbondale, Ill., 1968).

Historians disagree on whether the 1920s decade was an era of reaction or a continuation of the progressive movement. Most California history textbooks argue the former, taking their cues from Mowry, *California Progressives*. The contrary is argued in Jackson K. Putnam's "The Persistence of Progressivism in the 1920's: The Case of California," *PHR*, 35 (November 1966), *Modern California Politics* (2nd ed.; San Francisco, 1984), and *Old-Age Politics in California: From Richardson to Reagan* (Stanford, 1970); and in Daniel P. Melcher, "The Challenge to Normalcy: The 1924 Election in California," *SCQ*, 60 (Summer 1978). See also John L. Shover, "The California Progressives and the 1924 Campaign," *CHQ*, 51 (Spring 1971) and "Was 1928 a Critical Election in California?" *PNQ*, 58 (October 1957); and Russell Posner, "The Progressive Voters' League, 1923–1926," *CHSQ*, 36 (September 1957).

A continued polarization between right- and left-wing extremists during the 1920s is a generally agreed-upon phenomenon among historians. Howard A. De Witt, *Images of Ethnic and Radical Violence in California Politics, 1917–1930* (San Francisco, 1975) is exaggerated but significant. The difficulties faced by working classes is demonstrated in Jessica B. Peixoto, *Cost of Living Studies II: How Workers Spend a Living Wage* (Berkeley, 1929) and in Emily H. Huntington, *Unemployment Relief and the Unemployed in the San Francisco Bay Region, 1929–1934* (Berkeley, 1939). Radical efforts to gain strength during the decade are recounted in Ralph E. Shaffer, "Formation of the California Communist Labor Party," *PHR*, 36 (February 1967) and in "Communism in California, 1919–1924: 'Orders from Moscow' or Independent Western Radicalism?" *Science and Society*, 34 (Winter 1970). See also Martin Zanger, "Politics of Confrontation: Upton Sinclair and the Launching of the ACLU in Southern California," *PHR*, 38 (November 1969). On the right-wing reaction, see Edwin Layton, "The Better America Federation: A Case Study of Superpatriotics," *PHR*, 30 (May 1961) and Roger Lotchin, "The Darwinian City: The Politics of Urbanization in San Francisco Between the World Wars," *PHR*, 68 (August 1979); and two studies by Woodrow C. Whitten: *Criminal Syndicalism and the Law in California: 1919–1927, Transactions of the American Philosophical Society*, New Series, Vol. 59, Part 2 (Philadelphia, 1969) and "Trial of Charlotte Anita Whitney," *PHR*, 15 (September 1946).

The effects of Prohibition during this era are ably handled in Gilman Ostrander, *The Prohibition Movement in California, 1848–1933* (Berkeley, 1957). See also Wendell E. Harmon's "The Bootlegger Era in Southern California," *QHSSC*, 37 (December 1955); John R. Meers, "The California Grape and Wine Industry and Prohibition," *CHSQ*, 46 (March 1967); and Kenneth D. Rose, "'Dry' Los Angeles and Its Liquor Problems in 1924," *SCQ*, 69 (Spring 1987).

4

THE GREAT DEPRESSION AND WORLD WAR II, 1930–1945

JAMES J. RAWLS

A PROPER UNDERSTANDING of California history during the Great Depression and World War II requires the broadest possible context. Events far from the borders of California had a powerful impact on the state. One of the earliest efforts to analyze the economic effects of the depression is Paul N. Woolf, *Economic Trends in California, 1929–1934* (Sacramento, 1935). More comprehensive is Frank L. Kidner, *California Business Cycles* (Berkeley, 1946).

State efforts at providing economic relief and stimulating recovery generally were ineffective during the 1930s. For a discussion of state aid programs, see Leigh Athearn, *Unemployment Relief in Labor Disputes* (Los Angeles, 1939). In the early thirties, California experimented with conservation camps for unemployed men, as described in Harold D. Carew, "A Fair Deal Wins—A Foul Dole Loses," *Touring Topics*, 28 (November 1933).

Aid programs from the federal government provided substantial benefits to the state's economy during the depression. Leonard J. Arrington, "The Sagebrush Resurrection: New Deal Expenditures in the Western States, 1933-1939," *PHR*, 52 (February 1983), argues that the 1930s were a turning point in state and regional history because of the great contributions of federal agencies to western states. Likewise, Richard Lowitt, *The New Deal and the West* (Bloomington, Ind., 1984) stresses the enormous scale of federal aid to the western states, including funds to accelerate completion of the two great bridges across San Francisco Bay, although both were pre-New Deal nonfederal projects, and $38 million for Boulder Dam. A general history of the Boulder Dam/Hoover Dam project and its importance is Remi A. Nadeau, *The Water Seekers* (Garden City, N.Y., 1950).

Probably the greatest federal contribution was the funding of the Central Valley Project (CVP). Because the state was unable to pay for the project, the Federal Bureau of Reclamation took it over in 1935 and construction began two years later. Robert William de Roos, *The Thirsty Land: The Story of the Central Valley Project* (Stanford, 1948), offers a thorough account, including an introduction to the controversy over whether control of the electrical power generated should be public or private. Also generally supportive of the Bureau of Reclamation and public power is Marion Clawson, *The Effect of the Central Valley Project on the Agricultural and Industrial Economy and on the Social Character of California* (Berkeley, 1945). On the manifold legal issues surrounding the project, see "The Central Valley Project and Related Problems," a special edition of the *California Law Review*, 38 (October 1950). The best introduction to the subject, complete with illuminating maps and charts, is William Kahrl, ed., *The California Water Atlas* (Sacramento, 1979).

The political reaction to the Great Depression in California came slowly at first—and then it became extreme and frantic. The most conspicuous political result was the revival of the Democratic party, a turn of events well described in "The Resurgence of the Democratic Party in California," in Michael P. Rogin and John L. Shover, *Political Change in California* (Westport, 1970).

The power of the resurgent Democratic party was expressed early in the decade. In 1931 the state legislature adopted a reapportionment act which gave Democratic southern California a larger share of congressional and state assembly seats, best described in Thomas S. Barclay, "Reapportionment in California," *PHR*, 5 (June 1936). The following year California Democrats played an important part in the nomination and election of Franklin D. Roosevelt, as described in Russell M. Posner, "California's Role in the Nomination of Franklin D. Roosevelt," *CHSQ*, 39 (June 1960).

In spite of the rising Democratic tide, California's first elected governor in the 1930s was a Republican. At the time of the 1930 gubernatorial election, the economic stresses of the depression had not yet become critical and so James Rolph, Jr., the colorful Republican mayor of San Francisco for nineteen years. was elected. Most of the studies of Rolph's leadership concentrate on his mayoralty years. Morley Segal, "James Rolph, Jr., and the Early Days of the San Francisco Municipal Railway," *CHSQ*, 43 (March 1964) explores Rolph's role in the creation of America's first municipally owned railroad. Moses Rischin, "Sunny Jim Rolph: The First 'Mayor of All the People,'" *CHQ*, 53 (Summer 1974), characterizes Rolph as the "most picturesque and convivial figure ever to appear on the California political scene." Studies of Rolph's governorship are limited to general political histories such as H. Britt Melendy and Gilbert Gilbert, *The Governors of California* (Georgetown, Calif., 1965), which criticizes Rolph for his failure to provide effective leadership during the depression, and Jackson K. Putnam, *Modern California Politics* (2nd ed.; San Francisco, 1984), who describes Rolph as a "humane but weak man." The grim climax to Rolph's career is detailed in Brian McGinty, "Shadows in St. James Park," *CH*, 57 (Winter 1978-1979).

Rolph died while campaigning for renomination in 1934 and was succeeded by Lieutenant Governor Frank Merriam, a former Long Beach real estate agent, who won the Republican nomination. The Democratic primary was won by one of the nation's best-known socialists, Upton Sinclair. The 1934 election, in which Merriam defeated Sinclair, proved one of the hardest fought contests in California history. An indispensable source for the election is Sinclair's utopian novel *I, Governor of California, and How I Ended Poverty: A True Story of the Future* (Los Angeles, 1933), in which the candidate explains his EPIC (End Poverty in California) plan. See also Sinclair's retrospective *I, Candidate for Governor, and How I Got Licked* (Los Angeles, 1935) and Charles E. Larsen, "The Epic Campaign of 1934," *PHR*, 27 (May 1958).

Thorough political analyses of the 1934 election also appear in Rogin and Shover, *Political Change in California*. Leonard Leader, "Upton Sinclair's EPIC Switch: A Dilemma for American Socialists," *SCQ*, 62 (Winter 1980), chronicles the devastating effect of Sinclair's Democratic candidacy on the Socialist party in California. Russell M. Posner, "A. P. Giannini and the 1934 Campaign in California," *QHSSC*, 39 (June 1957), describes the vigorous efforts of the founder of the Bank of America to defeat Sinclair. Bob Barger, "Raymond L. Haight and the Commonwealth Progressive Campaign of 1934," *CHSQ*, 43 (September 1964), suggests that Haight's independent candidacy has been cast into undeserved obscurity. Walton Bean, "Ideas of Reform in California," *CHQ*, 51 (Fall 1972), concludes that the damage Sinclair did to the Democratic party and to New Deal liberalism was "apparent for decades." Fascinating recollections of the 1934 campaign, by several dozen participants, appear in Fay M. Blake and H. Morton Newman, "Upton Sinclair's EPIC Campaign," *CH*, 63 (Fall 1984).

The administration of the victor in that election has been almost completely neglected. Rogin and Shover, in *Political Change in California*, dismiss Merriam as a representative of the standpat wing of the Republican party. The judgment of Melendy and Gilbert, *Governors of California*, is especially harsh. Royce D. Delmatier, et al., eds., *The Rumble of California Politics* (New York, 1970) offers a more balanced appraisal. Putnam's *Modern California Politics* goes even further in rehabilitating Merriam's reputation.

The governor who is usually credited with bringing the New Deal to the Golden State is Culbert L. Olson, the Democrat who defeated Merriam in his bid for re-election in 1938. The definitive study of his administration is Robert E. Burke, *Olson's New Deal for California* (Berkeley, 1953). While openly sympathetic to Olson, Burke's analysis centers on the failure of Olson to accomplish all that he intended. For a laudatory campaign biography, see Frank Scully, *The Next Governor of California* (n.p., 1938).

Partly because of the failure of executive leadership in the thirties, California spawned an impressive number of social and economic panaceas. The most significant of these was the pension plan movement of Dr. Francis E. Townsend, described by its founder in *New Horizons: An Autobiography* (Chicago, 1943). The origins of the movement are presented in J. D. Gaydowski, "Eight Letters to the Editor: The Genesis of the Townsend National Recovery Plan," *SCQ*, 52 (December 1970). Abraham Holtzman, *The Townsend Movement: A Political Study* (New York, 1963), summarizes the historical literature on the subject. The best account of the movement and its relation to state politics is found in Putnam, *Old-Age Politics in California* (Stanford, 1970).

The wide range of California panacea movements during the depression is surveyed in Luther Whiteman and Samuel L. Lewis, *Glory Roads: The Psychological State of California* (New York, 1936). Entertaining as well as informative is Carey McWilliams' portrayal of the same phenomenon in *Southern California Country* (New York, 1946). On specific groups see Winston Moore and Maria Moore, *Out of the Frying Pan* (Los Angeles, 1939), an informal history of the rise of the Ham 'n Eggs movement; Tom Zimmerman, "Ham and Eggs Everybody!" *SCQ*, 62 (Spring 1980); William E. Akin, *Technocracy and the American Dream: The Technocrat Movement, 1900–1941* (Berkeley, 1977); and Gregory R. Woirol, "The American Technotax Society: Whittier, California: 1934–1935," *SCQ*, 65 (Fall 1983). The standard works on California utopianism are both by Robert V. Hine, *California's Utopian Colonies* (New York, 1966) and *California Utopianism* (San Francisco, 1981). The most popular of the "social messiahs" of the thirties was evangelist Aimee Semple McPherson. (See Chapter 9, *post*.)

The social history of California during the Great Depression is marked by several significant episodes. The arrival of more than a third of a million impoverished migrants from the Dust Bowl had a permanent impact on the state. A good introduction to this powerful human drama are the photographs and words of Dorothea Lange and Paul S. Taylor in *An American Exodus: A Record of Human Erosion* (New York, 1939). Walter J. Stein, *California and the Dust Bowl Migration* (Westport, 1973), examines the migration and describes the reaction which the migrants provoked.

As the Dust Bowl migrants arrived in California, farm labor organization revived. The classic account of the plight of the farmworkers and their efforts to unionize is Carey McWilliams, *Factories in the Field: The Story of Migratory Farm Labor in California* (Boston, 1939). A useful analysis is Clarke A. Chambers, *California Farm Organizations . . . 1929–1941* (Berkeley, 1952). Lloyd S. Fisher, *The Harvest Labor Market in California* (Cambridge, Mass., 1953), summarizes in a single sentence one of the most important qualities of California agriculture which determined worker-employer relations: "Farming in California is a business and not a way of life." Cletus E. Daniels, *Bitter Harvest: A History of California Farmworkers, 1870–1941* (Ithaca, 1981), explains why farmworker organization and strike activity reached a peak in the 1930s. The efforts to organize cannery and warehouse workers are described in Gerald A. Rose, "The

March Inland: The Stockton Cannery Strike of 1937," *SCQ*, 54 (Spring/Summer/ Fall 1972) and in Harvey Schwartz, *The March Inland: Origins of the ILWU Warehouse Division, 1934-1938* (Los Angeles, 1978).

Traditionally California farmworkers have been either alien or nonwhite—or both. The influx of native-born whites into the farm labor market during the depression thus disrupted a familiar pattern. *Unwanted Mexican Americans in the Great Depression: Repatriation Pressures, 1929-1939* (Tucson, 1974), by Abraham Hoffman, describes the efforts of the federal and local bureaucrats to rid the state of unneeded Mexican laborers. Francisco E. Balderrama, *In Defense of La Raza: The Los Angeles Mexican Consulate and the Mexican Community, 1929 to 1936* (Tucson, 1982), shows how the Mexican consul in Los Angeles supported and helped organize Mexicans in southern California. Meanwhile the efforts of Los Angeles employers to perpetuate "an unfree labor system" for Mexican workers is described in Douglas Monroy, "Like Swallows at the Old Mission: Mexicans and the Racial Politics of Growth in Los Angeles in the Interwar Period," *WHQ*, 14 (October 1983).

The most dramatic event in California labor history during the Great Depression was the San Francisco waterfront and general strike of 1934. Historiographical interest in the strike has centered on the role of union leader Harry Bridges and the extent of communist involvement. For its part, the Communist party claimed a major role in building solidarity among the waterfront workers. See William F. Dunne, *The Great San Francisco General Strike* (New York, 1934). Opponents of the strike have hammered away at Harry Bridges' alleged communist ties. Paul Eliel, *The Waterfront and General Strikes, San Francisco, 1934: A Brief History* (San Francisco, 1934), condemns Bridges as a man with "strong Communistic leanings if not actually Communistic connections." James Oneal and G. A. Werner, *American Communism: A Critical Analysis of its Origins, Development and Program* (New York, 1947), characterize Bridges as a "faithful follower of the 'party line.'"

Other scholars have denied the importance of the Communist party in the 1934 strike. Paul S. Taylor and Norman L. Gold, "The San Francisco and the General Strike," *Survey Graphic*, 23 (September 1934); Mike Quinn [*pseud.*], *The Big Strike* (Olema, Calif., 1949); Philip Taft, *Organized Labor in American History* (New York, 1964) and *Labor Politics American Style: The California State Federation of Labor* (Cambridge, Mass., 1968), are generally favorable to Bridges. The most complete, but decidedly unauthorized, biography of Bridges was written by Charles P. Larrowe, *Harry Bridges: The Rise and Fall of Radical Labor in the United States* (New York, 1972), who dispassionately considers the question of communist involvement in the 1934 strike and describes at length the subsequent and unsuccessful efforts by the federal government to deport Bridges. Harvey Schwartz, "Harry Bridges and the Scholars: Looking at History's Verdict," *CH*, 59 (Spring 1980), is an excellent overall historiographical essay.

The history of California during the 1930s is not just a story of collapse and conflict. Early in the decade, Los Angeles was the scene of the 1932 Olympic games. John Lucas, "Prelude to the Games of the Tenth Olympiad in Los Angeles, 1932," *SCQ*, 64 (Winter 1982), describes the planning that made the games a successful public event. The California Historical Society dedicated an issue of its quarterly to the 1932 Olympics: *Champions in the Sun*, *CH*, 63 (Winter 1984). San Francisco was host to the 1939 World's Fair. Richard Reinhardt, *Treasure Island: San Francisco's Exposition Years* (San Francisco, 1973), captures the glitter and excitement of the event.

The years between the Olympics and the World's Fair were a time of fluorescence in California's cultural history. Robinson Jeffers, the state's greatest poet, published some of his most memorable verse during this period. Among the many critical studies of Jeffers are Lawrence C. Powell, *Robinson Jeffers: The Man and His Work* (Los Angeles, 1934); James R. Squires, *The Loyalties of Robinson Jeffers* (Ann Arbor, 1956); and Frederic I. Carpenter, *Robinson Jeffers* (New York, 1962). It was also in the 1930s that California's most important novelist, John Steinbeck, produced his greatest work. Jackson K. Benson, *The True Adventures of John Steinbeck, Writer* (New York, 1984), is a thorough study. John St. Pierre, *John Steinbeck: The California Years* (San Francisco, 1984), is a brief but excellent discussion of Steinbeck's life and work in the thirties.

The dominant figure in California journalism in the 1930s was William Randolph Hearst. W. A. Swanberg, *Citizen Hearst* (New York, 1961), interprets the publisher as a man of magnificent triumphs and tragedies. A more indulgent biography is Cora B. Older, *William Randolph Hearst, American* (New York, 1936). On other major journalistic enterprises of the period, see Robert A. Rosenstone, "Manchester Boddy and the L.A. Daily News," *CHSQ*, 49 (December 1970) and Robert Gottlieb and Irene Wolt, *Thinking Big: The Story of the Los Angeles Times, Its Publishers, and Their Influence on Southern California* (New York, 1977).

California's most distinctive contribution to American culture is the Hollywood film. During the 1930s the film industry remained more prosperous than many other industries—largely because public demand for its products was higher than ever. Leo C. Rosten, *Hollywood: The Movie Colony, the Movie Makers* (New York, 1941), is a survey of the industry as it was in the late thirties. Two additional studies of note are Ken Jones and Arthur McClure, *Hollywood at War: The American Motion Picture and World War II* (Cranberry, N.J., 1973) and Charles Highan and Joel Greenberg, *Hollywood in the '40s* (New York, 1968).

José Rodríquez, et al., eds., *Music and Dance in California* (Hollywood, 1940) is a collection of original essays by California musicians and dancers. More traditional cultural histories of the period include Howard Swan, *History of Music in the Southwest* (San Marino, 1952), which describes the efforts of the Federal Music Project to aid destitute musicians, and Nancy D. W. Moure, *Painting and Sculpture in Los Angeles, 1900–1945* (Los Angeles, 1980), which discusses the support of the Federal Art Project for sculptors and painters. See also John A.

Emerson, "The WPA Federal Music Project in San Francisco: A Guide to Events and Sources," in Stephen M. Fry, ed., *California's Musical Wealth: Sources for the Study of Music in California* (Los Angeles, 1986). Isabel M. Jones, *Hollywood Bowl* (New York, 1936), tells the story of the Los Angeles Philharmonic Orchestra, while Arthur Bloomfield, *The San Francisco Opera, 1922-1978* (Sausalito, 1978), describes the grand conclusion to this institution's long-time search for adequate quarters, the triumphal opening of the San Francisco War Memorial Opera House in 1932.

Less than a decade after the dedication of the Opera House as a memorial to the Great War, the nation was again engaged in global conflict. World War II's impact on California's development during the twentieth century is comparable to that of the gold rush in the nineteenth. A comprehensive history of the impact of the war on California remains to be written. Gerald D. Nash, *The American WestTransformed: The Impact of the Second World War* (Bloomington, Ind., 1985), offers an original synthesis of major wartime developments throughout the Far West. He devotes a full chapter to the war's impact on California cities, including San Diego, Los Angeles, San Francisco, Oakland, Vallejo, and Richmond. The most valuable contribution is his analysis of the 10,000 cultural and religious refugees who came to southern California during the war. The emigrés included such luminaries as Thomas Mann, Bertold Brecht, and Arnold Schoenberg. A succinct overview is Jarrell Jackman, "Exiles in Paradise: German Emigrés in Southern California, 1933-1950," *SCQ*, 61 (Summer 1979).

Nedra B. Belloc, *Wages in California: War and Postwar Changes* (Berkeley, 1948), shows that while wages of California workers increased during the war years, the increases were far from uniform. Other general accounts of California's economic expansion are James J. Parsons, "California Manufacturing," *Geographical Review*, 39 (April 1949); Forest G. Hill, "The Shaping of California's Industrial Pattern," *Proceedings of the Thirtieth Annual Conference of the Western Economic Association* (Stanford, 1955); and Victor R. Fuchs, *Changes in the Location of Manufacturing in the United States Since 1929* (New Haven, 1962).

California's economic expansion during the 1940s led directly to a population increase, especially in the state's major metropolitan areas. Martin J. Schiesl, "City Planning and the Federal Government in World War II: The Los Angeles Experience," *CH*, 59 (Summer 1980), describes the war years as a time of cooperation between local planners and federal officials. Roger Lotchin has written three articles which provide essential background to the wartime expansion of California's cities: "The City and the Sword: San Francisco and the Rise of the Metropolitan Military Complex, 1919-1941," *JAH*, 65 (March 1979); "The Metropolitan Military Complex in Comparative Perspective: San Francisco, Los Angeles, and San Diego, 1919-1941," *JW*, 17 (July 1979); and "The Darwinian City: The Politics of Urbanization in San Francisco between the World Wars," *PHR*, 48 (August 1979).

Within a year of America's entry into World War II, new shipyards had sprung up at Richmond, Oakland, Sausalito, Vallejo, and San Pedro. The expansion of the shipbuilding industry during the war years is described in the Bureau of Labor Statistics, *Wartime Employment, Production, and Conditions of Work in Shipyards* (Washington, D.C., 1945). A more interpretive account appears in Wytze Gorter and George H. Hildebrand, *The Pacific Coast Maritime Shipping Industry, 1930-1948* (Berkeley, 1952, 1954). The expansion of the shipyards in the early 1940s placed a considerable strain on surrounding communities. "Richmond Took a Beating," *Fortune*, 31 (February 1945), describes the growing pains of one such community. Katherine Archibald, *Wartime Shipyard: A Study in Social Disunity* (Berkeley, 1947), analyzes the tense social environment of the shipyards and their accompanying boomtowns.

The other great enterprise to undergo rapid expansion during the war was the aircraft industry. Unlike the shipyard industry, the production of aircraft in California continued to expand after the war. The standard short account is John B. Rae, *Climb to Greatness: The American Aircraft Industry, 1920-1960* (Cambridge, Mass., 1968). See also Frank J. Taylor and Lawton Wright, *Democracy's Air Arsenal* (New York, 1947) and William G. Cunningham, *The Aircraft Industry: A Study in Industrial Location* (Los Angeles, 1951). Arthur P. Allen and Betty V. H. Schneider, *Industrial Relations in the California Aircraft Industry* (Berkeley, 1956), offers a more thorough analysis. The prewar background of the industry is well described in Arlene Elliott, "The Rise of Aeronautics in California, 1849-1940," *SCQ*, 52 (March 1970).

The man most responsible for managing California affairs during the expansive years of World War II was Earl Warren. Elected governor as the Republican candidate in 1942, Warren was returned to office four years later by winning both the Republican and Democratic primaries. He went on to become the only governor in the state's history to be elected to three terms. One of the first full-length studies of his life was a campaign biography by Irving Stone, *Earl Warren: A Great American Story* (New York, 1948). One of the best accounts of Warren's governorship is Richard B. Harvey, *Earl Warren: Governor of California* (New York, 1969). Following Warren's appointment as United States Chief Justice in 1953, he became the subject of several generally sympathetic, nonscholarly, journalistic biographies: Leo Katcher, *Earl Warren: A Political Biography* (New York, 1967) and John D. Weaver, *Warren: The Man, the Court, the Era* (Boston, 1967). A somewhat more balanced appraisal appears in Luther A. Huston, *Pathway to Judgement: A Study of Earl Warren* (Philadelphia, 1966).

Two of the most recent studies of Warren have viewed his career as a paradox. Jack Pollack, *Earl Warren: The Judge Who Changed America* (Englewood Cliffs, N.J., 1979), poses and probes "The Warren Paradox." How was it that a man of supposedly limited ability and moderate conservatism became a great and crusading liberal chief justice? G. Edward White, *Earl Warren: A Public Life* (New York, 1982), finds the answer to the paradox in a proper understanding of Warren's California years. White's biography stresses the inherent, inescapable connection between Warren's years as California public official and his decisions as chief justice, a similar theme found in the posthumously published *Memoirs of Earl Warren* (Garden City, N.Y., 1977).

As Putnam observes, in his *Modern California Politics*, one of the most controversial aspects of Warren's governorship was his stand on the "subversion" issue. Putnam credits Warren with helping to save the state from the deadly polarization of McCarthy-like extremism. Edward R. Long, "Earl Warren and the Politics of Anti-Communism," *PHR*, 51 (February 1982), argues that, as attorney general and governor, Warren "accepted the goals and on occasion used the tactics of anti-Communism associated with the Wisconsin senator." In 1941 the legislature created the Fact-Finding Committee on Un-American Activities, chaired by state assemblyman Jack Tenney. Ingrid W. Scobie, "Jack B. Tenney and the 'Parasitic Menace': Anti-Communist Legislation in California 1940–1949," *PHR*, 43 (May 1974), points out that as early as 1941 and 1942, Tenney proposed loyalty oaths for members of the legal and medical professions. Two other studies emphasize the role of the Tenney Committee in investigating non-Communist, right-wing, and authoritarian groups during the war years: Edward L. Barrett, Jr., *The Tenney Committee: Legislative Investigation of Subversive Activities in California* (Ithaca, 1951) and Robert L. Pritchard, "California Un-American Activities Investigations: Subversion on the Right?" *CHSQ*, 49 (December 1970).

In retrospect, the single most controversial action taken by Warren during his California career was his forceful recommendation in 1942 that the Japanese-American population of the state be relocated. Following Warren's recommendation—and that of other public officials on the West Coast—President Roosevelt issued Executive Order 9066 authorizing the relocation. (See Chapter 8, *post*.)

One of the most thorough accounts of relocation is Jacobus ten Broek, Edward N. Barnhart, and Floyd W. Matson, *Prejudice, War, and the Constitution* (Berkeley, 1954). Stetson Conn, Rose C. Engleman, and Byron Fairchild, eds., *The United States Army in World War II: The Western Hemisphere: Guarding the United States and Its Outposts* (Washington, D.C., 1964), reveals that the decision to relocate Japanese Americans was made at a meeting between President Roosevelt, Secretary of War Henry Stimson, and Assistant Secretary John McCloy. Nevertheless, Roger Daniels' *Concentration Camps USA: Japanese Americans and World War II* (New York, 1971), shows that Washington officials went out of their way to obtain military recommendations for a policy already decided upon. Michi Weglyn, *Years of Infamy: The Untold Story of America's Concentration Camps* (New York, 1976), offers a startling new analysis of relocation. In "The Decisions to Relocate the North American Japanese: Another Look," *PHR*, 51 (February 1982), Roger Daniels concludes that the argument that removal was a military necessity is "a mere fig leaf for a racism that had been endemic against Asians for nearly a century."

On the Supreme Court decisions which upheld the constitutionality of relocation, see Eugene V. Rostow, "The Japanese American Cases—A Disaster," *Yale Law Journal*, 54 (June 1945); Edward S. Corwin, *Total War and the Consti-*

tution (New York, 1947); and Sidney Fine, "Mr. Justice Murphy and the Hira-bayashi Case," *PHR*, 33 (May 1964).

The social history of California in the 1940s reveals that Japanese Americans were not the only minority group to be powerfully affected by World War II. The desperate shortage of labor in the state's war industries attracted blacks in unprecedented numbers to California. The percentage of blacks in the state rose from 1.8 in 1940 to 4.3 by 1950. (For historical background on the wartime migration of blacks, see Chapter 7, *post*.)

Expanding economic opportunity was also responsible for an increase in Hispanic immigration to California during the war years. In 1942 the United States and Mexico signed an agreement for the temporary immigration of farm laborers. This agreement marked the beginning of the formal bracero program, a "wartime emergency" program which lasted until 1964. The legislative history of the bracero agreement is contained in Otey M. Scruggs, "The Evolution of the Mexican Farm Labor Agreement of 1942," *AH*, 34 (July 1960). N. Ray Gilmore and Gladys W. Gilmore, "The Bracero in California," *PHR*, 32 (August 1963), traces the evolution of an informal program in the 1920s, the repatriation pressures of the 1930s, and the successful lobbying by California farmers for an international agreement in the 1940s. Ernesto Galarza, *Merchants of Labor: The Mexican Bracero Story* (Charlotte, N.C., 1964), shows how the original wartime measure was perpetuated long after the war by the continuing pressure of California agribusiness interests. One of the most thorough analyses of the condition of the braceros themselves is Henry P. Anderson's *The Bracero Program in California* (New York, 1976), which views the bracero program as actually worse than chattel slavery, a judgment shared by Truman E. Moore, *The Slaves We Rent* (New York, 1965).

Tensions between Anglo and Mexican Californians during the war erupted into violence in a series of bitter confrontations known as the "zoot-suit riots." The psychological dimensions of these outbreaks is examined in Mauricio Mazón, *The Zoot-Suit Riots: The Psychology of Symbolic Annihilation* (Austin, 1984). For a general account of the wartime Mexican experience and its historical background, see Carey McWilliams, *North from Mexico: The Spanish-speaking People of the United States* (Philadelphia, 1949). (See also Chapter 6, *post*.)

World War II was a catalyst for change in the status of California women, just as it was for the state's ethnic minorities. The demand for wartime workers led to a sharp increase in the number of women in the California labor force. On the status of women workers, see *Women at Work in California* (Sacramento, 1978), compiled by the California Employment Development Department. Among the many studies of the changing role of women in American society, see especially William Chafe, *The American Woman: Her Changing Social, Economic, and Political Roles, 1920–1970* (New York, 1972); Carol Ruth Berkin and M. B. Norton, *Women of America: A History* (New York, 1979); and Carl N. Degler, *At Odds: Women and the Family in America from the Revolution to the Present* (New York, 1980). (See also Chapter 9, *post*.)

As should be plain by now—from the present essay and the others in this volume—the historiography of California is rich. For just the period 1930 to 1945, hundreds of scholars have staked out their territories and made important contributions. Yet there remain major gaps in our knowledge. We do not yet have a comprehensive history of California in the Great Depression, nor of the impact of World War II on the state. California still is without a thorough political history, an economic or business history, a cultural history, a history of California agriculture, labor, education, ethnic minorities, or science and technology. The basic materials for such general histories surely are at hand.

5

CALIFORNIA SINCE 1945

PAUL BULLOCK

ONE OF THE BEST available overviews of California politics since 1945 is Gladwin Hill, *Dancing Bear: An Inside Look at California Politics* (New York, 1968), a journalistic but perceptive account. More scholarly is Michael P. Rogin and John L. Shover, *Political Change in California* (Westport, 1960). While agreeing with the authors on the perniciousness of southern California's "right-wing" politics, one reviewer, Jackson K. Putnam, "Political Change in California: A Review Essay," *SCQ*, 53 (December 1971), strongly dissents from their explanation of the psychological and sociological origins of such politics.

Another useful historical overview is *The Rumble of California Politics* (New York, 1970), ed. by Royce D. Delmatier, et al. Analytical profiles of the governors, through the administration of Edmund G. (Pat) Brown, may be found in H. Brett Melendy and Benjamin F. Gilbert, *The Governors of California* (Georgetown, Calif., 1965). A standard text on politics and government is Winston Crouch, John Bollens, and Stanley Scott, *California Government and Politics* (7th ed.; Englewood Cliffs, N.J., 1981).

Two of the key winners in the 1946 election, Richard M. Nixon and Earl Warren, have been the subjects of several biographies. Two of Nixon's few sympathetic biographers are Ralph de Toledano, *One Man Alone: Richard Nixon* (New York, 1969) and journalist Earl Mazo, *Richard Nixon: A Political and Personal Portrait* (New York, 1959), but their accounts of the 1946 campaign are superficial and, in some respects, inaccurate. Even the memoirs of the antagonists, Nixon's *Memoirs* (New York, 1978) and Jerry Voorhis' *Confessions of a Congressman* (New York, 1947), treat this campaign superficially. The most comprehensive description may be found in Paul Bullock, *Jerry Voorhis: The Idealist as Politician* (New York, 1978). Two hostile biographers of Nixon, Fawn

Brodie, *Richard Nixon: The Shaping of His Character* (New York, 1981) and Frank Mankiewicz, *Perfectly Clear: Nixon from Whittier to Watergate* (New York, 1973), borrow heavily from Bullock's account, as does Nixon himself in his *Memoirs*.

The equally controversial 1950 Nixon-Douglas campaign also has been discussed and debated in historical literature. The memoirs of Nixon and of Mrs. Douglas, *A Full Life* (New York, 1982), give their respective interpretations. Ingrid W. Scobie illuminates the campaign in "Helen Gahagan Douglas and Her 1950 Senate Race with Richard M. Nixon," *SCQ*, 58 (Spring 1976), while de Toledano and Mazo describe it from a viewpoint friendlier to Nixon. Unlike the Nixon biographies, the biographies of Earl Warren tend to be sympathetic. (See Chapter 4, *ante*.)

The political career of Ronald Reagan has been well chronicled. The better biographies which cover his governorship are Joseph Lewis, *What Makes Reagan Run: A Political Profile* (New York, 1968); Lou Cannon, *Reagan* (New York, 1982); George H. Smith, *Who Is Ronald Reagan?* (New York, 1968); and one from a journalist who has a balanced view of the controversial former governor, Bill Boyarsky, *Ronald Reagan: His Life and Rise to the Presidency* (New York, 1981). Edmund G. (Pat) Brown is responsible for two expectedly hostile studies: *Reagan and Reality: The Two Californias* (New York, 1970) and, with Bill Brown, *Reagan: The Political Chameleon* (New York, 1976).

Another controversial political leader is former Governor Edmund G. (Jerry) Brown, Jr. The enigmatic younger Brown is profiled in a biography by John C. Bollens and G. Robert Williams, *Jerry Brown in a Plain Brown Wrapper* (Pacific Palisades, 1978), which is generally favorable to Brown but overoptimistic and untimely in its consideration of his prospects as a future presidential candidate. Jackson K. Putnam's *Modern California Politics* (2nd ed.) contains an incisive analysis of Brown's gubernatorial record. A balanced appraisal of Brown as a governor may be found in Mary Ellen Leary, "What Makes Jerry Run," *The Nation*, 222 (March 27, 1976) and "California and The Two Browns," *The Nation*, 227 (December 2, 1978).

A few other California politicians of the postwar era have been profiled in political biographies. Eleanor Fowle, *Cranston: The Senator from California* (San Rafael, 1980), provides some interesting personal insights and reminiscences, but also has the usual limitations of a biography written by a close relative. One of the most principled of southern California politicians, long-time Los Angeles County Supervisor John Anson Ford wrote a useful autobiography, *Thirty Explosive Years in Los Angeles County* (San Marino, 1961). One of the most paradoxical figures in California politics has been Samuel Yorty, whose perennial candidacies and colorful career are examined in John C. Bollens and Grant B. Geyer, *Yorty: Politics of a Constant Candidate* (Pacific Palisades, 1973).

A particularly intriguing aspect of postwar politics in California has been the rise (and fall) of volunteer organizations outside the official party framework. The most visible and flamboyant of these organizations has been the California

Democratic Council (CDC), first organized in 1953-1954. It has been analyzed by James Q. Wilson, *The Amateur Democrat* (Chicago, 1966) and Francis Carney, *The Rise of the Democratic Clubs in California* (New York, 1958). Carney perceptively explains the decline of CDC in "The Palsy of the CDC," *The Nation*, 210 (May 4, 1970). Some consideration of the role of the California Republican Assembly may be found in Hugh A. Bone, "New Party Associations in the West," *American Political Science Review*, 45 (December 1951).

At the polar extreme from the volunteers are the party professionals, the lobbyists, and the profitmaking technicians who plan and administer campaigns. In the past, CDC's chief opponent within the Democratic professional ranks had been Jesse Unruh, popularly known as "Big Daddy" while he was Speaker of the Assembly, who derived his power from an ability to raise and distribute campaign contributions throughout the party ranks. He is well profiled in articles by Ed Cray, "Jesse Unruh, 'Big Daddy' of California," *The Nation*, 196 (March 9, 1963); Helen Fuller, "The Man To See in California," *Harper's*, 226 (January 1963); and Jeremy Larner, "Jess Unruh and His Moment of Truth," *Harper's*, 242 (April 1971).

In earlier years, the most powerful political professional in California had been lobbyist Arthur Samish, whose influence declined precipitously after August 1949 when a two-part "exposé" appeared in *Collier's* (see Lester Velie, "The Secret Boss of California," August 13 and 20, 1949). Prominent among the political technicians who moved into the power vacuum left by Samish's departure have been the California team of Whitaker and Baxter, who are examined by Irwin Ross in "The Supersalesmen of California Politics: Whitaker and Baxter," *Harper's*, 219 (July 1959).

Until the U.S. Supreme Court decisions in the *Baker* v. *Carr* and *Reynolds* (1964) cases, which mandated legislative apportionment based on the "One Person, One Vote" principle, the issue of possible reapportionment of the State Senate was a heated one in California. Governor Earl Warren discusses the legal issues involved in reapportionment in his *Memoirs* (Garden City, N.Y., 1977). A general survey of this issue may be found in *The Politics of Reapportionment*, ed. by Malcolm E. Jewell (New York, 1962).

"Red baiting" in California, which was at its height in the period from 1946 to the decline of "McCarthyism" in the mid-1950s, has been explored in a number of books and articles. An especially valuable source of information and analysis is Barrett, *The Tenney Committee*, a comprehensive and scholarly review of the committee's activities. Also of value is Ingrid W. Scobie, "Jack B. Tenney and the 'Parasitic Menace': Anti-Communist Legislation in California 1940-1949," *PHR*, 43 (May 1974).

Perhaps the best source on the Hollywood blacklist is John Cogley's *Report on Blacklisting: I, Movies; II, Radio and Television* (2 vols.; New York, 1956). A more recent work consisting largely of interviews with "blacklisters" and "informers" is Victor S. Navasky, *Naming Names* (New York, 1980), which focuses on the personal and moral dilemmas associated with the processes of blacklisting, The major judicial case arising out of blacklisting has been discussed in Larry M. Wertheim, "Nedrick Young, *et al.*, v. MPAA, *et al.*: The Fight Against the Hollywood Blacklist," *SCQ*, 57 (Winter 1975).

Labor relations in the immediate postwar period were troubled, with a rash of strikes throughout the nation. In California, the most dramatic dispute erupted in the movie studios, where a jurisdictional feud between the International Alliance of Theatrical and Stage Employees and the United Brotherhood of Carpenters and Joiners of America led to charges of Communism and racketeering. As a board member and (from 1947) president of the Screen Actors Guild, Ronald Reagan played a major role as self-styled "mediator" and gained some recognition in the local labor movement. The strike-lockout is described in Paul Bullock, et al., *Building California: The Story of the Carpenters' Union* (Los Angeles, 1982). Reagan's account is available in his autobiography, *Where's the Rest of Me?*, with Richard Hubler (New York, 1965). Another significant strike in the postwar period occurred in Oakland, where a dispute at a major retail store resulted in a short-lived general strike throughout the city, the first such strike in California since the San Francisco general strike of 1934, and is depicted by Philip J. Wolman, "The Oakland General Strike of 1946," *SCQ*, 57 (Summer 1975).

One of the controversial and influential labor leaders in California has been Harry Bridges, the former long-time president of the International Longshoremen's and Warehousemen's Union. Charles P. Larrowe's *Harry Bridges* (New York, 1972), is a biography by a Marxist writer. With increasing mechanization of longshore operations, in 1960 the union and the waterfront employers negotiated a precedent-setting agreement governing the introduction of automation in the industry and its impact on employment, wages, and benefits. A thorough analysis of this so-called "Mechanization and Modernization Plan" may be found in Lincoln Fairley, *Facing Mechanization: The West Coast Longshore Plan* (Los Angeles, 1979).

Undoubtedly the most publicized union organizing campaign has taken place in agriculture. In the late 1960s and early 1970s, after years of frustration and failure, the United Farm Workers succeeded in organizing large numbers of farm workers and winning some key contracts. UFW leader César Chávez has used the boycott weapon effectively, although a hostile state administration, opposition from the Teamsters' Union, growing employer resistance, and some internal problems within the union have recently reduced its effectiveness. Chávez and the union are the subjects of several books: Peter Matthiessen, *Sal Si Puedes* (New York, 1969); Jacques Levy, *Cesar Chavez: Autobiography of La Causa* (New York, 1975); Anne Loftis and Dick Meiser, *A Long Time Coming: The Struggle to Unionize America's Farm Workers* (New York, 1977); John G. Dunne, *Delano: The Story of the California Grape Strike* (New York, 1971); and Ronald Taylor, *Chavez and the Farm Workers* (Boston, 1975). Two sociologists who once were UFW boycott organizers, Linda C. and Theodore J. Majka, have co-authored a recent book, *Farm Workers, Agribusiness, and the State* (Philadelphia, 1982). A viewpoint antagonistic to Chávez and the union often is expressed by William F. Buckley and others in the journal *National Review* (see, for example, August 10, 1971).

Particularly valuable accounts of the conditions of farm workers and the organizing struggles are contained in the books of Ernesto Galarza, who himself was an active organizer as well as a scholar: *Farm Workers and Agribusiness in California, 1947-1960* (Notre Dame, 1977); *Merchants of Labor: The Mexican Bracero Story* (Charlotte, N.C., 1964); and *Spiders in the House and Workers in the Field* (Notre Dame, 1970). Issues related to the bracero immigrant workers program and Mexican immigration in general are examined in Richard B. Craig, *The Bracero Program: Interest Groups and Foreign Policy* (Austin, 1971) and Otey M. Scruggs, "The United States, Mexico, and the Wetbacks," *PHR*, 30 (May 1961). The extremely complex issues related to the inflow of illegal aliens from Mexico are explored in Walter Fogel, *Mexican Illegal Alien Workers in the United States* (Los Angeles, 1978).

Another complicated issue is the coverage of farm workers by California's Agricultural Labor Relations Act. Some Californians, most of them hostile to the union, argue that farm workers should be covered by the National Labor Relations Act, as amended by the 1947 Taft-Hartley Act, which outlaws the "secondary boycott." *Labor and Property Rights in California Agriculture: An Economic Analysis of the CALRA*, by Rex L. Cottle, Hugh H. Macaulay, and Bruce Yandle (College Station, Tex., 1982), is an attack on the California act by conservative economists. A more balanced appraisal of the issue, from all viewpoints, may be found in *California Farm Labor Relations and Law*, ed. by Walter Fogel (Los Angeles, 1985).

The California economy as a whole is examined, with forecasts of future economic trends, in annual reviews published by the Graduate School of Management at UCLA. The Southern California Research Council, based at Occidental and Pomona colleges, consists of economists and business executives who review the operations of the local economy and issue an annual report. An early study of postwar population trends is Warren S. Thompson, *Growth and Changes in California's Population* (Los Angeles, 1955). A useful regional socioeconomic study is Mellier G. Scott, *The San Francisco Bay Area: A Metropolis in Perspective* (Berkeley, 1959).

Some of the most heated issues in recent California history relate to the reclamation and irrigation of agricultural lands, the allocation of water resources, and ownership of the coastal tidelands. A particularly knotty issue has been the 160-acre limitation, established by the federal Reclamation Act, on the farm acreage which can be irrigated by a federally supported irrigation project. Congresswoman Helen Gahagan Douglas and labor economist Paul S. Taylor, also a social activist, were especially vocal defenders of the limitation, while U.S. Senator Sheridan Downey was a major opponent. Downey's tract, *They Would Rule the Valley* (San Francisco, 1947), was published by some of the large landowners. Taylor's views are expressed in his *Essays on Land, Water, and The*

Law in California (New York, 1979) and in "Central Valley Project: Water and Land," *WPQ*, 2 (June 1949); "California Water Project: Law and Politics," *Ecology Law Quarterly*, 5 (No. 1, 1975); and "Excess Land Law: Pressure versus Principle," *California Law Review*, 47 (August 1959). Clayton R. Koppes examines the 160-acre fight in "Public Water, Public Land: Origins of the Acreage Limitation Controversy, 1933-1953," *PHR*, 47 (November 1978), as part of a special issue devoted entirely to reclamation.

The distribution of water, among various parts of California, between California and Mexico, and between California and other Colorado River Basin states, has traditionally been another complex issue. Perhaps the definitive studies of these questions are the work of Norris Hundley, Jr., including *Dividing the Waters: A Century of Controversy between the United States and Mexico* (Berkeley, 1966) and *Water and The West: The Colorado River Compact and The Politics of Water in the American West* (Berkeley, 1975). Erwin Cooper's *Aqueduct Empire: A Guide to Water in California* (Glendale, 1968), takes a view somewhat similar to that held by Taylor. Harvey P. Grady, "From North to South: The Feather River Project and Other Legislative Water Struggles in the 1950s," *SCQ*, 60 (Fall 1978), offers another view.

The controversy over ownership and control of tidelands oil deposits has extended over many decades. A good account of this dispute is Ernest R. Bartley, *The Tidelands Oil Controversy: A Legal and Historical Analysis* (Austin, 1953).

An account of one of the major environmental campaigns is contained in Susan R. Schrepfer, *The Fight to Save the Redwoods: A History of Environmental Reform, 1917-1978* (Madison, 1983). Some of the growing environmental dangers are discussed in Raymond F. Dasmann, *The Destruction of California* (New York, 1965) and *California's Changing Environment* (San Francisco, 1981).

Although California has sometimes projected an image of a state in which race relations are reasonably smooth, the reality has been quite different. Works by Carey McWilliams, Roger Daniels, and Harry H. L. Kitano discuss prejudice against Californians of Japanese descent, and against other minority groups, during and after the war. Kitano has authored several studies of Japanese-American culture and history, including "Japanese Americans: The Development of a Middleman Minority," *PHR*, 43 (November 1974). Other essays in the same special issue of the *PHR* are: H. Brett Melendy, "Filipinos in the United States" and Roger Daniels, "American Historians and East Asian Immigrants." The essays have been published elsewhere in *The Asian American*, ed. by Norris Hundley, Jr. (Santa Barbara, ca.1976). Melendy is the author of *Asians in America: Filipinos, Koreans, and East Indians* (Boston, 1977). A recent history is Lorraine Crouchett, *Filipinos in California: From the Days of the Galleons to the Present* (El Cerrito, Calif., 1982). Publications of the Asian American Studies Center at UCLA analyze the history and experiences of Chinese, Japanese, and Filipino Americans. (See Chapter 8, *post*.)

Blacks have faced prejudice and discrimination of equal intensity. During and after the war, blacks migrated to southern California in large numbers, raising their population in Los Angeles County from about 25,000 just before the war to about 650,000 in 1965, the year of the Watts riot. Three previously separated ghettos—Watts, Central Avenue, and West Jefferson—were consolidated into one huge ghetto in south central Los Angeles. The growth of the ghetto is described in *Watts: The Aftermath*, ed. by Paul Bullock (New York, 1969). (See Chapter 7, *post*.)

With discrimination rampant both in the labor market and in housing, legislative action was needed, but it was not until 1959, when the Democrats came to power, that fair employment practices legislation was enacted in Sacramento. The original legislation covered only discrimination in the job market, leaving housing segregation untouched. In 1963, the state legislature enacted the Rumford Fair Housing law, but the infamous Proposition 14 repealing that law was overwhelmingly approved by the voters in 1964. Though the Supreme Court soon invalidated the proposition, its practical and psychological effects remained. This was the political and social atmosphere in which the Watts riot of 1965 erupted (a subject covered in Chapter 7, *post*).

The Hispanic population rose dramatically in the postwar period, with the expansion especially visible in southern California. Both the legal and illegal inflow from Mexico and high birth rates have made this population the largest minority in California, and the Hispanic, black, Asian, Pacific Island, and Native American populations, in sum, constituted a majority within Los Angeles County in 1985. In consequence, somewhat more attention recently has been directed to the history and culture of this previously underrecognized group. Probably the most useful short history now extant is Alberto Camarillo, *Chicanos in California* (San Francisco, 1985), which also contains suggested readings. (Useful essays and monographs on aspects of Chicano history and culture are discussed in Chapter 6, *post*.)

The somewhat unique culture of California, particularly of southern California, has been the focus of many sociological studies. Again, Carey McWilliams, in works such as *California: The Great Exception* (New York, 1949), *Southern California Country: An Island on the Land* (New York, 1946), and in his autobiography, *The Education of Carey McWilliams* (New York, 1979), offers perceptive insights. A highly personal interpretation of California living may be found in Remi Nadeau, *California: The New Society* (New York, 1963).

Donavan Bess examines the various "awareness" cults in *The Nation* (see, for example, the February 20, 1967, issue). Observers agree that southern Californians tend to be pleasure-seeking and sports-minded. In "Los Angeles and the Dodger War, 1957–1962," *SCQ*, 42 (Fall 1980), Cary S. Henderson explores one of the most controversial events in the history of California's professional sports. Books which analyze the social consequences of rapid growth include Neil Morgan, *The California Syndrome* (Englewood Cliffs, N.J., 1969) and R. L. Duffus, *Queen Califia's Island* (New York, 1965).

The place of the arts in California culture is discussed by Arthur Bloomfield,

The Arts in California (Sausalito, 1966). California Arts Commission, *The Arts in California* (Sacramento, 1965), provides the first general survey. A recent study focusing on the arts in Los Angeles, but with some consideration given to artistic innovations and trends in other communities, is *The Arts in the Economic Life of the City* (New York, 1979) by Harvey S. Perloff, et al. Artistic activity has flourished in postwar California as noted by Nancy D. W. Moure, *Painting and Sculpture in Los Angeles, 1900-1945* (Los Angeles, 1980) and *San Francisco Museum of Modern Art, the Painting and Sculpture Collection* (New York, 1985). A statewide perspective is provided by Peter Plagens, *Sunshine Muse: Contemporary Art on the West Coast* (New York, 1974).

While traditional interpreters have flourished, as described in Robert Frash, "A Regional Response to the Impressionistic Challenge: Painters of Laguna Beach," *CH*, 63 (Summer 1984), and in Nancy D. W. Moure, *The California Water Color Society: Prize Winners 1931-1954* (Los Angeles, 1973), artists like Karl Benjamin and Lorser Feitelson began portraying a strong, flat classicism which London critics soon dubbed "West Coast hard edge." Its essential characteristics are illustrated in *California: 5 Footnotes to Modern Art History*, ed. by Stephanie Barron (Los Angeles, 1977).

The emerging artistic individualism is reflected in the California Centennial Commission, *California Centennials Exhibition of Art* (Los Angeles, 1949) and extensively documented by the Long Beach Museum of Art, *Art in Southern California* (19 vols.; Long Beach, 1957-1966).

The onset of art's maverick decade 1958-1964 marked the national leadership of Californians Edward Ruscha, Richard Diebenkorn, and Ed Kienholz, whose contemporary commentaries utilized a variety of modes and materials but clearly asserted that there was a California school of art, although distinctly different in north and south as noted in "The Two Faces of California," *Newsweek*, 86 (September 6, 1976). Commentaries on the Bay area art scene are found in Lawrence Ferlinghetti, "Bay Region Painting and Sculpture," *Art Digest*, 29 (August 1955) and in Mary F. McChesney, *A Period of Exploration: San Francisco, 1945-50* (San Francisco, 1975).

The mood of experimentation led to significant contributions in printmaking, traced by Ebria Feinblatt and Bruce Davis, *Los Angeles Prints, 1883-1980* (Los Angeles, 1981). The internationally acclaimed lithographs produced at the Tamarind Studio organized in 1959 by June Wayne, are described more fully in Eleanor Munro, *Originals: American Women Artists* (New York, 1979).

Mural art, successfully executed by Kent Twitchell, Judy Baca, and others is explored in David Greenbury, et al., *Megamurals and Supergraphics: Big Art* (Philadelphia, 1977). Mural art by California Latinos is also discussed in "Now You Can Walk—See the Big Art Around L.A.," *Sunset Magazine*, 164 (February 1980). Discussions of issues surrounding minority involvement in the arts are examined by Paul Bullock in *Creative Careers: Minorities in the Arts* (Los Angeles, 1977) and by Mellier G. Scott in *Partnership in the Arts: Public and Private Support of Cultural Activities in the San Francisco Bay Area* (San Francisco, 1963).

Equally vital were postwar activities in crafts, ranging from the ceramics of Harrison McIntosh to the furniture by Gerald McCabe and Sam Maloof. The latter's elegant craftsmanship is reflected in the autobiography *Sam Maloof: Woodworker* (Tokyo, 1983). The most famous experiment in laminated wood, resulting in the famous chair created by Ray and Charles Eames, is described in Moure, *Painting and Sculpture in Los Angeles*.

Architecture in California has also experienced changes. After the war, high-rise buildings dotted the skyline of Los Angeles for the first time, and a new architectural style, popularly referred to as "California coffee shop," was widely adopted, as seen in David Gebhard and Susan King, *A View of California Architecture, 1960-1976* (San Francisco, 1976). San Francisco's heritage is examined in Gebhard, et al., *A Guide to Architecture in San Francisco and Northern California* (Santa Barbara, 1973); Joseph A. Baird, Jr., *Time's Wondrous Changes, San Francisco's Architecture, 1776-1915* (San Francisco, 1962); and Harold Gilliam and Phil Palmer, *The Face of San Francisco* (Garden City, N.Y., 1960).

The southern California tradition has been examined by Douglas Honnold, *Southern California Architecture, 1769-1956* (New York, 1956). Particularly thoughtful is Reyner Banham, *Los Angeles: The Architecture of Four Ecologies* (New York, 1971). Guides to current sites include Terry Sillo, *Excerpts from Southern California's Architectural Heritage* (Pasadena, 1976). Indispensable to the study of southern California architecture is David Gebhard and Robert Winter, *Architecture in Los Angeles: A Compleat Guide* (Salt Lake City, 1985).

More specialized works include Esther McCoy, *Modern California Houses: Case Study Houses, 1945-1962* (New York, 1962); Sally B. Woodbridge, "The California House," *The Wilson Quarterly*, 4 (Summer 1980), which traces the development of domestic architecture; and Harold Kirker, "California Architecture and Its Relationship to Contemporary Trends in Europe and America," *CHQ*, 51 (Winter 1972).

Postwar California photographers include Imogen Cunningham, portrayed in C. P. Le Warne, "Imogen Cunningham in Utopia," *PNQ*, 74 (April 1983). Precision modernist Edward Weston traces his development in *My Camera on Point Lobos* (Boston, 1950) and, with Charis W. Weston, in *California and the West* (New York, 1940). Ansel Adams' incomparable landscape photography is described in Wallace Stegner, "Ansel Adams and the Search for Perfection," *Arizona Highways*, 60 (January 1984). Reproductions are included in Adams (in collaboration with Nancy Newhall), *This Is the American Earth* (San Francisco, 1959) and *Yosemite Valley* (San Francisco, 1959). General works include Joyce R. Muench, ed., *West Coast Portrait* (New York, 1946) and Susan Muchnic and Leland Rice, *Southern California Photography 1900-65: An Historical Survey* (Los Angeles, 1981).

The vitality of California art was positively affected by increased postwar prosperity and philanthropy, a subject explored in Mellier Scott, *Partnership in the Arts: Public and Private Support of Cultural Activities in the San Francisco Bay Area* (Berkeley, 1963) and in Paul Bullock, *Creative Careers: Minorities in the Arts.* Support for the arts in the 1960s resulted in the construction of the Los Angeles County Museum of Art and a new multiple theatre complex described in *The Music Center Story: A Decade of Achievement, 1964–1974* (Los Angeles, 1974).

Musical histories include Grace G. Koopal, *Miracle of Music: The History of the Hollywood Bowl* (Los Angeles, 1972) and Orrin Howard, ed., *Festival of Music Made in Los Angeles* (Los Angeles, 1981), which contains a brief essay on the impact of Stravinsky and Schoenberg on California. Also useful is Philip S. Boone's oral history, "The San Francisco Symphony, 1940–1972" (San Francisco, 1978). The international dimension of this artistic activity was reflected in the 1984 Olympic Arts Festival described by Gloria Lothrop, "Los Angeles Twice Celebrates a Festival of Athletics and Art," *Biblio-Cal Notes*, 15 (Summer 1985).

Developments in West Coast dance are documented by Cobbett Steinberg, *San Francisco Ballet: The First Fifty Years* (San Francisco, 1985). See also David Vaughn, "Twyla Tharp: Launching a New American Classicism," *Dance Magazine*, 58 (May 1984). The conferring in 1978 of the Dance Magazine Award on Bella Lewitsky is discussed by L. Draegin, "Sean Greene's Dance Life with Bella Lewitsky," *Dance Magazine*, 52 (August 1978). Richard D. Saunders, ed., *Music and Dance in California and the West* (Hollywood, 1948), is useful.

While less dynamic, the influence of West Coast theatre represented by Emmy Award–winning *Children of a Lesser God* and Luis Valdez' *Zoot Suit* as well as *Shadow Box* and *Lady and the Clarinet*, all New York successes on Broadway, point to new leadership for California legitimate theatre, significantly enhanced by the contributions of the Equity-waiver theatres. The contribution of two veteran theatre groups is reviewed in Beth Mohr, "The Old Globe Theatre: Highlights from Fifty Years," *JSDH*, 31 (Spring 1985) and in Dan Eckley, "California's World Record 26-Year Theatrical Run: 'The Drunkard,' and 'The Wayward Way,'" *PH*, 26 (Winter 1982). Edmond M. Gagey has provided a comprehensive study in *The San Francisco Stage: A History* (New York, 1950). See also Robert G. Davis, *The San Francisco Mime Troup: The First Ten Years* (Palo Alto, 1975). *The Los Angeles Theatre Book: A Comprehensive Handbook for Playgoers* (Los Angeles, 1978), contains important essays by members of the Los Angeles Theatre Alliance.

"California's Literary Regionalism," *American Quarterly*, 7 (Fall 1955), attempts to identify several unifying themes, as does William Everson, *Archetype West: The Pacific Coast as a Literary Region* (Kensington, 1976). A common theme of rootlessness is identified by Lionel Rolfe, *Literary L.A.* (San Francisco, 1981). General surveys of recent literature include Gerald Haslam and James D. Houston, eds., *California Heartland: Writing from the Great Central Valley* (Santa Barbara, 1979). Ishmael Reed, ed., *Calafia: The California Poetry* (San Francisco, 1979), provides important insights into the work of less familiar poets.

New cultural values and life-styles are reflected in the "Beat" movement, whose major literary exemplars have been novelist Jack Kerouac (*On the Road* [New York, 1957]), poet Allen Ginsberg (*Howl, and Other Poems* [San Francisco, 1959]), and poet-bookstore owner Lawrence Ferlinghetti. The "Hippie" movement, centered largely in the Haight-Ashbury district and other parts of San Francisco, has been sympathetically evaluated by Lawrence Lipton in *The Holy Barbarians* (New York, 1959).

The work of Pulitzer Prize-winner Wallace Stegner, for *Angle of Repose* (New York, 1971), has been analyzed by Susan Tyburski, "Wallace Stegner's Vision of Wilderness," *Western American Literature*, 18 (Summer 1983). Instructive overviews of west coast fiction are provided by Lawrence C. Powell, *Creative Literature of the Golden State* (Los Angeles, 1971) and William S. Lee, ed., *California, A Literary Chronicle* (New York, 1968).

Jonas Spatz, *Hollywood in Fiction: Some Versions of the American Myth* (The Hague, 1969), introduces the visual medium as yet another facet of California cultural life which expanded after 1945. The motion picture industry has experienced fundamental changes in the postwar period. In the years immediately after World War II, the changes in public taste steadily reduced the size of the audience. A good history of the industry is Kenneth Macgowan, *Behind the Screen: The History and Techniques of the Motion Picture* (New York, 1965). Hortense Powdermaker takes a sociological look at Hollywood in *Hollywood: The Dream Factory* (London, 1951). Beth Day, *This Was Hollywood* (New York, 1960), documents the decline of the motion picture's popularity. The transition is traced in A. R. Fulton, *Motion Pictures: The Development of an Art from Silent Films to the Age of Television* (Norman, 1960). The relationship of contemporary music to the recording industry centered in southern California is touched upon in Anthony Fawcett, *California Rock, California Sound* (Los Angeles, 1979).

The rapid growth in the postwar period had a profound effect on the state's educational system. In the Pat Brown administration, a commission of educational experts produced a "Master Plan" for higher education, which was endorsed by the governor and approved by the legislature. A key member of the commission was its chair, Arthur G. Coons, who has described the issues and processes in development of the plan in *Crises in California Higher Education* (Los Angeles, 1968).

The growth of more socially conscious and militant student bodies led to explosive confrontations between students and campus administrations at institutions such as the University of California at Berkeley and San Francisco State University. Accounts of some of these struggles may be found in Seymour Lipset and Shelton Wolin, *The Berkeley Student Revolt* (Garden City, N.Y., 1965) and in Art Seidenbaum's *Confrontation on Campus* (Los Angeles, 1971).

In the late 1940s and early 1950s, an especially heated issue related to the imposition of a "loyalty oath" for faculty of the University of California. The Regents dismissed several faculty members for refusing to sign the non-Communist oath on principle, but the Supreme Court invalidated the Regents' oath two years later and reinstated the nonsigners. This occurrence has been analyzed by David P. Gardner, *The California Oath Controversy* (Berkeley, 1967) and by George R. Stewart, Jr., *The Year of the Oath* (Garden City, N.Y., 1950).

One of the most turbulent issues in recent California education has been the racial integration of previously segregated schools. The question of busing students to achieve integration has seemed to arouse special acrimony, although busing for other purposes has long been common. The experiences associated with attempted school integration have been explored by John and Laree Caughey, *To Kill a Child's Spirit: The Tragedy of School Segregation in Los Angeles* (Ithaca, 1973); Neil Sullivan and Evelyn S. Stewart, *Now Is the Time: Integration in the Berkeley Schools* (Bloomington, Ind., 1969); and, for Richmond, Lillian Rubin, *Busing and Backlash: White Against White in an Urban California School District* (Berkeley, 1972). Analytical overviews of the problem are contained in Charles A. Wollenberg, *All Deliberate Speed* (Berkeley, 1976) and in Irving G. Hendrick, *The Education of Non-Whites in California, 1849–1970* (San Francisco, 1977).

Lastly, any one investigating contemporary California politics and society will profit immeasurably from consulting the *California Journal*. This monthly publication dates back to 1969. It contains a wealth of information on all aspects of state politics and government, including bills introduced and passed in the legislature; the voting records of legislators; and detailed explanation of various laws or ballot propositions as well as general election coverage and candidates.

6

CALIFORNIA CHICANOS

FRANCISCO E. BALDERRAMA

THE FIELD OF CHICANO HISTORY has matured significantly since the initial dialogue over the structure of Chicano history began in the late 1960s and early 1970s. A new historiography has emerged exploring the Chicano experience and providing a new vantage point for viewing the historical development of California, as reflected in Alberto Camarillo, *Chicanos in California* (San Francisco, 1985), the only published survey. Written for the beginning student as well as the professional scholar, Camarillo accomplishes the difficult goals of integrating key secondary accounts and significant primary sources into an engaging narrative.

An understanding of California Chicanos may also be developed by examining the various general surveys of Chicano history. The volumes vary in quality. Matt S. Meier and Feliciano Rivera, *The Chicanos: A History of Mexican Americans* (New York, 1972), is generally competent but conceptually weak; Manuel A. Machado, *Listen Chicano: An Informal History of the Mexican American* (Chicago, 1978), is highly polemical; Julian Samora and Patricia Vandel Simon, *History of the Mexican American People* (Notre Dame, 1977), is directed to a secondary school audience. The best survey account is Rodolfo Acuña, *Occupied America: A History of Chicanos* (2nd ed.; New York, 1981), which synthesizes the earlier Southwest historiography with 1970s Chicano literature. Also familiarizing the reader with the major themes and issues for Chicanos in California is the concise essay of Carlos E. Cortés, "Mexicans," in the Stephen Thernstrom, ed., *Harvard Encyclopedia of American Ethnic Groups* (Cambridge, Mass., 1980). Helpful collections of articles in Chicano history are: Jack D. Forbes, ed., *Aztecas del norte: The Chicanos of Aztlán* (Greenwich, 1973); Matt S. Meier and Feliciano Rivera, eds., *Readings on La Raza* (New York, 1974); Renato Rosaldo, Robert Calvert, and Gustav Seligmann, eds., *Chicano: The Evolution of a People*

(Minneapolis, 1973); Manuel P. Servín, ed., *An Awakened Minority: The Mexican Americans* (2nd ed.; Beverly Hills, 1974); and for Spanish readers, David R. Maciel and Patricia Bueno, eds., *Aztlán: historia del pueblo chicano (1848-1910)* (Mexico, 1975). Significant information about the Mexican community of Los Angeles is also conveyed in José Antonio Ríos-Bustamante and Pedro Castillo, *An Illustrated History of Mexican Los Angeles, 1781-1985* (Los Angeles, 1986).

An introduction to the Chicano experience should include perusing key bibliographies, leading periodicals, and the foremost document publication series. The most comprehensive bibliography is Matt S. Meier, *Bibliography of Mexican American History* (Westport, 1984), which may be used with its accompanying volume, Matt S. Meier and Feliciano Rivera, comps., *Dictionary of Mexican American History* (Westport, 1981). Since the field of Chicano history is growing rapidly, serious investigators can only keep abreast by consulting the leading bibliography of Chicano bibliographies by Barbara J. Robinson and J. Cordell Robinson, *The Mexican American: A Critical Guide to Research Aids* (Greenwich, 1980) and by scanning bibliographies in the leading scholarly periodical for the field of Chicano Studies, *Aztlán: International Journal of Chicano Studies Research*. Equally important in uncovering historical materials for California Chicanos are published documents, especially the largest collections—*The Mexican American* (21 vols.; New York, 1974) and *The Chicano Heritage* (55 vols.; New York, 1976), ed. by Carlos E. Cortés.

Even though racially mixed people of Spanish and Indian background—ancestors of today's Mexican and Chicano—settled California first in the name of the Spanish crown and later under the Mexican Republic, a Spanish "Fantasy Heritage" has beclouded the historical figure of the Mexican. The emphasis on institutional history in the writings of frontier California has further obscured the Mexican image. (See Ch. 1, *ante*, for a more detailed assessment.) The Chicano-Mexicano perspective for early California and the Southwest is outlined in the research note of José Antonio Ríos-Bustamante, "A Contribution to the Historiography of the Mexican North in the Eighteenth Century," *Aztlán*, 7 (Fall 1976). A more detailed overview is Juan Gómez-Quiñones, "The Origins and Development of the Mexican Working Class North of the Río Bravo: Work and Culture Among Laborers and Artisans, 1600-1900," in Elsa Cecilia Frost, et al., *Labor and Laborers Through Mexican History* (Mexico City and Tucson, 1980). Heading the list of revisionist works for Spanish California are studies examining the long-neglected field of social history: David J. Langum, "California Women and the Image of Virtue," *SCQ*, 59 (Fall 1977) and "Californios and the Image of Indolence," *WHQ*, 9 (April 1978), as well as Gloria E. Miranda, "Gente de Razón Marriage Patterns in Spanish and Mexican California: A Case Study of Santa Barbara and Los Angeles," *SCQ*, 47 (Spring 1981). An especially controversial interpretation of the Spanish period is Manuel P. Servín, "The Beginnings of California's Anti-Mexican Prejudice," in his *An Awakened Minority* (2nd ed.; Beverly Hills, 1974). This article argues that the Spaniards in California, particularly the Franciscan missionaries, discriminated against persons of mixed blood or mestizos—the precursors of modern Mexicans and Chicanos. These findings appear to be an outgrowth of Servín's earlier study "The Secularization of the California Missions: A Reappraisal," *SCQ*, 47 (June 1965), which declared that the missionary fathers provoked secularization or the ending of the mission system by obstructing civilian settlers from receiving land grants. By far the most outstanding attempt at linking the Spanish and Mexican periods to Chicano developments after 1848 and beyond is the important document collection edited by David J. Weber, *Foreigners in Their Native Land: Historical Roots of the Mexican Americans* (Albuquerque, 1973). The Mexican era in California has never attracted the same attention as has the Spanish period. Nevertheless, David Weber's recent study, *The Mexican Frontier, 1821-1846: The American Southwest Under Mexico* (Albuquerque, 1982), may serve as an example for future studies of this era.

American expansion and the resulting Mexican American War is the critical issue for this period. Obviously, the war is the single most important event in Chicano history. It is the subject of the balanced and objective accounts of Glenn W. Price, *Origins of the War with Mexico: The Polk-Stockton Intrigue* (Austin, 1967) and Gene M. Brack, *Mexico Views Manifest Destiny, An Essay on the Origins of the Mexican War* (Albuquerque, 1975). Nevertheless, the war still requires further unbiased investigation, according to most Chicano historians. See David R. Maciel, "Comments on North America Divided: The Mexican War, 1846-1848," *Aztlán*, 2 (Fall 1971). Not only the war but also the peace treaty of Guadalupe Hidalgo is the subject of Ramón E. Ruiz and Mario T. García, "Conquest and Annexation," *New Scholar*, 7 (1978) and of Feliciano Rivera, "A Chicano View of the Treaty of Guadalupe Hidalgo," in George E. Frakes and Curtis B. Solberg, eds., *Minorities in California History* (New York, 1971).

The ending of the war in California did not drastically change the strong Mexican character of California. Even though the gold rush ushered in a sudden and overwhelming transformation of northern California, the transition was far more gradual in southern California where Mexican Californians remained a majority into the late nineteenth century. More importantly, Americanization was a tremendous transformation, for Mexicans were pushed from the center of the economic, political, and social life of the state to the margins of California society. The process of marginalization was examined first in the detailed study by Leonard Pitt, *Decline of the Californios* (Berkeley, 1966), which focused primarily on the lives and attitudes of upper-class Mexican Californians. Further exploration of the violent protest is Pedro Castillo and Alberto Camarillo, eds., *Furia y Muerte: Los Bandidos Chicanos* (Los Angeles, 1973). Castillo and Camarillo not only reprint important articles about Joaquín Murieta and Tiburcio Vásquez but define the convincing theory of social banditry for explaining lawlessness in late nineteenth-century California. Social banditry is also the subject of Carlos E. Cortés, "El bandolerismo social chicano," in David Maciel and Patricia Bueno, eds., *Aztlán: Historia contemporanea del pueblo chicano, 1848-1910* (Mexico, 1975). Another innovative study is the exploratory essay of Oscar Martínez, "On the Size of the Chicano Population: New Estimates 1850-1900," *Aztlán*, 6 (Spring 1975), determining the number of Mexicans for the nineteenth century.

The specific dynamics of Californio society in San Diego for the late nineteenth century are uncovered in Mario T. García, "The Californios of San Diego and the Politics of Accommodation," *Aztlán*, 6 (Spring 1975) and in "Merchants and Dons: San Diego's Attempt at Modernization, 1850-1860," *JSDH*, 21 (Winter 1975). The leading historian of the Los Angeles Mexican community for this era is unquestionably Richard Griswold del Castillo with his series of articles: "La Familia Chicana: Social Changes in the Chicano Family of Los Angeles, 1850-1880," *Journal of Ethnic Studies*, 3 (Spring 1975); "Myth and Reality: Chicano Economic Activity in Los Angeles, 1850-1880," *Aztlán*, 6 (Summer 1976); "Health and the Mexican American in Los Angeles, 1850-1887," *JMAH*, 4 (1974); and "Tucsonenses and Angelenos: A Socio-Economic Study of Two Mexican American Barrios, 1860-1880," *JW*, 18 (January 1979). Griswold also paints an interesting portrait of a prominent southland Californio clan: "The Fantasy Heritage in the Del Valle Family," *CH*, 59 (Spring 1980). Findings from the preceding articles are expanded and refined in Griswold del Castillo, *The Los Angeles Barrio, 1850-1890: A Social History* (Berkeley, 1980). Griswold has also explored family life during that period and later in "A Preliminary Comparison of Chicano, Immigrant and Native Born Family Structures, 1850-1880," *Aztlán*, 6 (Spring 1975) and in *La Familia: Chicano Families in the Urban Southwest 1848 to the Present* (Notre Dame, 1984).

Another significant new urban history study is Alberto Camarillo, *Chicanos in a Changing Society: From Mexican Pueblos to American Barrios in Santa Barbara and Southern California, 1848-1930* (Cambridge, Mass., 1979). This work is noteworthy because the author not only bridges the nineteenth-century experience with the present century, but also compares and contrasts the experience of Santa Barbara with the neighboring communities of Los Angeles, San Diego, and San Bernardino. It also defines and analyzes urbanization and barriozation, immigration and adaptation, as well as social and economic mobility. These important themes also appear in Ricardo Romo, *East Los Angeles: A History of a Barrio* (Austin, 1983), focused largely upon the years of 1900 to 1930 when massive Mexican immigration created a new eastside barrio. Los Angeles during the early twentieth century again appears as the focus of another new urban history study in Pedro Castillo, "Urbanization, Migration, and the Chicanos in Los Angeles, 1900-1920," in Maciel and Bueno, eds., *Aztlán: historia contemporanea del pueblo chicano*.

The preceding community studies of Chicanos during the early twentieth century all give some attention to the massive movement of Mexicans northward from Mexico to California, but immigration is also the central focus of the monographs of Mark Reisler, *By the Sweat of Their Brow: Mexican Immigrant Labor in the United States, 1900-1940* (Westport, 1976) and of Lawrence A. Cardoso, *Mexican Emigration to the United States, 1897-1931* (Tucson, 1980), which complement the classic accounts of Manuel Gamio and Paul S. Taylor. Less successful are the essays presented in Arthur F. Corwin, *Immigrants–and Immigrants: Perspectives on Mexican Labor Migration to the United States* (Westport, Conn., 1978), discussing immigration from 1900. Mexican immigration and adjustment to American life in California is a major theme in Ernesto Galarza, *Barrio Boy* (Notre Dame, 1971), an autobiography.

Another focal point of historical investigation is the Mexican immigrant community's ties to the Mexican motherland during the early twentieth century. For instance, the important influence of the Mexican Revolution of 1910 and the Mexican heritage of radicalism among Mexican nationals and Mexican Americans is detailed in William D. Raat, *Revoltosos: Mexico's Rebels in the United States, 1903-1923* (College Station, Tex., 1981). Juan Gómez-Quiñones, *Sembradores–Ricardo Flores Magón y El Partido Liberal Mexicano: A Eulogy and Critique* (Los Angeles, 1973), also discusses Mexican radicals in California as part of its analysis. The special relationship between the Mexican community and the Mexican consular service with specific references to consulates in California is investigated in Juan Gómez-Quiñones, "Piedras contra la luna; México en Aztlán y Aztlán en México: Chicano-Mexicano Relations and the Mexican Consulates, 1900-1920," in James Wilkie, et al., eds., *Contemporary Mexico: Papers of the IV International Congress of Mexican History* (Berkeley and Mexico City, 1976). A more detailed study of the Mexican Consular Service and Mexican community is Francisco E. Balderrama, *In Defense of La Raza* (Tucson, 1982). The study also reveals findings about Mexicano organization, *intercolonia* relations, *la raza* working class development, and *colonia* interaction with the Catholic church, educational institutions, and local, state, and national governments. The Spanish language press is an important institution of the Mexican immigrant community. This topic is the subject of articles by Francine Medeiros, "*La Opinión*, a Mexican Exile Newspaper: A Content Analysis of Its First Years, 1926-1929," *Aztlán*, 11 (Spring 1980); Richard Griswold del Castillo, "The Mexican Revolution and the Spanish Language Press in the Borderlands," *Journalism History*, 4 (Summer 1977); and Michael C. Neri, "A Journalistic Portrait of the Spanish-Speaking People of California, 1868-1925," *SCQ*, 60 (Summer 1973). The significance of the media for this era and later is also discussed in Felix Gutiérrez, "Spanish-Language Media in America: Background, Resources, History," *Journalism History*, 4 (Summer 1977).

Labor activity and union organizing is another major theme of great importance to the Mexican community at the beginning of the century. An insightful introduction to key issues and themes is Juan Gómez-Quiñones, "First Steps: Chicano Labor Conflict and Organizing, 1900-1920," *Aztlán*, 3 (Spring 1972). He emphasizes militant Chicano unionization and vigorous strike activity. A detailed analysis of Chicano participation in a turn of the century conflict is Charles Wollenberg, "Working on El Traque: The Pacific Electric Strike of 1903," *PHR*, 42 (August 1973). Receiving far greater attention than railroad laborers are farm workers. The leading scholarly study for farm workers and required reading for this era is Cletus E. Daniels, *Bitter Harvest* (Ithaca, 1981). Of the specific topics centering on Mexican farm workers, strike activity during the Great Depression is the topic receiving considerable attention: Juan Gómez-Quiñones and Devra Anne Weber, "'. . . down the valleys wild': Epilogue, Med-rasres still; the strikes of the thirties," *Aztlán*, 1 (Spring 1970); Abraham Hoffman, "The El Monte Berry Strike: International Involvement in a Local Labor Dispute," *JW*, 7 (January 1973); Ron L. López, "The El Monte Berry Strike of 1933," *Aztlán*, 1 (Spring 1970); Mark Reisler, "Mexican Unionization in California Agriculture, 1927-1936," *LH*, 14 (Fall 1973); Devra Anne Weber, "The Organizing of Mexicano Agricultural Workers: Imperial Valley and Los Angeles, 1928-1934, An Oral History Approach," *Aztlán*, 3 (Fall 1972); and Charles Wollenberg, "*Huelga* 1928 Style: The Imperial Valley Cantaloupe Strike," *PHR*, 38 (February 1969) and "Race and Class in Rural California: The El Monte Berry Strike of 1933," *CHQ*, 51 (Summer 1972). The preceding studies underscore the tradition of activism among Mexican farm workers, but investigation and analysis are usually limited to only union organizing and strike activity. Douglas G. Monroy, "Las Costura en Los Angeles, 1933-1939: The ILGWU and the Politics of Domination," in Magdalena Mora and Adelaida R. del Castillo, eds., *Mexican Women in the United States: Struggles of Past and Present* (Los Angeles, 1980), provides a larger context for understanding the Mexican working class during the depression years and continues his work in "An Essay on Understanding the Work Experience of Mexicans in Southern California, 1900-1939," *Aztlán*, 12 (Spring 1981) and "Like Swallows at the Old Mission: Mexicans and Racial Politics of Growth in Los Angeles in the Interwar Period," *WHQ*, 14 (October 1983). Equally important in going beyond the labor conflict viewpoint is Victor Nelson-Cisneros, "UCAPAWA and Chicanos in California: The Farm Worker Period, 1937-1940," *Aztlán*, 7 (Fall 1976), which discusses the various activities of the United Cannery, Agricultural, Packing, and Allied Workers of America.

While union organizing among Mexicans was occurring during the Great Depression, the economic crisis also provoked a massive flight of Mexican Nationals and Mexican Americans to Mexico. Important for understanding deportation-repatriation movement during the depression is the smaller yet significant drive of the 1920s described in Lawrence Cardoso, "La repatriación de braceros en época de Obregón, 1920-1923," *Historia Mexicana*, 26 (April/June 1977). Deportation-repatriation during the economic crisis of the 1930s is surveyed in the following articles: George C. Kiser and David Silverman, "Mexican Repatriation During the Great Depression," *JMAH*, 3 (1973) and Moisés González Navarro, "Los efectos sociales de la crisis del '29," *Historia Mexicana*, 20 (April/June 1970). The reaction of growers to relief policies, an important stimulus to repatriation, is described in David L. Zelman, "Mexican Migrants and Relief in Depression California," *JMAH*, 5 (1975). Abraham Hoffman contributes to understanding deportation-repatriation with "Mexican Repatriation Statistics: Some Suggested Alternatives to Carey McWilliams," *WHQ*, 3 (October

1972); "Stimulus to Repatriation: The 1931 Federal Deportation Drive and the Los Angeles Mexican Community," *PHR*, 42 (May 1973); and his monograph, *Unwanted Mexican Americans in the Great Depression* (Tucson, 1974).

United States entry into the Second World War signaled the beginning of a new era for Chicano history. While disproportionate numbers of Chicanos not only served on the battlefield but distinguished themselves with valor according to Raul Morín, *Among the Valiant* (Alhambra, 1966), other Mexicans suffered not only prejudice but persecution on the home front. Analyzing the prejudice and persecution of the war years is the recent and exciting application of psycho-history in Mauricio Mazón, *The Zoot-Suit Riots* (Austin, 1984). More importantly, a new political climate emerged after the war. Chicanos met this challenge by developing new organizations and strategies outlined in Alberto M. Camarillo, "Research Notes on Chicano Community Leaders: The G.I. Generation," *Aztlán*, 2 (Fall 1971). Among the key issues for Chicano organizations during this era is school segregation, and a critical case is analyzed by Charles Wollenberg, "Mendez v. Westminster: Race, Nationality and Segregation in California Schools," *CHQ*, 53 (Winter 1974). A larger context for studying school segregation in the Golden State is also provided by Charles A. Wollenberg's *All Deliberate Speed* (Berkeley, 1976). Chicano accomplishments receive a very negative assessment in Manuel P. Servín, "The Post-World War II Mexican American, 1945-1965: A Non-Achieving Minority," in Servín's *An Awakened Minority*. More recently, Rodolfo Acuña, *A Community Under Siege: A Chronicle of Chicanos East of the Los Angeles River, 1945-1975* (Los Angeles, 1984), uncovers new themes and issues in this chronicle of daily events in the life of East Los Angeles based upon two local community newspapers. The employment of the urban history of statistical analysis as well as oral history has been limited to only the case studies of Alberto M. Camarillo, "Chicano Urban History: A Study of Compton's Barrio, 1936-1970," *Aztlán*, 2 (Fall 1971) and Gilbert González, "Factors Relating to Property Ownership of Chicanos in Lincoln Heights," *Aztlán*, 2 (Fall 1971).

World War II also brought about the establishment of the infamous bracero program or farm labor procurement plan for Mexican workers. Ernesto Galarza contributes significantly to understanding the bracero program and the dynamics of farm labor in *Strangers in Our Fields* (Washington, D.C., 1956) and *Tragedy at Chular* (Santa Barbara, 1977). Other Galarza contributions include surveying the bracero experience in California from 1950 to 1964 in *Merchants of Labor* (Charlotte, N.C., 1964), describing the 1947 to 1950 National Farm Workers Union strike in *Spiders in the House and Workers in the Field* (Notre Dame, 1977), and analyzing the role of bracero labor and the National Farm Labor Union in *Farm Workers and Agribusiness in California, 1947-1960* (Notre Dame, 1977). Another important study is Richard B. Craig, *The Bracero Program: Interest Groups and Foreign Policy* (Austin, 1971). Not all Mexican workers entered under the bracero program, for many Mexicans entered as undocumented laborers seeking employment in southwestern agribusiness or border factories.

The Eisenhower administration reacted to this movement with a massive round-up and deportation of undocumented aliens without regard to civil liberties and basic human rights. This tragic episode is recounted in Juan Ramón García, *Operation Wetback: The Mass Deportation of Mexican Undocumented Workers in 1954* (Westport, 1980). In spite of this persecution many Mexicans returned to the American labor force and historians are now examining Mexican workers during this era. A specific research project is outlined in Luis L. Arroyo, "Chicano Participation in Organized Labor: The CIO in Los Angeles, 1938-1950. An Extended Research Note," *Aztlán*, 6 (Summer 1975). A pathfinding examination of Mexican women as workers is Vicki L. Ruiz's "Obreras y Madres," in *Renato Rosaldo Lecture Series: La Mexicana/Chicana* (Summer 1985).

While the Mexican community has a long history of addressing important needs and critical problems, the Chicano movement of the late 1960s and early 1970s was a time of intensive activism. A key work for understanding the political climate during these years and earlier is Ralph C. Guzmán, *The Political Socialization of the Mexican American People* (New York, 1976), describing organizational efforts, leadership models, voting patterns, and political ideologies. Readers should also examine Gerald P. Rosen, "The Development of the Chicano Movement in Los Angeles from 1967 to 1969," *Aztlán*, 4 (Spring 1973). There are also a number of preliminary yet insightful essays: C. S. Biliana and Harry Pachon, "Ethnic Political Mobilization in a Mexican American Community: An Exploratory Study of East Los Angeles," *WPQ*, 27 (September 1973); Richard A. García, "The Chicano Movement and the Mexican-American Community, 1972-1978: An Interpretative Essay," *Socialist Review*, 8 (July/October 1978); Miguel Tirado, "Mexican American Community Political Organizations, the Key to Chicano Political Power," *Aztlán*, 1 (Spring 1970); Joan Moore with Alfredo Cuellar, *Mexican-Americans* (Englewood Cliffs, N.J., 1970); Armando Gutiérrez, "The Evolution of Chicano Politics," *Aztlán*, 5 (Spring/Fall 1974). An examination of the Chicano movement from a Mexican perspective is presented in Jorge A. Bustamante, "El Movimiento Chicano y Su Relevancia Para los Mexicanos," in James Wilkie, et al., eds., *Contemporary Mexico; Papers of the IV International Congress of Mexican History* (Mexico City and London, 1975).

A critical phenomenon of the Chicano movement was the appearance of a third party and its activities, La Raza Unida. This subject is introduced in Richard Santillan, *Chicano Politics: La Raza Unida* (Los Angeles, 1973). Paralleling the campaign for political participation during the late 1960s and early 1970s was the student movement. Juan Gómez-Quiñones leads the way in understanding this generation of students with his article "Preliminary Remarks Toward a Tentative History of the Chicano Student Movement in Southern California," *Aztlán*, 1 (Fall 1970) and in his pamphlet *Mexican Students for La Raza: The Chicano Student Movement in California, 1967-1977* (Santa Barbara, 1978). One should also examine Carlos Munoz, Jr., and Mario Barrera, "La Raza Unida Party and the Chicano Student Movement," *Social Science Journal*, 19

(April 1982), and Kaye Briegel, "Chicano Student Militancy: The Los Angeles High School Strike of 1968," in Servín, ed., *An Awakened Minority*. The youth struggle is also presented in the memoirs of brown beret leader David Sánchez, *Expedition Through Aztlán* (La Puente, Calif., 1978), and in the article of Christine Marín, "Go Home, Chicanos: A Study of the Brown Berets in California and Arizona," in Servín, ed., *An Awakened Minority*. Relations between the police and Chicano community were particularly strained at this time, and Alejandro Morales addresses this issue in *Ando Sangando—I Am Bleeding: A Study of Mexican American-Police Conflict* (La Puente, Calif., 1972). A notorious episode between law enforcement officials and Chicanos is the subject of José Angel de la Vara, "1970 Chicano Moratorium and the Death of Rubén Salazar," in Servín, ed., *An Awakened Minority*. Gang activity is also explored in the leading work of Joan W. Moore, *Homeboys—Gangs, Drugs, and Prison in the Barrios of Los Angeles* (Philadelphia, 1978).

The farm workers and the leadership of César Chávez has attracted considerable scholarly as well as popular attention, and readers will find a number of works available. One can begin with the background material on California farm workers cited earlier. A selective bibliography of leading works for the present-day farm workers should include Sam Kushner, *The Long Road to Delano* (New York, 1975) and Ann Loftis and Dick Meiser, *A Long Time Coming: The Struggle to Unionize American Farm Workers* (New York, 1977). A legal perspective is also available in Salvador Enrique Alvarez, "The Legal and Legislative Struggles of the Farm Workers, 1965-1972," *El Grito*, 6 (Winter 1972/1973). César Chávez's leadership of the farm workers is the topic of John G. Dunne, *Delano: The Story of the California Grape Strike* (New York, 1967); Jacques Levy, *César Chávez: Autobiography of La Causa* (New York, 1975); and Ronald B. Taylor, *Chávez and the Farm Workers* (Boston, 1975). Readers might also want to read Chávez's own words in "César Chávez: A Conversation with César Chávez," *The Journal of Current Social Issues*, 9 (November/December 1970) and "The Mexican American and the Church," *El Grito*, 1 (Summer 1968). Fellow organizer Dolores Huerta also shares her views in "Dolores Huerta Talks About Republicans, César, and Her Home Town," in Servín, ed., *An Awakened Minority*.

Historians and other scholars of the Mexican experience have been giving increasing attention to uncovering the historical past of the Mexican woman or Chicana. The following articles question the lack of coverage of the Chicana and demand further research: María L. Apodaca, "The Chicana Woman: An Historical Materialist Perspective," *Latin American Perspectives*, 4 (Winter/Spring 1977); Adaliza Sosa Riddell, "Chicanas and el Movimiento," *Aztlán*, 5 (Spring/Fall 1974); and Shirlene A. Soto, "The Emerging Chicana: A Review of the Literature," *Southwest Economy and Society*, 2 (October/November 1976). Other articles exploring the Chicana are published in Magdalena Mora and Adelaida R. del Castillo, eds., *Mexican Women in the United States: Struggles Past and Present* (Los Angeles, 1980) and Rosaura Sánchez and Rosa Martínez

Cruz, eds., *Essays on La Mujer* (Los Angeles, 1977). Nevertheless, the only book-length study is Alfredo Mirandé and Evangelina Enríquez, *La Chicana—The Mexican American Women* (Chicago, 1980).

An equally important concern for historians and the Chicano community is the debate over contemporary Mexican immigration. An introduction to this critical issue may be obtained by reading Harry B. Cross and James A. Sandos, *Across the Border: Rural Development in Mexico and Recent Migration to the United States* (Berkeley, 1981); Dick J. Reavis, *Without Documents* (New York, 1978); and José Antonio Ríos-Bustamante, ed., *Mexican Immigrant Workers in the U.S.* (Los Angeles, 1981). Some investigators declare that the Mexican immigrant lowers American wages and displaces American workers. This view is developed in Vernon M. Brigg, "Illegal Alien: The Need for a More Restrictive Border Policy," *Social Science Quarterly*, 56 (December 1975) and Sidney Weintraub and Stanley Ross, *The Illegal Alien from Mexico: Policy Choices for an Intractable Issue* (Austin, 1980). Other scholars argue that Mexican immigrants are an economic asset to the United States economy and society. This view is presented in Thomas Muller, *The Fourth Wave: California's Newest Immigrants—A Summary* (Washington, D.C., 1983) and Kevin F. McCarthy and R. Burciaga Valdez, *Current and Future Effects of Mexican Immigration in California: Executive Summary for the California Roundtable* (Santa Monica, 1985). Immigration and its impact on urban areas in California are detailed in Wayne A. Cornelius, et al., *Mexican Immigrants and Southern California: A Summary of Current Knowledge* (San Diego, 1982) and *Mexican Immigrants in the San Francisco Bay Area: A Summary of Current Knowledge* (San Diego, 1982). An in-depth analysis of American reaction to undocumented workers with an analysis of pending legislation is Mauricio Mazón, "Illegal Alien Surrogates: A Psycho-historical Interpretation of Group Stereotyping in Time of Economic Stress," *Aztlán*, 6 (Summer 1975).

Closely related to the immigration issue is interaction between the Chicano community and Mexican society. Helpful in understanding contemporary relations between Chicanos and Mexicanos are the essays of Rodolfo O. de la Garza, "Chicanos and U.S. Foreign Policy: The Future of Chicano-Mexicano Relations," *WPQ*, 33 (December 1980) and "Chicano-Mexican Relations: A Framework for Research," *Social Science Quarterly*, 63 (March 1982). A brief yet noteworthy description of Mexican scholarly interest in the Chicano is also provided in David R. Maciel and Angelina Casillas, "Aztlán en México: Perspectivas Mexicanas sobre el Chicano," *Aztlán*, 11 (Spring 1980). Readers should also examine a leading collection of essays on relations between the United States and Mexico by Carlos Vásquez and Manuel García y Griego, eds., *Mexican-U.S. Relations: Conflict and Convergence* (Los Angeles, 1983).

The foregoing citations of recent Chicano historiography underscore the tremendous growth and rich vitality of the historical scholarship on the Mexican people in California.

7

CALIFORNIA BLACKS

LAWRENCE B. DE GRAAF

CONSULTING THE MULTIVOLUME classic state histories will be of little use on blacks except for scattered biographical sketches or events. Gerald D. Nash, "California and Its Historians: An Appraisal of the Historians of the State," *PHR*, 50 (November 1981), noted that early pioneer and romantic California historians largely ignored topics such as blacks which did not fit their political or optimistic viewpoints. Not until the 1930s did works on California in general yield much material on blacks. Even those works have severe limitations. The one-volume texts, such as those by John Caughey and Norris Hundley, Jr.; Walton E. Bean and James J. Rawls; Andrew F. Rolle and W. H. Hutchinson, largely treat themes in which race was a statewide issue, such as civil rights during the gold rush, ghetto riots, and school desegregation, or developments which profoundly altered the number or status of blacks in the state, such as World War II. Black culture, separate intellectual currents, and the evolution of communities and institutions are not widely treated.

A short overview that carries into the 1980s is Rudolph Lapp, *Afro-Americans in California* (2nd ed.; San Francisco, 1985). It is particularly rich on the gold rush era. Kenneth G. Goode, *California's Black Pioneers: A Brief Historical Survey* (Santa Barbara, 1974), is directed at high school readers. A survey of political issues involving blacks and their organizations from the gold rush to mid-twentieth century is James A. Fisher, "The Political Development of the Black Community in California, 1850–1950," *CHQ*, 50 (September 1971). A valuable source is Delilah L. Beasley, *The Negro Trail Blazers of California* (Los Angeles, 1919; reprint, 1969), though lacking footnotes, an index, and little overall interpretation.

Useful are relevant chapters in several anthologies and histories on minority groups in the state: Roger Olmsted and Charles Wollenberg, eds., *Neither Separate Nor Equal: Race and Racism in California* (San Francisco, 1971); Wollenberg, ed., *Ethnic Conflict in California History* (Los Angeles, 1970); Roger Daniels and Spencer C. Olin, Jr., *Racism in California* (New York, 1972); and George E. Frakes and Curtis B. Solberg, eds., *Minorities in California History* (New York, 1971).

The flowering of black history, beginning in the 1960s, has produced numerous bibliographies. For California and the West, one overshadows all others: James de T. Abajian, *Blacks and Their Contributions to the American West* (Boston, 1974), a bibliography and union list covering secondary works and primary documents to 1970. Periodical literature also remains a major source of information and ideas.

The history of blacks in California from their arrival in the late eighteenth century through the nineteenth century has been treated largely in scholarly journal articles and graduate theses. One overview is Odell Thurman, "The Negro in California Before 1890," *PH*, 19–20 (Winter 1975; Spring/Summer 1976). One intriguing question in the Spanish period is the African presence in exploration or settlement. An overview of Spanish settlers in the Southwest to 1790 is Jack D. Forbes, "Black Pioneers: The Spanish-Speaking Afro-Americans of the Southwest," *Phylon*, 27 (Fall 1966) and "Hispano-Mexican Pioneers of the San Francisco Bay Region: An Analysis of Racial Origins," *Aztlán*, 14 (Spring 1983). The African ancestry of most of the original settlers of Los Angeles is detailed in John Weatherwax, *The Founders of Los Angeles* (Los Angeles, 1954) and in William Mason, "Tracking the Founders of Los Angeles," *Museum Alliance Quarterly*, 6 (Summer 1967).

The presence of blacks among pioneer explorers and settlers in the Mexican and American eras is found in a compilation of brief biographical sketches by Sue B. Thurman, *Pioneers of Negro Origin in California* (San Francisco, 1949). Stories of black miners are compiled in W. Sherman Savage, "The Negro on the Mining Frontier," *JNH*, 30 (January 1945). Several blacks have been the subject of individual biographies. Preeminent is the explorer James Beckwourth, whose autobiography, *The Life and Adventures of James P. Beckwourth* (New York, 1856), has been reprinted in five editions. He has also attracted four book-length biographies; Elinor Wilson, *Jim Beckwourth: Black Mountain Man and War Chief of the Crows* (Norman, 1972), is the best. Other early studies include W. Shearman Savage, "Influence of William Leidesdorff on the History of California," *JNH*, 38 (July 1953) and E. Berkeley Tompkins, "Black Ahab: William T. Shorey, Whaling Master," *CHSQ*, 51 (Spring 1972). Two excellent monographs synthesize much of the nineteenth-century black experience in California: Rudolph Lapp, *Blacks in Gold Rush California* (New Haven, 1977) and Douglas H. Daniels, *Pioneer Urbanites: A Social and Cultural History of Black San Francisco* (Philadelphia, 1980).

Supplementing these are Philip Montesano, *Some Aspects of the Free Negro*

Question in San Francisco (San Francisco, 1973) and Howard Bell, "Negroes in California, 1849-1859," *Phylon*, 28 (Summer 1967). Biographical sketches of prominent black leaders throw added light on this period: Rudolph Lapp, "Jeremiah Sanderson: Early California Negro Leader," *JNH*, 53 (October 1968)—an educator; Mifflin W. Gibbs, *Shadow and Light* (Washington, D.C., 1902; reprint, 1969)—the autobiography of a San Francisco merchant who subsequently migrated to British Columbia; Helen Holdredge, *Mammy Pleasant* (New York, 1953) and Lerone Bennett, "The Mystery of Mary Ellen Pleasant," *Ebony*, 36 (April/May 1979)—a colorful San Francisco civil rights protestor.

Though California excluded slavery, there were cases of slaves being brought into the state and instances of slave owners recovering fugitives: see Clyde Duniway, "Slavery in California after 1848," *Annual Report of the American Historical Association, 1905* (Washington, D.C., 1906); Rudolph Lapp, *Archy Lee: A California Fugitive Slave Case* (San Francisco, 1969); and M. Eva Thacker, "California's Dixie Land," *California History Nuggett*, 5 (March 1938).

Blacks in antebellum California shared with others widespread denials of legal rights. Legislative and constitutional efforts to exclude blacks from the state are surveyed in Eugene Berwanger, "The 'Black Law' Question in Ante-Bellum California," *JW*, 6 (April 1967). The efforts of black leaders to repeal these laws are summarized in James A. Fisher, "The Struggle for Negro Testimony in California (1851-1863)," *SCQ*, 51 (December 1969). The exodus of California blacks in the late 1850s is summarized in Malcolm Edwards, "'The War of Complexion Distinction': Blacks in Gold Rush California and British Columbia," *CHQ*, 56 (Spring 1977). One of the few works that carried the history of blacks beyond the winning of legal rights to the end of the nineteenth century is Francis N. Lortie, Jr., *San Francisco's Black Community, 1870-1890: Dilemmas in the Struggle for Equality* (San Francisco, 1973).

Several writers have noted that the presence and rights of blacks became a significant issue in California politics in the 1850s and 1860s. Depicting both parties as appealing to anti-Negro attitudes are Gerald Stanley, "Racism and the Early Republican Party: the 1856 Presidential Election in California," *PHR*, 43 (May 1974) and "The Whim and Caprice of a Majority in a Petty State: the 1867 Election in California," *PH*, 24 (Winter 1980). Seeing the Republicans as deserving some credit for blacks gaining legal rights is Robert J. Chandler, "Friends in Time of Need: Republicans and Black Civil Rights in California during the Civil War Era," *A&W*, 24 (Winter 1982).

A comprehensive history of California blacks in the twentieth century remains to be written. Therefore, one must refer to works usually focusing either on one community or on a particular aspect of the black experience. Blacks coming to California have settled in metropolitan areas, especially Los Angeles and the San Francisco Bay area. Thus, much of the literature on them covers one of these communities. Though Los Angeles had the largest black community shortly after 1900, only a few works survey nineteenth-century origins. The transformation of the scattered black population into a segregated ghetto is analyzed in Lawrence B. de Graaf, "City of Black Angels: The Emergence of the Los Angeles Ghetto, 1890-1930," *PHR*, 39 (August 1970). Several prominent black residents have left useful memoirs or collections of writings, among them Charlotta Bass, *Forty Years: Memoirs from the Pages of a Newspaper* (Los Angeles, 1961); J. Alexander Somerville, *Man of Color* (Los Angeles, 1949)—an autobiography of a dentist and founder of the local NAACP chapter; and Baxter Scruggs, *A Man in Our Community* (Gardena, 1937)—a "rags to riches" biography of Louis A. Robinson. One of the most colorful of the late nineteenth-century residents' lives is treated in Donna Mungen's pamphlet, *The Life and Times of Biddy Mason* (Los Angeles, 1976).

The growth and expansion of the pre-World War II Los Angeles black community is detailed in Eugene S. Richard, "The Effects of the Negro's Migration to Southern California since 1920 upon his Sociocultural Patterns," *Sociology and Social Research*, 26 (March 1942). Surveying migration through World War II is Lawrence B. de Graaf, *Negro Migration to Los Angeles, 1930-1950*.

Beyond migration, the impact of World War II on the Los Angeles black community has been surveyed by Keith Collins, *Black Los Angeles: The Maturing of the Ghetto, 1940-1950* (Saratoga, Calif., 1980). Following the war, for nearly two decades little was written on Los Angeles save for articles proclaiming it as a potential Negro paradise, such as "Is Los Angeles a Utopia for Negroes," *Color*, 11 (November 1956).

Though its population grew little during the first four decades of the twentieth century, San Francisco's black community has attracted much historical study. "Organizing the Black Community in the San Francisco Bay Area, 1915-1930," *AW*, 23 (Winter 1981), studies the efforts of the NAACP and UNIA to deal with black community problems. Wartime migration and its impact is examined in Charles S. Johnson, et al., *The Negro War Worker in San Francisco* (San Francisco, 1944). Autobiographies of black residents of the city include Maya Angelou, *Now I Know Why a Caged Bird Sings* (New York, 1969), the first of four autobiographical works which discussed her life in wartime San Francisco. Subcommunities development after the war are studied in Robert E. Kapsis, "Black Ghetto Diversity and Anomie: A Sociopolitical View," *American Journal of Sociology*, 83 (March 1978).

Other bay area black communities have not been the subject of much study, though Oakland has long surpassed San Francisco in population. Wendell Bell, "The Social Areas of San Francisco Bay Region," *American Sociological Review*, 18 (February 1953), looks at patterns of segregation in black communities there compared to Los Angeles. Kathleen Archibald, *Wartime Shipyard: A Study of Social Disunity* (Berkeley, 1947), discusses wartime migration and resultant race friction in Richmond, continued into the postwar years by W. Miller Barbour, *An Exploratory Study of Socio-Economic Problems Affecting the Negro-White Relationship in Richmond, California* (New York, 1953).

Smaller black communities were formed elsewhere in the state, some dating from the nineteenth century. Best preserved has been the early history of blacks in San Diego. Glimpses of individual blacks there during the Mexican era are provided by David J. Weber, ed., "A Black American in Mexican San Diego: Two Recently Recovered Documents," *JSDH*, 20 (Spring 1974). Racial attitudes encountered by blacks are illustrated in Henry Schwartz, "The Mary Walker Incident: Black Prejudice in San Diego, 1866," *JSDH*, 19 (Spring 1973). The composition and development of a small black community are surveyed in Robert L. Carlton, "Blacks in San Diego County: A Social Profile, 1850-1880," *JSDH*, 21 (Fall 1975) and in Fail Madyun, et al., "Black Pioneers in San Diego, 1880-1920," *JSDH*, 26 (Spring 1981). The dislocations caused by wartime migration and resultant racial attitudes are surveyed by Laurence I. Hewes, Jr., *Intergroup Relations in San Diego: A Report to the City Council and the Board of Education of the City of San Diego* (San Francisco, 1946).

Blacks in other parts of the state are less well covered prior to 1960. The history of San Bernardino blacks to 1900 is summarized in Byron Skinner, *Black Origins in the Inland Empire* (San Bernardino, 1983). The absence of blacks from agricultural areas is one enigma that has been little studied. Most writings on black agricultural communities have dealt with Allensworth, now a state historical park. The veteran army chaplain who founded the colony is treated in Charles Alexander, *Battles and Victories of Allen Allensworth* (Boston, 1914).

Increased interest in black studies created by the civil rights activities and ghetto disorders of the 1960s brought forth more studies of black communities, Los Angeles being the focus of many. The movement of more affluent blacks to outlying communities is analyzed in William J. Siembieda, "Suburbanization of Ethnics of Color," *AAAPSS*, 422 (November 1975). The black population's expansion to neighboring cities outside of Los Angeles like Compton is examined in Stan Smith, "Compton . . . A Case Study in Gradual Integration," *California Sun Magazine*, 12 (Fall/Winter 1960-1961) and in Richard M. Elman, *Ill-At-Ease in Compton* (New York, 1967).

The largest body of literature focused on the Watts Riot of August 1965, which became the prism through which a wide array of social, economic, and political issues attending ghetto life came to light: Jerry Cohen and William S. Murphy, *Burn, Baby, Burn: The Los Angeles Race Riot, August 1965* (New York, 1966)—a narrative of the events; *The Los Angeles Riots: A Socio-Psychological Study* (New York, 1970), ed. by Nathan Cohen—the most extensive unofficial study; interpretive works such as Robert Conot, *Rivers of Blood, Years of Darkness* (New York, 1967); Paul Jacobs, *Prelude to Riot* (New York, 1967); David O. Sears and John B. McConahay, *The Politics of Violence: The New Urban Blacks and the Watts Riot* (Boston, 1973)—particularly useful for its bibliography; and Spencer Crump, *Black Riot in L.A.: Story of Watts Tragedy* (Los Angeles, 1966)—which summarizes widespread popular criticism of the riots.

The official analysis of the causes of the riot, the popularly named McCone Commission Report, became almost as much an item of study as the event itself. The official report, Governor's Commission on Los Angeles Riots, *Violence in the City—An End or a Beginning?* (Los Angeles, 1965), summarizes eighteen volumes of transcripts, depositions, and selected documents. Three of the most trenchant critiques of the reports are in Robert M. Fogelson, ed., *The Los Angeles Riots* (New York, 1969). An anthology of official reports from several riots that puts the McCone Commission in perspective is Anthony M. Platt, ed., *The Politics of Riot Commissions, 1917-1970* (New York, 1971).

The San Francisco Bay area had no event comparable to the Watts Riot, but minor incidents suggested similar racial tensions. Conditions at the start of the 1960s are surveyed in Wilson Record, *Minority Groups and Intergroup Relations in the San Francisco Bay Area* (Berkeley, 1963). A low-income black San Francisco neighborhood is studied in Arthur Hippler, *Hunter's Point: A Black Ghetto* (New York, 1974). Conditions in Richmond are summarized in Robert L. Wenkert, et al., *An Historical Digest of Negro-White Relations in Richmond, California* (Berkeley, 1967).

Much of the study of California blacks has been done by specialists in particular topical areas, especially housing and employment, where blacks have met historic discrimination, as well as the legal efforts to end such practices. An exhaustive bibliography on housing practices and related legal issues is James Kushner, "Apartheid in America: An Historical and Legal Analysis of Contemporary Racial Residential Segregation in the United States," *Howard Law Journal*, 22 (1979).

Numerous studies of housing discrimination through the 1950s led to the Unruh Act of 1960 and the Rumford Fair Housing Act of 1963, which in turn were challenged by a statewide initiative, Proposition 14. John H. Denton, *Apartheid American Style* (Berkeley, 1967) and Thomas Casstevens, *Politics, Housing and Race Relations: California's Rumford Act and Proposition 14* (Berkeley, 1967), are overviews through the *Mulkey* v. *Reitman* decision which overturned Proposition 14. The inadequacies of the Unruh Act are set forth in M. Kaplan, "Discrimination in California Housing: The Need for Additional Legislation," *California Law Review*, 50 (October 1962), while Raymond E. Wolfinger and Fred I. Greenstein detail "The Repeal of Fair Housing in California: An Analysis of Referendum Voting," *American Political Science Review*, 62 (September 1968), as does Harlan Hahn, "Northern Referenda on Fair Housing: The Response of White Voters," *WPQ*, 21 (September 1968).

Black workers in California prior to World War II were confronted with both limited access to occupations and competition as low-wage workers, as seen in Charles S. Johnson, "Negro Workers in Los Angeles Industries," *Opportunity*, 6 (August 1928); Lawrence B. de Graaf, "Race, Sex and Region: Black Women in the American West, 1850–1920," *PHR*, 49 (May 1980); and C. Wilson Record, "Negroes in the California Agricultural Labor Force," *Social Problems*, 6 (Spring 1959).

The labor shortage brought on by World War II opened manufacturing jobs to blacks and sparked racial labor issues. A contemporary exposé of discrimination in seeking defense industry jobs is National Negro Congress, *Jim Crow in National Defense* (Los Angeles, 1940). Experiences of black workers in wartime industries are covered in Archibald (above) and in Bernice Reed, "Accommodation Between White and Negro Employees in a West Coast Aircraft Industry, 1942-1944," *Social Forces*, 26 (October 1947). Peacetime problems are surveyed in "Postwar Status of Negro Workers in the San Francisco Area," *Monthly Labor Review*, 70 (June 1950) and in C. Wilson Record, "Willie Stokes at the Golden Gate," *Crisis*, 50 (June 1949).

Wartime discrimination brought the first of a series of efforts to end such practices through legislation. William H. Harris, "Federal Intervention in Union Discrimination: FEPC and West Coast Shipyards during World War II," *LH*, 22 (Summer 1981), reviews the most celebrated case of wartime federal fair employment activity in California.

California blacks long aspired to professional careers, but met patterns of discrimination that made some of them champions of civil rights. Best recorded are the medical professionals. Dietrich Reitzer, *Negroes and Medicine* (Cambridge, Mass., 1958), provides a national overview and a chapter on Los Angeles doctors; Orolee Ruffin, "Jim Crowing Nurses," *Crisis*, 37 (April 1930), portrays typical segregation in Oakland, and there are several physicians' autobiographies: Thomas Peyton, *Quest for Dignity* (Los Angeles, 1950); Helen K. Branson, *Let There Be Life: The Contemporary Account of Edna L. Griffin, M.D.* (Pasadena, 1947); and the above mentioned work by Somerville.

In recent decades, the outstanding model of success for many black males has been the professional athlete. The national literature on black athletes is extensive, as can be seen in Lenwood David and Belinda Daniels, *Black Athletes in the United States: A Bibliography ... 1800-1890* (Westport, 1981). Especially interesting are the several books and numerous articles by Los Angeles black sport historian Andrew S. N. (Doc) Young. Autobiographies provide glimpses of life in California and the experiences of blacks in sports. These include Jackie Robinson and Carl Rowan, *Wait Till Next Year* (New York, 1960) and Robinson's *Baseball Has Done It* (New York, 1964); William F. Russell, *Go Up for Glory* (New York, 1966) and Russell and Taylor Branch, *Second Wind: The Memoirs of an Opinionated Man* (New York, 1979); Frank Robinson, *My Life in Baseball* (Garden City, N.Y., 1968); *Willie Mays: My Life In and Out of Baseball* (New York, 1966); and Wilt Chamberlain and David Shaw, *Wilt* (New York, 1973).

Two comprehensive histories of minority group education in California emphasize the legal issues of segregation: Charles A. Wollenberg, *All Deliberate Speed* (Berkeley, 1976) and Irving G. Hendrick, *The Education of Non-Whites in California* (San Francisco, 1977). David L. Kirp, *Just Schools: The Idea of Racial Equality in American Education* (Berkeley, 1982), a national study using California cities as case studies, is useful. A select bibliography of various interpretations of the desegregation issue is William J. Holloway, "School Desegregation in the United States, 1973-1982: An Annotated Bibliography," *Negro Educational Review*, 34 (July/October 1983).

Increasing attention to civil rights issues in the late 1950s eventually brought a realization that many California blacks were relegated to de facto segregation that differed little in its effects from legalized separate schools. C. Wilson Record, "Racial Diversity in California Public Schools," *Journal of Negro Education*, 28 (Winter 1959), is an early overview of a problem thoroughly surveyed by the State Department of Education in *Racial and Ethnic Survey of California Public Schools* (Sacramento, 1967), the first of several such official studies.

The most extensive literature on school desegregation treats individual communities and emphasizes legal and political issues. These include: Robert Singleton and Paul Bullock, "Some Problems in Minority Group Education in the Los Angeles Public Schools," *Journal of Negro Education*, 32 (Spring 1963); John W. Caughey, *School Desegregation on Our Doorstep: The Los Angeles Story* (Los Angeles, 1967), co-authored by his wife, LaRee, and *To Kill a Child's Spirit* (Ithaca, 1973), which carries the issue through to the decision ordering desegregation in Los Angeles. Events through the California Supreme Court ruling upholding desegregation in 1976 are summarized in U.S. Civil Rights Commission, *A Generation Deprived: Los Angeles School Desegregation* (Washington, D.C., 1977). The defeat of the Los Angeles liberal school board members and the implications of the prolonged struggle are analyzed in M. Stephen Weatherford, "The Politics of School Busing: Contextual Effects and Community Polarization," *Journal of Politics*, 42 (August 1980) and Gary Orfield, "Lessons of the Los Angeles Desegregation Case," *Education and Urban Society*, 16 (May 1984).

While Los Angeles suggests the difficulties of achieving desegregation, the experiences of Berkeley portray the possibilities of success. The need for desegregation is set forth in Alan B. Wilson, *Educational Consequences of Segregation in a California Community* (Berkeley, 1966). Berkeley Superintendent of Schools Neil V. Sullivan, with Evelyn S. Stewart, provide both a history and personal insights on the desegregation effort in *Now Is the Time: Integration in the Berkeley Schools* (Bloomington, Ind., 1970). Useful is Alan Luneman, "Desegregation and Achievement: A Cross-Sectional and Semi-Longitudinal Look at Berkeley, California," *Journal of Negro Education*, 42 (Fall 1973) and the U.S. Civil Rights Commission, *School Desegregation in Berkeley, California* (Washington, D.C., 1977).

Politics has long been viewed as a vehicle for race advancement. Michael Goldstein, "The Political Careers of Fred Roberts and Tom Bradley: Political Style and Black Politics in Los Angeles," *The Western Journal of Black Studies*, 5 (Summer 1981), examines one of the earliest black elected officials and a successful recent one. The role of community groups is analyzed in Ernest F. Anderson, *The Development of Leadership and Organization Building in the Black Community of Los Angeles from 1900 through World War II* (Saratoga, 1980). Two other successful politicians are profiled in Clint Wilson, Jr., "Gilbert Lindsay: Once He Was a Lonely Janitor," *Sepia*, 28 (September 1979) and in Stephanie Sheppard, "Augustus F. Hawkins: Champion of the People," *Sepia*, 28 (July 1979).

Increased political activity after 1960 was first noticed on the local level. Herman Smith, in "Politics and Policies of the Negro Community," in Eugene P. Dvorin and Arthur J. Misner, eds., *California Politics and Policies: Original Essays* (Reading, Pa., 1966), surveys the state of Los Angeles at mid-decade. The impact of the Watts Riot on politics is analyzed in D. O. Sears and D. R. Kinder, "Racial Tensions and Voting in Los Angeles," in W. Z. Hirsch, ed., *Los Angeles: Visibility and Prospects for Metropolitan Leadership* (New York, 1971). Richard Young, "The Impact of Protest Leadership on Negro Politicians in San Francisco," *WPQ*, 22 (March 1969), concludes that black politicians and protest leaders shared common positions and appreciation for each other. Harriet Nathan and Scott Stanley, eds., *Experiment and Change in Berkeley: Essays on City Politics, 1950-1975* (Berkeley, 1978), trace that city's transformation from conservative Republican dominance to a coalition of white radicals and blacks.

The ascent of blacks to elected office is seen in the lives of individual politicians. Two have written extensively, Mervyn Dymally, ed., *The Black Politician: His Struggle for Power* (Belmont, 1971) and Ronald Dellums, "Responsibility of Black Politics," *Black Scholar*, 10 (January/February 1979). A biographical history of all black officeholders in the state to 1973 is Sethard Fisher, *Black Elected Officials in California* (San Francisco, 1978). The career of a leading advocate of state civil rights laws is provided in Lawrence P. Crouchett, *William Byron Rumford: The Life and Public Services of a California Legislator* (El Cerrito, Calif., 1984). For shorter biographical sketches see Robert Studer, "Willie Brown: California's Brash New Speaker," *Sepia*, 30 (April 1981) and Pamela Douglas, "West Coast Wonder Women," *Black Enterprise*, 12 (November 1981), a survey of black women in politics. The epitome of black political success and frustrations in California has been the political career of Tom Bradley. A detailed portrait is in *Tom Bradley: The Impossible Dream* (Los Angeles, 1986), by J. Gregory Payne and Scott C. Ratzan.

The history of black communities must also deal with various social problems and services available to treat them. The adequacy and acceptability of such public institutional services is surveyed in Agnes Wilson, *The Facilities for the Care of Dependent, Semi-Delinquent and Delinquent Negro Children in Los Angeles* (Los Angeles, 1925) and in Jerome Cohen, *A Descriptive Study of the Availability and Usability of Social Services in the South Central Area of Los Angeles* (Los Angeles, 1967).

The most important community institution to many blacks has been the church. In the nineteenth century it was a center of community life and political protest. That role is surveyed in Philip Montesano, "San Francisco Black Churches in the Early 1860s: Political Pressure Group," *CHQ*, 52 (Summer 1973) and in Larry G. Murphy, "The Church and Black Californians: A Mid-Nineteenth Century Struggle for Civil Justice," *Foundations*, 18 (April/June 1975). Aside from a few privately printed individual church histories, studies of black churches in the twentieth century are few.

The black press, like the church, was a central institution of early black communities in California and at times also served as a vehicle for protest. Most nineteenth-century newspapers are covered in William Snorgrass, "The Black Press in the San Francisco Bay Area, 1856-1900," *CH*, 60 (Winter 1981/1982). Useful for early Los Angeles and Bay Area papers is I. Garland Penn, *The Afro-American Press and Its Editors* (1891; reprint, New York, 1969). The career of a leading civil rights advocate among early editors is summarized in John H. Telfer, "Philip Alexander Bell and the San Francisco *Elevator*," *San Francisco Negro Historical and Cultural Society Monograph*, 9 (August 1966). The autobiography of Charlotta Bass, cited above, is of use. Ronald Wolseley, *The Black Press, U.S.A.* (Ames, Iowa, 1971), a national survey, has considerable information on Los Angeles papers.

Throughout the nineteenth century and into the twentieth, most California whites viewed blacks as inferior and excluded them from many activities and areas. These attitudes are especially treated by scholars of the racism school. But the presumption of those writers that whites held equally hostile attitudes toward all minorities is challenged by Luther Spoehr, "Sambo and the Heathen Chinee: Californians' Racial Stereotypes in the Late 1870s," *PHR*, 42 (May 1973). Contending that antiblack attitudes transferred to Chinese is Dan Caldwell, "The Negroization of the Chinese Stereotype in California," *SCQ*, 53 (June 1971). Even former abolitionists assumed less sympathetic attitudes, as is seen in Joan Jensen, "After Slavery: Caroline Severance in Los Angeles," *SCQ*, 48 (June 1966). By the second half of the twentieth century, overt expressions of prejudice are uncommon, but lingering manifestations are analyzed in Alphonso Pinkney, "Prejudice Toward Mexican and Negro Americans: A Comparison," *Phylon*, 24 (Winter 1963). The tendency of some whites in the 1960s to avoid any sign of criticism of blacks is discussed in Lillian Rubin, "The Racist Liberals—an Episode in a County Jail," *Trans-action*, 5 (September 1968). An omnipresent fear has been that hostile attitudes would translate into violence, tendencies which are surveyed in the Governor's Task Force on Civil Rights, *Report on Racial, Ethnic and Religious Violence in California* (3 vols.; Sacramento, 1982).

Before the 1960s, few writers considered radical or nationalist ideas and organizations an important component of the history of California blacks. Since then, the topic has received more attention than almost any other. The best treated is a turn-of-the-century San Diego preacher in Philip S. Foner, "Reverend George Washington Woodbey: Early Twentieth Century California Black Socialist," *JNH*, 61 (April 1976). For a collection of his teachings, see Foner, ed., *Black Socialist Preacher* (San Francisco, 1983). The widely popular Garvey movement was believed to have missed California until Emory Tolbert revealed an active and influential Los Angeles branch in *The UNIA and Black Los Angeles: Ideology and Community in the American Garvey Movement* (Los Angeles, 1980). The arrival of black Muslims in Los Angeles by the early 1960s is treated briefly in the standard work on that movement, C. Eric Lincoln, *The Black*

Muslims in America (Boston, 1964) and in Alfred Jarrette, ed., *Muslim's Black America* (Los Angeles, 1962).

Within a year of the Watts Riot, the Oakland ghetto gave birth to one of the nation's most celebrated radical groups, the Black Panthers. The rise of this organization and the lives of its leaders are treated in Reginald Major, *A Panther is a Black Cat* (New York, 1971) and in Gene Marine, *The Black Panthers* (New York, 1969). The leaders' thinking is best revealed in their own writings: *To Die for the People: The Writings of Huey P. Newton* (New York, 1972) and Bobby Seale, *Seize the Time: The Story of the Black Panther Party and Huey P. Newton* (New York, 1970).

The political and revolutionary nationalism of the Black Panthers, articulated by Eldridge Cleaver, was challenged by another form of black nationalism, cultural nationalism, espoused by the head of US, Maulana Ron Karenga. Eldridge Cleaver attained prominence with his autobiographical *Soul on Ice* (New York, 1967), and his *Post-Prison Writings and Speeches*, ed. by Robert Scheer (New York, 1969). Karenga's early thinking is set forth in C. Halisi and J. Ntume, eds., *The Quotable Karenga* (Los Angeles, 1967). Among Karenga's many articles, the most important is "Kawaida and Its Critics: A Sociohistorical Analysis," *Journal of Black Studies*, 8 (December 1977).

California in the late 1960s also produced one of the nation's few important black Communists, Angela Davis. Her evolution from a middle-class Southern family to an intellectual Communist is traced in *Angela Davis: An Autobiography* (New York, 1974) and in Regina Nadelson, *Who is Angela Davis: The Biography of a Revolutionary* (New York, 1972).

Artistic expression and performance have long been hallmarks of black culture, and California has been recognized for decades as an entertainment center of America. Yet, until recent times blacks have not been viewed as an important part of California arts, nor have historians credited California with playing a major role in the development of black culture. Theatre is a case in point. An overview of blacks in theatre with considerable information on California is Lindsay Patterson, comp., *Anthology of the American Negro in the Theatre: A Critical Approach* (New York, 1967).

The history of blacks in theatre became more meaningful in the 1960s, as the black arts movement sought to use the arts as a vehicle for defining a black consciousness and a sense of cultural uniqueness. This movement was particularly strong in theatre, as is seen in Larry Neal, "The Black Arts Movement," *Drama Review*, 12 (Summer 1968); Woodie King, Jr., "Black Theatre: Recent Condition," *Drama Review*, 12 (Summer 1968); playwright Ed Bullins, *The Theme is Blackness: 'The Corner', Other Plays* (New York, 1972); and Marvin X, "Manifesto: The Black Educational Theatre of San Francisco," *Black Theatre*, 6 (1972).

Music is also an area in which isolating "California blacks" is particularly difficult, for the product is universal and the conditions of work require constant travel. Little has been written exclusively on black music in California, so that the student must consult the several histories of blues and jazz or the collected biographies of black performers, such as Leonard Feather, *From Satchmo to Miles* (New York, 1972); Marshall W. Stearns, *The Story of Jazz* (New York, 1956); LeRoi Jones, *Blues People* (New York, 1963); and Charles Keil, *Urban Blues* (Chicago, 1966).

California has also been home to several prominent black artists, sculptors, and architects. As in other areas of culture, students must utilize national works such as Thomas D. Cedarholm, ed., *Afro-American Artists* (Boston, 1973) and Lynn M. Igoe, *250 Years of Afro-American Art: An Annotated Bibliography* (New York, 1981). The works of an early twentieth-century artist are collected in Oakland Museum, *Sargent Johnson Retrospective . . .* (Oakland, 1971). California's most prominent black architect, Paul Williams, is best studied in his own writings, *The Small Home of Tomorrow* (Hollywood, 1945) and in *New Homes for Today* (Hollywood, 1946). Nationally prominent as a depicter of black experiences is Charles White. His drawings and a biography are in *Images of Dignity: The Drawings of Charles White* (Los Angeles, 1967). See also Louie Robinson, "Charles White: Portages of Black Dignity," *Ebony*, 22 (July 1967) and for a prominent recent artist, Houston Conwill, "Interview with Betye Saar," *Black Art: An International Quarterly*, 3 (No. 1/1979).

The cultural medium most commonly associated with California, motion pictures, is also one of the best in which to measure changing conditions for blacks in cultural pursuits. Several works have traced the opportunities for blacks in the film industry primarily by analyzing their roles, the most scholarly being Thomas Cripps, *Slow Fade to Black: The Negro in American Films, 1900–1942* (New York, 1977), who analyzes the roles of blacks after World War II "The Death of Rastus: Negroes in American Films Since 1945," *Phylon*, 28 (Fall 1967). Categorizing most black film roles into stereotypes and concluding that Hollywood continues to think of blacks in such terms is Donald Bogle, *Toms, Coons, Mulattoes, Mammies and Bucks* (New York, 1973). Particularly detailed on films of the 1960s is Edward Mapp, *Blacks in American Films: Today and Yesterday* (Metuchen, N.J., 1972) and Lindsay Patterson, comp., *Black Films and Film Makers* (New York, 1975).

A common theme of literature since World War II is whether the opportunities for blacks in terms of jobs and roles has notably improved, as reflected in Edward Mapp, "Black Women in Films," *Black Scholar*, 13 (Summer 1982), which surveys roles from the 1920s through the 1970s, and in U.S. Commission on Civil Rights, *Behind the Scenes: Equal Employment Opportunity in the Motion Picture Industry* (Washington, D.C., 1978). Further insights are found in numerous autobiographies. One of the few analyses of the status of blacks in the television industry is U.S. Commission on Civil Rights, *Window Dressing on the Set: Women and Minorities in Television* (Washington, D.C., 1977).

A topic in itself is black filmmakers and companies that for several decades were known only to people in black communities. A survey of early black companies is Thomas Cripps, "Movies in the Ghetto B.P. (Before Poitier)," *Negro*

Digest, 18 (February 1969), and an early black filmmaker is profiled in Bernard L. Peterson, Jr., "Films of Oscar Micheaux: America's First Fabulous Black Filmmaker," *Crisis*, 86 (April 1979). The entry of blacks into the mainstream of filmmaking is surveyed in Charles D. Peavy, "Through a Lens Darkly: America's Emerging Black Film Makers," *Journal of Popular Culture*, 4 (Winter 1971).

A historical synthesis of black culture in California remains to be written; to date we have only the pieces to be assembled. In this characteristic, black culture epitomizes much of California black history after the nineteenth century. It has been researched and written to the point of dissertations, theses, case studies, and articles, but little of it has been synthesized into broad patterns that will enable historians of California to assess the full meaning of the black presence in all facets of state history, or scholars of the black experience nationwide to appreciate the role of California. The writing of such syntheses is the central challenge of black history today.

8

CALIFORNIA ASIANS

DONALD T. HATA, JR., AND NADINE I. HATA

AS THE NATION NEARS the twenty-first century, Los Angeles and San Francisco now rival the earlier East Coast role of Ellis Island as ports of entry for new Americans from throughout Asia and the Pacific. Due to acknowledgment of the multicultural dimensions of American history since World War II, a variety of bibliographies on Asian and Pacific Americans are available. Comprehensive are Isao Fujimoto, et al., *Asians in America: A Selected Annotated Bibliography* (Davis, 1983) and Paul M. Ong and William Wong Lum, *Theses and Dissertations on Asians in the United States with Selected References to Other Overseas Asians* (Davis, 1974). A key supplement is the "Annual Bibliography," introduced in 1977 in *AJ*. Bibliographic essays include a number by Roger Daniels: "Westerners from the East: Oriental Immigrants Reappraised," *PHR*, 35 (November 1966), "American Historians and East Asian Immigrants," *PHR*, 43 (November 1974), and "North American Scholarship and Asian Immigrants, 1974–1979," *Immigration History Newsletter*, 11 (1979), which annotates publications on nineteenth- and twentieth-century Asian immigration.

Bibliographies also exist on individual Asian communities: Gladys C. Hansen and William F. Heintz, *The Chinese in California: A Brief Bibliographic History* (Portland, Oreg., 1970); Yuji Ichioka, et al., *A Buried Past: An Annotated Bibliography of the Japanese American Research Project Collections* (Berkeley, 1974); Helen E. Henefrund and Orpha Cummings, *Bibliography of the Japanese in American Agriculture* (Washington, D.C., 1943); Helen D. Jones, *Japanese in the United States: A Selected List of References* (Washington, D.C., 1946); Yuji Ichioka, "A Buried Past. A Survey of English-language works on Japanese American History," in Emma Gee, ed., *Counterpoint: Perspectives on Asian America* (Los Angeles, 1976); Christopher Kim, *Annotated Bibliography on*

Koreans in America (Los Angeles, 1976); Fortunato U. Macadangdang, *A Selective Bibliography of Filipino Experiences in America* (San Jose, 1973); Irene P. Norell, *Literature of the Filipino-American in the United States: A Selective and Annotated Bibliography* (San Francisco, 1976); Irene F. Rockman, *Understanding the Filipino-American, 1906-1976* (Monticello, Ill., 1976); and Shiro Saito, *Filipinos Overseas: A Bibliography* (New York, 1977).

Strategies enabling Asian immigrants and their descendants to survive are described in H. Brett Melendy, *The Oriental Americans* (New York, 1972)—on Chinese and Japanese—and his *Asians in America: Filipinos, Koreans, and East Indians* (Boston, 1977). Norris Hundley, Jr., ed., *The Asian American, The Historical Experience* (Santa Barbara, 1976), examines Chinese, Japanese, Filipino, Korean, and East Indian communities, while Tricia Knoll, *Becoming Americans: Asian Sojourners, Immigrants, and Refugees in the Western United States* (Portland, Oreg., 1982), adds Vietnamese, Laotians, Boat People, and Kampucheans. Multidisciplinary collections include Amy Tachiki, et al., eds., *Roots: An Asian American Reader* (Los Angeles, 1971); Gee, ed., *Counterpoint: Perspectives on Asian America*; and Stanford M. Lyman, *The Asian in North America* (Santa Barbara, 1977).

Asian/Pacific American immigration history is largely a California story, with the exception of Hawaii. The earliest arrivals, Chinese, responded to California's gold rush and railroad labor needs. General treatments are: Betty Lee Sung, *Mountain of Gold: The Story of the Chinese in America* (New York, 1967); Rose Hum Lee, *The Chinese in the United States of America* (Hong Kong, 1960)—empathetic but factually flawed; and S. W. Kung, *The Chinese in American Life: Some Aspects of Their History, Status, and Contributions* (Seattle, 1962). Thomas W. Chinn, comp., *A History of the Chinese in California: A Syllabus* (San Francisco, 1969) remains a basic reference. Specialized histories of the early Chinese experience in various occupations include Alexander Saxton, "The Army of Canton in the High Sierra," *PHR*, 35 (May 1966); Ping Chiu, *Chinese Labor in California, 1850-1880* (Madison, 1963); Robert J. Schwendinger, "Chinese Sailors: America's Invisible Merchant Marine, 1876-1905," *CH*, 57 (Spring 1978); and Rodman M. Paul, *California Gold* (Reprint; Lincoln, 1947). Chinese contributions to railroading, agricultural, and urban occupations are treated by: Gunther Barth, *Bitter Strength: A History of the Chinese in the United States, 1850-1870* (Cambridge, Mass., 1964) and "Chinese Sojourners in the West: The Coming," *SCQ*, 46 (March 1964); Julius L. Jacobs, "California's Pioneer Wine Families," *CHQ*, 54 (Summer 1975); Arthur F. McEvoy, "In Places Men Reject: Chinese Fishermen at San Diego, 1870-1893," *JSDH*, 23 (Fall 1977); Charles Choy Wong, "Black and Chinese Grocery Stores in Los Angeles' Black Ghetto," *Urban Life*, 5 (January 1977) and "The Continuity of Chinese Grocers in Southern California," *Journal of Ethnic Studies*, 8 (Summer 1980); Thomas W. Chinn, "New Chapters in Chinese American History," *CH*, 57 (Spring 1978); Andrew Griego, ed., "Rebuilding the California Southern Railroad: The Personal Account of a Chinese Labor Contractor, 1884," *JSDH*,

25 (1979); Paul M. Ong, "An Ethnic Trade: The Chinese Laundries in Early California," *Journal of Ethnic Studies*, 8 (Winter 1981); and Peter Leung, "When a Haircut Was a Luxury: A Chinese Farm Laborer in the Delta," *CH*, 64 (Summer 1985).

Histories of Chinese communities are: George Chu, "Chinatowns in the Delta: The Chinese in the Sacramento-San Joaquin Delta, 1870–1960," *CHSQ*, 49 (March 1970); Gloria Sun Hom, ed., *Chinese Argonauts: An Anthology of the Chinese Contributions to the Historical Development of Santa Clara County* (Los Altos, 1971); Susan W. Book, *The Chinese in Butte County, California, 1860–1920* (San Francisco, 1976); Jean Rossi, "Lee Bing: Founder of California's Historical Town of Locke," *PH*, 20 (Winter 1976); and Sandy Lyon, *Chinese Gold: The Chinese in the Monterey Bay Region* (Capitola, Calif., 1985). Inner dynamics of Chinese settlements are explored by Stanford Lyman in *The Asian in the West* (Reno, 1970), who focuses on San Francisco and other local sites, and Victor G. and Brett De Bary Nee, *Longtime Californ': A Documentary Study of An American Chinatown* (Boston, 1974).

For diverse insights into the lives of Chinese women in the nineteenth and twentieth centuries, see Otis Gibson, "Missionary Work among Chinese Women in California," *Chinese in America* (Cincinnati, 1877); Joyce Mende Wong, "Prostitution: San Francisco Chinatown, Mid- and Late-Nineteenth Century," *Bridge Magazine*, 6 (Winter 1978); Lucie Cheng Hirata, "Chinese Immigrant Women in Nineteenth Century California," in C. R. Berkin and M. B. Norton, eds., *Women in America* (Boston, 1979); and Lucie Cheng, et al., *Linking Our Lives: Chinese American Women of Los Angeles* (Los Angeles, 1984).

The nativist assault, which led to a series of federal laws prohibiting Chinese immigration after 1882, was supported by H. H. Bancroft, who dismissed the Chinese as alien, inferior, and unassimilable. Mary R. Coolidge, *Chinese Immigration* (New York, 1909) and the Rev. Otis Gibson, *The Chinese in America* (Cincinnati, 1877) refuted the nativists' charges of Chinese unassimilability, but had little influence on legislators and politicians who recognized the appeal of the nativist movement among working-class voters. Studies documenting the anti-Chinese issue and its unifying impact on the California labor movement include: Lucille Eaves, *A History of Labor Legislation in California* (Berkeley, 1910); Ira B. Cross, *A History of the Labor Movement in California* (Berkeley, 1935); Rodman M. Paul, "The Origin of the Chinese Issue in California," *MVHR*, 25 (September 1938); Ralph Kauer, "The Workingmen's Party in California," *PHR*, 13 (September 1944); Leonard Pitt, "The Beginnings of Nativism in California," *PHR*, 30 (February 1961); Philip C. Choy, "Golden Mountain of Lead: The Chinese Experience in California," in Roger Olmsted and Charles Wollenberg, eds., *Neither Separate Nor Equal* (San Francisco, 1971) and Delber L. McKee, *Chinese Exclusion Versus the Open Door Policy, 1900–1906: Clashes over China Policy in the Roosevelt Era* (Detroit, 1977). Elmer C. Sandmeyer's *The Anti-Chinese Movement in California* (Urbana, 1939), with a foreword and supplementary bibliography by Roger Daniels in its reprinted version (1973), remains the best work on the subject, along with Alexander Saxton, *The Indispensable Enemy* (Berkeley, 1971); Stuart C. Miller, *The Unwelcome Immigrant: The American Image of the Chinese, 1785-1882* (Berkeley, 1969) and "An East Coast Perspective to Chinese Exclusion, 1852-1882," *Historian*, 33 (February 1971). The anti-Chinese movement was not limited to legal and legislative harassment. Mob violence and murders are the subjects of Chester P. Dorland, "Chinese Massacre at Los Angeles in 1871," *APHSSC*, 3 (1894); Paul M. De Falla, "Lantern in the Western Sky," *QHSSC*, 42 (March/June 1960); William R. Locklear, "The Celestials and the Angels: A Study of the Anti-Chinese Movement in Los Angeles to 1882," *QHSSC*, 42 (September 1960); Lynwood Carranco, "Chinese Expulsion from Humboldt County," *PHR*, 30 (November 1961); and "The Chinese in Humboldt County, California: A Study in Prejudice," *JW*, 12 (January 1973).

Other perspectives on the anti-Chinese movement have expanded the historiography of the subject: Shih-shan Tsai, "Chinese Immigration Through Communist Eyes: An Introduction to the Historiography," *PHR*, 43 (August 1974); Robert McClellan, *The Heathen Chinee: A Study of American Attitudes toward China, 1890-1905* (Columbus, Ohio, 1971); Dan Caldwell, "The Negroization of the Chinese Stereotype in California," *SCQ*, 53 (June 1971); Luther W. Spoehr, "Sambo and the Heathen Chinee: Californians' Racial Stereotypes in the Late 1890s," *PHR*, 42 (May 1973); and Francis N. Lortie, Jr., *San Francisco's Black Community, 1870-1890: Dilemmas in the Struggle for Equality* (San Francisco, 1973)—describing differences between the *Elevator* and *Pacific Appeal* on the Chinese and the Workingmen's party.

While historians agree that Asian immigration to California began with the arrival of Chinese amidst the gold rush, Richard Dillon, "Kanaka Colonies in California," *PHR*, 25 (February 1955) and Henry Taketa, "1969, the Centennial Year," *PH*, 13 (Winter 1969), a study of the Wakamatsu Tea and Silk Farm Colony of Eldorado County and probably the first Japanese settlement in the continental United States, suggest the need to research the early presence of other trans-Pacific migrants as well.

The cheap labor vacuum created on the West Coast by the Chinese exclusion laws was a major factor in the large influx of Japanese immigrants after 1890. The newcomers were soon perceived as a more dangerous version of the "Yellow Peril" than were their Chinese antecedents; see Donald T. Hata, Jr., *"Undesirables": Early Immigrants and the Anti-Japanese Movement in San Francisco, 1892-1893* (New York, 1979). The arrival of women is the subject of Yuji Ichioka, *"Amerika Nadeshiko*: Japanese Immigrant Women in the United States, 1900-1924," *PHR*, 48 (May 1980) and Akemi Kikumura, *Through Harsh Winters: The Life of a Japanese Immigrant Woman* (Novato, Calif., 1981).

By 1906 two events drew national attention to the anti-Japanese ferment led by the Asiatic Exclusion League. The first was the 1906 San Francisco School Board's decision to force all Japanese to attend the one public school designated for Chinese pupils. The Japanese government issued a strongly worded protest, and Theodore Roosevelt forced the board to rescind its order. Meanwhile, Japan suddenly posed a threat to the balance of power in Asia and the Pacific by its unexpected victory in the Russo-Japanese War. Nativists and xenophobes joined to accuse Japanese immigrants as the vanguard of an invasion from within and without. Two early works on these issues were Herbert B. Johnson, *Discrimination Against Japanese in California* (Berkeley, 1907) and William G. Burke, *The Japanese School Segregation Case: Respondents' Brief* (San Francisco, ca.1907).

In opposition to the Asiatic Exclusion League's *Proceedings* (San Francisco, 1907–1912) and the Native Sons of the Golden West's *Grizzly Bear Magazine*, a forum for nativist views, were equally polemical defenders of Japanese immigration such as Sidney L. Gulick, *The American Japanese Problem* (New York, 1914), who published two dozen books and numerous articles, and K. K. Kawakami, *Asia at the Door, A Study of the Japanese Question in the Continental United States, Hawaii and Canada* (New York, 1914) and *The Real Japanese Question* (New York, 1921). Other works on the issue include Yosaburo Yoshida, "Sources and Causes of Japanese Immigration," *AAAPSS*, 34 (September 1909); U.S. Immigration Commission, *Reports of the Immigration Commission: Japanese and Other Immigrant Groups in the Pacific Coast and Rocky Mountain States*, 23 (Washington, D.C., 1911); H. A. Millis, *The Japanese Problem in the United States: An Investigation for the Commission on Relations with Japan Appointed by the Federal Council of Churches of Christ in America* (New York, 1911); Yamato Ichihashi, *Japanese Immigration: Its Status in California* (San Francisco, 1913); Thomas A. Bailey, "California, Japan and the Alien Land Act Legislation of 1912," *PHR*, 1 (March 1932); "The Oriental on the Pacific Coast—A Symposium," *The Pacific Review*, 3 (December 1920); and Herbert P. LePore, "Prelude to Prejudice: Hiram Johnson, Woodrow Wilson and the California Land Law Controversy of 1913," *SCQ*, 61 (Spring 1979).

Subsequent controversies included the alien land laws of 1912 and 1920, forbidding purchases by "aliens ineligible to citizenship," and the convergence of nationwide nativist movements, which demanded immigration quotas and total exclusion of the Japanese. George Shima, *An Appeal to Justice* (Stockton, 1920), defended immigrants on behalf of the Japanese Association of America, headquartered in San Francisco, but the nativist-xenophobic alliance was far more prolific. Alarmists warned of Imperial Japan's plans to invade the West Coast in Homer Lea, *The Valor of Ignorance* (New York, 1909); Peter B. Kyne, *The Pride of Palomar* (New York, 1921); and Wallace Irwin, *Seed of the Sun* (New York, 1921). The California State Board of Control, *California and the Oriental: Japanese, Chinese and Hindus* (Sacramento, 1920; rev. ed., 1922), published statistics documenting official support for exclusion. Social scientists examined the anti-Japanese immigration movement, including Raymond L. Buell, "The Development of Anti-Japanese Agitation in the United States," *Political Science Quarterly*, 37 (December 1922) and 38 (March 1923); R. D.

McKenzie, *Oriental Exclusion* (Chicago, 1928); and M. Fujita, "The Japanese Association of America," *Sociology and Social Research*, 13 (January/February 1929). Diplomatic and legal dimensions of the complex issue appeared in Thomas A. Bailey, *Theodore Roosevelt and the Japanese American Crisis* (Stanford, 1934); Milton R. Konvitz, *The Alien and the Asiatic in American Law* (Ithaca, 1946); and Frank F. Chuman, *The Bamboo People: The Law and Japanese Americans* (Del Mar, 1976). Also see David J. Hellwig, "Afro-American Reactions to the Japanese and the Anti-Japanese Movement, 1906-1924," *Phylon*, 38 (March 1977). The standard reference on the arrival of Japanese immigrants and the multiplicity of factors which led to their exclusion is Roger Daniels, *The Politics of Prejudice* (New York, 1969). Two general works which include these issues are Hilary Conroy and T. Scott Miyakawa, *East Across the Pacific: Historical and Sociological Studies of Japanese Immigration and Assimilation* (Santa Barbara, 1972) and Robert A. Wilson and Bill Hosakawa, *East To America: A History of the Japanese in the United States* (New York, 1980).

Other studies of economic contributions, biographies, and local communities include Masakazu Iwata, "Japanese Immigrants in California Agriculture," *AH*, 36 (January 1962); William M. Mason and John A. McKinstry, *The Japanese of Los Angeles, 1869-1920* (Los Angeles, 1969); Buddhist Churches of America, *Buddhist Churches of America, Volume I: 75 Year History, 1899-1974* (Chicago, 1974); Cheryl L. Cole, *History of the Japanese Community in Sacramento, 1883-1972* (San Francisco, 1975); Don Estes, "Kondo Masaharu and the Best of All Fishermen," *JSDH*, 23 (Summer 1977) and "Before the War: The Japanese in San Diego," *JSDH*, 24 (Fall 1978); Kuchi Kanzaki, "Landless by Law: Japanese Immigrants in California Agriculture to 1941," *Journal of Economic History*, 38 (March 1978); Roger Daniels, "The Japanese," in John Higham, ed., *Ethnic Leadership in America* (Baltimore, 1978); Toshio Yoshimura, *George Shima, Potato King and Lover of Chinese Classics* (Tokyo, 1981); Kesa Noda, *Yamato Colony: 1906-1960* (Livingston, Calif., 1981); San Mateo Chapter, Japanese American Citizens League, *1872-1942—A Community Story* (San Mateo, 1981); Eileen Sarasohn, *The Issei, Portrait of a Pioneer: An Oral History* (Palo Alto, 1983); Karl G. Yoneda, *Ganbatte: Sixty-Year Struggle of a Kibei Worker* (Los Angeles, 1983); Timothy Lukes and Gary Okihiro, *Japanese Legacy in Farming and Community Life in California's Santa Clara Valley* (Santa Clara, 1985); and Don and Nadine Hata, "George Shima: The Potato King of California," *JW*, 25 (January 1986).

By 1924, in response to a nationwide anti-immigration movement, Congress passed an immigration bill containing a specific provision for the exclusion of Asians. From 1924 until the relaxation of national quotas in 1952, Japanese immigration ceased. The 1924 law also stopped the trickle of East Indians and Koreans who arrived after 1900. Some 6,400 East Indians settled mainly in California between 1907 and 1920 after being forced out of western Canada and the Pacific Northwest. The arrival of some 2,000 East Indians in San Francisco, in response to a need for railroad construction laborers in 1910, briefly diverted the Asiatic Exclusion League's attention from the Japanese. Articles appeared on the "Hindu invasion" in *Colliers*, 45 (March 1910); Herman Schef-fauer, "The Tide of Turbans," *Forum*, 43 (June 1910)—referring to Sikhs; as well as overtly exclusionist pieces in the *Proceedings of the Asiatic Exclusion League* (April/September 1910). H. A. Millis, head of the Immigration Commission's investigations on the Pacific Coast, reinforced exclusionists' polemics in "East Indian Immigration to the Pacific Coast," *Survey*, 28 (June 1912). These events are summarized in Joan M. Jensen, "Apartheid: Pacific Coast Style," *PHR*, 38 (August 1969) and in Gary R. Hess, "The Forgotten Americans: The East Indian Community in the United States," *PHR*, 42 (November 1974). Support for Indian independence from England among California's East Indians during World War I is the subject of Giles T. Brown, "The Hindu Conspiracy, 1914–1917," *PHR*, 17 (August 1948); Mark Naidis, "Propaganda of the Gadar Party," *PHR*, 20 (August 1951); Gary R. Hess, "The 'Hindu' in America: Immigration and Naturalization Policies and India, 1917–1946," *PHR*, 38 (February 1969); Don K. Dignan, "The Hindu Conspiracy in Anglo-American Relations during World War I," *PHR*, 40 (1971); and Joan M. Jensen, "The Hindu 'Conspiracy': A Reassessment," *PHR*, 48 (February 1979), on the prosecution of twenty-nine East Indians for conspiracy to violate the neutrality law.

Summary treatments are Rajani Kanta Das, *Hindustani Workers on the Pacific Coast* (Berlin, 1923); Harold S. Jacoby, *A Half Century Appraisal of East Indians in the United States* (Stockton, 1956); Lawrence A. Wenzel, "The Rural Punjabis of California: A Religio-Ethnic Group," *Phylon*, 29 (Fall 1968); H. Brett Melendy, *Asians in America: Filipinos, Koreans, and East Indians* (Boston, 1977); and Parmatma Saran and Edwin Eames, *The New Ethnics: Asian Indians in the United States* (New York, 1980).

Korean immigration began in 1902, first to Hawaii, and soon thereafter to California and other parts of the Pacific Slope. Isolated from other Asian immigrants due to distinctive differences in language, and often mistaken for Japanese, Koreans did not receive attention from historians until significant numbers arrived after World War II. See Lee Houchins and Chang-su Houchins, "The Korean Experience in America, 1903–1945," in Hundley, ed., *The Asian American*; Hyung-Chan Kim and Wayne Patterson, eds., *The Koreans in America, 1882–1974* (Dobbs Ferry, N.Y., 1974); Hyung-Chan Kim, ed., *The Korean Diaspora: Historical and Sociological Studies of Korean Immigration and Assimilation in North America* (Santa Barbara, 1977); Bong-Youn Choy, *Koreans in America* (Chicago, 1979); and Eui-Young Yu, et al., eds., *Koreans in Los Angeles: Prospects and Promises* (Los Angeles, 1982).

Filipinos and Pacific Islanders were the only groups untouched by the 1924 federal immigration law's exclusion of Asian immigrants. Parts of Samoa, Guam, Hawaii, and the Aleutians came under American control during the late nineteenth-century application of Manifest Destiny imperatives beyond the West Coast, and the Philippine Islands were annexed as a result of the Spanish American War in 1898; see Stuart C. Miller, *"Benevolent Assimilation": The*

American Conquest of the Philippines, 1899-1903 (New Haven, 1982). Few Pacific Islanders entered the continental United States until after World War II. Filipinos were ambivalently defined in the 1917 federal immigration law which stated that they were neither U.S. citizens nor aliens, but "nationals." Bruno Lasker, *Filipino Immigration to the Continental United States and to Hawaii* (Chicago, 1929); Emory S. Bogardus, "American Attitudes Toward Filipinos," *Sociology and Social Research*, 14 (September/October 1929); and Maximo C. Manzon, *The Strange Case of Filipinos in the United States* (New York, 1938), observe that the exclusion of Japanese and other Asians in 1924 created a cheap migrant labor vacuum, and Filipinos were seen as convenient colonial replacements. Migrant teams of stoop laborers roamed the Sacramento-Stockton Delta, and the San Joaquin, Salinas, and Imperial valleys. Stockton became known as "Little Manila," and other enclaves were established in San Francisco, Los Angeles, and San Diego as seasonal workers sought fishing and domestic jobs in the cities. Histories of pioneer Filipino communities include Benicio Catapusan, *The Filipino Occupational and Recreational Activities in Los Angeles* (San Francisco, 1975), on the period 1924-1933; Adelaida Castillo, "Filipino Migrants in San Diego, 1900-1946," *JSDH*, 22 (Summer 1976); and Carol Hemminger, "Little Manila: The Filipino in Stockton—Prior to World War II," *PH*, 24 (Spring/Summer 1980).

By 1928, race riots flared against Filipino laborers as exclusionists described them as "the third wave," after the Chinese and Japanese, that had to be halted. Emory Bogardus, *Anti-Filipino Race Riots* (San Diego, 1930), analyzed the much publicized violence against Filipinos at Watsonville in 1930; more recent studies include several works by Howard A. DeWitt, *Anti-Filipino Movements in California: A History, Bibliography and Study Guide* (San Francisco, 1976); "The Watsonville Anti-Filipino Riot of 1930: A Case Study of the Great Depression and Ethnic Conflict in Southern California," *SCQ*, 61 (Fall 1979); and *Violence in the Fields: California Filipino Farm Labor Unionization during the Great Depression* (Saratoga, Calif., 1980). Two accounts by Filipinos who experienced intense discrimination during this period are Manuel Buaken, *I Have Lived With the American People* (Caldwell, Idaho, 1948) and Carlos Bulosan, *Sound of Falling Light: Letters in Exile* (Quezon City, P.I., 1960). Exclusionists were confronted by a unique problem in that the Philippines were American territory; thus Filipino arrivals remained unrestricted until 1934, when the Tydings-McDuffie Act imposed an annual quota of fifty, along with a promise of future Philippine independence. As citizens of a sovereign foreign nation, Filipinos would be subject to laws against immigration and settlement of Asians in America. See H. Brett Melendy, "Filipinos in the United States," *PHR*, 42 (November 1974) and *Asians in America: Filipinos, Koreans, and East Indians* (Boston, 1977).

The period following the 1924 exclusion act until the eve of World War II saw the various Asian communities isolated from infusions of new immigrants and left to their own resources as the nation staggered through the Great Depression.

See Ivan Light, "From Vice District to Tourist Attraction: The Moral Career of American Chinatowns, 1880-1940," *PHR*, 43 (August 1974); Stanford Lyman, "Conflict and the Web of Group Affiliations in San Francisco's Chinatown, 1850-1910," *PHR*, 42 (November 1974); and Jade Snow Wong's account of life in San Francisco's Chinatown, *Fifth Chinese Daughter* (New York, 1945).

Merchants became the ruling elite in California's urban Asian communities and dominated relations with public officials and outsiders. Yuji Ichioka, "Japanese Associations and the Japanese Government: A Special Relationship, 1909-1926," *PHR*, 46 (August 1977), reinforces the co-optive role of merchants. John Modell, *The Economics and Politics of Racial Accommodation: The Japanese of Los Angeles, 1900-1942* (Urbana, 1977), "Class or Ethnic Solidarity: The Japanese American Company Union," *PHR*, 38 (May 1969) and "Tradition and Opportunity: The Japanese Immigrant in America," *PHR*, 40 (May 1971), supplement the accommodationist strategies and limited gains analyzed by Harry H. L. Kitano in *Japanese Americans: The Evolution of a Subculture* (Englewood Cliffs, N.J., 1969) and "Japanese Americans: The Development of a Middleman Minority," *PHR*, 42 (November 1974); and David J. O'Brien and Stephen S. Fujita, "Middleman Minority Concept: Its Explanatory Value in the Case of the Japanese in California Agriculture," *Pacific Sociological Review*, 25 (April 1982).

On February 19, 1942, two months after the outbreak of war with Imperial Japan, Executive Order 9066 authorized the Army to evacuate all "persons of Japanese ancestry," irrespective of U.S. citizenship. By the end of June 1942, over 110,000 Japanese Americans were moved from temporary assembly centers on the West Coast to more permanent and distant concentration camps administered by the War Relocation Authority. (See Chapter 4, *ante*.) The scope of this essay precludes a comprehensive review of evacuation and incarceration materials, which continue to expand with new information and diverse historiographical perspectives. California's concentration of Japanese Americans makes them integral to standard works, including popular accounts by Carey McWilliams, *Prejudice: Japanese Americans: Symbol of Racial Intolerance* (Boston, 1944); Allan R. Bosworth, *America's Concentration Camps* (New York, 1967); Audrie Girdner and Anne Loftis, *The Great Betrayal: The Evacuation of the Japanese Americans During World War II* (New York, 1969); Bill Hosokawa, *Nisei: The Quiet Americans* (New York, 1969) and *JACL in Quest of Justice: The History of the Japanese American Citizens League* (New York, 1982); and Dillon S. Myer, *Uprooted Americans: The Japanese Americans and the War Relocation Authority During World War II* (Tucson, 1971).

The incarceration experience from the view of the victims is the subject of Mine Okubo, *Citizen 13660* (New York, 1946), with sketches by the author beginning with the temporary assembly center at Tanforan Racetrack; Sue Kunitomi Embrey, *The Lost Years, 1942-1946* (Los Angeles, 1972), about the WRA camp at Manzanar; Arthur A. Hansen and Betty E. Mitson, *Voices Long Silent, An Oral Inquiry Into The Japanese American Evacuation* (Fullerton, 1974)—a product of the Japanese American Project, CSU, Fullerton, Oral

History Program; and Yoshiko Uchida, *Desert Exile* (Seattle, 1982). The annual New Year's supplementary editions of Japanese-American newspapers are also a source of biographical articles.

Other sources include Thomas and Nishimoto, *The Spoilage*; Grodzins, *Americans Betrayed*; Thomas, *The Salvage*; Jacobus ten Broek, Edward N. Barnhart, and Floyd W. Matson, *Prejudice, War, and the Constitution* (Berkeley, 1954); Edward N. Barnhart, *Japanese American Evacuation and Resettlement* (Berkeley, 1958); Cecil H. Uyehara, *Checklist of Archives in the Japanese Ministry of Foreign Affairs, Tokyo, Japan, 1868-1945* (Washington, D.C., 1954)—incorporating microfilmed materials on California's alien land laws and the wartime concentration camp at Tule Lake; William Magistretti, "A Bibliography of Historical Materials in the Japanese Language on the West Coast Japanese," *PHR*, 12 (March 1943); Edward H. Spicer, et al., *Impounded People: Japanese Americans in the Relocation Centers* (Tucson, 1969); Frank Chuman, *The Bamboo People: The Law and Japanese Americans* (Del Mar, 1976); Michi Weglyn, *Years of Infamy* (New York, 1976); Roger Daniels, *Concentration Camps, U.S.A.* (New York, 1971) and his expanded *Concentration Camps, North America, The Decision to Relocate the Japanese Americans* (New York, 1975). Also see Anthony L. Lehman, *Birthright of Barbed Wire, The Santa Anita Assembly Center for the Japanese* (Los Angeles, 1970); Gerald Schlenker, "The Internment of the Japanese of San Diego County during the Second World War," *JSDH*, 18 (Winter 1972); Harvey Schwartz, "A Union Combats Racism: The ILWU's Japanese American 'Stockton Incident' of 1945," *SCQ*, 62 (Summer 1980); Tule Lake Committee, *Kinenhi: Reflections on Tule Lake* (San Francisco, 1980); and Donald E. Collins, *Native American Aliens* (Westport, Conn., 1985).

In 1980 Congress created the Commission on Wartime Relocation and Internment of Civilians. Its report, *Personal Justice Denied: Report of the Commission on Wartime Relocation and Internment of Civilians* (Washington, D.C., 1982), refuted the rationale of "military necessity" preferred by government officials and confirmed by the U.S. Supreme Court in three key decisions during the war. Peter Irons, *Justice at War, The Story of the Japanese Internment Cases* (New York, 1983), influenced the recent reversal of the U.S. Supreme Court decision in *Korematsu* v. *U.S.* for insufficient evidence. New works have reinforced the growing movement among Japanese Americans for "redress," as reflected in the Japanese American Citizens League, National Committee for Redress, *The Japanese American Incarceration: A Case for Redress* (San Francisco, 1978), and in Roger Daniels, "Japanese Relocation and Redress in North America: A Comparative View," *PH*, 26 (Spring 1982) and *Japanese Americans, From Relocation to Redress* (Salt Lake City, 1986).

Since the end of World War II, the Golden State's older and larger Chinese and Japanese communities have been enriched by the infusion of immigrants from virtually every national and ethnic group from across the Pacific: East Indians, Pakistanis and Sri Lankans from South Asia; Thais, Burmese, Malaysians, Cambodians, Laotians, Vietnamese, Filipinos, and Indonesians from

Southeast Asia; mainland Chinese, as well as Hong Kong, Taiwan, and other overseas areas; Koreans from East Asia; Samoans, Hawaiians, Guamanians, Fijiians, and Tongans from the Pacific Islands.

There is evidence that some Asian/Pacific Americans are moving rapidly into the mainstream. The new arrivals continue to play the traditional first and second generation immigrant survival game of being "two hundred percent Americans." The accommodationist strategy has, by some accounts, worked well. Asian/Pacific immigrants and their American-born descendants have been hailed as members of a "model minority" whose inscrutable "don't rock the boat" and "up by their own bootstraps" posture in the face of adversity should be emulated by more militant minority groups; see Ivan Light, *Ethnic Enterprise in America: Business and Welfare Among Chinese, Japanese and Blacks* (Berkeley, 1972); Thomas Sowell, *Ethnic America: A History* (New York, 1981); as well as journalistic accounts by William Petersen, "Success Story, Japanese American Style," *New York Times Magazine* (January 9, 1966), "Success Story: Outwhiting the Whites," *Newsweek* (June 21, 1971), and "Japanese in U.S. Outdo Horatio Alger," Los Angeles *Times* (October 17, 1977).

The post-World War II focus on one-dimensional success stories has produced the popular but mistaken belief that trans-Pacific immigrants "take care of their own" and require little support from public social services. The California State Advisory Committee to the U.S. Commission on Civil Rights (USCCR), *Asian Americans and Pacific Peoples: A Case of Mistaken Identity* (Washington, D.C., 1975) and *A Dream Unfulfilled: Korean and Filipino Health Professionals in California* (Washington, D.C., 1975) revealed that discrimination against Asian/ Pacific Americans resulted from identification as white, ignoring national origins, thus denying minority status. In *Success of Asian Americans: Fact or Fiction?* (Washington, D.C., 1980), the USCCR concluded: "the success stereotype appears to have led policymakers to ignore those truly in need." The view is supported by: State of California, Department of Industrial Relations, Division of Fair Employment Practices, *Californians of Japanese, Chinese, Filipino Ancestry: Population, Employment, Income, Education* (San Francisco, 1965); U.S. Department of Commerce, Social and Economic Statistics Administration, *1970 Census of Population. Subject Reports. Japanese, Chinese and Filipinos in the United States* (Washington, D.C., 1973); Betty Lee Sung, *Statistical Profile of the Chinese in the United States. 1970 Census* (Washington, D.C., 1975); and ASIAN, Inc. (Asian American Service Institute for Assistance to Neighborhoods), *Discriminatory Employment of Asian Americans: Private Industry in the San Francisco-Oakland SMSA* (San Francisco, 1977). The USCCR's *Civil Rights Digest* (Fall 1976) focused entirely on Asian/Pacific Americans. Critiques of omissions and other distortions of Asian Americans in history textbooks include Roger Zuercher, "The Treatment of Asian Minorities in American History Textbooks," *Indiana Social Studies Quarterly*, 22 (Autumn 1969); Dennis Ogawa, *From Japs to Japanese: The Evolution of the Japanese American Stereotype* (Berkeley, 1971); and Don and Nadine Hata, "I Wonder Where the Yellow

Went? Distortions and Omissions of Asian Americans in California Education,"
Integrated Education, 12 (May/June 1974).

A pervasive theme in the historiography of the Asian/Pacific experience, which
is at once a problem and an opportunity for future studies, is reflected in Roger
Daniels, "American Historians and East Asian Immigrants," *PH*, 42 (November
1974), who observed that "Asian Americans are still seen largely as the objects
rather than the subjects of history." To what extent revisionist criticisms have
influenced an integrated perspective and new information in current scholarship,
which still largely focuses on topics that lend themselves to English language
resources, remains unclear due to factors such as limited foreign language skills
among American scholars and graduate students, and the largely untapped
wealth of research materials available in Asian languages both here and across
the Pacific.

9

CALIFORNIA WOMEN

GLORIA RICCI LOTHROP

WHILE THE HISTORY of women is no longer in its "pioneer" stage, it is not yet "mature." Women's achievements have remained generally undocumented, recorded in artifact and ephemera rather than in published sources. This is especially true with respect to California history where feminine contributions have been only marginally examined. Much research is needed before we can portray accurately the influence exerted by California women of all classes and ethnic groups throughout the history of the Golden State. At the same time, scholars of the future will owe much to the efforts of those whose work is summarized in the following pages.

The study of California women's history can be facilitated by referring to a number of guides. Among the most comprehensive are: *Women's History Sources: A Guide to Archives and Manuscript Collections in the United States* (New York, 1979), ed. by Andrea Hinding, Ames Bower, and Clarke Chambers; *Women's Collections* (New York, 1985), ed. by Suzanne Hildenbrand and Lee Ash; and "Women's History: A Listing of West Coast Archival and Manuscript Sources," *CHSQ*, 55 (Spring/Summer 1976), comp. by Joan H. Wilson and Lynn B. Donovan. Comprehensive bibliographies include *Women, A Bibliography of Bibliographies* (Boston, 1980), comp. by Patrick K. Ballou. Current scholarship is well represented in Cynthia Harrison, *Women in American History: A Bibliography* (Santa Barbara, 1979). Another instructive guide is *Women's Studies: A Bibliography of Dissertations, 1870-1982* (New York, 1985), comp. by Victor F. Gilbert. A special issue, "Women in the American West," *PHR*, 24 (May 1980), features a comprehensive bibliographical essay by Joan M. Jensen and Darlis A. Miller.

A few women can be traced through the *Historical Biographical Dictionary Master Index* (Detroit, 1980); *An Index to the Biographies in 19th Century California Histories* (Detroit, 1979); and *Notable American Women, 1607-1905: A Biographical Dictionary* (4 vols.; Cambridge, Mass., 1971, 1980). This author has illustrated, in "Rediscovering California's Forgotten Women: A Survey of California History Texts," *CH Courier*, 28 (May 1986), that women's contributions have received only marginal attention. Works specifically focusing on California include Reda Davis, *California Women 1885-1911* (San Francisco, 1967); Harry Gray, *Women of California* (Benecia, 1972); and *California Women: A History* (San Francisco, 1987) by Joan M. Jensen and Gloria R. Lothrop.

A "Women of California" theme issue of the *PH*, 28 (Fall 1984), included current research which updates such respected studies as Rockwell D. Hunt, "Great Women of California," *QHSSC*, 31 (September 1949). Also see Lothrop, "Westering Women and the Ladies of Los Angeles: Some Similarities and Differences," *South Dakota Review*, 19 (Spring/Summer 1981).

Volumes which provide brief sketches of important California women include *A Woman of the Century* (Detroit, 1967), ed. by Frances Willard and Mary A. Livermore; Sandra Myres, *Westering Women and the Frontier Experience* (Albuquerque, 1982); Dorothy Gray, *Women of the West* (Millbrae, 1976); Irene Philips, *Women of Distinction Under Three Flags* (San Diego, 1972); and Elinor Richey, *Eminent Women of the West* (Berkeley, 1975). Christiane Fischer in her anthology, *Let Them Speak for Themselves: Women of the West, 1849-1900* (New York, 1978), draws from diaries and letters describing California life.

A large body of biographical literature describes California life from a woman's perspective, including Margaret H. Easton, *Diary of a Sea Captain's Wife: Tales of Santa Cruz Island* (Santa Barbara, 1980); Mary Ritter, *More than Gold in California, 1849-1933* (Berkeley, 1933); Helen Holdredge, *Firebelle Lillie, The Life and Times of Lillie Coit of San Francisco* (New York, 1967); Dorothy Joraleman, "Growing Up in Berkeley, 1900-1917," *AW*, 20 (July/August 1983); and Dorothy Geissinger, "922 Oak Street," *AW*, 14 (January/February 1977), both of which provide personal views of the 1900s Bay area. Helpful is Patricia K. Addis, *Through A Woman's I: An Annotated Bibliography of American Women's Autobiographical Writings, 1946-1976* (Metuchen, N.J., 1983).

A review of historical sources should begin chronologically with Robert F. Heizer, ed., *Handbook of North American Indians: California* (Washington, D.C., 1978). Useful insight into the details of daily Indian life is provided in Burt W. Aginsky, "Population Control of the Shanel (Pomo) Tribe," *American Sociological Review*, 4 (April 1939); Thomas Buckley, "Menstruation and the Power of Yurok Women: Methodology in Cultural Reconstruction," *American Ethnologist*, 9 (No. 1/1982); and Peter Howorth, *Foraging along the California Coast* (Santa Barbara, 1977).

The tension represented by Spanish advances into California is addressed in Victoria Brady, et al., "Resist: Survival Tactics of Indian Women," *CH*, 68 (Spring 1981). Another response to the missionizing aspect is examined in

Laura E. King, "Hugo Reid and His Indian Wife," *APHSSC*, 4, Pt. 2 (1898). The processes of Indian survival and adaptation are reflected in the post-Mission period in *The Autobiography of Delfina Cuero* (Morongo, 1980), ed. by Florence Shipek, and Wylackie Indian Lucy Young, "Lucy's Story," *Family Heritage*, 1 (October 1978). See also Elizabeth Colsen, ed., *Autobiographies of Three Pomo Women* (Berkeley, 1974) and Ruby Modesto and Guy Mount, *Not For Innocent Ears: Spiritual Traditions of a Cahuilla Medicine Woman* (Angeles Oaks, 1981).

The generally unexamined role of women as recipients of land grants in the Mexican period is explored in J. N. Bowman, "Prominent Women of Provincial California," *SCQ*, 39 (June 1957) and David Langum, "Sin, Sex and Separation in Mexican California," *The Californians*, 5 (June/July 1987). Important is Gloria E. Miranda's "Hispano-Mexican Childbearing Practices in Pre-American Santa Barbara," *SCQ*, 65 (Winter 1983) and Susanna B. Dakin, *Rose or Rose Thorn? Three Women of Spanish California* (Berkeley, 1963).

Other accounts yielding rich insights into individual personal lives in the Mexican period are: Sister Mary Theresa Wittenberg, "A California Girlhood: Reminiscences of Ascension Sepulveda y Avila," *SCQ*, 64 (Summer 1982); Terry Stephenson, "Tomas Yorba, His Wife Vicenta and His Account Book," *QHSSC*, 23 (September 1957); Esther B. Black, *Rancho Cucamonga and Doña Merced* (San Bernardino, 1975); and Bess Garner, *Windows in an Old Adobe* (Pomona, 1939), which describes life at Rancho San José de Palomares. (Also see Chapter 1, *ante*.)

The arrival of foreigners was to elicit additional commentary about California which Langum has analyzed in "California Women and the Image of Virtue" and "Californios and the Image of Indolence." Despite these criticisms, a large number of marital unions ensued as described by Hattie Stone Benefield, *For the Good of the Country* (Los Angeles, 1951), which tells of an Anglo-Californio marriage. The same blending of cultures is explored by Raymond S. Brandes, "Times Gone By in Alta California: Recollections of Señora Juana Machado de Ridington," *QHSSC*, 41 (September 1959).

The blending of Mexican and American legal traditions resulting from provisions of the Treaty of Guadalupe Hidalgo concluding the Mexican War were, for a time, advantageous to women, an issue touched on by David Langum, "Expatriate Domestic Relations Law in Mexican California," *Pepperdine Law Review*, 1 (1979) and Peter T. Commy, *The Historic Origins of California's Community Property Law* (San Francisco, 1957). Donald E. Hargis reviews the debate surrounding the adoption of Section 13 in the first California constitution in "Women's Rights in California, 1849," *QHSSC*, 37 (December 1955).

The rush of gold-seeking argonauts who flooded California were generally young male sojourners. By 1850 women represented only 10 percent of the influx. Among them were visitors as well as settlers, none of whom provided a more articulate account of life among the gold seekers than Louise Amelia Knapp Smith Clappe in *The Shirley Letters Written in 1851-1852 . . .*, ed. by Carl I. Wheat (New York, 1949). Female visitors ventured from afar. Emma H.

Adams, *To and Fro in Southern California* (Cincinnati, 1887), included accounts of her visits to several southern California ranches, while Evelyn Hertslet, *Ranch Life in California* (London, 1886), reported on life in Lassen County. See also Sheldon Jackson, "An English Quaker Tours California: The Journal of Sarah Lindsay, 1859–1860," *SCQ*, 51 (March 1969) and Caroline H. Dall, *My First Holiday: or, Letters Home* (Boston, 1881), who describes her youthful adventure through Colorado, Utah, and California. The personal diary of Harriet Bunyard provided the substance of "From Texas to California in 1868," *APHSSC*, 13, Pt. 1 (1924). Unique experiences are shared in Malinda Jenkins, *Gambler's Wife* (New York, 1933) and by Mrs. E. J. Guerin, whose successful deceit, resulting in her being the first woman to vote in California, is described in *Mountain Charley or the Adventures of Mrs. E. J. Guerin, who was thirteen years in male attire* (Norman, 1968).

The enthusiasm of the foregoing accounts belies the rigors of overland travel that preceded arrival in California. Several significant studies have recently contributed to an understanding of that treacherous journey shadowed by fear of ambush, limited forage, tainted water, and sheer monotony, elements captured in Lillian Schlissel, *Women's Diaries of the Westward Journey* (New York, 1982) and John M. Faragher, *Women and Men on the Overland Trail* (New Haven, 1979). In *Ho for California!* (San Marino, 1980), Sandra L. Myres uses firsthand accounts to portray the daily wagon train routine not as unbelievably burdensome but as a welcome opportunity for pioneer women to socialize and enjoy intermittent leisure. Women's relative advantage over men as trail cooks is explored in Joseph Conlin, "Eating on the Rush: Organizing Meals on the Overland Trail," *CH*, 64 (Summer 1985). The place of children is examined in John Faragher and Christine Stansill, "Women and Their Families on the Oregon Trail to California and Oregon, 1842–1867," *Feminist Studies*, 2 (No. 2/3, 1975) and in Ruth B. Moynihan, "Children and Young People on the Overland Trail," *WHQ*, 6 (July 1975).

Representative women's accounts of the arduous overland journey have been published: Harriet Ward, *Prairie Schooner Lady* (Los Angeles, 1959); "Overland by Ox-Train in 1870: The Diary of Maria Hargrove Shrode," *QHSSC*, 26 (March 1944); and Charles G. Clarke, ed., "Journal Kept While Crossing the Plains by Ada Millington," *SCQ*, 56 (Spring/Summer/Fall 1977). Sea voyage accounts include Dora Hart, *Via Nicaragua: A Sketch of Travel to California* (London, 1887) and Annegret Ogden, "Go West, Young Women," *The Californians*, 3 (May/June and July/August 1985), selections from the diary of Sophia Eastman while sailing aboard the *Niantic*.

On occasion, the dangers anticipated in these accounts became realities. Snowy isolation in the steep Sierra is described by Eliza D. Houghton, *The Expedition of the Donner Party and Its Tragic Fate* (Chicago, 1911). Perils of another sort awaited the gold-seeking Jayhawkers who ventured southward into Death Valley. Their escape and the doughty triumph of Juliet Brier are described in William L. Manly, *Death Valley '49* (Los Angeles, 1949). The numerous accounts of the fate of the Oatman sisters include William B. Rice, "The Captivity of Olive Oatman—A Newspaper Account," *CHSQ*, 21 (March 1942) and the recently republished R. B. Stratton, *Captivity of the Oatman Girls* (Reprint ed., Lincoln, 1983).

Several significant studies of women in the mid-nineteenth century include Ralph Mann, "The Decade After the Gold Rush: Social Structure in Grass Valley and Nevada City, California, 1850-1860," *PHR*, 41 (November 1972) and Christiane Fischer, "Women in California in the Early 1850's," *SCQ*, 60 (Fall 1978). The developing role of women is described with vividness and detail in three classics: Sarah B. Royce, *A Frontier Lady, Recollections of the Gold Rush and Early California* (Lincoln, 1977); Eliza W. Farnham, *California In-Doors and Out* (Nieuwkoop, Netherlands, 1972); and Robert G. Cleland, ed., *Apron Full of Gold: The Letters of Mary Jane Megquier from San Francisco, 1849-1856* (San Marino, 1949). Important insights into the nineteenth-century woman's world of work is provided by the cookbooks of the era, which in addition to describing culinary tastes, dietary patterns, and common holiday festivities, served as etiquette guides and indispensable guidebooks on home health care, household cleaning, preserving, and canning. Consult the checklist of cookbook imprints, 1870-1932, by Liselotte and William K. Glazer, comp., *California in the Kitchen* (Berkeley, 1960).

The mid-nineteenth-century relationship between men and women is explored by Andrew J. Rotter, "Matilda for Gods Sake Write: Women and Families on the Argonaut Mind," *CH*, 58 (Summer 1979); "Commandments to California Wives," *The Californians*, 4 (May/June 1986); and Elisabeth Margo, *Taming the Forty-Niner* (New York, 1955).

The history of children, integral elements in the family unit, has thus far been overlooked, the exception being John E. Baur, *Growing Up with California* (Los Angeles, 1978). An overdue discussion of infant rearing among California's residents is found in Jean Sherrell, "The Western Baby," *The Californians*, 1 (January/February 1983). Information and statistics on mortality, child welfare, and institutional care is available in *Welfare Activities of Federal, State and Local Government in California, 1850-1934* (Berkeley, 1936) and in Sara E. Heminger, *The Care of Dependent Children in California, 1850-1879* (San Francisco, 1880). See also J. S. Holliday, "A Historian Reflects on Edgewood Children's Center," *CHS*, 64 (Spring 1985).

Childhood letters and diaries are frequently overlooked resources. Among the few published accounts are Jean H. Hannah and Shirley Sargent, eds., *Dear Papa: Letters Between John Muir and His Daughter Wanda* (Fresno, 1985) and Victoria Jacobs, *Diary of a San Diego Girl—1856* (Santa Monica, 1974). Important reminiscences include five looks at girlhood in Los Angeles: Louise Lenz, ed., "Memoirs of Caroline Van der Leck Lenz," *QHSSC*, 36 (September 1974); Sarah Bixby Smith, *Adobe Days: A Book of California Memories* (Reprint ed., Lincoln, 1987); Katherine Bixby Hotchkis, *Christmas Eve at Rancho Los Alamitos* (San Francisco, 1971) and *Trip with Father* (San Francisco, 1971); and Susanna Bryant Dakin, *The Scent of Violets* (San Francisco, 1968).

While family appears to have been an essential part of the pioneer pattern, the problems presented by migration and settlement in new communities often affected the family ties, an issue considered by Barbara Laslett, "Social Change and the Family: Los Angeles, California, 1850-1870," *American Sociological Review*, 44 (April 1977). Los Angeles family units are again the focus in Elaine T. May, *Great Expectations: Marriage and Divorce in Post-Victorian America* (Chicago, 1980). An important assessment of the status of divorced women is provided by Robert L. Griswold, "Apart But Not Adrift: Wives, Divorce and Independence in California, 1850-1890," *PHR*, 49 (May 1980). Griswold's *Family and Divorce in California, 1850-1890: Victorian Illusions and Everyday Realities* (New York, 1982), sheds light upon male and female role expectations of the period.

Needed investigation into the ethnic aspects of family formation has been initiated by Marc Raphael, "Jewish Marital Patterns, 1910-1913," *WSJHQ*, 7 (January 1974) and by Richard Griswold del Castillo, "La Familia Chicana: Social Changes in the Chicano Family of L.A.," *JES*, 3 (Spring 1975). (Also see Chapter 6, *ante*.)

After the Civil War an increasing number of women teachers were active agents in the preservation of cultural continuity as detailed in Polly Kaufman, *Women Teachers on the Frontier* (New Haven, 1984). Women's contributions to California education has been sporadically researched, among these are: Henry W. Splitter, "Education in Los Angeles: 1850-1900," *QHSSC*, 33 (Spring/Fall/ Winter 1951); Laura E. King, "Pioneer Schools and Their Teachers," *APHSSC*, 4, Pt. 2 (1898); and Mary Bowman, "California's First American School and Its Teacher," *APHSSC*, 10, Pts. 1-2 (1915/1916), a sketch of early school teacher Olive Mann Isbell.

California's leadership in the kindergarten movement has not been adequately reported but informative biographical profiles in *Notable American Women* describe the contributions of early proponents of the movement in the state— Emma Marwedel, Kate Douglas Wiggin, and Sarah Ingersoll Cooper. See also Richard H. Peterson, "Philanthropic Phoebe: The Educational Charity of Phoebe Apperson Hearst," *CH*, 64 (Fall 1985). Georgette McGregor, "The Educational Career of Susan Miller Dorsey," *History of Education Journal*, 4 (Autumn 1953), is a pioneer study of women in school administration.

The role of women in higher education has been documented at Mills College by Elias O. James, *The Story of Cyrus and Susan Mills* (Stanford, 1953); Mary Atkins, *The Diary of Mary Atkins, A Sabbatical in the 1860's* (Mills College, 1937); and George Hedley, *Aurelia Reinhart: Portrait of a Whole Woman* (Mills College, 1961). Jane Stanford's influential role in the development of Stanford is presented by David S. Jordan, *The Story of a Good Woman: Jane Lathrop Stanford* (Yonkers-on-Hudson, 1922) and Gunther W. Nagel, *Jane Stanford, Her Life and Letters* (Stanford, 1975). Another is Albert Britt, *Ellen Browning Scripps: Journalist and Idealist* (Oxford, Eng., 1960).

Among the few articles discussing women's important contributions as librarians are Marco R. Newmark, "Miss Mary Foy," *QHSSC*, 37 (December 1955) and Raymund F. Wood, "The Traveling Libraries of California," in *Los Angeles Corral of Westerners Branding Iron*, 125 (March 1977), which describes the contributions of Laura Steffens and Harriet G. Eddy.

Unquestionably western education was substantially affected by the efforts of women's religious teaching orders whose records in many cases are comprehensive, but whose accomplishments have not resulted in general interpretive study as supplements to existing institutional histories. First among the religious women to come to California were the Dominican Sisters, who established a convent in Monterey in 1851. The community's extensive archival holdings are delineated in *Religious History Sources: A Guide to Repositories in the United States*, ed. by Evangeline Thomas, CSV (New York, 1983).

The arrival in San Jose in 1851 of a contingent of Sisters of Notre Dame de Namur is described in Sister Mary Anthony, *In Harvest Fields by Sunset Shores* (San Francisco, 1926). Mary D. McNamee, *Light in the Valley: The Story of California's College of Notre Dame* (San Diego, 1967), examines the sisters' successful organization of a college in Belmont. The arrival of the Daughters of Charity of St. Vincent de Paul, the first to come to Los Angeles, resulted in the opening of the Institute and Orphan Asylum in 1856 and in the following year an infirmary. Details are provided in W. H. Workman, "Sister Scholastica," *APHSSC*, 5, Pt. 3 (1902) and in *Sixty Years in Southern California, 1853-1913, Containing the Reminiscences of Harris Newmark*, ed. by Maurice and Marco Newmark (4th rev. ed.; Los Angeles, 1970).

In 1854, in the midst of San Francisco's turbulent development, a group from County Cork arrived. *Oak Leaves, 1854-1904* (San Francisco, 1904) and the *Memoir of Rev. Mother Mary Teresa Comerford* (San Francisco, 1882) trace the successes of the Presentation Sisters who opened their first school in 1856. The pioneer effort of another teaching group is recounted in Mary Fields, "Reminiscences of the Sisters of St. Joseph Corondolet," *JSDH*, 28 (Summer 1982). Additional information on religious women can be found in a useful booklet, "Life of Mother Michael Cummings, Foundress of the Sisters of Mercy in San Diego, California" (San Diego, 1912).

The important role of a second contingent of the Sisters of Mercy is documented in *Mother Mary Baptist Russell: California's Pioneer Sister of Mercy*, by Sister Mary Aurelia McCardle, SM (San Francisco, 1954). See also Mathew Russell, SJ, *The Life of Mother Mary Baptist Russell, Sister of Mercy* (New York, 1901).

Also important are D. J. Kavanaugh, SJ, *The Holy Family Sisters in San Francisco, 1872-1922* (San Francisco, 1922); Bernard Cronin, *California Caravan of Charity: Historical Sketch of the Nursing Sisterhoods: Their Hospitals in California* (San Francisco, 1949); and Theodore Maynard, *Too Small a World: The Life of Francesca Cabrini* (Boston, 1945).

Another facet of women's religious involvement is explored in Thomas C. Marshall, *Into the Streets and Lanes: The Beginnings of the Social Work of the*

Episcopal Church in the Diocese of Los Angeles, 1887–1947 (Claremont, 1948), which describes the leadership of Sister Mary in establishing the Hospital of the Good Samaritan in Los Angeles in 1887. Further discussions of contributions to the Christian ministry include Otis Gibson, "Missionary Work Among Chinese Women in California," *Chinese in America* (New York, 1978) and Patricia R. Hill, *The World Their Household: The American Woman's Foreign Mission Movement and Cultural Transformations, 1870–1920* (Ann Arbor, 1985).

Other accounts of women's participation in California church work include: Osgood C. Wheeler, *The Story of Early Baptist History of California* (n.p., 1889); E. B. Wave, *History of the Disciples of Christ in California* (Healdsburg, 1916); Edward A. Wicher, *The Presbyterian Church in California, 1849–1927* (New York, 1928); Josephine F. Washburn, *History and Reminiscences of Holiness Church Work in Southern California and Arizona* (South Pasadena, 1912); and Martha Rowlett, "Women in Ministry: California-Nevada Conference of the United Methodist Church," *PH*, 22 (Spring 1978).

Perhaps because change and innovation were more easily accepted in the West, women assumed a comparatively large number of church leadership roles. In the late nineteenth century most prominent were the proponents of Theosophy, including Ojai resident Annie Besant whose life is captured in Arthur H. Nethercot, *The Last Four Lives of Annie Besant* (Chicago, 1963). Her contentions with Katherine Tingley, sometimes called the "purple mother of Theosophy," are recorded in Thomas D. Clarke, "Battle of the Fair Theosophists Is On: Annie Besant's Lecture Tour of San Diego," *JSDH*, 23 (Spring 1977). A full account of Katherine Tingley's work can be found in Paul Kagain and Marilyn Ziebarth, "Eastern Thought on a Western Shore: Point Loma Community," *CHSQ*, 52 (Spring 1973).

There are numerous popular accounts focusing on the more flamboyant aspects of the life of Aimee Semple McPherson, as well as her official autobiography, *The Story of My Life* (Hollywood, 1951) and in Robert Bahr, *Least of All the Saints* (Englewood Cliffs, N.J., 1979). Her successful use of radio as well as professionally staged pageantry to accompany sermons are described in David Clark, "Miracles for a Dime—From Chautauqua Tent to Radio Station with Sister Aimee," *CHQ*, 57 (Winter 1978/1979) and William G. McLoughlin, "Aimee Semple McPherson: Your Sister in the King's Glad Service," *Journal of Popular Culture*, 1 (Winter 1967).

Women's service as nurses and doctors is recounted in Adelaide Brown, "The History of the Development of Women in Medicine in California," *California and Western Medicine*, 23 (May 1925); the contribution to the success of these efforts made by Dr. C. Annette Buckel is in Margaret Martin, "Dr. C. Annette Buckel: The 'Little Major,'" *CHSQ*, 19 (March 1940); and in Helen D. Macknight's autobiography, *A Child Went Forth* (New York, 1934). See also Reva Clar, "First Jewish Woman Physician of Los Angeles," *WSJHQ*, 14 (October 1981) and Lois Brock, "The Hospital for Children and Training School for

Nurses, 1875-1949," *American Medical Woman's Journal*, 35 (January 1950).

California women pursued a variety of endeavors. Agriculturist Harriet Strong wrote a persuasive article in *Business Folio*, 1 (January 1895), calling for more farm training schools for women. Her plea was echoed by colleague Jeanne Carr who envisioned the establishment of such training at her own Rancho Carmelita in Pasadena. See Jane Apostal, "Jeanne Carr: One Woman and Sunshine," *AW*, 15 (July/August 1978). One woman's role in the citrus industry is found in Vincent Moese, "Mrs. Tibbets' Fabulous Fruit," *The Californians*, 3 (July/August 1985); success in the production of dried fruit, cut flowers, seeds, and perfume essences is described in Maggie Brainard, "Women in Commercial Horticulture," *California Illustrated Magazine*, 3 (December 1892) and Gloria Lothrop, "Women Pioneers and the California Landscape," *The Californians*, 4 (May/June 1986). A leading California botanist's life has been sensitively captured in Carol G. Wilson, *Alice Eastwood's Wonderland: The Adventures of a Botanist* (San Francisco, 1955). The long-lasting influence of horticulturist and landscape designer Kate Sessions has been detailed in a special issue of *California Garden*, 45 (Autumn 1953) and in *Kate Sessions: Pioneer Horticulturist* (San Diego, 1976) by Elizabeth MacPhail. Horticultural study has been further enhanced by Lester Rowntree, *Hardy Californians* (Salt Lake City, 1980).

The land offered a variety of business opportunities as described by Jeannine Oppenwall, "Turning Butterflies into Gold: This Subtle Art Is Discovered by a California Girl," *Westways*, 72 (May 1980) and by Shirley Sargent, *Yosemite and Its Innkeepers* (Yosemite, 1975), which documents women's role in the recreation industry. See also Shirley Sargent, *Pioneers in Petticoats: Yosemite's Early Women, 1856-1900* (Yosemite, 1966).

Business opportunities for California women were manifold. Some understanding of the challenge confronting the businesswoman is offered in Robert Chandler, "A Woman Printer Battles the All-Male Union," *The Californians*, 4 (March/April 1986), which also provides information on the early days of the *Pacific Monthly*. A very different enterprise is aptly described by Marie De Santis, *Neptune's Apprentice: Adventures of a Commercial Fisherwoman* (Novato, 1984). More generalized accounts are Gloria Lothrop, "Women Workers in the West, 1860-1900," *San Diego Corral of Westerners Brandbook*, 8 (San Diego, 1987) and Lillian B. Mathews, "Women in the Trade Unions of San Francisco," *University of California Publications in Economics*, 3 (June 19, 1913).

The history of prostitution in California has been recorded from differing perspectives. Traditional treatments, marred by stereotypical images and exploitive interpretations, include Ronald D. Miller, *Shady Ladies of the West* (Los Angeles, 1964); Curt Gentry, *The Madams of San Francisco: An Irreverent History of the City* (Garden City, N.Y., 1964); Ron Miller, "Hell's Belles," *Los Angeles Corral of Westerners Brandbook*, 12 (Los Angeles, 1965); and

David A. Comstock, *Gold Diggers and Camp Followers* (Grass Valley, 1982). A more objective portrayal is provided by Herbert Asbury, *The Barbary Coast* (New York, 1933). Jacqueline Barnhart, *The Fair but Frail: Prostitution in San Francisco, 1849–1900* (Reno, 1986), considers the urban conditions that influenced public attitudes toward prostitution. Particularly revealing is Neil Shumsky and Larry M. Springer, "San Francisco's Zone of Prostitution, 1880–1934," *Journal of Historical Geography*, 7 (January 1981). See also Joyce Wong, "Prostitution: San Francisco Chinatown, Mid- and Late-Nineteenth Century," *Bridge Magazine*, 6 (Winter 1978) and Yuji Ichioka, "Ameyuki-san: Japanese Prostitutes in Nineteenth Century America," *AJ*, 4 (No. 1/1977). The response of American religious groups is documented in Carol G. Wilson, *Chinatown Quest: The Life Adventures of Donaldina Cameron* (San Francisco, 1931) and in Mildred C. Martin, *Chinatown's Angry Angel: The Story of Donaldina Cameron* (Palo Alto, 1977). A reassessment of the missionary crusade is advanced by Laurence Wu McClain, "Donaldina Cameron: A Reappraisal," *PH* 27 (Fall 1983).

The tedium of frontier life was occasionally relieved by the arrival of professional entertainers. Lured by the inflated gold rush economy, American and European performers flocked to the Pacific slope to be presented by the impressaria described by Marie D. Dun in "Hannah Lloyd Neal: A Literary Philadelphian in Post-1853 California," *CHSQ*, 31 (September 1952). The fortunes of others are described in Constance M. Rourke, *Troopers of the Gold Coast: or, The Rise of Lotta Crabtree* (New York, 1928); David Dempsey and Raymund Balderi, *The Triumph and Trials of Lotta Crabtree* (New York, 1968); Helen Holdredge, *The Woman in Black: the Life of Montez* (New York, 1955); and Oscar Lewis, *Lola Montez: the Mid-Victorian Bad Girl of California* (San Francisco, 1938).

Native-born Californians who became popular nineteenth-century entertainers include opera singer Emma Nevada cited by Rockwell Hunt in *California's Stately Hall of Fame* (Stockton, 1950) and stage actress Caroline Chapman described in Helen T. Pratt, "Souvenirs of an Interesting Family," *CHSQ*, 7 (September 1928). Articles about visiting thespians include Lois F. Rodescape, "'Quand Même,' California Footnotes to the Biography of Sarah Bernhardt," *CHSQ*, 20 (March 1941) and Helen R. Goss, "Lillie Langtry and Her California Ranch," *QHSSC*, 37 (June 1955). Among the many studies of Helena Modjeska, the Polish actress who settled in California, two of the most careful are Mamie Krythe, "Madame Modjeska in California," *QHSSC*, 35 (March 1953) and Ellen Lee, "Modjeska and Paderewski: Polish Californians," *Biblio-Cal Notes*, 13 (Spring/Summer 1982).

The international aspect of California settlement is extensively explored in a special issue of the *PH*, 26 (Summer 1982), devoted to the experiences of ethnic women. The life of Irish women in San Francisco is represented by Hasia R. Diner, *Erin's Daughters in America: Irish Immigrant Women in the Nineteenth Century* (Baltimore, 1983). *The Italians of San Francisco, 1850–1930* (New York, 1978), by Deanna Gumina, provides important information on the social networks of San Francisco's Italian women, a subject also examined by Mary Grace Paquette, *The Seven Sisters* (Fresno, 1985). An important addition is Micaela Di Leonardo, *The Varieties of Ethnic Experience, Class and Gender Among California Italian-Americans* (Ithaca, 1984), which underscores the importance of economic opportunity in assuring social mobility. See also Sally M. Miller and Mary Wedegaertner, "Breadwinners and Builders: Stockton's Immigrant Women," *The Californians*, 4 (July/August and September/October 1986).

The *WSHJQ* is a rich source of information on the experience of women settlers. Representative studies are Norton B. Stern, "Charitable Ladies of San Bernardino and Their Woman of Valor, Henrietta Ancker," 13 (July 1981) and Helen Newmark, "A Nineteenth Century Memoir," 6 (April 1974). The relationship of Jewish social reformers and unskilled non–English-speaking immigrants is explored by Lynn Fanfa, "The Emanu-El Sisterhood: Agent of Assimilation," *The Californians*, 4 (March/April 1986). See also "Immigrant Jewish Women in Los Angeles: Occupation Family and Culture," in J. R. Marus and A. J. Peck, eds., *Studies in the American Jewish Experience* (Cincinnati, 1981).

The study of Asian immigration has been enhanced by Corine Hoexter, *From Canton to California: The Epic of Chinese Immigration* (New York, 1976). A memorable view of life within an immigrant Chinese family has been provided by Jade Snow Wong in *Fifth Chinese Daughter* (New York, 1945) and by Maxine Hong Kingston, *The Woman Warrior: Memoirs of a Girlhood Among Ghosts* (New York, 1977). Specific aspects of immigration have been explored by Vincente Tang, "Chinese Women Immigrants and the Two-Edged Sword of Habeas Corpus," *Chinese Historical Society of America Bulletin*, 18 (October 1983). (See Chapter 8, *ante*, for additional Asian sources.)

The experiences of increasing numbers of Japanese who arrived after the turn of the century are studied by Yugi Ichioka, "Amerika Nadishiko: Japanese Immigrant Women in the United States, 1900-1924," *PHR*, 48 (May 1980). See also Ellen Nakano Glenn, "The Dialectics of Wage Work: Japanese-American Women and Domestic Service, 1905-1940," *Feminist Studies*, 6 (Fall 1980). Similar lines of inquiry are pursued by Eun Sik Yang, "Korean Women of America: From Subordinates to Partnership, 1903-1930," *AJ*, 2 (Fall/Winter 1984). See also John Modell, "The Japanese American Family: A Perspective for Future Investigators," *PHR*, 37 (February 1968). The story of black women in California awaits comprehensive historical analysis. (See Chapter 7, *ante*, for references to this group.)

Overviews of the literary life of California women have been provided by Gustave O. Arlt, "California's Literary Women," *QHSSC*, 36 (June 1954) and by Ella S. Mighels in *The Story of the Files: A Review of California Writers and Literature* (San Francisco, 1983) and *Literary California . . .* (San Francisco, 1918). The works of nineteenth- and early twentieth-century women writers were frequently published in Millicent Shinn's *Overland Monthly* (1880-1925), Charles F. Lummis' *Land of Sunshine*, which often featured the writings of Mary Austin, Nora French, and Sharlot Hall, and the *Hesperion* discussed by

Marion Tinling in "Hermione Day and the Hesperion," *CH*, 59 (Winter 1980/ 1981).

California's most astute interpreter of the land in both geography and symbol has been Mary Austin, author of such familiar titles as *Land of Little Rain* (New York, 1903), *The Land of Journey's Ending*, and her biography describing life on Rancho Tejon, *Earth Horizon* (New York, 1932). She has been the subject of numerous journal articles as well as several biographies, including *Mary Austin, Woman of Genius* (New York, 1939) by Helen Doyle and *I, Mary* (Tucson, 1981) by Augusta Fink.

One of Hubert H. Bancroft's able researchers is described by Hazel E. Mills, "Frances Fuller Victor, 1826-1902," *AW*, 12 (Summer 1970). Personal accounts of some of California's most historic events were also described by Jessie B. Fremont in *Recollections* (New York, 1912) and in Pamela Herr, "Jessie Benton Fremont: The Story of a Remarkable Nineteenth-Century Woman," *AW*, 16 (March/April 1979). Helen Hunt Jackson's dramatic retelling of the history of California Indians during the Mission period, *Ramona* (Boston, 1898) and *Glimpses of California and the Missions* (Boston, 1919), have generated continued commentary, including Allan Nevins, "Helen Hunt Jackson, Sentimentalist vs. Realist," *American Scholar*, 10 (Summer 1941) and John R. Byers, "The Indian Matter of Helen Hunt Jackson's *Ramona*," *American Indian Quarterly*, 2 (Winter 1975/1976). John E. Keller has edited a biography, *Anna Morrison Reed, 1849-1921* (Lafayette, 1979), documenting the life of a journalist and suffragist who also shared in the poetric tradition long associated with California's first Poet Laureate, Ina Coolbrith, whose most comprehensive biography is *Ina Coolbrith: Librarian and Laureate of California* (Provo, 1973) by Josephine Rhodehamel and Raymund F. Wood.

Women writers of California fiction include Ida Meacham Storbridge, Mrs. Fremont Older, and Gertrude Atherton, whose oeuvre is well described in Henry J. Forman, "A Brilliant California Novelist, Gertrude Atherton," *CHSQ*, 40 (March 1961). Atherton's contributions as historical observer are reflected in *California: An Intimate History* (1914), *The Splendid Ideal Forties* (1915), and *Adventures of a Novelist* (1932). Active participants in California's literary scene have included over the years novelist Kathleen Norris, whose work was positively appraised by Kenneth Rexroth, "Mrs. Norris' Story," *New York Times Book Review*, February 6, 1955. International literary figures with ties to California are represented in Lois Rather, *Gertrude Stein and California* (Oakland, 1974) and Gunther Stuhlman, ed., *The Diary of Anais Nin* (New York, 1967). See also Tillie Olsen, *Tell Me a Riddle* (New York, 1960). An overview is provided in Marilyn Yalom, ed., *Women Writers of the West Coast: Speaking of Their Lives and Careers* (Santa Barbara, 1983).

Among the few gifted interpreters who captured the western scene in both word and picture, Mary Hallock Foote remains pre-eminent. Her life is treated with understanding and insight by Rodman Paul, ed., *A Victorian Gentlewoman in the Far West: The Reminiscences of Mary Hallock Foote* (San Marino, 1972). In addition to numerous journal articles Wallace Stegner's Pulitzer Prize-winning fictionalized account, *Angle of Repose* (New York, 1971), effectively conveys Foote's increasing attachment to the western landscape.

California, as reflected through the daily life of the Pomo Indians, defines the emphasis of *The Painter Lady: Grace Carpenter Hudson* (Eureka, 1978) by Searles R. Boynton. A description of a wide range of California women artists including Eva Scott Fenyes and Helen Tanner Brodt can be found in Phil Kovnick, *The Woman Artist in the American West, 1860-1960, Exhibit Catalogue* (Fullerton, 1976). Women's participation in the movement inspired by William Morris is the subject of Linda Roth's, "Ramona Castle: Irene Strong's Home and Craftsman Movement," *JSDH*, 28 (Summer 1982). See also Bruce Kammerling, "Anna and Albert Valentien: The Arts and Crafts Movement in San Diego," *JSDH*, 24 (Summer 1978). The work of San Francisco sculptor Alice Rideout has been overlooked except for descriptions in Jeanne M. Weinman, *The Fair Women* (Chicago, 1981).

More recent California artists Helen Lundeberg, June Wayne, and Bettye Saar are profiled in Eleanor Munro, *Originals: American Women Artists* (New York, 1979). Judy Chicago is well represented in Karen Peterson and J. J. Wilson, *Women Artists: Recognition and Reappraisal* (New York, 1976), while *Big Art*, ed. by David Greenberg, et al. (Philadelphia, 1977), presents the work of several women muralists including *Mujeres Muralistas*. The work of June Wayne and Mary Corita is described in Ebria Feinblatt and Bruce Davis, *Los Angeles Prints, 1883-1980* (Los Angeles, 1980). Works of sculptresses Beulah Woodard and Ray Eames among others are described in Nancy D. W. Moure, *Painting and Sculpture in Los Angeles, 1900-1945* (Los Angeles, 1980). See also Elizabeth McCausland, "Dorothy Liebes, Designer for Mass Production," *Magazine of Art*, 40 (April 1947) and Tressa Miller, *Self-Portraits by Women Artists Exhibit Catalogue* (Los Angeles, 1985). The work of Dorothy Wormser is discussed by Norton Stern in "First Jewish Lady Architect of the West," *WSJHQ*, 7 (October 1984). There are numerous studies on architect Julia Morgan.

The majority of California women directed their creative energies to the development of their local communities. Their roles as culture bearers and city builders are described in Dorothy Huggins, "Women in Wartime San Francisco, 1864," *CHSQ*, 24 (September 1945) and in Jane E. Collier, "Early Club Life," *APHSSC*, 4, Pt. 3 (1899); also in Marco Newmark, "La Fiesta De Los Angeles of 1894," *QHSSC*, 21 (June 1947) and Jane Apostal, "They Said It with Flowers: The Los Angeles Flower Festival Society," *SCQ*, 62 (Spring 1980).

Two early biographies of Caroline Severance, organizer of the Friday Morning Club of Los Angeles and founder of the International Federation of Women's Clubs, are Ella G. Ruddy, ed., *The Mother of Clubs: Caroline Severance* (Los Angeles, 1906) and Mary S. Gibson, *Caroline M. Severance, Pioneer* (Los Angeles, 1925). Insights into the work of this remarkable woman are provided by

Joan Jensen, "After Slavery: Caroline Severance in Los Angeles," *QHSSC*, 48 (June 1966) and Thelma Hubbell and Gloria Lothrop, "The Friday Morning Club: A Los Angeles Legacy," *SCQ*, 50 (1963).

In her autobiography, *The Answer: Memoirs of Clara Bradley Burdette* (Pasadena, 1951), this prominent woman organizer describes the expansion of the woman's club movement. Informative official histories include Mary Wood, *The History of the General Federation of Women's Clubs* (New York, 1912); Mrs. Dorcus James, *The History of the WCTU of Northern and Central California* (Oakland, 1913); and Rowena Beans, *"Inasmuch . . ." The 100 Year History of the San Francisco Ladies Protective and Relief Society, 1853-1953* (Berkeley, 1953). See also Reva Clar, "San Francisco's Emanu-El Residence Club," *WSJHQ*, 15 (July 1982) and Virginia Katz, "The Ladies Hebrew Benevolent Society of Los Angeles," *WSJHQ*, 11 (January 1978).

The suffrage struggle has been examined in Jean Loewy, "Katherine Philips Edson and the California Suffragist Movement, 1919-1920," *CHSQ*, 47 (December 1968) and in Amelia Fry, "Along the Suffrage Trail: From West to East for Freedom Now," *AW*, 6 (January 1969). Documenting community responses are Marilyn Kneeland, "Modern Boston Tea Party—The San Diego Suffrage Campaign of 1911," *JSDH*, 23 (Fall 1977) and Jean Smith, "The Voting Women of San Diego, 1920," *JSDH*, 26 (Spring 1980). Two historical appraisals include the important analysis by Ronald Schaffer, "The Problem of Consciousness in the Woman Suffrage Movement: A California Perspective," *PHR*, 45 (November 1976) and Reda Davis, *California's Guide to Their Politics, 1885-1911* (San Francisco, 1967).

Armed with supportive social networks and suffrage, California women leaders committed themselves to many reforms. The range of endeavors is represented by David S. Jordan, "Women Workers for Peace," *Outwest*, 43 (January 1916) and Patricia Schaelchlin, "Working for the Good of the Community: Rest Haven Preventarium for Children," *JSDH*, 29 (Winter 1983). One prominent woman reformer is treated by Mary Hill, *Charlotte Perkins Gilman: The Making of a Radical and Feminist* (Philadelphia, 1980) and "Making Her Fame: Charlotte Perkins Gilman in California," *CH*, 64 (Summer 1985) by Gary Scharnhorst, who has also compiled *Charlotte Perkins Gilman: A Bibliography* (Metuchen, N.J., 1985).

The causes that frequently carried women into the courts were often argued by California's Clara Shortridge Foltz described by Nicholas Polos in "Portia of the Pacific: California's First Woman Lawyer," *JSDH*, 26 (Summer 1980). Other reformers, like Annette Adams and Florence Edson, affected policies even more widely while holding federal office. See Joan Jensen, "Annette Abbott Adams, Politician," *PHR*, 35 (May 1966); Norris Hundley, Jr., "Katherine Philips Edson and the Fight for the California Minimum Wage, 1912-23," *PHR*, 29 (August 1960); and Jacqueline Braitman, "California Stateswoman: The Public Career of Katherine Philips Edson," *CH*, 65 (June 1986).

The story of political activist Anita Whitney is told by Al Richard, *Native*

Daughter (San Francisco, 1942) and by Woodrow Whitten, "The Trial of Charlotte Anita Whitney," *PHR*, 15 (September 1946). The opposite pole of the political spectrum is represented by Congresswoman Florence Prag Kahn in "The Lady from California," by Frances Parkinson Keyes, *Delineator*, 118 (February 2, 1931). A relatively unknown event is examined in Gerald Gill, "Win or Lose—We Win: The 1952 Presidential Campaign of Charlotte A. Bass," in *Afro-American Women: Struggles and Images*, ed. by Sharon Harley and Rosalyn Terborg (New York, 1978). The career of Helen Gahagen Douglas is examined in her autobiography, *A Full Life* (New York, 1982).

The commitment to social betterment also led women to initiate historic preservation projects and champion the cause of environmental protection. Mrs. Armitage S. C. Forbes, pioneer mission preservationist, attempted to capture the "romance of the missions" in *Mission Tales in the Days of the Dons* (Chicago, 1909). With equally earnest dedication, Christine Sterling restored the historic heart of Los Angeles, an effort she described in *Olvera Street, Its History and Restoration* (Los Angeles, 1933).

Countless other community institutions were sustained by public spirited women philanthropists. Articles discussing several of them are: Barbara Lowney, "Lady Bountiful: Margaret Crocker of Sacramento," *CHSQ*, 47 (June 1968); G. Allan Hancock, "Madame Ida Hancock Ross, with Views of Her Home, Villa Madonna," *QHSSC*, 30 (March 1952); and Parke Rouse, Jr., "Westways Women: That Huntington Woman," *Westways*, 70 (December 1978).

A crusader for environmental conservation before the phrase was coined is captured by Grace T. Sargent, "Forgotten Mother of the Sierra: Letters of Julia Tyler Shinn," *CHSQ*, 38 (June 1959). Articles about conservationists include Jane Apostol, "Margaret Collier Graham, First Lady of the Foothills," *SCQ*, 63 (Winter 1981) and Connor Sorenson's study of Minerva Hamilton Hoyt, "Apostle of the Cacti: The Society Matron as Environmental Activist," *SCQ*, 58 (Fall 1976).

The outdoors also beckoned to increasing numbers of women cyclists and climbers, some daring enough to scale the tallest peaks as described by Leonard Daughenbaugh, "On Top of Her Wold: Anna Mills Ascent of Mt. Whitney," *CH*, 64 (Winter 1985). Sports as well are seen in a profile of Hazel Hotchkiss Wightman by Barbara Klaw, "Queen Mother of Tennis," *American Heritage*, 27 (August 1975). Some of the early aviators, attracted by California climate and weather, were women. Existing autobiographies include *The Fun of It* (New York, 1932) by Amelia Earhart and Jacqueline Cochran Odlum, *Stars at Noon* (Boston, 1954). Two additional studies are "The Ninety-nines," *Palm Springs Life*, 17 (October 1974) and "Sky Climber," *Westways*, 69 (February 1977).

Although women are an established part of the California entertainment world, the limited number of studies include Wallace Smith's article on Lucretia del Valle Grady, "The Last of the Senoritas," *The Californians*, 4 (March/April 1986) and Keith Lummis, "A Singer Remembers," *The Californians*, 2 (May/June 1984). Stephen Fry's *A Bibliography of the Story of the All-Women's*

Orchestras in California (Los Angeles, 1985) begins with the work of nineteenth-century violinist Camilla Curso and traces women musicians to the more recent era of Ina Rae Hutton. The life of popular nineteenth- and early twentieth-century composer Carrie Jacobs Bond, author of "The End of a Perfect Day," is reflected in her autobiography *The Roads of Melody* (New York 1927). One of the most prolific composers of the first half of the twentieth century is described by Catherine P. Smith and Cynthia S. Richardson in *Mary Carr Moore, American Composer* (Ann Arbor, 1987). Internationally acclaimed vocal artist and long-time Santa Barbara resident, Ernestine Schumann-Heink, is remembered in Hermann Klein, *Great Women Singers of My Time* (New York, 1931). Women in dance are represented by Walter Terry, *Miss Ruth: the "More Living Life" of Ruth St. Denis* (New York, 1969). Numerous studies of Isadora Duncan include Terry's *Isadora Duncan: Her Life* (New York, 1963).

The clarity of the California landscape attracted photographers as well as filmmakers, many of whom are represented in *Women and Photography: An Historical Survey* (San Francisco, 1975). Very important individual studies include *With Nature's Children: Emma B. Freeman (1880-1928)—Camera and Brush* (Eureka, 1976) by Peter Palmquist; Laverne M. Dicker, "Laura Adams Armer, California Photographer," *CH*, 56 (Summer 1977); and Milton Meltzer, *Dorothea Lange: a Photographer's Life* (New York, 1978). For additional insights consult the oral histories of Lange, "The Making of a Documentary Photographer" (Berkeley, 1959) and Imogen Cunningham, "Portraits, Ideas and Design" (Berkeley, 1959). See also Steven M. Gelber, "The Eye of the Beholder: Images of California by Dorothea Lange and Russell Lee," *CHS*, 64 (Fall 1985).

Depression-driven migrants pictured in Lange's photos are captured in Margo McBane and Mary Winegarden, "Labor Pains: An Oral History of California's Women Farmworkers," *CH*, 57 (Summer 1979). See also Elizabeth Nicholas, "Working in California Canneries," *Harvest Quarterly*, 3-4 (September/December 1976). Additional material on farm women during the Great Depression can be found in Glen H. Elder, *Children of the Great Depression* (Chicago, 1974), a report of longitudinal observations of an Oakland sample, 1934-1964.

The California Commission on the Status of Women has compiled the comprehensive *Campesinas: Women Farm Workers in the California Agricultural Labor Force* (Sacramento, 1978). This often unexamined segment of the labor market has been studied by Laura Arroyo, "Industrial and Occupational Distribution of Chicana Workers," *Aztlán*, 4 (Fall 1973) and in Vicki Ruiz, *Cannery Women; Cannery Lives* (Albuquerque, 1987).

World War II, which clouded the years following the Depression, also introduced Rosie the Riveter. The major movement of women to the paid workforce was observed at the time in such articles as Llewellyn Toland, "Women Are Doing Everything"; Harriet J. Eliel, "Wartime Child Care," and B. H. Crocheron, "Harvest Volunteers Respond," in *California Magazine of the Pacific*, 33 (September 1943). A special issue of *Radical America*, 9 (July/August 1975), contains a number of articles on women workers during World War II as well as studies of postwar consumer boycotts. See also Sherna B. Gluck, "What Did 'Rosie' Really Think? Creativity, Change and Subject Experience: Lessons from Oral History," *Southwest Economics and Society*, 6 (Fall 1983). D'Ann Campbell has drawn some thoughtful intergenerational connections in "Was the West Different? Values and Attitudes of Young Women in 1943," *PHR*, 47 (August 1978).

The social dislocation and fragmentation aggravated during wartime called for increased assistance of social welfare agencies staffed by professionals in a relatively new field. The development of one segment of the profession is described by Loretta R. Lawler, *Full Circle: The Story of the National Catholic School of Social Service, 1918-1947* (Washington, D.C., 1951), which provides an account of the work of a pioneer San Francisco social reformer. Two works that document important contributions to the field are Jean Barton, *Katharine Felton and Her Social Work in San Francisco* (Palo Alto, 1947) and Sanford Katz, ed., *Creativity in Social Work: Selected Writings of Lydia Rappoport* (Philadelphia, 1975), which contains the major works of a leading theorist in the analysis of social work interactions.

Wartime exigencies also led to the acceptance of more women scientists, many of them recent emigrés. Joan Dash's *A Life of One's Own* (New York, 1973) provides insight into the life of Berkeley's Nobel Prize Laureate, theoretical physicist Maria Gertrude Goeppert Mayer. Also see Robert and Suzanne Massie, *Journey* (New York, 1975), a biography of Stanford physiologist Judith Graham Pool and "Elsie Frankel-Brunswick: Selected Papers," ed. by Nanette Heiman and Joan Grant, *Psychological Issues* (Monograph 3), 8 (1974).

The life of a respected archeologist is highlighted in Ross Parmenter, "Glimpses of a Friendship: Zelia Nuttall and Franz Boas," *Pioneers in American Anthropology*, ed. by June Helm MacNeish (Seattle, 1966). Efforts to attract women to medicine are reported by Judith G. Pool, "The Case for More Women in Medicine: The Stanford Program," *New England Journal of Medicine*, 285 (July 1971). The pioneer in a specialized area of medicine, gerontology, is presented in Marian A. de Ford, *Psychologist Unretired: The Life Pattern of Lillian J. Martin* (Palo Alto, 1948). A latter day supporter of such study has been honored with an "Ethel Percy Andrus Special Issue," *Modern Maturity*, 11 (January 1968).

Postwar prosperity also touched California's businesswomen. The virtually unexamined area of clothing manufacture has been explored in Gloria Lothrop, "A Trio of Mermaids—Their Impact Upon the Southern California Sportswear Industry," *JW*, 25 (January 1986). Reva Clar, "Tillie Lewis of Stockton," *WSJHQ*, 16 (January 1984), describes success in tomato processing and diet food manufacturing. See also the widely diverse John Poppy, "Adelle Davis and the New Nutrition Religion," *Look*, December 15, 1970, and the autobiography of gourmet food maven M. F. K. Fisher, *Among Friends* (San Francisco, 1983). Sara Boynoff, "Reporting for Work," *Westways*, 70 (February 1978) and Anthony Del Balso, "The Lordly Ladies of the Press," *Town and*

Country, 140 (January 1986), examine the lives of women journalists in California.

The women's movement has not only increased awareness of the place of women in society, but has also attempted to assure equality of opportunity with governmental assistance. Resulting documents compiled by the California Commission on the Status of Women provide fruitful areas of research: *California Women* (1973); *Child Care Issues* (1975); *Statistical Report on the Status of Displaced Homemakers in California* (1982); *Pay Inequities for Women: Comparable Worth and Other Solutions* (1983), among many others.

More recent state history includes an increasing number of elected women public officials described in Chuck Buxton, "Old Girls' Network," *California Journal*, 11 (January 1980); Janet Flamming, "Female Officials in the Feminist Capital: The Case of Santa Clara County," *WPQ*, 38 (March 1985); Carola Lazzareschi, "Rose Bird, Criminal Lawyer, as the Complete Bureaucrat," *California Journal*, 7 (March 1976); and Rivian Taylor and James Richardson, "Rose Bird and the Press," *California Journal*, 17 (September 1986).

While prominent figures and popular issues in California women's history have been highlighted in the works cited above, there is need (as was indicated at the beginning of this chapter) for further research. Resources, including unpublished diaries, reminiscences and dissertations as well as a wealth of unexamined archival material, invite additional investigation. Such effort should produce a comprehensive profile of women of all classes and ethnic groups—an essential step toward the eventual goal: an integrated, synthesized inclusion of women in the story of California's people.

10

URBAN CALIFORNIA

GUNTHER BARTH

THE EMERGENCE and the development of the city in California has been the subject of a great number of books and articles. The adjective "urban" is frequently a convenient catchall for a classification of activities that do not fall readily into the many loosely drawn categories of historical enterprise. Confronted with an abundance of riches, any guide to urban California literature must be selective.

The most significant feature in the history of the city in California is the role of Los Angeles as pioneer of a new course of urbanization. Its worldwide reverberations seem to justify the use of the superlative, so judiciously avoided in any scholarly assessment. In the Los Angeles area there emerged a new form of the spatial organization of people, under the influence of climate and topography, technology and suburbanization. It combined features of rural and urban life into a world that was neither rural nor urban, but seemed as ingenious a mixture of both as the word rurban, which Carey McWilliams, *Southern California Country* (New York, 1946) seems to have coined to describe the phenomenon.

A great number of books have touched on aspects relating to the significance of the Los Angeles area for urbanization, but no single study has as yet treated it comprehensively. The bibliography by Doyce B. Nunis, Jr., comp., *Los Angeles and Its Environs in the Twentieth Century: A Bibliography of the Metropolis* (Los Angeles, 1973), provides a good understanding of the magnitude of the subject. Several studies dealing with the entire history of the city identify significant components of the development. W. W. Robinson compressed them into *Los Angeles: A Profile* (Norman, 1968). Other pastmasters of the subject are Remi Nadeau, *Los Angeles: From Mission to Modern City* (New York,

1960); Andrew F. Rolle, *Los Angeles* (San Francisco, 1980); John and LaRee Caughey, eds., *Los Angeles: A Biography of a City* (Berkeley, 1976); and Lynn Bowman, *Los Angeles: Epic of a City* (Berkeley, 1974).

The remaking of the physical and social environment, which assured durability to the land of magical improvisation, fell into the age of the camera and has been captured in many photographs. They account for several of the books that celebrated the bicentennial of the city. Art Seidenbaum, *Los Angeles 200: A Bicentennial Celebration* (New York, 1980); David L. Clark, *Los Angeles, a City Apart: An Illustrated History* (Woodland Hills, Calif., 1981); and David Lavender, *Los Angeles Two Hundred* (Tulsa, 1981)—all chronicle the essentials. The centennial of a newspaper that extensively shaped the area and the residents' outlook is Digby Diehl, *Front Page: 100 Years of the Los Angeles Times, 1881-1981* (New York, 1981).

The juxtaposition of dated and recent pictures of the same setting accounts for the stunning features of Robert W. Cameron, *Above Los Angeles: A Collection of Nostalgic and Contemporary Aerial Photographs of Greater Los Angeles* (San Francisco, 1976); Bruce Henstell, *Los Angeles: An Illustrated History* (Los Angeles, 1980); and Guernot Kuehn, *Views of Los Angeles: 125 Black and White Photographs Contrasting the Past with the Present* (Los Angeles, 1978). Fred E. Boston, *Beverly Hills: Portrait of a Fabled City* (Los Angeles, 1975), is indeed something special; another of his collection of pictures covers the towns around Santa Monica Bay. In a pair of books Zelda Cini brings together photographs in *Hollywood, Land and Legend*, with Bob Crane (Westport, Conn., 1980), and of Encino and Northridge in *El Valle de Santa Catalina de Bononia de Los Encinos, 1769-1975* (Sherman Oaks, 1975) and *The Romantic History of Northridge, 1765-1975* (Northridge, 1976). Judy Wright, *Claremont: A Pictorial History* (Claremont, 1980) and Maureen R. Michelson and Michael R. Dussler, *Pasadena: One Hundred Years* (Pasadena, 1984), are equally helpful.

A useful guide to the urban world of Orange County, somewhat dated, is David T. Rocks, comp., *Orange County Local History, 1869-1971: A Preliminary Bibliography* (Santa Ana, 1972). Mildred Y. MacArthur, *Anaheim: "The Mother Colony"* (Los Angeles, 1959), studies the city before the urban sprawl stimulated by Disneyland inundated it. The early years are also the focus of Charles Swanner, *Santa Ana: A Narrative of Yesterday, 1870-1910* (Claremont, 1953). Gladys D. Alex, et al., *Santa Ana's 100 Years: Prelude to Progress, 1869-1969* (Santa Ana, 1969), fastens on the transition as theme, as does Larry L. Meyer and Patricia L. Kalayjian, *Long Beach: Fortune's Harbors* (Tulsa, 1983) and Hortense Hoffman, *Long Beach from Land to City* (Long Beach, 1957). An attractive balance in the choice of emphasis characterizes Tom Patterson, *A Colony for California: Riverside's First Hundred Years* (Riverside, 1971).

The details of the physical growth of the Los Angeles area have received much attention. Of particular interest is Judith W. Elias, *Los Angeles: Dream to Reality, 1885-1915* (Northridge, 1983). The creation of the harbor, which seemed to emerge out of nowhere, is surveyed in a well-illustrated book by the

Los Angeles Harbor Department, Charles F. Queenan, *The Port of Los Angeles: From Wilderness to World Port* (Los Angeles, 1983). The disputes surrounding the appropriation of water from Inyo County, about 250 miles north of the city, sustaining an expansion of the sprawling housing developments, is traced by Abraham Hoffman, *Vision or Villainy* (College Station, Tex., 1981) and by William Kahrl, *Water and Power* (Berkeley, 1982).

The complex role of the automobile is discussed in articles by Ashleigh Brilliant, "Some Aspects of Mass Motorization to Southern California, 1919-1929," *SCQ*, 47 (June 1965); Mark S. Foster, "The Model-T, the Hard Sell, and Los Angeles's Urban Growth," *PHR*, 44 (November 1975); and with quantitative analysis by Martin Wachs, "Autos, Transit, and the Sprawl of Los Angeles: the 1920's," *Journal of the American Planning Association*, 50 (Summer 1984). Oil as another factor heightening the rurbanization of the area is treated by Fred W. Viehe, "Black Gold Suburbs: The Influence of the Extractive Industry on the Suburbanization of Los Angeles, 1890-1930," *Journal of Urban History*, 8 (November 1981).

For the new urban and social development of the Los Angeles area, architecture is at once stimulus and result, and quite a number of insights come from good studies of the built environment. Montgomery Schuyler, "Round About Los Angeles," *Architectural Record*, 24 (December 1908), discusses early solutions to housing and considers them an encouraging social phenomenon. A thorough pioneering effort, Anton Wagner, *Los Angeles: Werden, Leben und Gestalt der Zweimillionenstadt in Suedkalifornien* (Leipzig, 1935), explores the initial stages of the urban world from a geographic perspective that rarely suffers from his quaint view of the social forces behind the development. Of interest is Rodney Steiner, *Los Angeles: Centrifugal City* (Dubuque, 1981).

Another good starting point for an exploration of the physical setting is David Gebhard and Robert Winter, *A Guide to Architecture in Southern California* and *Architecture in Los Angeles: A Compleat Guide* (Salt Lake City, 1985). The intricate architectural heritage of the area is surveyed with good illustrations by Paul Gleye, in collaboration with the Los Angeles Conservancy, Julius Shulman, and Bruce Boehner, *The Architecture of Los Angeles* (Los Angeles, 1981). Reyner Banham, *Los Angeles: The Architecture of Four Ecologies* (New York, 1971), makes a spirited defense for the leading role of the city's architecture in the world, based on his evaluation of the creative interactions between natural and human mechanisms. A balanced discussion of a complex issue is provided by David Brodsly, *L.A. Freeway: An Appreciative Essay* (Berkeley, 1981).

Crucial for an awareness of the orientation of the Los Angeles area toward the future is an understanding of municipal history and civic spirit, and these tasks are successfully fused in a critical assessment by Robert M. Fogelson, *The Fragmented Metropolis: Los Angeles, 1850-1930* (Cambridge, Mass., 1967). The foundation for grasping the relationship between politics, planning, and building have been laid by Mellier G. Scott, *Metropolitan Los Angeles: One Community* (Los Angeles, 1949); Richard Bigger and James Kitchen, *How the*

Cities Grew: A Century of Municipal Independence and Expansionism in Metro-politan Los Angeles (Los Angeles, 1952); and Winston W. Crouch and Beatrice Dinerman, *Southern California Metropolis* (Los Angeles, 1963). The slim study by George W. Bemis and Nancy Basche, *From Rural to Urban: The Municipal-ized County of Los Angeles* (Los Angeles, 1947), emphasizes politics. The ability of the area to sustain expansion and thrive on a series of business booms is presaged by Glenn S. Dumke, *The Boom of the Eighties* (San Marino, 1944). See also the annual publication, *Sixty-Mile Circle: The Economy of the Greater Los Angeles Area*, Security Pacific Corporation, Los Angeles.

Los Angeles has replaced the platonic unity of the traditional city with the Aristotelian diversity of a new kind of urban world. Belles lettres reflect the change, but only a few writers have captured compassionately the impact of the altered way of life on people. Arna Bontemps, *God Sends Sunday* (New York, 1931) and Nathanael West, *The Day of the Locust* (New York, 1939), tower over this group of writers. A mystery story by Raymond Chandler, *Farewell, My Lovely* (New York, 1940), forces the changing world into focus. The "city western," as a genre of American literature reflecting stages of urbanization west of the Rocky Mountains, depends in a happy measure on Chandler, as Joseph C. Porter indicates in "The End of the Trail: The American West of Dashiell Ham-mett and Raymond Chandler," *WHQ*, 6 (October 1975).

More often than not, writers dealing with the Los Angeles area are satisfied mixing humor and satire in their castigations. Evelyn Waugh, *The Loved One* (Boston, 1948), fortifies his satire with art. Other authors use the area primarily as the setting for their strictures on a decaying world in general, as does Aldous Huxley, *After Many a Summer Dies the Swan* (New York, 1939). A collection of essays is in David Fine, ed., *Los Angeles in Fiction* (Albuquerque, N.M., 1984). It recognizes the emergence of a dominant literary region of the country in the entire genre of writing from the tough-guy tale and the barrio fiction to the Los Angeles novel and the Southern California story. Walter Wells had earlier reduced a fraction of the subject to two themes, *Tycoons and Locusts: A Regional Look at Hollywood Fiction of the 1930's* (Carbondale, 1973), initially probed by Franklin Walker, "Hollywood in Fiction," *Pacific Spectator*, 2 (Spring 1948).

The diversity of the Los Angeles area speaks directly from the composition of the heterogeneous population. W. W. Robinson, *The Indians of Los Angeles: Story of the Liquidation of a People* (Los Angeles, 1952), discusses a part of the topic, before the so-called urban Indian became recognized as a social force. Oscar Winther, "The Rise of Metropolitan Los Angeles, 1870-1900," *HLQ*, 10 (August 1947), delineates the shifting areas of origin of migrants from the East Coast and the Midwest.

Carey McWilliams' writings have frequently exposed the plight of the Mexican American. More recent scholarship has put the barrio into historical perspective, as depicted in Chapter 6, *ante*.

The Watts riots of 1965 brought the palm tree ghetto into dramatic focus, and with it came a sequence of studies of blacks in the changing urban setting of Los Angeles, a matter thoroughly discussed in Chapter 7, *ante*.

The turmoil of wartime Los Angeles of 1943 is the context of Mauricio Mazón, *The Zoot-Suit Riots* (Austin, 1984). For the riot of 1871, which took the lives of eighteen or nineteen Chinese, see the articles by Paul M. De Falla, "Lantern in the Western Sky," *QHSSC*, 42 (March/June 1966) and William R. Locklear, "The Celestials and the Angels: A Study of the Anti-Chinese Movement in Los Angeles to 1882," *QHSSC*, 42 (September 1960). Earlier forms of vigilantism are discussed by Robert W. Blew, "Vigilantism in Los Angeles, 1835-1874," *SCQ*, 54 (Spring 1972).

Quite frequently the Los Angeles area is linked with studies of ethnic groups, but the interrelation of people with distinct variants of the changing urban scene plays only a minor role in the analysis. Although the area is predominantly the setting for such studies, it is not a factor in the influences which shape the conditions and the behavior of ethnic and racial groups. Neil C. Sandberg, *Ethnic Identity and Assimilation: The Polish-American Community; A Case Study of Metropolitan Los Angeles* (New York, 1974), is strong on methodology and data, but less so on Los Angeles. Other books built the connection on economics, identity, and assimilation. Among them are John Modell, *The Economics and Politics of Racial Accommodation: The Japanese of Los Angeles, 1900-1942* (Urbana, 1977); Sheila E. Henry, *Cultural Persistence and Socio-Economic Mobility: A Comparative Study of Assimilation among Armenians and Japanese in Los Angeles* (San Francisco, 1978); and Helen Givens, *The Korean Community in Los Angeles County* (San Francisco, 1974). (See Chapter 8, *ante*.)

The ongoing interplay between the social and psychological facets of urbanization receive the attention of Max Vorspan and Lloyd P. Gartner, *History of the Jews of Los Angeles* (San Marino, 1970); and of Gregory H. Singleton, *Religion in the City of Angels: American Protestant Culture and Urbanization, Los Angeles, 1850-1930* (Ann Arbor, 1979).

At first glance, the contribution of the Los Angeles area to the course of urbanization points to the future, that of the Bay area to that segment of California's past marked by the spectacular rise of San Francisco during the gold rush. And so do many books dealing with the history of San Francisco. They focus on the span of time from the middle of the nineteenth century to the early decades of the twentieth century, when San Francisco was the metropolis of the Pacific Coast. The Bay area, as a new form of urban entity, emerged only after Los Angeles regained its position as the dominant urban center of California.

Historical studies seem to approach the subject of the Bay area as a new entity of urbanized life rather hesitantly, unlike natural histories that appear more direct in their approach to what for them has always been a unit, as in T. John Conomos, ed., *San Francisco Bay, the Urbanized Estuary: Investigations into the Natural History of San Francisco Bay and Delta with Reference to the Influence of Man* (San Francisco, 1979).

Both Oakland and Berkeley histories continue to depend on the excellent compilations by the Works Projects Administration as a solid base for investigations, Edgard J. Hinkel and William E. McCann, eds., *Oakland, 1852-1938: Some Phases of the Social, Political, and Economic History of Oakland, California* (2 vols.; Oakland, 1939) and WPA Writers' Program, comp., *Berkeley: The First Seventy-five Years* (Berkeley, 1941). In recent years there appeared Beth Bagwell, *Oakland: Story of a City* (Novato, 1982); George Pettitt, *A History of Berkeley* (Oakland, 1976); and Phil McArdle, ed., *Exactly Opposite the Golden Gate: Essays on Berkeley History, 1845-1945* (Berkeley, 1983). Well-selected photographs characterize Elinor Richey, *The Ultimate Victorians on the Continental Side of San Francisco Bay* (Berkeley, 1970). Bennett Maurice Berger, *Working Class Suburb: A Study of Auto Workers in Suburbia* (Berkeley, 1960), dealing with Milpitas, and Frank M. Stanger, *South from San Francisco: San Mateo County, California; Its History and Heritage* (San Mateo, 1963), show how the subject of settlements along the rim of the bay can be handled successfully. And so do Vallie Jo Whitfield, in *History of Pleasant Hill, California* (Pleasant Hill, 1981), who accounts for the transformation of agricultural land into suburbia some twenty miles east of the bay, and Helen B. Kerr, *Sausalito: Since the Days of the Spanish Dons* (Berkeley, 1967).

Recent attempts to tackle the topic of the urban world of the Bay area show the long shadow of Mellier G. Scott, *The San Francisco Bay Area: A Metropolis in Perspective* (Berkeley, 1959), who skillfully probes the beginning of the trend to examine major cities in a perspective framework, coupled with his unique concept of regional planning. James E. Vance, Jr., *Geography and Urban Evolution in the San Francisco Bay Area* (Berkeley, 1964), emphasizes the roles of San Francisco and Oakland in urban development. While searching for a large framework, Charles Wollenberg, *Golden Gate Metropolis: Perspectives on Bay Area History* (Berkeley, 1985), keeps his focus on San Francisco. Roger W. Lotchin, "The City and the Sword: San Francisco and the Rise of the Metropolitan Military Complex, 1919-1941," *JAH*, 65 (March 1979), somewhat broadens the perspective, as does Frank M. Stanger, *South From San Francisco: San Mateo County . . .* (San Mateo, 1963). A consideration of San Jose and the Silicon Valley also tends to expand the orientation, somehow stripping the South Bay of its separate role in Edith Brockway, *San Jose Reflections: An Illustrated History of San Jose, California, and Some of Surrounding Area* (Campbell, Calif., 1977). However, an early study of the appearance of the new technology in the Bay area, Dirk Hanson, *The New Alchemists: Silicon Valley and the Micro-Electronics Revolution* (Boston, 1982), has not yet much to say about its influence on patterns of urbanization.

Concepts of the Bay area as a unit of scholarly investigation can still be gleaned from Bulletin 154 of the California Division of Mines, Olaf P. Jenkins, ed., *Geological Guidebook of the San Francisco Bay Counties: History, Landscape, Geology, Fossils, Minerals, Industry, and Routes of Travel* (San Francisco, 1951). The publications of the Association of Bay Area Governments, the Save-the-Bay Campaign, and People for Open Space contain valuable ideas for the importance of thinking in terms of the large entity.

Quite naturally, studies of the technology forging transportation links penetrate the broader setting more readily. Allen Brown, *Golden Gate: Biography of a Bridge* (Garden City, N.Y., 1965), is the best work on the magnificent structure. Joseph B. Strauss, *The Golden Gate Bridge: Report of the Chief Engineer to the Board of Directors of the Golden Gate Bridge and Highway District* (2 vols.; San Francisco, 1938), provides a good starting point. Historical description of the Bay Bridge still depends largely on an early publication, *The San Francisco–Oakland Bay Bridge* (Chicago, 1936). Richard H. Dillon, Don de Nevi, and Thomas Moulin, *High Steel: Building the Bridges Across San Francisco Bay* (Millbrae, 1979), partly fill the gap.

The beginning and the end of the period that nostalgia has identified as the city's great age are successfully marked by Roger W. Lotchin, *San Francisco, 1846–56: From Hamlet to City* (New York, 1974) and by Judd L. Kahn, *Imperial San Francisco: Politics and Planning in an American City, 1897–1906* (Lincoln, 1979). Gunther Barth, *Instant Cities: Urbanization and the Rise of San Francisco and Denver* (New York, 1975), relates the sudden rise of the city to a distinct phenomenon of urban growth. The sudden end is detailed by William K. Bronson, *The Earth Shook, the Sky Burned* (Garden City, N.Y., 1959), which deals well with one of the frequently talked-about events in the city's history.

Doyce B. Nunis, Jr., ed., *The San Francisco Vigilance Committee of 1856* (Los Angeles, 1971), furnishes a good overview of one of the city's controversial affairs. Dwight L. Clarke, *William Tecumseh Sherman: Gold Rush Banker* (San Francisco, 1969), mirrors the events of the 1850s through the eyes of a shrewd observer of the city scene. The leading role of merchants in the 1856 Vigilance Committee and the 1877 Committee of Safety is discussed by Peter R. Decker, *Fortunes and Failures: White Collar Mobility in Nineteenth-Century San Francisco* (Cambridge, Mass., 1978).

The claims for San Francisco's hegemony speak clearly from the titles of three nineteenth-century works still helpful on account of the wealth of detail they amassed: Frank Soule, John H. Gihon, and James Nisbet, *The Annals of San Francisco . . .* (New York, 1855); John S. Hittell, *A History of the City of San Francisco and Incidentally of the State of California* (San Francisco, 1878); and John P. Young, *San Francisco: A History of the Pacific Coast Metropolis* (2 vols.; San Francisco, 1912). This approach also characterizes Zoeth Eldredge, *The Beginnings of San Francisco from the Expedition of Anza, 1774, to the City Charter of April 15, 1850* (2 vols.; San Francisco, 1912), who sees the city as the inevitable climax of the development of California. Almost sixty years earlier, John W. Dwinelle, *The Colonial History of the City of San Francisco* (San Francisco, 1863) had shown rather remarkable restraint.

The second half of the nineteenth century has received a considerable degree of attention from political historians who probe the variety of San Francisco's machines and bosses. (See Chapter 4, *ante*.)

The urban setting of two of those decades is captured well in the work of the period's eminent photographers, G. R. Fardon of the 1850s and Eadweard

Muybridge of the 1870s, whose pictures have been reproduced frequently. Harold Kirker, *California's Architectural Frontier* (Rev. ed.; Santa Barbara, 1973), comments extensively on the city's architecture in the second half of the nineteenth century. Wesley D. Vail, *Victorians: An Account of the Domestic Architecture in San Francisco, 1870–1890* (San Francisco, 1964), is also helpful. Joseph A. Baird, *Time's Wondrous Changes: San Francisco Architecture* (San Francisco, 1963), offers the most extensive treatment. Michael R. Corbett, et al., *Splendid Survivors: San Francisco's Downtown Architectural Heritage* (San Francisco, 1979), is a good overview of the relics that survived earthquake, fire, and Manhattanization.

Three types of studies move in time beyond the limits of Old San Francisco: general histories, picture books, and ethnic studies. John B. McGloin, *San Francisco: The Story of a City* (San Rafael, 1978), represents well the full-length histories. T. H. Watkins and R. R. Olmsted, *Mirror of the Dream: An Illustrated History of San Francisco* (San Francisco, 1976), works effectively with conflicting images of the changing setting. Douglas Daniels, *Pioneer Urbanites: A Social and Cultural History of Black San Francisco* (Philadelphia, 1980), is one of the investigations of ethnic and racial groups, which carries its story successfully into the 1930s. Several, like R. A. Burchell, *The San Francisco Irish, 1848–1880* (Berkeley, 1980), re-examine the extensively covered ground of the nineteenth century. Another important study is Deanna Gumina, *The Italians of San Francisco, 1850–1930* (New York, 1978).

Like San Francisco, other California cities rose rapidly at mid-nineteenth century and survived the hectic experience. They all thrived on the population movement unleashed by the gold rush that decisively oriented the development of the young state toward the city. The emphasis on the town had been embodied in the concept of Spanish colonization from its beginnings. Promulgated formally with the Laws of the Indies in 1573, the sections dealing with the establishment of settlements were first published in English by Zelia Nuttal, "Royal Ordinances Concerning the Laying Out of New Towns," *Hispanic American Historical Review*, 4 (November 1921), 5 (May 1922). The lack of material and human resources, as well as the distance from the centers of authority, stifled urban growth in Alta California.

That urban vision, ignored by weak officials and modified by settlers who had their own ideas about their most pressing needs, has rarely been used as a yardstick to evaluate the urban features of the local scene in the studies of the Spanish-Mexican experience in California. The pertinent sections in Dora P. Crouch, Daniel J. Garr, and Axel I. Mundigo, *Spanish City Planning in North America* (Cambridge, Mass., 1982) pursue the task, not altogether successfully, but the book contains insights into the issues.

Romances or chronicles frequently serve as accounts of the early settlements in Alta California. Their capital provides a case in point. It inspired Tirey L. Ford, *Dawn and the Dons: The Romance of Monterey* (San Francisco, 1926). During the Junípero Serra Year, so designated by the California State Legislature of 1933 in commemoration of the sesquicentennial of the death of the founder of Franciscan California, appeared Laura Powers, *Old Monterey: California's Adobe Capital* (San Francisco, 1934). Jeanne Van Nostrand, *A Pictorial and Narrative History of Monterey: Adobe Capital of California, 1770-1847* (San Francisco, 1968), is notable, as is Augusta Fink, *Monterey: The Presence of the Past* (San Francisco, 1972).

Aspects of the intriguing seed years of cities in Alta California are gaining wider attention, such as in Mary Tucey and David Hornbeck, "Anglo Immigration and the Hispanic Town: A Study of Urban Change in Monterey, California, 1835-1860," *Social Science Journal*, 13 (April 1976). Starting points for analogous investigations can be found in several good studies of other early towns. (See Chapters 1-2, *ante*.)

The historiography of the mining towns in the foothills of the Sierra Nevada has produced studies dealing with individual towns, but relatively little concern for their position within the context of urbanization. Earle Ramey, *Beginnings at Marysville* (San Francisco, 1936) and Catherine Phillips, *Coulterville Chronicle: The Annals of a Mother Lode Mining Town* (San Francisco, 1942), are substantial pieces of work. A glimpse beyond Marysville and on to Yuba City can be found in William Ellis, *Memories: My Seventy-two Years in the Romantic County of Yuba, California* (Eugene, Ore., 1939), but the growth of Yuba City as an example of urban development fostered in part by the almost fifty agricultural settlements designed by Vernon de Mars for the Farm Security Administration in rural California between 1937 and 1943 still awaits comprehensive historical treatment.

There has been no recent attempt to deal comparatively with California mining towns, as with some of their counterparts in the Rocky Mountains, or to trace the implications of a mining heritage for contemporary urban life, although Charles H. Shinn, *Mining Camps: A Study in American Frontier Government* (New York, 1885), demonstrated the usefulness of the comparative approach for his field of interest many years ago. A contribution to the "new urban history," Ralph Mann, *After the Gold Rush: Society in Grass Valley and Nevada City, California, 1849-1870* (Stanford, 1982), relates two nearby towns to each other as well as his conclusions about models of social interaction applied in studies of Eastern cities.

Quite a number of studies treat racial and ethnic groups in mining camps and towns, but they bypass the opportunity of linking the life of a group with features of urbanization. At times the contact between miners and their urban setting is visible in collections of pictures and photographs, such as Harry T. Peters, *California on Stone* (Garden City, N.Y., 1935) and Otheto Weston, *Mother Lode Album* (Stanford, 1948). Discussions of ghost towns favor the tall story, but Paul Fatout, *Meadow Lake: Gold Town* (Bloomington, Ind., 1969), is an exception, partly because no building reminds the tourist now of the town once bustling in the High Sierra.

The San Joaquin Valley and the Sacramento Valley have not yet produced the urban histories keeping up with the galloping urbanization that seems intent on linking Marysville with Sacramento and Stockton with Fresno. Raymond W. Hillman and Leonard A. Covello, *Cities & Towns of San Joaquin County since 1847* (Fresno, 1985), have made many variants of the urban form, incorporated cities, unincorporated towns, little settlements of today, and ghost towns, the subject of their engaging book that reaches the present.

George P. Hammond, *The Weber Era in Stockton History* (Berkeley, 1982), is a splendid example of a one man, one generation study of a city. R. Coke Wood and Leonard A. Covello, *Stockton Memories: A Pictorial History of Stockton, California* (Fresno, 1977); Olive Davis, *Stockton: Sunrise Port on the San Joaquin* (Woodland Hills, 1984); and Nicholas Hardeman, *Harbor of the Heartlands ...* (Stockton, 1986), extend the coverage of city life into our days. Modesto, one of the stations in the San Joaquin Valley the Central Pacific Railroad named in 1870 when it reached the place, now thrives in the automobile age in Jeannette Maino, ed., *One Hundred Years: Modesto, California, 1870-1970* (Modesto, 1970).

For the study of the intensified urbanization of the San Joaquin Valley, with Fresno as its center, the publication of about 1,000 of Claude C. Laval's magnificent photographs covering the first half of the twentieth century is an inspiring beginning, in Jerome D. Laval, *As "Pop" Saw It: The Great Central Valley of California as Seen Through the Lens of a Camera* (2 vols.; Fresno, 1975-1976). For the literature on the city itself Joan Dinkin, comp., *Fresno: A Bibliography* (Fresno, 1977) is useful. Other pictorial histories give Fresno and Bakersfield their due: Edwin M. Eaton, *Vintage Fresno: Pictorial Recollections of a Western City* (Fresno, 1965) and Richard C. Bailey, *Heart of the Golden Empire: An Illustrated History of Bakersfield* (Woodland Hills, 1984). The emerging metropolis near the southern junction of the two great valley highways is also the theme of Eugene Burmeister, *City Along the Kern: Bakersfield, California, 1869-1969* (Bakersfield, 1969). Another centennial history does justice to the major town at the northern end of the Central Valley in Edward Petersen, *Redding, 1872-1972: A Centennial History* (Redding, 1972).

The history of the capital of the state still depends for details on the *Sacramento Guide Book*, published by the Sacramento *Bee* in 1939 and on Sophie Price, *The Sacramento Story* (New York, 1955). However, two attractive picture books also offer glimpses on the capital scene, Julie E. and Kevin M. Mims, *Sacramento: A Pictorial History of California's Capital* (Virginia Beach, Va., 1980) and Joseph A. McGowan and Terry R. Willis, *Sacramento: Heart of the Golden State: An Illustrated History* (Woodland Hills, 1983). Sacramento's early years are covered by Vernon Neasham and James E. Henley, *The City of the Plain: Sacramento in the Nineteenth Century* (Sacramento, 1969) and Thor Severson, *Sacramento: An Illustrated History, 1839-1874; From Sutter's Fort to Capital City* (San Francisco, 1973). The state capital, as well as all earlier capitals, is served well by Marion Murphy, *Seven Stars for California: A Story of the Capitals* (Sonoma, 1979).

About half a century ago, *Coast and Valley Towns of Early California* (San

Francisco, 1938), pointed at relations among the towns along the coast, but no study has pursued the idea further. Santa Barbara has attracted considerable attention, as evidenced by Dewey Schurman, ed., *Headlines: A History of Santa Barbara from the Pages of Its Newspaper, 1855-1982* (Santa Barbara, 1982); Rochell Bookspan, ed., *Santa Barbara by the Sea* (Santa Barbara, 1983); and Bruce Muench, *Santa Barbara* (Toronto, 1984), which offers a pictorial view. The classic account of Carmel, before it was embraced by almost everyone, is Franklin Walker, *The Seacoast of Bohemia: An Account of Early Carmel* (San Francisco, 1966).

A large number of communities in the greater Los Angeles area have been the focus of local histories. Among the most outstanding are: Esther Klotz, *Riverside and the Day the Bank Broke* (Riverside, 1972); Donald Pflueger, *Covina* (Claremont, 1961) and *Glendora* (Claremont, 1964); Henry M. Page, *Pasadena: Its Early Years* (Los Angeles, 1964); Thomas D. Carpenter, *Pasadena: Resort Hotels and Paradise* (Azusa, 1984); Jane Apostal, *South Pasadena, 1888-1988* (South Pasadena, 1987); Bruce T. Torrence, *Hollywood, The First Hundred Years* (New York, 1982); Betty L. Young, *Pacific Palisades: Where the Mountains Meet the Sea* (Pacific Palisades, 1983); and Augusta Fink, *Time and the Terraced Land* (Berkeley, 1966).

Of all the coastal cities, San Diego stands out where published histories are concerned. A splendid seven-volume history, commissioned by James C. Copley and Helen K. Copley and written by a former editor of the San Diego *Union*, covers the history of the area from 1542 to 1970, Richard F. Pourade, *History of San Diego* (7 vols.; San Diego, 1960-1977). A condensed treatment is in Iris H. W. Engstrand, *San Diego: California's Cornerstone* (Tulsa, 1980). Also useful are Ray Brandes, *San Diego: An Illustrated History* (Los Angeles, 1981) and Raymond G. Starr, *San Diego: A Pictorial History* (Norfolk, Va., 1987). Two founders of the city, their actions somewhat separated in time, are treated by Engstrand, *Serra's San Diego: Father Junípero Serra and California's Beginnings* (San Diego, 1982) and Elizabeth C. MacPhail, *The Story of New San Diego and of Its Founder Alonzo E. Horton* (2nd rev. ed.; San Diego, 1979). Additional contributions to the city's historiography can be located through Walter H. Posner, comp., *A List of Master's Theses on the History of San Diego Written at San Diego State University* (San Diego, 1975).

Many helpful hints about the contours of urban California can be found in a variety of splendid reference works. They are well represented through James D. Hart, *A Companion to California* (Rev. ed.; New York, 1988), and in the works of Erwin G. Gudde and Elisabeth K. Gudde, *California Place Names: The Origin and Etymology of Current Geographic Names* (3rd ed.; Berkeley, 1969) and *California Gold Mining Camps . . .* (Berkeley, 1975).

For the nineteenth century, the text and the illustrations of the seventeen California county histories, published by Thomas Thompson and Albert West, contain valuable details about urban life. Despite their casual identification as "subscription histories," which tend to accentuate the accomplishments of the affluent, they record many aspects of the interaction of people with the environment, through a great amount of information on roads and railroads, ferries and bridges, inns and factories, land holdings, and other indices of accelerated urbanization.

Accounting for that intricate process of urbanization also produces a considerable number of rather diverse stories about the rise of cities and the development of citified regions. Justice can hardly be done to all these publications here. However, a few of them should be mentioned as types of writings on urban California because they somehow stimulate the frequently quite elusive feeling of community, so often considered endangered by intensified urbanization. Frequently, their research, writing, and publication bring people together, heightening an awareness that community is where community happens.

The Vacaville City Council published the splendid history by Ronald H. Limbaugh and Walter A. Payne, *Vacaville: The Heritage of a California Community* (Vacaville, 1978). On the coast in Mendocino County, the "Greenwood Hobbyists" put together old photographs and much local lore and published Walter Matson's account of their work, *Reminiscences of a Town with Two Names: Greenwood, Known also as Elk* (Greenwood, 1980). Betty Lewis' extensive gleanings, *Watsonville: Memories That Linger* (2 vols.; Fresno, 1976; Santa Cruz, 1980), are yet another variant of a communal reliving of phases of urban California.

At times, historic buildings have inspired care for their preservation, and one might hope that the writings devoted to them will also inspire histories of the urban settings sustaining them. Eureka has seen a beginning with Laurence Beal, *The Carson Mansion: America's Finest Victorian Home and the Man Who Built It* (Eureka, 1973) and Benjamin Sacks, *Carson Mansion & Ingomar Theatre: Cultural Adventures in California* (Fresno, 1979). Perhaps the Bidwell House and the Stansbury House will provide an impetus for a history of Chico, in the same way that the Woodland Opera House is one nucleus for the work of the Yolo County Historical Society, *Woodland House Tour, 1976* (Woodland, 1976). In the case of Red Bluff, buildings also account for a beginning of historical consciousness, in Oscar Lewis, "Victorian Shadows on Walnut and Main: Red Bluff, California," in Thomas C. Wheeler, ed., *A Vanishing America: the Life and Times of the Small Town. Twelve Regional Towns by Hodding Carter*... (New York, 1964).

Much of the urbanization of California took place under the watchful eyes of the camera, which explains in part the profusion of fascinating picture books that enrich the genre of historical writings on settlements. In turn they bring to life again older histories that are often bypassed. John Gabbert's solid study, *History of Riverside City and County* (Riverside, 1935), has acquired a new dimension through the publication of James T. Brown, *Harvest of the Sun: An Illustrated History of Riverside County* (Northridge, 1985). Eventually, it is to be hoped, the accompanying prose in all these photographic studies will be as insightful as the pictures, as soon as we have learned to fathom them more extensively as historical evidence and to express the meaning of these signs of the past somewhat independent of their images. Then any selection of materials on urban California will also be less arbitrary because each publication will reflect the meaning of the infinite complexity of people's responses to the environment when caught in the whirlpool of accelerated urbanization.

PART TWO
ARCHIVES
AND SOURCES

11

NATIONAL ARCHIVES FEDERAL RECORDS CENTERS

DIANE S. NIXON AND MICHAEL ANDERSON

NATIONAL ARCHIVES—LOS ANGELES BRANCH

DIANE S. NIXON

Street address:	24000 Avila Road
	Laguna Niguel, CA 92677
Mailing address:	P.O. Box 6719
	Laguna Niguel, CA 92677-6719
Telephone:	(714) 643-4220
Days and hours:	Monday–Friday, 8:00 A.M. to 4:30 P.M.;
	first Saturday of each month, 8:00 A.M.
	to 4:30 P.M.

THE LOS ANGELES BRANCH of the National Archives is a repository of the permanently valuable records created by federal agencies in southern California, Arizona, and Clark County, Nevada. Also included are the Pre-Presidential Papers of Richard M. Nixon, and microfilm publications of important original record holdings of the National Archives in Washington, D.C., including many sources of special interest to genealogists, such as the Federal Population Censuses, 1790–1910, and the Compiled Service Records and Pension and Bounty-Land-Warrant Application Files of the Revolutionary War.

The Los Angeles Branch holds over 14,500 cu. ft. of original federal records, dating from 1851 through 1982. These records were created by federal agencies located in the following states: California (the eleven southern counties only: San Luis Obispo, Santa Barbara, Ventura, Kern, Inyo, San Bernardino, Riverside,

Los Angeles, Orange, San Diego, and Imperial); all of Arizona; and Nevada (Clark County only, which includes Las Vegas). Each year this collection is augmented by additional records transferred from agencies within the region.

Among the oldest records are the files created by the U.S. District Court and the U.S. Circuit Court of Los Angeles. The Los Angeles National Archives Branch currently holds the records of the U.S. District Court for the Central District of California (Los Angeles) for the years 1851-1961 (2,532 lin. ft.), and the Circuit Court (Los Angeles) for 1887-1911 (126 lin. ft., 6 in.). Records created by these federal courts consist of (1) case files, which may include subpoenas, pleadings, depositions, affidavits, judgments, and often, exhibits; and (2) indexes and listings of cases (many of which are in bound volumes), such as docket books, minutes, and orders.

Holdings of the U.S. District Court, Los Angeles, include case files (general, 1887-1907; civil, 1907-1950; equity, 1913-1938; admiralty, 1890-1929; and criminal, 1907-1957), and docket books (civil, 1907-1958; bankruptcy, 1907-1947; referee, 1923-1952; equity, 1913-1938; and criminal, 1907-1942). The branch also holds the following Los Angeles District Court naturalization records: Indexes (1887-1931); declarations of intention (1887-1959); petitions for naturalization (1887-1957); and naturalization depositions (1925-1961). Other naturalization records relate to military petitions and repatriations (primarily covering the years 1918-1954). Records of the Circuit Court, Los Angeles, include civil and criminal case files, docket books, and minute books (1887-1911).

The branch also holds the records of the U.S. District Court, San Diego. Prior to 1929, the San Diego area was in the same jurisdiction as the District Court, Los Angeles. Researchers interested in federal legal matters affecting the San Diego area should therefore refer to the Los Angeles files for cases prior to 1929, and to the San Diego records for the years thereafter. Holdings of the U.S. District Court, San Diego, consist primarily of case files (civil, 1929-1959; equity, 1929-1938, and criminal, 1929-1956); dockets (civil, 1929-1942; bankruptcy, 1929-1961; equity, 1929-1938, and criminal, 1929-1943); and minutes (1929-1952).

The branch also holds over 85 cu. ft. of donated naturalization records from two nonfederal courts. The naturalization records of the Los Angeles County Superior Court include: Naturalization index (1852-1915); naturalization records (1852-1888); certificates (1876-1906); declarations of intention (1887-1915); and petitions (1907-1915). The San Diego County Superior Court has contributed the following records: Index (1853-1955); declarations of intention (1941-1955); certificates (1883-1903); and petitions (1906-1956). There is also a microfilm set of the *Declarations of Intention filed at the San Diego Superior Court* (1871-1941; 8 reels).

Among the topics for possible study in the legal case files are the nature of federal legal proceedings; famous trials, judges, and defendants in California history; Chinese exclusion and deportation; violation of liquor laws; counterfeiting; the avoidance of selective service regulations; industrialization; economic depression; the status of ethnic groups; labor, radical, and pacifist movements. The Los Angeles District Court holdings may be used for studies related to the Hollywood motion picture industry.

Southern California federal court records for 1960 and later years will be transferred on a scheduled basis to the Los Angeles National Archives Branch. At present, these later cases and their indexes are housed by either the Los Angeles Federal Records Center or the court of origin. Files held by the Records Center legally belong to the originating agency. All court records (except for those files sealed by a judge), however, may be consulted by the public. Any researcher wishing to consult a case held by the Federal Records Center must know the specific court, year, case number, and shipment (accession) number of the case. The researcher must obtain this information from the court of origin prior to making an appointment with the Records Center to examine the records.

Useful for studies relating to the federal government's relations with native Americans are the records of the Bureau of Indian Affairs (BIA), RG 75. There are over 1,000 cu. ft. of BIA records relating to the Indians of southern California, 1880-1964. The BIA is responsible for the well-being of Indians living on reservations. Its records are useful for analyzing the operation of federally administered Indian programs, and they provide some documentation on the history and culture of various tribes.

Individual Indian case files have a seventy-five-year privacy restriction; therefore, files of this type which were created after 1914 are not yet open for research. Fortunately, however, individual Indian case files constitute only a small portion of the BIA holdings, and almost all of the other records in this record group are not subject to restrictions.

Most important for researchers studying the Indians of southern California are the records of the Mission Indian Agency, its predecessor offices (such as the Campo, Pala, and Soboba superintendencies), and its successor office (the Riverside Area Field Office). The records of these various offices (1880-1960s) measure approximately 325 cu. ft.

The records of the Mission Indian Agency include the New Central Classified Files (1920-1953; 17 lin. ft., 6 in.), and the General Subject File (1939-1947; 10 in.). These files include correspondence, reports, newspaper clippings, and other records relating to such topics as general administration, finances and accounts, land transactions, medical and dental services, agricultural extension, education and social relations, and employment activities. Valuable narrative and statistical summaries of all types of agency activities are included in the Annual Reports (1921-1942; 4 lin. ft., 4 in.). Other important individual series include Records Relating to the Second World War (1941-1945; 10 in.); Photographs (1936-1942; 2 lin. ft.) taken by farm agents and other agency employees to document progress under various New Deal programs; Maps and Plats (1909-1950; 1 lin. ft., 3 in.) of the reservations in San Diego, Riverside, and San Bernardino counties, and Censuses (1922-1940; 2 lin. ft.). *Indian Census Rolls* (1884-1940), for many tribes, are also available on microfilm. The Los Angeles

Branch also holds many records of the various subagencies and superintendencies which were once under the jurisdiction of the Mission Indian Agency. The records of the Colorado River Indians are also available.

Another important collection in RG 75 relates to the Sherman Institute, a boarding school for nonresident Indian students located in Riverside, which was established by an Act of Congress in 1900. The records of the school (244 lin. ft.) include the Central Classified Files (1907-1939; 16 lin. ft., 4 in.), consisting of correspondence, memoranda, orders, reports, and telegrams relating to the administration of the school; Letters Sent (1902-1948; 16 lin. ft., 4 in.), relating primarily to financial matters; and many other smaller series containing information about curricula and enrollment, teachers and administrators, student outings, organizations, and special events.

The third largest record group in the holdings of the branch is the Bureau of Land Management (BLM), RG 49. The BLM was established in 1946 by the consolidation of the General Land Office (GLO) and the Grazing Service. The General Land Office was established in 1812, and the Grazing Service in 1934. The branch holds over 750 cu. ft. of records originated by the GLO and the BLM during the period 1853-1973. The GLO records include those created by the Los Angeles District Office (1853-1939), the land offices in Independence (1903-1929), and Visalia (1925-1928). The BLM records were originated by the district offices in Los Angeles (1908-1969), Riverside (1930-1971), and Bakersfield (1935-1973). There is a considerable overlap in the date spans of the records originated by the Los Angeles District Office (under the jurisdiction of both GLO and BLM), and the Los Angeles and Riverside District Offices (under BLM). Because of this overlap, researchers should consult the finding aids for both GLO and BLM (and for Los Angeles and Riverside) to determine if specific series originated by one office were continued by its successor.

Records of land entries constitute the largest series of GLO/BLM records of this branch (over 1,085 cu. ft. alone for the Los Angeles and Riverside District Offices, 1908-1973). Records of land entries prior to 1908 are arranged by enabling act (e.g., the Homestead Act), and then alphabetically by the land claimant's name. Mineral entries are arranged by the name of the specific claim. After 1908, GLO and then BLM assigned a serial number to each land entry; all documents relating to that entry were filed under the same serial number. This branch holds an alphabetical card index to serialized land entries of the Los Angeles District Office (1948-1956) and the Riverside District Office (1957-1967). All other alphabetical card indexes have been retained by the BLM Sacramento Office.

Perhaps the most interesting records of the Los Angeles District Office were originated in the years prior to 1908, when the office was a part of GLO. Among these are the Case Files for Homestead and Pre-Emption Entries (1869-1908; 15 lin. ft., 4 in.). Arranged alphabetically by the surname of the land applicant, these files contain such documents as the initial application, notice of publication, statement of final intention, and sometimes, the testimony of witnesses who corroborated statements made by an applicant. There is also a Register of Homestead Entries (1869-1908; 8 in.). This four-volume register, with entries arranged by chronologically assigned application numbers, records each homestead application, including such information as the number and date of the application, a legal description of the land, the name of the applicant and address, and the ultimate patenting, contesting, or cancellation of the application. Two smaller series of note relate to land entries under the Military Bounty Land Acts; Abstracts of Military Bounty Land Acts (1859-1901; 2 in.); and Records of Entries Filed Pursuant to the Soldiers and Sailors Act (1872-1896; 5 in.). These records provide data about servicemen and the land they or their widows claimed. The Records of Entries Filed Pursuant to the Soldiers and Sailors Act are primarily declaratory statements of service; each document includes the name of the soldier or sailor (and his widow's name, if the serviceman was deceased), a statement of loyalty to the United States, a description of the individual's service in the Civil War, and a legal description of the land claim.

The Los Angeles Branch has begun to acquire some administrative subject files of various National Park Service (NPS), RG 79, facilities in this region—primarily in Nevada and Arizona, but with one California facility represented, Death Valley National Monument for the period 1954-1966 (6 in.).

Another Department of the Interior agency represented is the U.S. Geological Survey, RG 57. Included are the Hydrographic Survey Sheets of California counties (1891-1906; 7 in.). These records document the existence of wells, and provide data on water quality and use. Prominent landowners are represented in this turn-of-the-century hydrographic census—including J. W. Bixby, A. B Chapman, and William MacFadden.

The U.S. Coast Guard, RG 26, Customs Service, RG 36, and the discontinued Bureau of Marine Inspection and Navigation, RG 41, have originated many similar records series relating to navigation, and vessel inspection and documentation. These three record groups are represented by more than 400 cu. ft. of records.

The Los Angeles Collection District originated as the Wilmington Collection District in 1882. The branch's holdings cover 1876-1966 and include correspondence of the district, quarterly vessel documentation abstracts, and various records of specific ports (Los Angeles, Redondo Beach, Port Hueneme, and San Luis Obispo).

The San Diego Collection District is even older than its Los Angeles counterpart, being established in 1873. It originally included Santa Barbara, Los Angeles, San Bernardino, and San Diego counties. Following official designation as District 25 in 1920, it was assigned responsibility for only San Diego and Imperial counties. In 1923 the district was placed under the jurisdiction of the Los Angeles Collection District, but was returned to separate status in 1930. The records of the district include correspondence (1880-1913), circulars, annual narrative, and statistical reports (1948-1955). Also included are records of the following specific offices: the Port of San Diego (1885-1966), the Calexico Customs Office (1902-1922), and the Tijuana Customs Office (1894-1922).

Two small but important series, originated by both the Los Angeles and San Diego districts, are the Wreck Reports. These reports of shipwrecks off the southern California coast cover the period 1883-1917 (Los Angeles; 1 in.) and 1885-1934 (San Diego; 1 in.).

Customs Service and Bureau of Marine Inspection and Navigation holdings include many series relating to the purchase and registry of vessels. These records contain such information as the name of the vessel, the year and place built, dimensions and capacities, home port, and the owner's name and address.

Official Merchant Marine Log Books are included in the records of both the Bureau of Marine Inspection and Navigation, RG 41, and the Coast Guard, RG 26. Log books retained under RG 41 cover the period 1916-1942 (3 lin. ft., 2 in.); the Coast Guard log books are dated 1942-1953 (100 lin. ft., 10 in.). The log books of both agencies contain the name and number of each merchant marine vessel, the port of registry, registered tonnage, name of master, number of master's certificate, the dates and type of voyage, and a listing of the crew and a report on their character. Among the many vessels represented by individual log books is the *Montebello*, sunk by a Japanese torpedo in December 1941. The Unit Logs of the U.S. Coast Guard are useful for locating data on Coast Guard vessels and units in the Los Angeles area. The records cover the period 1970-1982 (38 lin. ft., 2 in.) and include information on operations, navigation, and weather conditions.

A record group of growing importance at the branch is RG 181, Naval Districts and Shore Establishments. In 1985 the branch accessioned over 1,300 cu. ft. of Navy records originated by the 11th Naval District Headquarters in San Diego, the San Diego and Long Beach Naval Stations, the Long Beach Naval Shipyard, and other shore installations in the southern California area. These records cover 1916-1959, with most dating from 1941 to 1959. A small but interesting collection of naval records relates to the Los Angeles Zoot Suit riots of 1943 (1 lin. ft.).

There are also over 63 cu. ft. of records originated by the Los Angeles District of the Army Corps of Engineers, RG 77, for the years 1899-1963, including Project Administration Records of the Los Angeles District (1899-1935; 50 lin. ft.). This series includes correspondence, memoranda, narrative and statistical reports, procedures, maps, and photographs. Files in this series relate to such topics as the mining of the San Diego Channel during the Spanish-American War, the development of the Los Angeles harbors, the sinking of vessels in the Santa Barbara Channel, the construction of the San Francisco-Oakland Bay Bridge, the damming of Bolsa Chica Creek, the St. Francis Dam failure, and the purchase of private land for the construction of Ft. Rosecrans. Other series include Monthly River and Harbor Reports (1912-1940; 4 lin. ft., 3 in.); Monthly and Annual Fortification Reports (1912-1935; 1 lin. ft., 3 in.); and Cartographic Records Relating to Reservoir and Dam Projects (1957-1963; 1 in.).

Recently transferred from the Atlanta Branch to the Los Angeles Branch were records of the Selective Service System (World War I), RG 163, for southern California and Arizona (approx. 10 cu. ft.). Holdings relating to World War II are primarily to be found in RG 26 (Coast Guard), 36 (Customs Service), 77 (Corps of Engineers), and 181 (Naval Districts and Shore Establishments), and some are also included in RG 75 (BIA). One other record group representing an agency disestablished after the war is the Petroleum Administration for War (PAW), RG 253. PAW was responsible for establishing policies, plans, and programs relating to wartime conservation, development, and production of petroleum products. The branch holds the only known remaining records of the District Five (Los Angeles) Petroleum Industry Committee (106 cu. ft.). Included are reports, minutes, press releases, and correspondence.

The topics of aviation and aeronautics are well represented in the holdings of the Federal Aviation Administration, RG 237, and the National Aeronautics and Space Administration, RG 255. There is also a small collection of records relating to the 659th Aerospace Test Wing (1961–1965; 1 lin. ft.) in RG 342, Air Force Commands, Activities, and Organizations.

The Federal Aviation Administration is represented by various records of the Western Region Air Traffic Division (1960–1971; 26 cu. ft.). Records already arranged and described include those pertaining to airport terminal control areas in Los Angeles (as well as San Francisco, Las Vegas, Seattle, and Denver), and cases involving unsatisfactory airport conditions at airports within the region.

The National Aeronautics and Space Administration (NASA) is represented by 132 cu. ft. of records, covering 1939 through 1967. NASA, and its predecessor, the National Advisory Committee for Aeronautics (NACA), which was founded in 1915, have been involved in the scientific study of flight and aeronautical research and experimentation. The Los Angeles Branch's holdings primarily relate to the activities of the Dryden Flight Research Center (1946–1959) and the Western Support Office (1939–1959).

The Dryden Flight Research Center was located at Muroc (later Edwards) Air Force Base; its records document the first era of high-speed aeronautical research. Memoranda and other records document the testing of such aircraft as the X-1, X1-A, X1-B, X1-E, X-2, X-3, X-4, and X-5; also the D-558 I and II, and the F-51, F-100, and F-100A.

Presently stored at the Los Angeles National Archives Branch, awaiting eventual transfer to the Nixon Presidential Library (if it is administered by the National Archives), are the Richard M. Nixon Pre-Presidential Papers—over 400 lin. ft. of papers, primarily relating to Nixon's Vice-Presidency. These papers, originally deeded to the federal government in 1968 and 1969 and transferred to the Laguna Niguel facility in 1975 and 1979, are, with some exceptions, open to research.

Over 50,000 reels of microfilm, which reproduce several hundred original records series held at the National Archives Building in Washington, D.C., are also available. Most of these microfilm publications deal with topics of national and international interest. Some microfilm publications relate specifically to California history or may be used for research about Californians or their descendants. Perhaps the most useful are the Federal Population Censuses, 1790–

1910. These records contain very valuable data about the residents of California cities and counties. (Note: Due to a seventy-two-year privacy restriction, more recent Federal Population Censuses are not yet available for research.)

California first appeared in the Sixth Census of the United States, 1850. This census, arranged by state, county, enumeration district, and street address, includes the following types of data for each person listed: Name, address; age; sex; color; whether deaf mute, blind, or insane; the value of real estate owned; occupation/trade; place of birth; whether married within the year; whether attended school during the year; literacy; and whether a pauper or a convict. The 1850 census relating to California (4 reels) includes all counties then in existence, with the exception of Contra Costa, San Francisco, and Santa Clara.

All counties are included in the 1860 and 1870 censuses of California (44 reels); these censuses include the same types of data as the 1850 census. Alphabetical name indexes for California are available for both the 1850 and 1860 censuses, but not yet for the 1870 census.

The 1880 census (California segment—33 reels) represents a number of firsts. It was the first federal census to show the relationship of each person in the family to the head of the household, and the first to have a "soundex" (a name index which groups together all surnames which sound similar but have variant spellings). The greatest deficiency of the 1880 soundex is that it only lists households which include at least one child who was ten years of age or younger. Households with only older children are listed in the census, but not in the soundex.

The 1890 Federal Population Census for California no longer exists. Most of the population schedules for that year, including California, were destroyed by a 1921 fire in the Department of Commerce Building, Washington, D.C. However, the 1900 and 1910 censuses are complete and detailed (79 reels relating to California), and soundexes for California are available for both years.

Most of the military records on microfilm relate to the Revolutionary War and the War of 1812. However, an Index to Compiled Service Records of Volunteer Union Soldiers from California (7 reels) is available. This index provides such information as the name and unit of a soldier, and sometimes his rank, profession, and office. The actual compiled service records, in contrast to this index, are available only at the National Archives, Washington, D.C. Copies of records pertaining to military service prior to World War I may be obtained by completing an NATF Form 80 (Order for Copies of Veterans Records) and by forwarding the form to the Military Service Branch of the National Archives. Records of Californians who served in the armed forces during and after World War I are scattered in various repositories, including the National Archives Building, the Military Personnel Records Center, and a number of other centers operated by the various branches of the military.

A number of microfilm series relate to land acquired by individuals during the Mexican rule of California. California's Spanish Archives (14 reels) is a reproduction of a set held by the California State Archives, Sacramento. California's

Spanish Archives include transcripts and translations of private land grant cases. The records on the microfilm are handwritten, some in Spanish and others in English translation. An index volume and five volumes of surveys and plats relating to the land claims are also included. Much of the material in this series is duplicated in another microfilm series: California Private Land Claim Dockets (1852-1903; 117 reels). Only those private land cases which were brought before the U.S. Land Commission appear in this later series, however. Some of the cases documented in the California's Spanish Archives were never brought before the commission.

There are several other indexes to private land grant cases, for both northern and southern California (1853-1903). Included are the names of the parties involved, and a chronology of the documents and actions filed. The indexes are arranged roughly in chronological order. A name index is included for northern California, but not for southern California.

Several other microfilm series documenting the early years of the state are worth noting. Baptismal Records, Los Angeles County (1771-1873; 2 reels) reproduces the Thomas W. Temple II collection of baptismal records of the Mission San Gabriel and the Plaza Church of Los Angeles. Letters Sent by the Governors and the Secretary of State of California (1847-1848; 1 reel) concerns such topics as administration, trade, Indian affairs, customs duties, property rights, and the discovery of gold. The letters sent and proclamations issued by the military governors and the secretary of state were addressed to local and federal officials, representatives of foreign countries residing in California, military officers, and private individuals. The Returns from United States Military Posts (1800-1916) show the movement of troops or detachments to and from various posts, and includes information about the post, detachments in the field, and battles with Indians. Lists of commanders and officers of the various posts are often included. Among the military posts represented are the Presidio of San Francisco (1847-1916; 6 reels); the Presidio of Monterey (1847-1916; 3 reels); San Diego Barracks (1849-1903; 5 reels); and Ft. Tejon (1854-1864; 1 reel). Finally, there are the Indian Census Rolls (1884-1940). The earlier years include the English and/or Indian name of each person, age or date of birth, sex, and relationship to the head of the family. Beginning in 1930, additional information is shown, including degree of Indian blood, marital status, ward status, and place of residence. The Mission Indians (1929-1939, 8 reels) are included in this series.

Individuals wishing to use the original records or the Nixon Pre-Presidential Papers are urged to contract the Branch in advance of each prospective visit. It is not necessary, however, for researchers wishing only to use the microfilm publications to provide advance notification. The researcher must use the finding aids and conduct his/her own research on site, although the staff will perform brief searches to provide answers to very specific, concise requests received through the mail or by telephone.

There are forty microfilm readers, available on a first-come, first-served basis. Descriptive pamphlets, listing the contents of each reel in a microfilm series, may be consulted at the Branch. There are free brochures available to assist those who are about to use census records for the first time, and a video introduction to genealogical records held by the National Archives may be viewed in the Microfilm Research Room.

Reproductions of original records, papers from the Nixon collection, and portions of the microfilm publications are available upon request. Prices vary with size, quantity, method of reproduction, and handling difficulty.

Introducing the National Archives—Los Angeles Branch, a brochure about the Branch's services and holdings; *Research Opportunities* (a forty-page guide to the original materials available at the branch); and a listing of all microfilm holdings will be provided without charge when requested by prospective researchers.

NATIONAL ARCHIVES—SAN FRANCISCO BRANCH

MICHAEL ANDERSON

Street address:	1000 Commodore Drive
	San Bruno, CA 94066
Mailing address:	Same
Telephone:	(415) 876–9009
Days and hours:	Monday, Tuesday, Thursday, Friday, 8 A.M.
	to 4:30 P.M.; Wednesday, 8 A.M. to 8:30 P.M.

The San Francisco Branch of the National Archives is one of eleven field branches established in 1969. It serves a region consisting of northern and central California, Hawaii, the Pacific Ocean area, and Nevada (except for Clark County). Holdings include over 20,000 cu. ft. of records.

The holdings are identified by "record group" number, assigned by the National Archives for administrative purposes. A record group usually corresponds to a department, bureau, independent agency, or comparable unit within the government's organizational hierarchy. The branch contains records from sixty-four record groups (RG), including a wealth of materials relating to the history of California.

Federal involvement and regulation in California predated the formal granting of statehood in 1850. The oldest records are those of the Bureau of Customs (RG 36), which established an office in San Francisco in 1849. Records of the San Francisco Customs Office include correspondence (1869-1928; 669 vols.); coded administrative files (1913-1947; 325 cu. ft.); records of vessel arrivals and departures (1849-1950; 68 vols.); and records of collection of tonnage duties (1872-1919, 6 vols.).

Two other record groups also contain records closely related to San Francisco Customs Bureau activities. Customs officers served as part of the field force of the Bureau of Marine Inspection and Navigation (RG 41). Documents in RG 41 relating to San Francisco Customs activities include records of registry, enrollment, and licensing of vessels (1849-1951; 215 vols.); records of tonnage admeasurement (1865-1945; 29 vols.); and records of mortgage of vessels (1897-1925; 17 vols.).

Records of the Coast Guard (RG 26) are also closely related to those of the Customs Bureau. The functions of admeasuring and documenting American vessels were the responsibility of the Bureau of Customs until 1967, when these duties transferred to the Coast Guard. Coast Guard records relating to the San Francisco Customs Bureau include vessel folders (1913-1937; 1 cu. ft.); wreck reports (1898-1935; 26 vols.); and shipping articles and crew lists (1854-1950; 134 cu. ft.).

In addition to the San Francisco Customs records the archives branch has records of the Customs Bureau office at the port of Eureka. Included are such items as records of tonnage and measurement (1882-1930; 2 vols.), an index of conveyance of sale for vessels over twenty tons (1852-1949; 11 vols.), wreck reports (1898-1933; 3 vols.), and various records of registry, licensing, enrollment, and mortgage of vessels.

Court documents created as a result of the implementation of federal justice in California constitute a significant portion of the holdings of the archives branch. The branch has over 5,000 cu. ft. of records from United States District Courts in the Northern and Eastern Districts of California (RG 21).

In 1851 California joined the federal judicial system with the establishment of a Northern District Court at San Francisco and a Southern District Court at Los Angeles. With the exception of the period 1866-1886 when the Southern District was temporarily abolished and the Northern District Court exercised its duties over all of California, this division of the state remained in effect until 1966. Since 1966 California has been divided into four districts, Northern (San Francisco), Eastern (Sacramento and Fresno), Central (Los Angeles), and Southern (San Diego).

Records of the District Court for the Northern District of California include case files, dockets, and minutes. The records relate to proceedings in admiralty, bankruptcy, criminal, common law, equity, and civil cases.

Admiralty records include case files (1851-1934; 626 cu. ft.); case registers (1855-1860; 2 vols.); case indexes (1867-1921; 2 microfilm reels); an index of habeas corpus cases filed by Chinese attempting to gain admission to the United States (1882-1906; 1 microfilm reel); and a record book of habeas corpus cases filed by Chinese (1892-1899; 1 vol.). The Chinese habeas corpus record book and index as well as most of the case files between 1882 and 1902 relate to the so-called "Exclusion Acts" passed by Congress which prohibited Chinese laborers from entering the United States.

Bankruptcy records of the District Court for the Northern District of California include docket books (1867-1932; 37 vols.); indexes (1898-1928; 3 vols.); and case files (1867-1878; 101 cu. ft.). Criminal records include a register of cases (1851-1853; 1 vol.); an index to cases (1904-1921; 1 microfilm reel); and case files (1851-1934; 449 cu. ft.). Common law and equity records include a general index to defendants in common law and equity cases (1863-1927; 1 microfilm reel); a general list of common law cases (1923-1927; 1 microfilm reel); equity case files (1913-1938; 396 cu. ft.); and common law case files (1912-1938; 325 cu. ft.). Civil records consist of case files (1938-1953; 450 cu. ft.).

Naturalization records are primarily used for genealogical purposes but they are also an excellent source for demographic studies. Northern District Court naturalization records include indexes to declarations and petitions for naturalization (1906-1928; 2 vols.); petitions and records of naturalization (1907-1956; 444 vols.); certificates of naturalization (1852-1906; 17 vols.); and naturalization certificate stubs (1908-1926; 192 vols.).

In 1912 the Northern District Court assumed the records and duties of the Ninth Circuit Court for the District of Northern California (1887-1912) and its predecessor courts, the Circuit Court for the District of California (1856-1863), the Tenth Circuit Court for California and Oregon (1863-1866), and the Ninth Circuit Court for the District of California (1866-1887).

Records of the Circuit Court for the District of California include a judgment docket index (1855-1863; 1 vol.); minutes of meetings at Los Angeles (1857-1861; 1 in.); and common law and equity case registers (1855-1863; 5 vols.). Case files of circuit "U.S. Cases" (1855-1863; 1 vol.) include civil, criminal, and admiralty cases in which the federal government acted as plaintiff. Criminal charges in U.S. cases include cruelty to seamen, murder, tax evasion, and encouragement of soldiers to desert. The majority of the circuit civil case files (1855-1863; 17 cu. ft.) concern land matters, including claims on Spanish-Mexican land grants.

Records of the Tenth Circuit Court for California and Oregon include a general index to registers of U.S. cases (c. 1863-1867; 1 vol.); a general index to registers of private cases (1863-1867; 1 vol.); an equity docket register of U.S. cases (1863-1867; 1 vol.); an equity docket register of private cases (1863-1867; 1 vol.); and a register of U.S. cases (1863-1867; 1 vol.).

Records of the Ninth Circuit Court for the Northern District of California are intermixed with the records of the Ninth Circuit Court for the District of California. They include an index to certificates of naturalization (1868; 1 vol.); case records for consular courts held at Hong Kong, Nagasaki, and Yokohama (1863-1876; 1 in.); a general index to civil case files (1863-1891; 1 in.); civil case files (1856-1912; 602 cu. ft.); records of the appointment of court officials (1864-1897; 1 cu. ft.); records of the appointment of supervisors of congressional elections (1871-1888; 1 cu. ft.); several series of naturalization records such as declarations of intentions to become citizens (1855-1911; 10 vols.); a register of applications for naturalization (1879-1903; 1 vol.);

petitions and records of naturalization (1903-1911; 5 vols.); and naturalization certificates and stubs (1855-1912; 24 vols.).

The archives branch has records of the District Court for the Eastern District of California which was created in 1966 with divisions at Fresno and Sacramento. The Fresno court was originally established in 1900 when the Southern District was split into a Northern Division located at Fresno and a Southern Division located at Los Angeles. The Sacramento court was founded in 1916 when the Northern District was similarly divided into two divisions, a Northern Division holding sessions at Eureka and Sacramento and a Southern Division holding sessions at San Francisco.

Fresno records include minute books (1900-1951; 6 cu. ft.); mixed case files (1900-1907; 7 cu. ft.); civil case files (1938-1967; 171 cu. ft.); common law and equity case files (1907-1938; 108 cu. ft.); criminal case files (1907-1942; 37 cu. ft.); a criminal case index (1907-1944; 1 vol.); and civil, common law, and equity case indexes (1900-1941; 2 vols.).

Sacramento records include civil case files (1938-1973; 356 cu. ft.); equity case files (1916-1940; 79 cu. ft.); common law case files (1916-1944; 60 cu. ft.); and criminal case files (1916-1961; 175 cu. ft.). Naturalization records include declarations of intention (1917-1956; 5 vols.); civil petitions for naturalization (1922-1956; 29 vols.); military petitions for naturalization (1944-1946; 3 vols.); and overseas military certificates of naturalization (1944-1945; 1 vol.).

Another source in the archives branch for information concerning the federal judicial history of California are the records of the United States Ninth Circuit Court of Appeals (RG 276). The Courts of Appeals are intermediate courts created in 1891 to relieve the Supreme Court of the necessity of considering all appeals in federal cases. Decisions of the court are final except when subject to discretionary review or appeal to the Supreme Court.

For appellate purposes the United States is divided into eleven judicial circuits. The Ninth Circuit's jurisdiction includes the states of California, Arizona, Nevada, Oregon, Washington, Idaho, Montana, Alaska, and Hawaii. Records held by the branch include case files, copies of briefs, and opinions of the court (1903-1955; 2,594 cu. ft.).

The archives branch has the records of the United States Mint and Assay Office at San Francisco (RG 104). The gold rush prompted the California legislature to petition Congress to establish a mint in San Francisco; Congress complied by passing the necessary legislation in 1852. The first gold dust was received on April 3, 1854. Over the years the facility was responsible for the assaying, smelting, and refining of precious metals, and for coinage for the United States as well as for many foreign governments.

Mint records include correspondence of the Superintendent (1853-1938; 106 cu. ft.); records of assays (1854-1936; 40 cu. ft.); records of bars, coins, and coinage (1854-1960; 102 cu. ft.); records relating to gold and silver deposits and purchases (1854-1963; 65 cu. ft.); records relating to smelting and refining (1870-1934; 3 vols.); records relating to weighings (1854-1931; 15 cu. ft.);

fiscal and accounting records (1854-1935; 73 vols.); and records relating to the locality of producing mines (1878-1940; 14 vols.).

The gold rush and its aftermath brought new settlers to California, settlers anxious to acquire land upon which to establish homes. Documents relating to acquisitions and other land transactions are in the California records of the Bureau of Land Management (RG 49) and its predecessor offices. The bureau, an office of the Department of the Interior, is responsible for classification, management, and disposition of public lands. It also administers federally owned mineral resources on nonfederal lands. The bureau was established in 1946 by consolidating the General Land Office and the Grazing Service.

The land records include materials from the Office of the Surveyor General of California such as correspondence (1906-1921; 106 vols.); press copies of instructions to United States Surveyors (1912-1918; 3 vols.); records relating to mineral surveys (1873-1921; 7 vols.); and field notes of national forest area surveys (1904-1906; 1 cu. ft.).

Records of the California District Office of the Field Surveying Service include a register of appointments of mineral surveyors (1906-1950; 1 vol.); an index to mineral claim surveys (1916-1957; 1 vol.); and national forest homestead entry case files (1908-1928; 1 cu. ft.).

There are records of district land offices at Humboldt (1858-1899)/Eureka (1899-1925); Independence (1873-1878)/Bodie (1878-1887)/Independence (1887-1925); Marysville (1855-1905); Shasta (1870-1890)/Redding (1890-1913); Sacramento (1867-1976); Benicia (1853-1857)/San Francisco (1857-1906)/Oakland (1906-1911)/San Francisco (1911-1927); Stockton (1858-1906); Susanville (1871-1925); and Visalia (1858-1927). Materials from these offices include applications for mineral lands, registers of mineral entries, township tract books and survey plats, and records of patents delivered.

California was inhabited by Native Americans long before these land claims were made, long before even the Spanish and Mexican settlers arrived. The archives branch has a wealth of information concerning California's indigenous population of the late nineteenth and twentieth centuries included in the records of the Bureau of Indian Affairs (RG 75).

Documents relating to the administration of Indian affairs on a statewide basis are contained in the records of the Sacramento Area Office and its predecessor, the California Agency. The Area Office was responsible for the administration of all Bureau of Indian Affairs programs within California except for the Sherman Institute (Indian High School) at Riverside, the Fort Yuma Reservation, and the California portions of the Fort Mohave, Chemehuevi, and Colorado River reservations. Established in 1950, its records include those of earlier agencies, subagencies, and schools dating from 1900.

The coded subject records of the Area Office (1900-1956; 70 cu. ft.) include a large portion of documents from the Sacramento Agency, its predecessors, and subagencies at Greenville, Round Valley, Fort Bidwell, Tule River, Hoopa Valley, Mission, and Carson. Other records of the Area Office include case records of land transactions (1909-1956; 55 cu. ft.); irrigation project case records (1909-1958; 6 cu. ft.); records of roads projects (1933-1950; 2 cu. ft.); tribal roll cards (1955; 23 cu. ft.); and administrative subject files (1850-1923; 4 cu. ft.).

The archives branch has records from several Indian agency offices. Records of the Round Valley Agency include correspondence of the superintendent (1863-1914; 50 vols.); agency narrative and statistical reports (1872-1913; 3 cu. ft.); court records (1874-1886; 1 vol.); records relating to land transactions (1859-1922; 1 cu. ft.); tribal census records (1896-1923; 2 cu. ft.); birth and death registers and certificates (1901-1924; 3 vols.); and records of the Fort Bidwell Hospital (1906-1940; 1 cu. ft.).

Records of the Digger Agency include tribal census rolls (1911-1920; 1 in.) and school censuses of children on the Digger and Tuolumne reservations (1915-1917; 1 in.).

Fort Bidwell School and Agency records include administrative files (1898-1937; 5 cu. ft.); tribal censuses (1910-1929; 3 in.); records of the Fort Bidwell Hospital (1906-1938; 1 cu. ft.); and day school reports (1909-1918; 2 in.).

Records of the Greenville School and Agency include correspondence (1894-1923; 41 vols.); administrative files (1895-1923; 11 cu. ft.); annual narrative and statistical reports (1912-1919; 1 cu. ft.); and various school records.

Hoopa Valley Agency records include correspondence (1900-1945; 16 vols.); administrative files (1896-1947; 26 cu. ft.); tribal census rolls (1902-1941; 6 cu. ft.); records relating to land allotments (1899-1926; 3 cu. ft.); and records relating to schools (1907-1943; 6 cu. ft.).

Sacramento Agency records include a register of land allotments (1906-1928; 1 vol.); Central Valley project records concerning construction of Shasta Dam (1930-1934; 2 vols.); records of the Indian Emergency Conservation Work Program and the Civilian Conservation Corps–Indian Division (1933-1943; 7 cu. ft.); and correspondence of the educational field agent (1930-1938; 1 cu. ft.).

In 1916 an "Outing Center" was established in Berkeley to place Indian girls and women in domestic employment positions within the Bay Area residences. The archives branch has correspondence and employment records of the outing matron and placement officer (1916-1933; 4 in.). The records consist of "outing" and other employment contracts, service history records, and applications.

In the late nineteenth century, as immigration continued to bring new arrivals to California's shore, advances in medical science and our understanding of disease control led to the federal government's implementation of quarantine procedures requiring inspection of vessels possibly exposed to diseases in foreign ports. The archives branch has the records of the Bureau of Public Health Quarantine Station on Angel Island (RG 90, 22 cu. ft.). The station was established in 1892 and remained in operation until 1948. Correspondence (1890-1926; 10 cu. ft.) concerns planning and construction of the facility, finance, disease control, reports of quarantines and quarantine procedures, fumigation, and all other phases of the station's operations. General administrative files (1918-1948;

10 cu. ft.) concern station finances, relations with the military, alien inspection, hospital matters, fumigation, and disinfection.

The archives branch has many records relating to the 1906 San Francisco earthquake and fire. The documents tell of federal efforts to assist citizens and to re-establish or repair offices in order to continue with the mechanics of government. Some of the most significant documents concerning the earthquake and its aftermath are included in the records of Letterman Army Hospital, 1898–1913 (RG 112, 408 cu. ft.), located on the Presidio in San Francisco.

The largest series of Letterman Hospital records are the medical case files of patients (1898–1913; 385 cu. ft.). Other records include a name index to civilians hospitalized as a result of earthquake related injuries (April 1906; 1 vol.) and medical reports and related correspondence pertaining to the refugee camps established in Golden Gate Park and elsewhere following the earthquake (April 1906; 1 cu. ft.).

Additional hospital records include numerous correspondence series, a register of physical examinations of recruits (1898–1908; 1 vol.); muster rolls of patients (1898–1908; 4 cu. ft.); and registers of deaths and burials of patients (1898–1910; 19 vols.).

The branch has California records from many of the federal agencies established to battle the economic depression of the 1930s, including records concerned with California operations of the Farm Security Administration (RG 96, 28 cu. ft.). The Farm Security Administration, successor agency to the Resettlement Administration, was established in 1935 to provide loans and grants for rural rehabilitation and relief to needy farmers, farm tenants, and sharecroppers; to establish resettlement projects for low-income families; and to set up soil erosion, reforestation, flood control, and other projects.

The FSA also operated rural labor camps, furnishing shelter, medical care, sanitation facilities, and community services to domestic and foreign migrant farm laborers. The branch has records of seventeen of these migrant labor camps (1933–1945; 17 cu. ft.), including Camp Arvin in Kern County which was a model for the camps which John Steinbeck described in *The Grapes of Wrath* (1939).

The records of the Corps of Engineers, United States Army (RG 77, 200 cu. ft.) are a valuable source for studying the Corps' activities in California. The Corps' military responsibilities have included constructing and repairing fortifications and other installations. Civil duties have included maintaining and improving inland waterways and harbors, formulating and executing plans for flood control, operating dams and locks, and approving plans for the construction of bridges, wharves, piers, and other works over navigable waters.

Records of the San Francisco District Office include fortification files (1884–1944; 8 cu. ft.); photographs relating to harbor projects (1913–1938; 2 cu. ft.); a journal of operations pertaining to fortifications on Alcatraz Island (1853–1877; 2 vols.); and a journal of operations pertaining to the fort at Lime Point (1867–1876; 1 vol.). Records of the subordinate office at Fort Point include correspondence (1858-1902; 1 cu. ft.); daily reports of operations (1854-1864; 4 vols.); and a register of materials received (1858-1863; 1 vol.). There are also letters and reports of operations (1902-1907; 2 vols.) of the subordinate office at Fort Winfield Scott.

Records of the Sacramento District Office and the California Debris Commission include administrative files (1906-1943; 156 cu. ft.). These records concern such subjects as gold dredging, flood and debris control, land surveys, and fire reports.

The branch also has records documenting the activities of the United States Navy in California included in records of Naval Districts and Shore Establishments (RG 181, 5,000 cu. ft.). This group includes the Twelfth Naval District, headquartered at San Francisco, and Mare Island Naval Yard. Mare Island records (482 cu. ft.) include correspondence (1854-1940), issuances (1858-1883), records relating to personnel (1882-1910), and records relating to fiscal matters (1859-1869).

Twelfth Naval District records (1925-1959; approx. 1,500 cu. ft.) consist of documents accumulated by the commandant's office and filed according to the Navy Filing Manual, a subject-numeric filing system. The Twelfth District served an area consisting of northern California, Nevada except Clark County, Colorado, and Utah, but most of its activities were concentrated in California. The records contain a great deal of information concerning naval operations during World War II.

The records discussed in this chapter are the larger holdings of the National Archives—San Francisco Branch which relate to California. However, many of the smaller groups of records held also contain valuable information.

The 1917-1919 records of the California State Food Administration (RG 4) document an interesting attempt by the government to maintain control over the supply, distribution, and conservation of food chiefly by means of voluntary agreements and a licensing system. Records of the San Francisco Office of the National Recovery Administration (RG 9) highlight efforts to rehabilitate industry and trade, expand employment, and improve labor conditions during the Great Depression.

Records of another depression era agency, the Works Projects Administration (RG 69), include survey sheets of records in federal agencies in California compiled between 1936 and 1938 by the Survey of Federal Archives. Interfiled with the survey sheets are notes and drafts on agency histories, with emphasis on their creation and activities in California.

Records of the Bureau of Agricultural Economics (RG 83) include studies of the impact of World War II Japanese-American relocation and internment upon California agriculture. The records of the General Services Administration (RG 269) contain 1958-1963 correspondence and reports directed at identifying government property connected with Howard Hughes' "Spruce Goose," built under contract with the Defense Plant Corporation.

A wide range of federal records are available at the archives branch for the study of California history. The federal government has played an active role in the state, resulting in the creation of numerous government offices. The National Archives—San Francisco Branch has records of many of the statewide federal agencies and is the primary source for conducting research in the records of federal offices located in northern and central California.

12

CALIFORNIA STATE ARCHIVES

DAVID L. SNYDER

Street address:	1020 "O" Street, Room 130
	Sacramento, CA 95814
Mailing address:	Same
Telephone:	(916) 445–4293
Days and hours:	Monday–Friday, 8:00 A.M. to 5:00 P.M.

CALIFORNIA IS SOMEWHAT unique in that the first legislative act signed into law by the first legislative session of 1850 provided for public archives within the Office of the Secretary of State. The California State Archives' current holdings occupy 55,000 cu. ft. of space, in which is found 51,057 ft. of records in various formats, both hard copy and microform.

Supreme Court RG (1850–1972; 6,352 cu. ft.); Appellate Court RG (1905–1980; 13,224 cu. ft.). No other record groups in the State Archives provide such a commentary on life and conditions in California over the whole span of the state's history since 1850. The court case files, including lower court transcripts on appeal, trial court and clerk's transcripts, legal briefs and opinions, document the evolution of California's legal history and much more. Name indexes, both by plaintiff and by defendant, exist for Supreme and Appellate courts and cover most case files up through the mid-1930s. Little or no subject indexing is available. A detailed finding aid, *Records of the Supreme Court of California*, California State Archives Inventory No. 1 (1970), describes all series comprising this record group. In all other cases shelf lists, by court case numbers, control access.

Legislative Papers RG (1849–date; 6,610 cu. ft.). The records of the California Senate and Assembly document the legislative process and the workings of the individual houses. The largest subgroups include the Legislative Bill File

(1849–date; 1,600 cu. ft.), all measures as introduced, amended, and chaptered; original laws (1850–date, 134 cu. ft.); and Senate and Assembly Journals (1849–date; 1,078 cu. ft.). More significant to current research are the papers of individual Senators, Assemblymen and women, and legislative committee files (ca. 1960–date; 1,750 cut. ft.).

The most actively used archival records are legislative and Governor's Office resources relating to "legislative intent." Author's Bill Files include: analyses; proposed and adopted amendments; communications, testimony, and position statements in support or opposition; legal opinions; author's floor and committee statements; press releases and other background information germane to a measure. Committee Bill Hearing Files contain similar information as found within Author's Bill Files, with sometimes more information on individuals and organizations appearing before the committee to testify, and roll calls of votes cast. Such sources are extremely important in dealing with legislative intent and the legislative process because committee proceedings and floor debates are not recorded or published verbatim as is the case at the federal level.

Legislators' papers and committee files include other records series pertinent to operations of the legislature. A legislator's papers normally include subject/correspondence files covering such diverse matters as constituent requests and problems resulting in the creation of case files; issue files relating to important matters before the legislature; district affairs and problems sometimes serving as the background for legislation; press and publicity files including invitations to attend various meetings, functions, etc., and/or deliver speeches; election and reelection campaign files, sometimes including political party documentation and committee activity files which sometimes duplicate information as found in committee files.

Committee files, other than those associated with the bill hearing process, are generally subject-oriented hearings held between legislative sessions or during adjourned breaks. Subject matter varies from current legislation referred to committee for interim hearings and recommendations to matters assigned by house officers, resolution or other legislative mandate. Unlike regular session hearings, most interim hearings produce a hearing transcript or, as in more recent sessions, audio tapes which provide a verbatim record of proceedings. The committee working files also include agendas, complete texts of testimony, statements, and other presentations made before committee, publicity releases, and staff background papers, reports, and other information. Full texts of testimony and statements are important because not all are included as presented in the hearing transcripts.

Committee and legislator's papers are individually catalogued. In-house inventories exist for some individual legislators' papers where the collections are relatively complete. Restrictions exist on the use of some individuals' papers and researchers are advised to contact the Archives in advance to determine if any restrictions exist. Hearing transcripts and committee working files (1935–1970) are described in *Records of the California Legislature*, California State Archives Inventory No. 2 (1971).

Governor's Office RG (1849–date; 3,555 cu. ft.). Governor's Office records document the day-to-day transactions of that office and reflect, to a considerable degree, the overall operations of state government. Governor's Office administrative papers, the correspondence, memoranda, and other records that flow between the office and other branches of state, federal, and local government, as well as to and from the general public, are not on deposit in the State Archives because the California Public Records Act makes no provision for their disposition. Despite the haphazard disposition practices of the past, a considerable body of Governor's Office records do exist. Many of these records constitute separate series reflecting specific functions, programs, and operations. Examples include: "Registers of Official Transactions" (1852-1903; 19 vols.); "Letterbooks" (1851-1887; 13 vols.); Petitions to the Governor (1850-1909; 1 cu. ft.); Proclamations (1849–date; 5 cu. ft.); and Offers of Rewards (1850–date; 2 cu. ft.).

Records concerning the governor's power to grant pardons, reprieves, and commutations of sentence after conviction constitute a sizeable Prison Papers subgroup (1850–date; 1,500 cu. ft.). In the operations of these powers, and in those functions pertaining to the extraditions of prisoners to and from California (1856–date), the Governor's office has created a mass of data pertaining to crimes and punishment as well as biographic data on thousands of individuals. Applications for Pardon, Historical Case Files (1850–c.1935); Executive Clemency Case Files (ca.1930–date); and Extreme Penalty Case Files (ca.1948–date) make up the largest series. All three series are similar in types of documentation. The Extreme Penalty series differs only in that the applicants are all subject to the death penalty. Any of these records less than twenty-five years old from date of activity are closed to public use and access must be cleared through the Governor's Office, Legal Affairs Secretary.

Major collections of papers of two of California's governors, Earl Warren (1943-1953; 550 cu. ft.) and Goodwin J. Knight (1953-1959; 186 cu. ft.) are deposited in the California State Archives. The three principal subgroups of Warren's and Knight's papers include Administrative, Federal, and Legislative files. Warren's papers additionally include records series created as Alameda County District Attorney (1924-1938); State Attorney General (1939-1943); Political and Campaign Files (1932-1950); and Personal and Family Affairs (1927-1953). They are described in *The Earl Warren Papers: 1924-1953*, California State Archives Inventory No. 5 (1976).

Governor's Chaptered Bill Files (GCBF), a part of the Governor's Legislative Files, have been regularly deposited in the State Archives since Warren's administration. The current holdings (1943-1982; 504 cu. ft.) are important, along with legislative committee and legislators' papers described above, for the information they include on legislative intent, on the arguments for and against a measure, and on the issues and interests involved respecting the bill's enactment into law. A separate file exists for each measure signed into law and for each measure vetoed. The file jacket in part serves as a checklist of agencies, organizations, and individuals to whom inquiries were directed for views and comments. The index to the published Final Calendars/Histories for each session serves as a subject guide to the Chaptered Bill Files.

Secretary of State RG (1849–date; 6,414 cu. ft.). The Secretary of State is California's chief elections officer. The records of the Elections and Political Reform divisions (1849–date; 1,216 cu. ft.) include several series having high research value. Election returns, county abstracts of votes cast down to the precinct level, reflect voting patterns which may or may not be representative of national trends and moods. Vote analyses can be augmented by the use of Precinct Maps (1972–date). Election returns also serve as an index to population growth and shifts, and for some periods serve as a register of contemporary place names. Other prominent series include candidate and committee Campaign Statements of Receipts and Expenditures (1894–date); Reports of Voter Registration (1912–date); Nomination Papers (1894–date); Ballot Measures and Arguments (1911–date), including the exercise of the initiative and referendum process; Statements of Votes (1849–date); State Party Central Committee Records of Appointments; and a sampling of nineteenth- and twentieth-century ballots. Elections papers are described in *Records of the Elections Division, California Secretary of State*, California State Archives Inventory No. 3 (1972).

Incorporation Records (1850–1959; 2,124 cu. ft.) cover a vast cross-section of California economic, business, cultural, and social history. To date (1959–date; filings are available on microform through the Corporate Division) over one million articles of incorporation, amendments—including change of name or place of business, increase or limitation of capital stock, and applications for and decrees of dissolution—have been filed. Corporate records are arranged alphabetically by corporate name, and a master index of active and inactive corporations is maintained by the Corporate Division in the Secretary of State's main office.

Trademark filings (1861–date; 436 cu. ft.) is another subgroup which reflects a part of California business and economic history. Applications usually include the name(s) of applicant(s), company name, business address, identification of product, a detailed description of the trademark, and a facsimile of the specimen of trademark. Trademark specimens are frequently lithographs, often done with great skill and in multiple colors, and represent an art form. Also included within this subgroup are Container Brands (1862–date), Farm and Ranch Names (1911–date), Fraternal Names and Insignia (1933–date), Linen Marks (1937–date), and Service Marks (1968–date). All series include active and inactive filings and are controlled by a master index by name of applicant and trademark or other category as maintained by a Trademark Examiner in the Secretary of State's main office.

As the principal recipient of filed or deposited documents, the Office of the Secretary of State receives a variety of filings. A sampling of these includes:

scrapbooks and administrative papers of Frank C. (1911-1940) and Frank M. Jordan (1942-1970), father and son Secretaries of State; Secretary of State letterbooks (1850-1860, 1855-1910); registers of motor vehicles, dealers in motor vehicles, and chauffeurs-drivers (1905-1913); the original Constitutions and Constitutional Convention working papers of 1849 and 1878-1879; Administrative Rules and Regulations of state agencies (1941-date); Register of Governor's Appointments (1850-date); records of the California Heritage Preservation Commission (1963-date); original manuscript enumerations of the 1852 State Census and 1860 and 1880 U.S. Census; special censuses of cities and towns (1897-1938); County, City, and Town Annexation and Reorganization Documents (1883-date); and records relating to Spanish-Mexican Land Grants (1784-1846; 19 vols.). The Land Grant papers are unique because, as official state copies created in the 1860s, they are receivable as prima facie evidence with like force as the originals. All are indexed by name of grant and grantee and exist in both Spanish and English. A complete description is in *Records of the Secretary of State*, California State Archives Inventory No. 6 (1978).

Administrative agencies and departments make up the greatest part of the Executive Branch of California government. The following entries are illustrative of agency records containing substantive and significant subject matter. The absence of reference to specific agencies is because the records have not been accessioned or processed and described. In-house inventories and finding aids exist for many agencies and record groups. In all cases, researchers are advised to contact the California State Archives in advance to determine the status of a given agency's records.

Agriculture Department RG (1919-1973; 263 cu. ft.). Agriculture has been a primary California industry since the gold rush, and government became involved fairly early, evolving from a number of commissions and boards, with a department established in 1919. It is unfortunate that few pre-1919 records have survived. Subjects covered include such matters as: labor problems—World War II loss of Japanese-American labor force, Bracero program, labor boycotts, farm labor housing, and illegal workers; insect and pest control—development of agricultural inspection stations, Oriental and Mediterranean fruit flies, Japanese beetle, and other pests; regulation of the use and disposal of pesticides and agricultural chemicals such as DDT; operations of the Milk Stabilization Act of 1935; marketing and labelling of agricultural products; impact of urban sprawl; cooperative research efforts with the USDA, other federal agencies, and the University of California; wetlands development; drought; and agricultural water policy. Closely related are the Records of the State Agricultural Society (1868-1953) and the California State Fair and Exposition (1953-1968; 16 cu. ft.).

Records of the Board of State Capitol Commissions (1856-1911; 5 cu. ft.) and Capitol Restoration Project (1975-1982; 63 cu. ft.). These document efforts in Sacramento to secure a site for and the construction of a suitable capitol building, along with the acquisition and development of the land which now makes up Capitol Park. These records have proven their importance by being used as part of the Capitol Resotration Project. Basic to these records is a master project report of all work accomplished and a master set of architectural drawings on polyester film. See also *Records of the Board of State Capitol Commissioners, 1856–1911*, California State Archives Inventory No. 7 (1979).

Constitutional Revision Commission RG (1964–1974; 20 cu. ft.). Revision of the California Constitution has been carried out on several occasions. The latest major attempts at revision, the techniques and procedures, and the use of a large number of people from the public sector in studying, drafting proposals, conducting hearings, and making recommendations to the legislature and eventually to the electorate, are represented here. Changes initiated as a result of the commission's activities continue to have impact on current endeavors for constitutional revision.

Department of Corrections RG (1850–1980; 384 cu. ft.). The history of penology in California is in large part the stories of San Quentin and Folsom State prisons. The heart of this RG are the inmate case files for San Quentin (1890–1958; 57 cu. ft.) and Folsom (1881–1942; 37 cu. ft.). The inmate case files are complemented by mug books, warden's correspondence, daily log books, and records of the Board of Prison Terms and Paroles and Adult Authority dealing with the sentencing and parole of inmates. The records of the Department of Corrections, formed in 1944, trace the more modern development and operations of correctional facilities.

Education Department/State Board of Education RG (1861–date; 737 cu. ft.). The Common School Reports (1861–1958), one of the most significant series, covers the historical operations of individual schools or school districts. Initially these were County Superintendents of Schools' Annual Reports to the State Superintendent and included statistical data on school-aged children, attendance, length of school years, tax base and support, size and value of school library, names of teachers and salaries paid, names of district officers, and space for narrative observations on local conditions. Complementing the reports are selected records of local school districts, about 100 different districts currently represented, which provide additional detail on the educational processes and operations at the local level, encompassing records of local school boards down to and including daily activities in the classroom.

Fish and Game Department/Commission RG (1885–1972; 42 cu. ft.). Although the commission was established in 1870, few records concerning fish and wildlife management exist prior to 1900. Major subject areas covered in this RG include hatchery operations for restocking fresh and saltwater species; cooperation with state and federal agencies in wildlife enhancement programs; Pittman-Robertson wildlife projects; conservation and environmental concerns and education; competition between commercial and sportfishing; Russian and Japanese commercial fishing in California waters; off-shore oil drilling; nuclear power plant pollution and radioactive waste disposal; and pollution monitoring and enforcement activities dating back to 1920.

Forestry Department Board RG (1885-1975; 75 cu. ft.). The mission of the Department of Forestry (CDF) is the protection and management of 38 million acres of state, private, and intermingled federal lands and includes timber protection, recreation, range lands, and watershed values. A significant historical research collection concerns the CDF state labor camp program. Started in 1931 to assist the depression unemployed, the program was later federally funded and became known under the popular names of SERA (State Emergency Relief Administration) and CCC (Civilian Conservation Corps) camps. The California camp records include considerable detail on camp plans and specifications, construction costs, camp operation and activity reports, photographs of camp conditions as evidenced in camp newspapers, and transcripts of oral history interviews of participants and CDF employees (1968). Other subject areas include forest management—regulation of timber harvesting and the Forest Practices Act (1945); reforestation; operations of state nurseries and state forests; pest control; law enforcement; range and watershed management and soil conservation; research and cooperation with federal and state agencies and the University of California; and timber taxation.

Board of State Harbor Commissioners RG (1863-1950; 104 cu. ft.). The origins and early development of the Port of San Francisco were haphazard and under private ownership until 1863. The largest series of this collection is made up of wharf and pier books recording ship arrivals and departures and cargoes carried with the greatest traffic documented in the period between 1875 and 1914. Other series include the President's and Secretary's correspondence files and engineering records on port development and maintenance, and operational records relating to the Belt Line Railroad. Small and related collections on the Port of Eureka (1887-1938; 18 vols.) and the Board of Pilot Commissioners for the bays of San Francisco, San Pablo, and Suisun (1907-1936 and 1960-1979; 3 cu. ft.) are also deposited in the California State Archives.

Law Revision Commission RG (1954-1978; 27 cu. ft.). The primary function of the Law Revision Commission is the examination of common law statutes and judicial decisions in order to discover defects and anachronisms in the law and to recommend needed reforms. The study files and hearings frequently document legislative intent and reflect the input and impact of such organizations as the American Law Institute, National Conference of Commissioners of Uniform State Laws, bar associations, judges, lawyers, law enforcement organizations, public officials, and the general public.

Department of Mental Hygiene—State Hospitals RG (1885-1972; 137 cu. ft.). This collection, to be enlarged as additional records become available, consists of the records of four state hospitals: DeWitt (1947-1972), Mendocino (1889-1972), Modesto (1947-1972), and Sonoma (1885-1952), and includes sizeable series of patient files statistically sampled for DeWitt, Mendocino, and Modesto. Hospital administration and operations are included in the records of Mendocino and Sonoma. Patient files are retained because of the information disclosed on the care and treatment or rehabilitation of the mentally ill or deficient, alcoholic, drug addicted, and criminally insane. Restrictions on use do apply to these records. Researchers are requested to make written applications in advance of a proposed visit to the State Archives.

Military Department RG (1849-1941; 398 cu. ft.). The records of the California Militia and State Guard constitute one of the most active record groups in the State Archives. Although the collection is not fully catalogued, one of the most active series comprises the records of militia units and companies formed between 1849 and 1865. A majority of these were organized during the Civil War, eventually totaling 126 companies and more than 14,000 men. Company records include muster rolls and record duty stations and military posts occupied. Another series of high research activity are papers relating to the Indian wars (1850-1880; 2.5 cu. ft.), principally between the years of 1850 and 1862. This series documents the formation and muster of the citizen militia, usually different from the units referred to above, to suppress or eliminate the "Indian menace" and to pacify the frontiers. Of particular importance are the large number of letters and field reports which present first hand observations and commentary by individuals involved. A detailed calendar of the Indian War Papers describing 1,035 documents is available.

Natural Resources Department RG (1902-1961; 45 cu. ft.). This department consisted of the divisions of Fish and Game, and Forestry (described above), Mines (and Geology), Beaches and Parks, Oil and Gas (1929-1961), and Soil Conservation (1941-1961). Research value is best represented in records relating to: Emergency Conservation Work accomplished by CCC labor, WPA, and SERA Projects; development of conservation education programs (1947-1953); beach and park development, including a statewide system of riding and hiking trails; activities of Save-the-Redwoods League; creation of the first state park, California Redwood Park (1902-1905); construction and restoration project files for historic places; and the California Historic Landmarks Projects (1936-1940), the basis for the current program of registered state historical landmarks and sites.

Public Utilities (Railroad) Commission (PUC) RG (1861-1976; 676 cu. ft.). Economic and social history are significantly represented in the records of the PUC. In this RG, facility and operational information is found on steam and electric railroads, electric and gas companies, telephone and telegraph companies, water carriers, water companies, and warehouse companies. The two largest series consist of selected Formal Applications and Formal Complaints covering the period 1908-1955 and include transcripts, reports, statistical data, engineers' valuations, exhibits, and other records providing in-depth information on various aspects of company operations. Another major series contains annual reports of regulated utilities including those of railroads dating back to 1861. Series 21 of the inventory *Records of the Public Utilities Commission*, Part I, California State Archives Inventory No. 8 (1979), deserves special attention. (Part II is in preparation.) In 1912 the Commission required all operational railroads to file a complete set of maps showing their lines and facilities. Ninety-five companies filed over 5,000 hand-drawn maps and blueprints containing a wealth of information on rights-of-way, station plats, depots, yards, other owned facilities along the lines, and geographic features. The map collection came with a card index listing maps by railroad and/or geographical location with distinct divisions for (1) alignments, (2) profiles, and (3) station plans. The card index is further separated between the facilities of the Southern Pacific Company and all other operating railroads.

Highway Division, Department of Public Works RG (1895-1972; 430 cu. ft.). No state is as dependent on highway transportation as California. This is reflected in a large volume of records covering the planning, construction, and maintenance of California highways. Of special interest are field survey notebooks and road survey files, some dating back to the turn of the century. Information recorded covers subjects such as soil and vegetation, existing buildings or structures, landmarks, topography, and construction needs. In addition, highway construction projects are documented by the use of photographs. No agency of California has exposed more film over the past seventy-five years than Highways. Virtually every aspect of highway work, from the purchase of the right-of-way to bank protection and traffic stripes, is covered. From such photographs, and from a larger photo collection maintained by the Department of Transportation (see *Guide to the Caltrans "Transportation Library History Center"* [1985]), most aspects of California highways are documented. Other subjects include flood and natural disaster relief, use of convict labor in highway construction (1915-1955), and highway beautification. A separate subgroup, Bridge Construction Project Files (1918-1974), covers the evolution of bridge design and function for the greater part of the twentieth century. Photographs again represent important documentation because they depict bridges replaced, in some cases dating back before 1900, and other structures in existence at the time of the project. Another collection documents the construction of the San Francisco-Oakland Bay Bridge from inception through opening (1933-1936). A major part of the collection is several thousand photos taken on a daily basis and on every construction phase.

Reclamation Board RG (1859-1965; 42 cu. ft.). This record group primarily covers the period 1913-1964 and, to a lesser extent, predecessor agency records concerning the use, management, and disposal by sale of tide and submerged lands. The Reclamation Board's principal concern was flood control planning in the central valley, which included the Sacramento and San Joaquin River watersheds, the preservation and protection of navigation, and the reclamation and protection of lands susceptible to overflow.

Reconstruction and Reemployment Commission RG (1934-1949; 12 cu. ft.). The commission was created in 1943, and its predecessor agency was a planning body to prevent postwar reconversion problems similar to those experienced at the end of World War I and to assist local community planning and development. Of special interest is the extensive use of citizens' advisory committees in the role of decision and policymakers.

Recreation Commission RG (1947-1961; 16 cu. ft.). The primary responsibilities of the commission were to devise ways to use state resources to meet the needs of people's expanding leisure time, improve the coordination in existing services of federal, state, and local agencies, and aid in the development of recreational facilities and programs. Included are numerous recreational studies and surveys of needs as done by various municipalities, park and recreation, school, and other special districts.

Social Welfare-War Services Bureau (1941-1948; 5 cu. ft.). This wartime agency was set up at the request of the Federal Security Agency to administer three programs, Civilian War Assistance, Enemy Alien Assistance, and Japanese Evacuation. The first two programs provided temporary aid necessitated by enemy action to civilians who were disabled, dependents of civilians killed, disabled, interned, or reported as missing. Japanese evacuation and relocation was the most difficult program to handle. Record Series 87 documents the operations at eighty control stations in the evacuation of Japanese Americans. Reports covering these operations include a good deal of commentary on such problems as mixed marriages, the separation of families caused by illness of a family member, orphaned children, community attitudes, and the resultant confusion and misunderstandings which often accompany hastily conceived programs.

State Relief Administration (SRA) RG (1933-1942; 6 cu. ft.). The SRA was created to meet depression conditions. Relief activities were inextricably bound up with federal agencies and local activities. Relief operations documented include: Interstate immigration as it affected the SRA; agricultural migratory labor in the San Joaquin Valley; re-employment; surplus commodity distribution; and transient CCC and WPA work camps and programs.

Youth Authority RG (1889-1975; 54 cu. ft.). This RG is similar to that of the Department of Corrections. The principal series relates to the operations of Preston School of Industry, Ione, and the Fred C. Nelles School for Boys, Whittier. The most valuable series for either institution are the inmate histories which detail the individual's life inside the institution from date of reception to release. These files also contain a great deal of biographical information. The files for Whittier (1892-1948; 59 vols.) are more complete than those of Preston (1909-1914, 1924-1926, 1931-1948; 3 vols., 15 ft.). Admission registers maintained by the Governor's Office, described above, fill in portions of missing information. It is interesting to note that girls were detained at Whittier until 1919, when the Ventura School for Girls was opened.

Audio-Visual Materials (ca.1870-date; 175,000-200,000 items). Audiovisual materials of all physical types are maintained separately from state agency records for preservation purposes although they are identified and described by agency of origin. Audio records consist principally of untranscribed cassette and reel-to-reel tapes of hearings and other agency activities. Photographic prints and negatives, including a sizeable volume of aerial photographs, make up the largest part of this collection. The bulk of photographic materials was generated or collected by various agencies during the normal conduct of state business, and date from 1910 to the 1960s. Specific detail on major agency collections is provided above.

Numerous other administrative agency collections are also deposited in the California State Archives. The following list is provided to indicate those collections and record groups for which some form of inventory exists: Alcoholic Beverage Control/Alcoholic Beverage Control Appeals Board (1941-1973; 15 cu. ft.); American Revolution Bicentennial Commission (1968-1977; 12 cu. ft.); California Arts Commission (1964-1975; 9 cu. ft.); Business and Transportation Agency (1967-1972; 16 cu. ft.); Cosmetology Board (1927-1960; 5 cu. ft.); California Council on Criminal Justice (1968-1974; 4 cu. ft.); Districts Securities Commission (1922-1977; 36 cu. ft.); Office of Economic Opportunity (1964-1971; 7 cu. ft.); Education-California State Historical Association (1916-1947; 4 cu. ft.); Employment-Social Workers Placement Service (1941-1953; 2 cu. ft.); Employment Stabilization Commission (1935-1946; 15 cu. ft.); General Services-Building Standards Commission (1958-1971; 1.5 cu. ft.); Advisory Commission on Indian Affairs/California Indian Assistance Project (1964-1972; 5 cu. ft.); Industrial Relations Department (1911-1970; 14 cu. ft.); Investment Department (1907-1971; 5 cu. ft.); Lieutenant Governor's Office (1963-1974; 22 cu. ft.); Medical Examiners, Board of (1876-1978; 69 cu. ft.); Poultry Improvement Commission (1935-1969; 3 cu. ft.); Savings and Loan Department (1922-1971; 20 cu. ft.); and State War Council (1940-1945; 1 cu. ft.).

A final category is included to cover the unprocessed or marginally under control records which make up the remaining holdings of the California State Archives. Of these the largest part is a backlog of 5,900 cu. ft. of unprocessed records representing a wide spectrum of state programs and operations. Control over these materials is maintained by accession register worksheets indexed by agency of origin. In the area of marginally under control are included: local government records for the counties of Humboldt, Marin, Mendocino, Nevada, Sonoma, and Sutter (variously dated between 1850 and 1960; 675 cu. ft.); and "Selected Archives," various agency records processed prior to 1960 with minimal application of modern archival standards (1850-1950; 2,520 cu. ft.). Included in this latter grouping are records of the Department of Consumer Affairs (previously Professional and Vocational Standards), Board of Control, State Controller, Board of Equalization, Department of Justice, State Lands Commission, and State Treasurer, amounting to 1,414 cubic feet. Catalog control over the "Selected Archives" is by agency card index entries.

In conclusion, it is important to note two important facts. Many records of historical value remain in agency custody, although most are available for reference purposes as provided for under the California Public Records Act and the Information Practices Act. Not all records in the State Archives are described here, underscoring the necessity of making direct contact with this institution on research matters. Lastly, new accessions are constantly added. Those having significant or other historical values are announced quarterly in *California Originals*, newsletter of the California State Archives.

13

COUNTY RECORDS

KENNETH N. OWENS

RESEARCH IN COUNTY RECORDS can provide vital evidence for virtually any type of localized study that involves property or people, local government, or regional society. As beginning points, two publications are extremely helpful. H. G. Jones, *Local Government Records: An Introduction to Their Management, Preservation, and Use* (Nashville, 1980), explains the use of local archives for historians and other researchers.

Indispensable for California researchers is Laren W. Metzer, comp., *Identification of the Historical Records of County Government in California* (Sacramento, 1981), a manual that identifies the classes of county records with research importance. Because county government has historically been fairly uniform in California, these records are generally similar in title, information, use, arrangement, and even format from one county to another. There is no certainty, however, that a particular class of documents will have been preserved.

Metzer treats the records of fifteen different county offices and agencies, totalling 168 separate record series. He provides a short description of the functions served by each office or agency, then lists the records related to that particular entity, series by series. Along with the listing, Metzer supplies a "Research Note" for each series that suggests the most likely use the particular records will have for historical investigators. Adding to the publication's merit are appendices that summarize the history of county government organization, the county court system, and the statutes regulating the disposition of county records in California. Omitted from Metzer's listing are record series found only in a few counties, such as placer mining claims books in the Mother Lode counties or Sacramento County's Chinese poll tax rolls. A free copy of Metzer's guide can be obtained by request from the California State Archives at 1020 O Street, Sacramento, CA 95814.

Researchers, like archivists, must be concerned about more than the preservation of a county's historical records. They must be able to locate the records that have been preserved, gain access to them, and make use of them under reasonable working conditions. Deed books and similar property records—the one category of documents seldom if ever discarded—are usually available through the office of the county recorder, but few jurisdictions promote or actively accommodate the public's use of other types of records having historical importance.

County court records, bulky and organized in ways that may at first baffle historians, constitute a special problem. Ordinarily they remain the property of the court system, supervised nominally by the county judiciary, with access subject to conditions fixed by the sitting judges. In some instances, older court records have been transferred to the jurisdiction of county historical agencies or other local repositories, where access should be unrestricted. By chance, the historical court records of six northern counties—Humboldt, Marin, Mendocino, Nevada, Sonoma, and Sutter—have found a resting place in the stacks of the State Archives in Sacramento. Name indexes are available for Marin and Sonoma county court records. Opportunities for research in such records are pointed out in W. N. Davis, Jr., "Research Uses of County Court Records, 1850–1879," *CHQ*, 52 (Fall/Winter 1973).

For all the reasons mentioned above, it can become a challenging research problem in itself to determine what records are available in a specific county and where those records can be found. One publication may be cited as a detailed statewide finding aid for county records, but it is a finding aid now lamentably outdated: Owen C. Coy, comp., *Guide to the County Archives of California* (Sacramento, 1919). A county-by-county inventory undertaken between 1915 and 1917, it provides a capsule geographical and administrative sketch of each county, then catalogs the county's archives according to each county office. Usually the same records can still be located somewhere, although some have been destroyed and others have strayed or decayed in the interim. In addition, new classes of records have been added to each county's holdings since the survey.

Between 1939 and 1942, as a New Deal aid for local government, the federal Works Projects Administration sponsored a series of county records inventories to revise and update the Coy work. These WPA inventories are guidebooks that should be consulted by researchers in the counties where the effort was carried to completion. Like the Coy volume, they are ordinarily accurate and reliable. The California State Archives has identified WPA inventories for eleven individual counties: Alameda, Fresno, Kern, Los Angeles, Mono, Napa, San Benito, San Diego, San Francisco, San Luis Obispo, and Santa Clara. Perhaps others may be found in county libraries and local repositories. Typescript inventories for Marin, San Diego, and San Mateo counties are reported in *California Local History: A Centennial Bibliography* (Stanford, 1950), but after more than thirty years there is no assurance that these inventories, located in local libraries, are still available.

A handful of California counties have completed modern inventories of their archives for records management purposes. Nine are known: Alpine, Napa, Orange, Sacramento, San Bernadino, San Mateo, Santa Clara, Sonoma, and Yolo. Most remain unpublished, but records inventories have been published for three counties either as a related effort or as a separate project: Sonoma County Records Inventory Project, *Inventory of Records, 1834-1978, Office of the Recorder* (Rohnert Park, 1979), and *Inventory of Records, 1847-1980, Office of the Clerk* (Rohnert Park, 1982); John Caswell, comp., *Records and Archives Survey, Stanislaus County Government* (Turlock, 1977); and Ventura County Historical Records Commission, *Historical Records Manual of Ventura County: An Inventory of the County Agency and Department Records Having Historical Value* (Ventura, 1982). An unpublished inventory of Yolo County records has also gained circulation through the wonders of cheap photoduplication: Susan C. Hawthorne, comp., "Draft Report: Inventory of Yolo County Archives" (N.p., 1976; copies are in the California State Archives and the California Room of the California State Library). In addition, there exist published guides to select records in the holdings of Mendocino and Shasta counties: Jacqueline L. Lowe, comp., *Guide to Public School Records, Mendocino County California, 1861-1962* (Willits, 1983), and Shirley Rodgers Hart, Corinne Graves Hoffpauir, and Hazel McKim, comp., "Records in [the] Clerk's Archives, Shasta County" (Redding, 1984).

Where records have been moved from their office of origin, researchers may find record series divided between the county agency and one or more alternative repositories. In extreme cases, the dispersion of records defies any logical order. Fresno County records, for example, are scattered between the county library, the city and county historical society, the library of CSU, Fresno, and at least four separate county facilities. In Santa Clara County, the county's non-current documentary resources are spread among repositories that include the San Jose State University library, the San Jose Historical Museum, the county library, the Santa Clara County Heritage Commission, and a half dozen county offices. A recent guide is Charlene A. Gilbert, "Santa Clara County's Historical Museums and Societies and Their Archival Holdings of California History," *Passports* (CSU, San Jose), 8 (1984). Los Angeles County provides still another illustration of records dispersion taken to an extreme, with an estimated fifteen different county offices, located all across the Los Angeles basin, now having custody of some significant group of historical records. In addition, the county's Museum of Natural History provides a home for a large body of noncurrent tax records, while the Huntington Library has become the curator for an invaluable collection of county brand books that date from the Hispanic period.

Repositories that have acquired county records may have available their own finding aid—a preliminary inventory or a shelf list, for example—to help researchers locate the needed materials in their collections. At latest report, published guides have been prepared by only three agencies with county records included in their holdings. Two of these guides, describing the Sacramento local government records held by the Sacramento City-County Museum and History Division and the Butte County archives in the holdings of the Meriam Library on the campus of CSU, Chico, are devoted entirely to the public records in that repository: Susan E. Searcy, comp., *For the Record: Catalog of Public Records, City of Sacramento 1849-1982 [and] Sacramento County 1848-1982* (Sacramento, 1982) and Mary Ellen Bailey, comp., *Public Records of Butte County, California, Meriam Library, California State University, Chico* (3rd ed.; Chico, 1985). The third is a guide to manuscripts in the San Diego Center for Regional History, located on the campus of San Diego State University, which lists records from five county agencies among the general holdings in that repository: Stephen Colston, comp., *A Catalog of the Manuscript and Oral History Collections of the Center for Regional History* (San Diego, 1986). Included are records from the Office of the County Clerk, the Department of Agriculture, the Department of Transportation, and the Office of Public Information. The papers of the Metropolitan Water District, 1938-1977, are also located in the San Diego Center for Regional History. A larger collection of San Diego County records is held by the San Diego Historical Society.

Until a comprehensive modern inventory of California public records has been completed, researchers must proceed with but few other reference works for guidance. A useful reference is the volume entitled *Archival and Manuscript Repositories in California*, compiled by the staff of the California State Archives and published in 1984 by the Society of California Archivists. This guidebook, which updates and expands the 1975 SCA *Directory*, gives information on more than fifty institutions that report government records holdings, including eleven public libraries and twenty-four local museums and historical societies. These holdings, however, are not described in detail. Another well-known reference is Margaret M. Rocq, ed., *California Local History: A Bibliography and Union List of Library Holdings* (2nd ed.; Palo Alto, 1970) and the same editor's *Supplement to the Second Edition* (Palo Alto, 1976). County records are included among the items listed by Rocq where located in local libraries. Two additional reference sources may also provide a lead to local repositories that contain county records. The National Historical Publications and Records Commission, *Directory of Archives and Manuscript Repositories in the United States* (Washington, D.C., 1978) surveys the same type of repositories covered by the SCA guide, but includes some institutions that did not respond to the SCA's inquiry. The annual *Roster and By-Laws* put out by the Conference of California Historical Societies prints an extensive listing of local libraries, historical societies, museums, and related organizations that are part of the CCHS network. Although these guides are all incomplete for county records, they share the advantage of being organized by locality, thus enabling a researcher to check easily for possible repositories within any particular area.

At this point in the finding process, the staff of the California State Archives can often be helpful. Staff members have recently made a statewide assessment of the condition of local records and their access status, especially checking current county holdings against Coy's 1919 *Guide*. This quick, rough inventory has given the staff a good sense of the situation from county to county, and they are pleased to assist researchers in an advisory capacity. Because California lacks a modern survey of local government records, however, the State Archives staff can provide very little precise or detailed information, such as the location of individual records series in one county or another.

In some places, prospective researchers may find their inquiries actively discouraged. If an official objection or denial is made to a request for access to county records—a denial, that is, to a researcher's right to see the records, and not just a testy complaint because it is inconvenient to haul out the records on short notice—the researcher should be prepared to cite the California Public Records Act. This measure, which is the chief instrument for effecting the public disclosure of government records in California, is found in the California Government Code, sections 6250–6265. It declares that "access to information concerning the conduct of the people's business is a fundamental and necessary right of every person in this state." Public records, according to the act, include "any writing containing information relating to the conduct of the public's business prepared, owned, used, or retained by any state or local agency regardless of physical form or characteristics." Every citizen, the act declares, has a right to inspect any public record, with certain specified exemptions.

The matter of exemptions is critical, since state law seeks to balance the public's right to know with the individual's right to reasonable privacy. Hence, the exemption provisions of the Public Records Act are supplemented by the provisions of the 1977 Information Practices Act, found in Civil Code section 1798 *et seq.*, both of which relate directly to the researcher's right to examine all types of government records in California. Excluded from the open access rule are, among other categories, records that pertain to pending litigation to which the public agency is a party, and any personnel, medical, or similar files, "the disclosure of which would constitute an unwarranted invasion of personal privacy."

Under the Information Practices Act, even data that are clearly defined as "personal or confidential information" may be disclosed to researchers under certain carefully defined conditions. Information can be given "to a person who has provided the agency with advance adequate written assurance that the information will be used solely for statistical research or reporting purposes, but only if the information to be disclosed is in a form that will not identify any individual." The data may also be made available "to the University of California or a nonprofit educational institution conducting scientific research, provided the request for information includes assurances of the need for personal or confidential information, procedures for protecting the confidentiality of the information, and assurances that the personal identity of the subject shall not be further disclosed in individually identifiable form."

14

CALIFORNIA STATE LIBRARY

GARY F. KURUTZ

Street address:	California State Library
	California Section
	Library and Courts Bldg.
	914 Capitol Mall
	Sacramento, CA 94237-0001
Mailing address:	P.O. Box 942837
	Sacramento, CA 94237-0001
Telephone:	(916) 445-4149
Days and hours:	Monday–Friday, 8:00 A.M. to 5:00 P.M.

THE CALIFORNIA SECTION formally came into existence in 1903 and was mandated "to collect, preserve, and disseminate information regarding the history of the state." Long before that, however, the State Library demonstrated a deep commitment to California history. Founded in January 1850, with donations of books from General John C. Frémont and Colonel Jonathan D. Stevenson, the legislature created the library to support state government and preserve its history. In July of that year, the library's first book catalog, a one-page manuscript, was compiled, and it listed several important California titles. Twenty-five years later, the library produced a printed book catalog and devoted an entire section to its Californiana collection. Numbering over 1,000 titles, this represented one of the earliest known bibliographies of California history.

As with any research library with an emphasis on its state's history, the book collection forms a major component. Today, the collection numbers over 70,000 volumes (excluding government documents and law books) and ranks as one of the largest such collections in the Far West. In date, the books range from accounts of early explorers to the latest guidebook to San Francisco restaurants.

Geographically, all fifty-eight counties are represented, as well as works related to neighboring states, Baja California, and areas where California has had a significant influence. A majority of these titles are listed in the standard bibliographies of California history, early book catalogs of the State Library; more recently, Section holdings are included in the Research Libraries Information Network data base.

Found on the shelves are thousands of county and local histories, biographies, printed diaries, travel accounts, guidebooks, promotional works, cook books, WPA publications, business and institutional histories, essays, bound volumes of oral history transcriptions, fine press books, catalogs from private colleges, biographical encyclopedias, etc. In short, just about every imaginable subject is represented. One of the finest and least known special collections is the Section's superb fiction collection, which now ranks among the finest regional fiction collections. The books are supported by a vast selection of bound pamphlets covering such categories as mining, railroads, education, religion, agriculture, Southern California, and political speeches. Also available are complete or near complete runs from every major California city directory, as well as fine runs of general multicounty and Pacific Coast directories. While contemporary directories are continually added to the collection, the Section also acquires and maintains a near complete file of California telephone books dating back to the 1880s.

Demographic historians have come to rely extensively on the collection of Great Voting Registers. The "Registry Act" passed in 1866 caused the State Library to become the official repository of these locally printed documents. By no means complete, they represent the largest such concentration. They date from 1866 to the 1970s and contain interesting data on names, occupation, address, date of arrival in California, and place of origin. Many have been microfilmed and are available for interlibrary loan.

As far back as 1862, the Legislature appropriated the then handsome sum of $2,500 to purchase runs of the *Californian, California Star,* and *Alta California.* Since then, the library has consistently acquired California newspapers, and the collection totals over 2,400 titles, making it one of the largest of its kind. Every major city and region is represented, as well as a wide variety of special interest and ethnic groups. To keep abreast of current affairs, the Section subscribes to over 150 California newspapers. The microfilm collection now numbers over 70,000 reels and all are available for interlibrary loan. For such holdings consult *Newspaper Holdings of the California State Library*, comp. by Marianne Leach (Sacramento, 1986).

Equal in size, scope, and value to the newspaper files are the periodicals. Over 4,000 titles are found in the California Section ranging in date from the first issue of the state's first periodical, the *Pioneer* (1856), to the latest issue of *Low Rider*, a monthly devoted to Chicano popular culture. Presently, the library subscribes to over 500 magazines and newsletters published in California. All the major periodicals published in the state are represented, including complete or near complete runs which are represented in the *California Union List of Period-icals* (San Jose, 1987) and Thomas M. Fante's *General Magazine Index, California Section* (Sacramento, 1983).

The map collection serves as a major attraction. Its cartographical holdings number over 3,000 loose maps and hundreds of maps found in bound volumes. They are superb for locating routes of early explorers, shipwrecks, overland trails, gold mines, stage routes, railroad routes, historic sites, development of cities and counties, early land grants, freeways, and for scores of other historical and legal applications.

In addition to specialized maps, the Section offers a full range of state, regional, county, and city maps issued by tourist associations, chambers of commerce, homestead associations, railroads, moving companies, automobile clubs, oil companies, and by such well-known publishing houses as Briton and Rey, Butler, Chevalier, and Bancroft and Company. Also on hand are a number of precinct maps, block books, real estate maps, pictorial souvenir maps, a microfilm copy of the Library of Congress' Sanborn Fire Insurance Maps of California, and a microfilm of Los Angeles precinct maps from 1896 to 1942. Researchers gain access to the Section's maps via a card catalog organized by place, subject, and cartographer. Bound atlases and portfolios of maps are also listed in the Section's book catalogs.

Since its inception, the Section has carefully and consistently collected ephemeral materials to represent all aspects of California life. Today, it ranks as one of the largest and best organized statewide collections. Wonderfully diverse, it consists of campaign buttons, badges, bumper stickers, pennants, citrus labels, sheet music, certificates, menus, calendars, business cards, programs, transportation timetables, coasters, tickets, ballots, posters, book plates, dust jackets from books, and promotional literature distributed by chambers of commerce, amusement parks, housing developments, and athletic teams.

Not surprisingly, the Section offers a vast quantity of political ephemera. The Campaign Literature File contains buttons, ribbons, brochures, flyers, announcements, and bumper stickers printed for hundreds of candidates, constitutional amendments, and propositions stretching back to the administration of 1850. Also on hand is a large selection of ballots, invitations to gubernatorial inaugurations, and handbills and flyers distributed during the Vietnam War era.

The key to the ephemera collection is through a special card catalog labelled "Textual File Materials." The cards are arranged by type of ephemera from abstracts of title to timetables. This, in turn, is supplemented by a useful subject index.

The California Section's manuscript collection presently numbers over 500 processed collections. While covering a variety of subjects, the manuscripts focus on the history of the Sacramento Valley, pioneers, gold rush and mining, northern California business history, politics, and historic sites. Most of these collections have been described in previous publications. Helpful are Thomas Fante's

"Fragments of the Past: the Manuscript Collections of the State Library's California Section," *News Notes of California Libraries*, 74 (No. 1, 1979), and *Cataloged Manuscripts and Diaries of the California Section* (Sacramento, 1981).

Access to the manuscripts is gained through the summary sheets created for each collection. These sheets, located in ring binders at the reference desk, include such useful information as the formal name of the collection, dates, box number(s), contents, biography or history of the creating individual or institution, subjects covered, major correspondents, collection arrangement, provenance, and restrictions (if any). Many of the bound diaries, ledger books, hotel registers, etc., have been cataloged as books and carry either Library of Congress or Dewey Decimal numbers. Access is found through the card catalogs under main entry, subject, and the general category of manuscripts.

California's social, economic, and political history is superbly documented through the Section's Photograph Collection. Over 24,000 portraits and tens of thousands of views of places and subjects are readily available. These are supplemented by scores of photograph albums, lantern slides, portfolios, and books with original photographs. Nearly all photographic media are found, ranging from silvery daguerreotypes of the 1840s to video tapes of the last gubernatorial debates. Because of the library's location, photographs of San Francisco, Sacramento Valley, and Mother Lode counties dominate. The subject collections are particularly strong on mining, agriculture, state government, transportation, and historic sites. A card index by subject, place, and portrait provides the researcher with access to this important visual resource.

Besides photographs, the Section houses pictorial materials representing a variety of mediums such as oil on canvas paintings, pencil sketches, watercolors, woodcuts, etchings, and lithographs. These have been popular not only for illustrating publications but also as visual documentation. Areas of strength include letter sheets from the 1850s and 1860s; bird's eye views of California cities and towns; prints of California scenic wonders, buildings, people and parades; cartoons lampooning politicians and capitalists; and prints produced by the Federal Art Project during the WPA era. Many of these illustrations have been indexed. It is important to mention here that the library also has a number of illustrated periodicals from the nineteenth century.

One of the attractive features of the California Section is that its librarians have created over the generations a number of unique card indexes and card files. These resources not only save the researcher quantities of time but also reveal sources and information that otherwise might not have been found.

The California Information File (now available on microfiche) is recognized as one of the most powerful research tools on California history. In fact, most researchers visiting the library begin their research with this card file. It consists of references to people, places, and events. Presently the file holds over 640,000 cards bearing about one million citations to information appearing in California magazines, newspapers, county histories, theses, government documents, biographical encyclopedias, correspondents in manuscript collections, biographical cards filled out by notable Californians and pioneers, and cards of World War I soldiers. Examples of periodicals indexed for the file are *The Wave* (1893-1894), *The Overland Monthly* (1867-1916), and *Hutching's California Magazine* (1856-1861). Among newspapers indexed are the *Californian* of Monterey and San Francisco (1846-1848), Sacramento *Union* (1850-1900), and San Francisco *Alta California* (1849-1881). To give an idea of size and scope, there are over 11,000 card references to fires in California, 14,000 to railroads, 13,500 to Californians named Smith, and 4,500 to Chinese in California.

While the Section has made a long and enduring commitment to collecting newspapers, it has not neglected access. Newspapers without indexes represent a time-consuming chore for the historian. In addition to the newspapers indexed for the Information File, the librarians have also created the San Francisco Newspaper Index. This unique card file holds indexes to the San Francisco *Chronicle* (1913-1980), San Francisco *Call* (1882-1889; 1904-1913), and San Francisco *Examiner* (1913-1928). (Two of these are available on microfiche.) These, in turn, are supported by microfilm and microfiche indexes of newspapers produced by other newspapers or libraries. One of the most useful is a microfiche index of the San Diego *Herald* and *Union* created by the staff of the San Diego Public Library. Finally, more recent years are covered by the Bell and Howell indexes to the Los Angeles *Times* and San Francisco *Chronicle*.

Besides these invaluable indexes, the Section has other special files and collections which prove useful for tracking down individual names. Among these are compilations of vital statistics, cemetery records, pioneer family histories donated by the Daughters of the American Revolution; the Pioneer Roster of the Native Daughters of the Golden West (microfilm); United States Census records from 1850 to 1910; mortuary records from Sacramento (1847-1885); Sacramento City Cemetery Records (1886-1914); indexes to the San Francisco (1866, 1888-1904), and Sacramento County (1867-1872) voter registers. The biographical card files form another unique resource. When the Section was established in 1903, the librarians sent out cards to pioneers, authors, musicians, actors, artists, and politicians in an effort to collect biographical data on important Californians. These cards, filled out by the biographer or his or her family, contain information on full name, place and date of birth, education, residence, publications, exhibitions, and other accomplishments.

The collections of the library's Government Publications Section, General Collection, and Law Library provide a superb complement to the California Section. Within the Library-Courts Building, the researcher will have at his/her disposal a vast array of resources. The Government Publications Section offers a collection of over 2.5 million documents plus thousands of government issued maps. The size of the collection is due to the fact that the library serves as a United States Government regional depository and a complete depository of California documents. The latter consists of published reports, bulletins, newsletters, transcripts, periodicals, and maps issued by the various state agencies. As well, the documents section houses a large number of county and municipal documents.

Historians will find useful a number of publications in the Law Library. Important sources include California bills, 1867 to date; California Supreme Court briefs, 1850 to date; California Appellate Court briefs, 1904 to date; California statutes dating from 1850; and California codes since 1872. A highlight is a rare twenty-eight-volume set of records and briefs before the courts and Board of United States Land Commissioners during the 1850s and 1860s.

Finally, the General Collection of the library houses a splendid gathering of classic Western Americana, reference works, and one of the finest history-related periodical collections in the western United States. Nonrare materials are available for interlibrary loan, as are the newspapers on microfilm.

15

THE BANCROFT LIBRARY

WILLIAM M. ROBERTS

Street address:	The Bancroft Library
	University of California
	Berkeley, CA 94720
Mailing address:	Same
Telephone:	(415) 642–3781
Days and hours:	Monday–Friday, 9:00 A.M. to 5:00 P.M.
	Closed University holidays.

THE BANCROFT LIBRARY was purchased by the University of California in 1905, with Bancroft himself donating a portion of the cost. Since that time the collection has continued to grow in the subject areas first defined by Bancroft: California, Mexico, the western United States, and Central America. At present most of the growth of archival materials is in Californiana. In 1970 The Bancroft Library was expanded to include the rare books and special collections of the General Library at UCB, in part because of similar requirements for the physical care and use of the collections.

Unfortunately it would be impossible to provide, in such a short account, a complete record of all the manuscript materials which touch upon the history of California to be found in the Bancroft Collection. A few categories of material are not covered in depth because, however valuable the information they contain may be, they are too numerous to mention here. One of these categories is H. H. Bancroft's "dictations," an early form of oral history, usually recorded as straight narrative rather than the question and answer form we usually think of today. These dictations run to several hundred items, from Mariano Guadalupe Vallejo's five-volume reminiscences to the many of only a few pages. Many of these are accompanied by biographical sketches prepared either by the subject himself or by one of the compilers of Bancroft's *Chronicles of the Builders* (San Francisco, 1890–1892).

Also omitted from the present study are the hundreds of reels of microfilm and the thousands of pages of transcripts of materials in foreign archives, such as the Archivo General de la Nación in Mexico City, as well as from the United States National Archives, and films of individual items from various public and private collections.

There are a number of important sources for the exploration of California under Spanish and Mexican leadership, especially a number of diaries, ranging from 1725 to 1821. The earliest of these are two records of Juan Bautista de Anza's second expedition of 1775–1776. One of these is a copy of Anza's "Diario" made for H. H. Bancroft; the other is a contemporary copy of the diary of Pedro Font, a member of the expedition, which covers the period from September 1775 to June 1776.

Mission history sources are numerous in the Bancroft collection: the largest single collection is known as the "Archivos de la Misiones" (1796–1856; 2 ft.), a gathering of original documents and contemporary copies which includes correspondence, reports, accounts, circular letters, a few *padrones* (censuses), and a book of marriages. Extracts of the "Libros de Misión" of nearly all the missions were prepared for Bancroft, but there are many original documents to be found.

An important item demonstrating the use of music in the missions is a choir book in Gregorian notation (1813) prepared for the neophytes at Mission San José by Narciso Durán. "Documentos relativos a las Misiones de Nueva España" (1781–1790; 519 pp.) contain original and contemporary copies assembled by Alphonse Pinart on the ex-Jesuit missions of New Spain. The papers of William Edward Petty Hartnell (1815–1852; 1 ft.) contain a photocopy of a letterbook relating to trade with the missions; his diaries relate his visits of inspection as "visitador general" of the missions of Alta California (1839–1840). In addition to the transcripts mentioned above, there are many others prepared by Alphonse Pinart of correspondence and various documents relating to the missions, as well as several compendia of mission statistics, notably those prepared by historian Zoeth S. Eldredge.

One of the primary sources for the study of Spanish and Mexican governmental affairs is the "Archives of California" (63 vols.) covering the period 1767–1848. This collection consists of manuscript copies prepared for H. H. Bancroft of original government records which were subsequently lost in the San Francisco earthquake and fire in 1906. Bancroft's copies are not complete: occasionally an entire document was copied, but some documents were only summarized. Since the original pagination is noted, we know also that some documents were omitted entirely. Nevertheless, these transcripts contain as complete a record as it is possible to find of the day-to-day functioning of the Spanish and Mexican governments of California.

California's Spanish and Mexican eras, especially the latter, are amply documented by the many collections of private papers of Californios acquired by Bancroft, almost all of which bear the generic title "Documentos para la Historia de California." The largest of these and the most important is the collection of Mariano Guadalupe Vallejo (1780-1875; 36 ft.). See Doris M. Wright's *A Guide to the Mariano Guadalupe Vallejo Documentos para la Historia de California, 1780-1875* (Berkeley, 1953). Other important collections like Vallejo's are: the Alviso Family Documents (1817-1850; .5 ft.); the Manuel de Jesús Castro Documentos, including Castro's personal papers (1836-1863; 1.5 ft.); the Estudillo Family Papers (1772-1848; .5 ft.), which contain the papers of José María Estudillo; the Antonio María Pico Papers (1781-1872; 2 ft.); the Juan Bandini's Documentos (1776-1850; 45 items); and the Rafael Pinto Papers (1832-1847; 1 ft.).

There are also important collections on Americans for this period. The papers of Thomas Oliver Larkin, the United States' only consul to Mexican California, provide a look at both his official position and his business affairs. (*The Larkin Papers*, ed. by George P. Hammond, were published by the University of California Press in 10 vols., 1951-1968.) The Thomas Ap Catesby Jones' taking of Monterey in 1842 is documented in two small collections of Jones material. Henry S. Burton's diary and letterbook (1846-1848) tell of his activities as a member of the New York Volunteers. John S. Griffen's "Documents for the History of California" (1846-1876) comment particularly on his participation in the Battle of San Pascual. John Gallegher's "Personal Reminiscences of the War in Upper and Lower California" are an account by a member of Stevenson's Regiment. Robert W. Whitworth's diary (1846-1847) was written as a member of the Mormon Battalion. Other notable collections of this era include the papers of: Nathan Spear (1830-1849; 1 ft.); Henry Delano Fitch (1827-1858; 1.5 ft.); and William McKendree Gwin (1833-1897; 1 ft.), which relate mainly to his political activities in Mississippi, California, and Mexico. The Weber Family Papers (1836-1915; 25 ft.) contain the papers of Charles M. Weber, including correspondence and accounts relating to his various activities and extensive land holdings, as well as the papers of his descendants. Among the other important early American California collections are the papers of: Jacob P. Leese (1837-1849; 1 ft.); John C. Frémont (1839-1927; 2.5 ft.); William Heath Davis (1840-1905; 1.5 ft.); Joseph L. Folsom (1846-1855; .7 ft.); John A. Sutter (1846-1870; 1 ft.), including a copy made for H. H. Bancroft of "New Helvetia: Diary of events from 1841-8" (214 leaves), kept variously by John Bidwell, William F. Swasey, W. N. Locker, and by Sutter himself; Richard B. Mason (1847-1848; .2 ft.); H. Burnett (1849-1885; 63 items); and the Bidwell Papers (1792-1934; 7 ft.).

Land was an important issue in Mexican California and in the early statehood period, and many collections of personal papers from these periods contain information on the holdings of the individuals concerned. The Bancroft Library has on deposit from the United States District Court its Land Case Records documenting the prosecution by the United States of all Spanish and Mexican land grants. These records consist of transcripts of the original grants, depositions by the landholder and testimony of acquaintances, original diseños (maps), and formal surveys of the tracts of lands. The Halleck, Peachy & Billings Papers (1852-1862; 4.5 ft.) record that firm's extensive participation in land grant litigation. Benjamin I. Hayes' 1875 compilation, "Land Matters in California," relates to land grant matters in Los Angeles and San Diego counties.

Vigilance committees were not uncommon in the early statehood period, the most famous being the well-organized San Francisco Committees of 1851 and 1856. The 1851 Committee is well documented by its records (1851-1852; 4 ft.), and in addition a number of diaries and other personal collections comment upon the committee: William D. Bickham's "Notes of Travel" (1851; 212 pp.), Phineas U. Blunt's "Journal" (1848-1852; 169 leaves), the Robert S. and Harry La Motte family letters (1849-1872; 1 ft.), John McCrackan's "Letters to his family" (1849-1853; 1 ft.), and Benjamin Wingate's "Letters to his wife" (1852-1854; .5 ft.) are examples of these.

The San Francisco Vigilance Committee of 1856 is represented by a smaller collection of records (1856; .5 ft.); by the papers of Joseph B. Crockett (1849-1879; .5 ft.) and James M. Grover (1854-1905; .2 ft.); and the papers of Governor John N. Johnson (1848-1860; .5 ft.), which relate mainly to his difficulties with the committee.

The diaries of William A. Z. Edwards (1843-1908; 68 vols.) include comments on vigilance committee activities in the mines, as well as documenting his own mining ventures in Tuolumne and Placer counties and his later ranching and political positions in Santa Clara County. Many of Bancroft's dictations contain observations on vigilance activities in San Francisco and elsewhere.

Collections of political figures form a large and important part of Bancroft's holdings. While every California governor is represented in the collection to some degree, several are represented by substantial collections. Among these are the Waterman Family Papers (1839-1906; 21 ft.); the papers of Governors George C. Pardee (1890-1941; 73 ft.); Frank F. Merriam (1897-1948; 40 ft.); Culbert L. Olson (1912-1949; 9 ft.); and Edmund G. Brown (1950-1966; 812 ft.). The papers of Hale Champion (1961-1966; 77 ft.), Brown's director of finance, complement Brown's papers for the period.

Papers of United States congressmen often contain a fascinating mix of local, national, and even international political concerns. The papers of Hiram W. Johnson (1895-1945; 135 ft.) document his career both as governor of California and as U.S. senator, 1917-1945. The papers of John D. Works (1910-1917; 5 ft.) document his position on such issues as intervention in Mexico, United States entry into World War I, Hetch Hetchy legislation, irrigation, and the 1916 presidential campaign in California. The papers of James D. Phelan (1880-1930; 80 ft.) relate mainly to his work in state and national politics, but also include material on Japanese exclusion, prohibition, Hetch Hetchy, his interest in the arts, and his participation in the life of San Francisco. The papers of Jesse W. Carter (1912-1939; 94 ft.) contain material on his law practice in

Shasta County, particularly on water rights cases, on Democratic politics in California during the 1930s, on prohibition enforcement as district attorney, and on his activities as a state senator. The collection also includes the papers of Oliver J. Carter (1941-1948; 17 ft.) relating to his career as state senator. The Sheridan Downey Papers (1929-1961; 10 ft.) consist primarily of his political career as U.S. senator, 1939-1950, with considerable information on his investigation of the Central Valley Project. George Miller's Papers (1951-1968; 27 ft.) document his career as state senator from Contra Costa County, while William F. Knowland's Papers (1946-1958; 300 ft.) contain correspondence files, U.S. Senate committeee files, much documentation of his work concerning the Far East and the State Department, and files on federally assisted California water projects. The papers of Joseph R. Knowland (1914-1952; 58 ft.) contain materials on parks in California, his lumbering activities, and the Oakland *Tribune*. The papers of Charles Brown (1947-1962; 7 ft.) document his interests in Inyo County Indians, land, and water. The papers of William T. Bagley (1961-1974; 18 ft.) consist primarily of bill files. The Jerome Waldie Papers (1966-1972; 150 ft.), in addition to his correspondence, bill, and general legislation files, contain his water projects files, constituent correspondence, and district office files.

The papers of Chester H. Rowell (1887-1946; 26 ft.) consist of correspondence; editorials for the Fresno *Republican*; and other items relating to California politics, the Lincoln Roosevelt Republican League, the Progressive party, and the Republican party, as well as to other interests. John T. Gaffey's Papers (1884-1934; 1.5 ft.) describe his activities in the Democratic party and in Los Angeles civic organizations. The papers of John F. Heney (1903-1957; .5 ft.) consist primarily of letters written to him concerning the San Francisco graft prosecution trials, the Progressive Era, and the Democratic party. The papers of John W. Stetson (1912; 81 items) document his presidency of the Roosevelt Progressive Republican League of California and the election of 1912. The papers of Arthur Arlett (1912-1921; 3 ft.) concern his activities with the Panama-Pacific International Exposition, the California Board of Harbor Commissioners, and the Progressive party. The Robert W. Kenny Papers (1920-1947; 30 ft.) are chiefly his papers as attorney general of California, 1942-1946, and his private law practice. The Roger Kent Collection (1947-1974; 18 ft.) documents his long involvement with the Democratic party, including his tenure as the chairman of the State Central Committee. The papers of Clara Shirpser (1948-1968; 2.5 ft.) relate to her political activities, particularly as Democratic National Committee-woman for California, 1952-1956.

California lawyers and their interests are represented by the papers of Elbert P. Jones (1846-1852; 1 ft.); Shafter Family Papers (1855-1877; 5 vols.); Hittell Family Papers (1855-1916; 6.5 ft.); Charles A. Storke (1856-1936; 5 ft.); St. Sure Family Papers (1886-1966; 3 ft.); William Denman (1900-1959; 55 ft.), and Austin Lewis (1913-1944; 4.5 ft.); and the John Francis Neylan Collection (1911-1960; 90 ft.) which also documents his activities as publisher of the San Francisco *Call*, a UC regent, and his association with William Randolph Hearst.

The Bancroft Library has numerous printed sources of information about various ethnic groups in California. Manuscript sources are not nearly so numerous but nevertheless document the ethnic diversity of the state to some degree. There are two collections of Chinese business records in Nevada and Placer counties (1870-1915; 4.5 ft.). The John J. Manion Papers (1926-1946; .2 ft.) contain his writings on San Francisco's Chinatown and on narcotics. Materials on Japanese Americans center around the extensive collection of United States War Relocation Authority records (1941-1953; 250 ft.), which include materials collected by and/or generated by the UCB's Japanese-American Evacuation and Resettlement Study. The records of the California Federation for Civic Unity (1945-1956; 5.5 ft.) include material on conferences relating to racial discrimination and segregation, immigration, and employment practices, much of it pertaining to the resettlement period. Other useful collections are the papers of Evelyn McCool (1942; .4 ft.) and Gerda Isenberg (1942-1946; .8 ft.), and a collection of material prepared by the California Attorney General's Office (1942; 1 ft.) documenting the preevacuation location of Japanese Americans in California.

Material relating to Afro Americans include the Jeremiah Burke Sanderson Papers (1857-1912; 1 ft.) of a black family in the San Francisco Bay Area which contain correspondence and other materials on the African Methodist Episcopal Church and the Livingstone Institute. The Records of the West Coast Regional Office of the National Association for the Advancement of Colored People (1946-1970; 52 ft.) contain correspondence, minutes, fund raising and financial records, and files for particular programs, such as education, employment, housing, youth activities, legislation, political, and legal action. These records also include those of the Los Angeles field office. The records of the Governor's Commission on the Los Angeles Watts Riots (1965; 28 ft.) contain reports, testimony and depositions, interviews, correspondence, exhibits, and statistical data gathered by or prepared for the Commission. The papers of Wayne Collins (1945-1964; 28 ft.) consist of case files of Japanese renunciants, Peruvian-Japanese and East Indian deportation cases, as well as personal and family correspondence.

There is a wide range of materials concerning the Indians of California. Many of Bancroft's dictations as well as early diaries and papers contain comments on the native populations; these consist for the most part of short, untrained observations which, nonetheless, express the views of both the Spanish and Mexican settlers as well as those of the Americans. American Indian agents are represented by a dictation of Oliver M. Wozencraft; the papers of Pierson B. Reading (1841-1868); and those of James W. Denver (1845-1892; .5 ft.) as United States Commissioner of Indian Affairs. Early observations on the languages and history of the Indians of California are found in two works by Felipe Arroyo de la Cuesta (1815 and 1837) which include vocabularies and grammars of many Indian groups, in two collections of notes and vocabularies recorded or collected by Alphonse Pinart (1852-1880; 27 items), and in three collections of historical

notes and vocabularies of Stephen Powers (1873-1874; 8 items). The papers of
Henry B. Brown (1851-1853; .25 ft.) record his experiences (including collecting
vocabularies) while sketching California Indians and scenes. The journal of
Paul E. Botta (1826-1829), kept while on the ship *Le Héros* under the command
of Auguste Bernard du Hautcilly, includes descriptions of California Indians. The
Charles L. Patridge Papers (1901-1924; .5 ft.) concern the resettlement of
Warner's Ranch Indians. The struggle for Indian rights is documented in the
records of the California League for American Indians (1918-1941; 13 ft.) and
in the Kenny Papers already mentioned.

In the field of anthropology there are several important collections dealing in
whole or in part with California Indians. The papers of Alfred L. Kroeber (1900-
1960; 35 ft.) contain correspondence, writings, field notebooks, phonetic trac-
ings, and other linguistic materials, notes on Indian music, and various subject
files relating to his work with California tribes. The C. Hart Merriam Collection
of Data Concerning California Tribes and Other American Indians (1902-1935;
22 ft.) contains ethnological, linguistic, historical, and geographical notes arranged
according to his classification of tribes by linguistic group. Accompanying this
collection is an important file (ca. 3,300 items) of photographs of informants,
artifacts, and dwellings taken primarily by Merriam himself. The papers of Anna
Gayton Spier (1925-1965; 1 ft.) contain some correspondence and many field
notes relating primarily to the Yokuts Indians. Robert Spier's field notes (1949-
1950; 1 vol.) record linguistic and ethnological data gathered among the Chuk-
chansi Yokuts, and Leslie Spier's Papers (1924-1961; 2 ft.) contain materials on
the Klamath Indians. The papers of Sherburne F. Cook (1896-1974; 14 ft.) contain much material on his research into California Indian population figures.

Many collections deal extensively with the question of agricultural labor in
the state. "Source materials gathered by Federal Writers' Project on Migratory
Labor, District No. 8" (1936-1939; 36 ft.) are composed chiefly of abstracts
and clippings from various publications covering the period 1849-1939. The
Federal Writers' Project "Monographs Prepared for a Documentary History of
Farm Labor" (1938; .5 ft.) contains seventeen typescripts on such specific
topics as child labor, labor on specific crops, labor by various ethnic groups, etc.
The papers of Simon J. Lubin (1912-1936; 4 ft.) relate primarily to his service
with the State Commission of Immigration and Housing and include material on
agricultural labor camps and the 1913 Wheatland hopfield riots. The records of
the Simon J. Lubin Society (1927-1940; 15 ft.) concern the society's interest in
farmer organization, cooperatives, migrants, housing, and farm tenancy. Agricultural strikes during the 1930s are documented in a collection of papers of
Paul S. Taylor (1933-1942; 3 ft.), the diary of Fred Maloy (1933; 1 vol.), and
Gerald A. Rose's "The Brentwood Plan for Agricultural Labor" (1962; 56
leaves), which studies strikes in Contra Costa County in 1934 and the adoption
of the plan. Additional collections of papers of Paul S. Taylor (1925-1975;
125 ft.) document his long interest in agricultural labor, migrant labor, Mexican
laborers, and housing, as well as in California's water problems, and generally in

all phases of agricultural economics. The records of the California Division of Immigration and Housing (1913-1937; 92 ft.) contain correspondence, reports, county files, and inspection reports (including of labor camps). The papers of Harry E. Drobish (1917-1954; 11 ft.) relate to his career as agricultural economist with the State Emergency Relief Association and the United States Resettlement Administration.

In addition to farm labor, other labor movements are represented by important collections. Perhaps the earliest of these is the Record Book of the Eureka Typographical Union, No. 21, of San Francisco (1853-1859). The Haskell Family Papers (1878-1951; 7 ft.) include documentation on Burnett G. Haskell and Hanna F. Haskell's involvement in the Coast Seamen's Union, the International Workmen's Association, and other trade unions, and socialist movements of San Francisco and Kaweah Colony, California. The International Typographical Union of North America, No. 46, Sacramento, is represented by ten volumes of minutes (1859-1940). Also in the printing trades, the papers of Luis A. Ireland (1910-1960; 4.5 ft.) relate to his career as secretary of the Printers' Board of Trade and the Employing Printers' Association. The records of the San Francisco Labor Council (1905-1965; 175 ft.) document all phases of the Council's activities. The Subject Files of the International Longshoremen's and Warehousemen's Union (1936-1976; 21 ft.) contain publications, reports and studies, press releases, statistical data, legislative bills, etc., relating the various seamen's and maritime unions. The Paul Sharrenberg Papers (1918-1960; 6.5 ft.) document his career in the labor movement, in the California State Federation of Labor, and his position on the California Commission of Immigration and Housing and the California Department of Industrial Relations. The papers of Walter MacArthur (1905-1944; 7 ft.) describe his activities as United States Shipping Commissioner, including relations with various maritime unions. The Thomas Mooney Collection (1906-1942; 75 ft.) documents the activist's career, particularly his trial and conviction in connection with the bombing at the Preparedness Day Parade in San Francisco in 1915 and efforts to secure his release. The papers of C. L. Dellums (1932-1960; 43 ft.) primarily concern his work for the Brotherhood of Sleeping Car Porters. The legal files of Gladstein, Leonard, Patsey & Anderson (1933-1957; 77 ft.) document the firm's labor union cases. The Proceedings before the United States National Longshoremen's Labor Board (1934-1936; 21 vols.) document arbitration efforts in the longshoremen's strike of 1934. The Arthur Dupuy Eggleston Papers (1935-1941; 3 ft.) contain his writings, clippings, and some correspondence as labor editor of the San Francisco *Chronicle*.

The lumber industry is documented in the records of several companies. The records of T. B. Joy & Company (1854-1934; 24 vols.) consist of daybooks, journals, ledgers, and miscellaneous correspondence and accounts for operations near Bodega. The Pacific Lumber Company's records (1865-1938; 5 ft.), although fragmentary, contain financial records and correspondence, including some with the Save-the-Redwoods League and state agencies pertaining to negotiations for purchase of land between 1925 and 1932. The records of the Sonoma Lumber Company (1877-1884; 6 vols.) consist of minutes of meetings of the directors, records of sales, ledgers, and cash books. The extensive records of the Union Lumber Company (1883-1946; 13 ft. and 531 vols.) document all phases of the company's activities and include some records of affiliated companies such as the Glen Blair Redwood Company, the Fort Bragg Lumber Company, the Mendocino Lumber Company, etc. The records of the Elk River Mill and Lumber Company (1884-1933; 74 vols.) include cash books, journals, ledgers, letterbooks, invoices and receipts, cargo records, and inventories. The records of the Dolbeer and Carson Lumber Company (1884-1941; 54 vols.), consisting of correspondence and accounts, include records of the Bucksport and Elk River Railroad Company, the Humboldt Northern Railway Company, and the William Carson Estate Company. The records of the Pacific Coast Redwood Company (1903-1929; 6 vols.) include its minute book, journals, and ledgers. The collection of business records formed by R. R. Chaffee (1909-1954; 18 ft. and 15 vols.) include records of the Wolf Creek Timber Company, the California Coast Lumber Company, the Trask Timber Company, and others. The papers of Jacob C. Hawley (1862-1896; 14 vols.) relate to his service as San Francisco agent for the Elk River and Arcata Mill and Lumber companies. The records of the California Redwood Association (1927-1962; 4 ft.) contain primarily samples of statistical tabulations and reports, annual reports, distribution of shipments reports, and grading rules and pattern books.

The shipping industry is represented by the John Kentifield & Company records (1853-1923; 60 ft. and 184 vols.) which includes ships' papers for numerous ships owned by the firm. The Dollar Collection (1872-1967; 78 ft. and 72 vols.) includes business records of the Robert Dollar Company and its divisions, Dollar Steamship Lines, Dollar Portland Lumber Company, Globe Wireless Ltd., Admiral Oriental Line, Egmont Timber Company, etc. Adele Ogden's "Trading Vessels on the California Coast, 1786-1848" (1,493 leaves) is a chronological compilation of voyages which includes names of vessels, owners and captains, cargo carried, itineraries. The work includes an index by name of vessel and reference citations.

Several collections trace the growth of the conservation and parks movements, the largest of these being the records of the Sierra Club (1896-present; ca. 300 ft.); the Sierra Club has designated The Bancroft Library as the permanent repository of its records, so these files continue to grow. They include mountain registers, reference files on the many issues of interest to the club, financial records, files of the History Committee, and files of many individuals prominent in the club. The records of the Point Lobos League (1929-1945; 5 ft.) document the preservation of Point Lobos as a natural reserve and include many reports on the biology and ecology of the region. The Save-the-Redwoods League records (1920-1944; 10 ft.) include extensive correspondence files of John C. Merriam, William Kent, Duncan McDuffie, and Stephen T. Mather, as well as office memoranda, reference files, and publicity materials. The records of

Friends of the Earth (1973-1981; 32 ft.) include materials on various California water plans, on Redwood and Yosemite National Parks, and on the Mineral King controversy.

Several collections from an earlier date treat the natural history of the region and are in a sense related to be above. The records of the California Geological Survey of 1861-1864 (22 folders) is accompanied by 332 manuscript maps drawn as a result of the survey's work. Related to these collections are the papers of George Davidson (1845-1911; 61 ft.) which deal in large part with his work for the United States Coast and Geodetic Survey.

The manuscript collections of The Bancroft Library span the entire gamut of subjects that might be considered part of California's history. While the library has published guides to its non-California manuscripts, the sheer size and complexity of its California collections have mitigated against the publication of such a desirable and valuable work, although it has normally supplied collection descriptions for inclusion in the National Union Catalog of Manuscript Collections. The library has recently begun to enter records into the RLIN network in an effort to make its holdings more widely known. The library has long assisted bibliographers in their work with the result that its holdings are to be found in such bibliographies as *American Literary Manuscripts* (Athens, Ga., 1977) and *Women's History Sources* (New York, 1979), which incidentally lists more Bancroft sources for women's history studies than are mentioned in this chapter.

Despite its location on the Berkeley campus of the University of California, The Bancroft Library is open to all researchers at the college level or above who have a need to use its materials; university affiliation is not necessary. While staff limitations make it impossible to answer extremely general questions about California history, it welcomes letters of inquiry on specific topics or persons and will make every attempt to answer in as full a manner as possible. The resources of the library are available to all.

16

THE HUNTINGTON LIBRARY

PETER J. BLODGETT AND WILLIAM P. FRANK

Street address:	The Huntington Library, Art Gallery
	and Botanical Gardens
	1151 Oxford Road
	San Marino, California 91108
Mailing address:	Same
Telephone:	(818) 405-2275
Public hours:	Tuesday–Sunday, 1:00 to 4:30 P.M.
	(for those people visiting the gardens
	or the galleries)
Research library hours:	Monday–Saturday, 8:30 A.M. to 5:00 P.M.
	(Access to the Research Library is by
	advance application only.)

SEVENTY YEARS AGO, Henry Huntington dedicated his enormous personal collection of rare books and manuscripts to an institution whose primary responsibility would be not merely "the advancement of learning, the arts and sciences, and to promote the general welfare" but also "to prosecute and encourage study and research of original sources of history, literature, art, science and kindred objects." Upon his death in 1927, he left behind a research library equipped with intellectual resources of unparalleled breadth and depth. For detailed accounts of Huntington's book collecting and the research library's creation, see James Thorpe, et al., *The Founding of the Henry E. Huntington Library and Art Gallery* (San Marino, 1969; hereafter cited HEH).

Among Huntington's varied interests he counted the history of California, beginning with early episodes of European exploration and settlement. His purchases of California materials laid a foundation upon which the Huntington as an institution has continued to build with great success. Today, in addition to its manuscript holdings, the HEH possesses a marvelously comprehensive collection of printed Californiana including early maps, newspapers, and periodicals, as well as an extensive photographic archive.

An indispensable source for information on the permanent settlement of Alta California itself is the José de Gálvez Collection (1763-1794; 734 pieces), which includes correspondence and documents on the organization of the expeditions under Portolá in 1769 as well as on some of the first reports sent back that year by Pedro Fages, Miguel Costansó, and other members of the expeditions. Subsequent efforts to open direct communication between Sonora and the new settlements can be followed in the "Diario" kept by Juan Bautista de Anza of his 1774 expedition and in a similar diary written by the peripatetic Francisco Garcés (1775-1776). Meanwhile, Spanish scientific exploration of the coast of Alta California was being actively pursued, as represented here in the observations made by José Longinos Martínez (1792).

Spanish settlement of California gradually established itself over the next decades, and that process can be seen in several HEH collections. The California File is a synthetic and still-growing collection of individual items and small groups of papers from all periods of California history, including those of Spanish (1765-1821; 144 pieces) and Mexican (1822-1845; 59 pieces) rule. The California Historical Documents Collection (1812-1912; 162 pieces) is similar, dealing with political and legal matters. Concerned with one specific locality is the Monterey Collection (1785-1877; 1,337 pieces), which chiefly concerns municipal government during the period 1828-1854.

Political, commercial, and social life under Mexican and the first decades of American rule can be seen with particular fullness in the papers of Abel Stearns (1821-ca.1934; approx. 12,500 pieces). A *Californio* perspective emerges from the Mariano Guadalupe Vallejo Collection (1833-1888; 257 pieces), which has material in particular on the defense of the northern frontier of California, relations with the missions, and the treatment of Indians. Commerce and shipping is at the heart of the William Leidesdorff Collection (1840-1867; 502 pieces). The papers of William Heath Davis (1843-1906; 634 pieces) contain not only information on shipping and commerce, but also on land titles, and include manuscripts and source material for Davis' *Sixty Years in California*. Land records and rancho life are at the center of the Henry Dalton Collection (1819-1942; 2,430 pieces). Other pertinent collections include those of Grant Jackson (1828-1954; 155 pieces), and Charles Wolter (1792 and 1827-1970; 448 pieces).

The transfer of control of California to the United States is well represented in the California File (1846-1848; 65 pieces) and in the California Historical Documents, Abel Stearns, Monterey, Leidesdorff, and Vallejo collections. C. E. S. Wood Collection (1846-1974; approx. 30,000 pieces) has some information on the conquest of California, as does the Fort Sutter Collection (1845-1862; 161 pieces). The Sherman Otis Houghton Collection (1831-1914; 195

pieces) relates to the relief of the Donner Party. Views of California made during this period are in the William Rich Hutton Collection (1847-1861; 147 pieces, 95 drawings).

During the era of transition from Mexican to American rule, conditions in California were further complicated by the discovery of gold in 1848 and the vast, frantic migration that ensued. Within the California File nine boxes contain hundreds of individual letters written during the crucial decade 1848-1858. These letters are arranged chronologically. Similarly, among the scores of original western diaries on file, there are dozens kept by eager argonauts which provide detailed accounts of daily life in the diggings and in the towns.

Supplementing these single items are many significant collections of personal papers from this period. Two of the most notable are the Joseph Pownall Collection (1840-1926; approx. 1,775 pieces), which contains many letters that recount conditions in the northern and southern mines, and the papers of Amos P. Catlin (1849-1871; approx. 2,760 pieces), a New York lawyer who settled in the Mormon Island area, documenting mining in that location as well as the development of later water and mining companies.

From the era of the ranchos to the present day, land, its ownership, and use have been fundamental to the development of California. Stearns amassed a group of contiguous ranchos that at one time made him the largest landowner in southern California, and his papers have a great deal of material on his voluminous holdings. The records of his brother-in-law, Cave Couts (1832-1951; approx. 16,000 pieces) are especially rich for San Diego County. Other material on ranchos is scattered through numerous collections, such as those of Lewis Wolfskill (1830-1946; 1,622 pieces); Henry Dalton and Henry A. Barclay (1867-1908; ca.150 pieces).

The transfer to American rule meant that title to the ranchos had to be confirmed and their boundaries determined with some degree of precision, providing work for years to lawyers and surveyors. The law firm of Halleck, Peachy & Billings (1837-1861; 80 pieces) was especially prominent in land cases, while the Chipman-Dwinelle (1845-1943; approx. 435 pieces) and Brophy-Beeson collections also have material. The surveying process in southern California can be studied in daunting detail for the whole second half of the century in the Solano-Reeve (pre-1849–ca.1910; 3,225 pieces, including 2,100 maps) and William Moore (1851-1891; approx. 100 pieces) collections. Material on San Francisco is in the Jasper O'Farrell (ca.1845-1924; 76 pieces) and Milo Hoadley (1849-1886; 65 pieces) collections, for example. Information on land development and land titles in San Francisco is in the John Center (1849-1884; 362 pieces); Rodman M. Price (1842-ca.1890; 256 pieces); and Adolph Sutro (1853-1931; 2,786 pieces) collections. For land issues in the Monterey area, the David Jacks (ca.1845-1926; approx. 200,000 pieces); and Charles Wolter collections are especially valuable. The Charles Fernald Collection (1852-1904; 8,160 pieces) focuses in particular on the Santa Barbara area, while the El Dorado County Archives (1850-1906; ca.1,600 pieces) and the Lowden Collection (1856-1929;

ca.12,500 pieces) have land records on the far northern portion of the state. Other miscellaneous material can be found in the Gerald John Kane Nevada (1839-1952; ca.12,500 pieces) and John H. H. Peshine (1849-1903; ca.850 pieces) collections.

It is for southern California, however, that the HEH has its largest concentration of material on land issues and the growth of agriculture, suburban, and urban development. In addition to those already mentioned, the papers of Matthew Keller (1851-1959; 525 pieces) and of his son Henry W. Keller (1827-1966; 7,985 pieces) between them have a great deal on both Los Angeles and other regions in the state. Equally broad and voluminous are the records and correspondence of James de Barth Shorb (1816-1931; ca.10,600 pieces); George S. Patton, Sr. (1887-1966; ca.20,000 pieces); and Benjamin D. Wilson (1847-1920; ca.3,500 pieces). The Banning Company Collection (1859-1948; 12,104 pieces) is important for the development of Wilmington and its harbor, Santa Catalina Island, and other scattered locations. Two prominent lawyers, one later a banker, who were involved in land development were Henry O'Melveny (1874-1941; approx. 6,300 pieces) and Jackson Alpheus Graves (1878-1903; approx. 14,000 pieces). The William H. Weinland Collection (1853-1946; 2,100 pieces) has papers on the Banning region, while the John Wesley North Collection (1849-1947; approx. 1,500 pieces) concerns in part the promotion of Riverside, which is also a focus of the South Riverside Land and Water Company (ca.1885-1960; ca.7,500 pieces). There are a number of smaller collections relating to other southern California localities. The most valuable source in the HEH, however, on land subdivision, urbanization, and suburban growth in southern California in the twentieth century is the Henry E. Huntington Collection (1794-1970; approx. 150,000 pieces). It is complemented by several far smaller collections as well.

In the mining field, HEH holdings include business papers about numerous California mining ventures. Two examples are the papers of Henry D. Bacon (ca.1766-1906; ca.4,000 pieces), California financier, who had a stake in many California mining properties, and those of Henry H. Markham (1867-1899; ca.2,494 pieces), congressman and governor late in the nineteenth century, who counted gold and silver mining in California and Arizona among his varied business enterprises. Another good example is the business correspondence of Robert C. Turner (1887-1921; 1,286 pieces), vice president of the Brunswick Consolidated Gold Mining Company, which deals with company affairs and other mining enterprises in California. California's petroleum industry appears in the business correspondence (1909-1914) of Henry H. Sinclair (1819-1937; ca.1,300 pieces), including that of the Palmer Oil Company.

Of equal interest are the numerous collections that chronicle the careers of leading American mining engineers. The papers of James D. Hague (1824-1936; ca.24,000 pieces) contain dozens of Hague's reports evaluating California mining projects. One subgroup of the collection consists of the Clarence King Collection (ca.1860-1903; 752 pieces). Numbered among this assortment of scientific papers are notebooks and manuscripts compiled during his years with the California Geological Survey as well as several drafts of chapters from *Mountaineering in the High Sierras* (Boston, 1872). Several collections of engineering papers from our own century mirror the continuing importance of the mining industry and the increasing significance of petroleum to the state's economy. Harley Sill (1901-1964; ca.1,445 pieces), a Los Angeles mining engineer, made a number of reports on mines and ores in California. Clarence E. Van Gundy (1930-1960; ca.3,000 pieces), petroleum geologist, prepared many studies for major oil companies on the location of oil-bearing formations all over the state. The Ralph Arnold Collection (1836-1961; ca.200,000 pieces) possesses hundreds of field reports and maps describing mining and petroleum properties throughout California, as well as several manuscripts outlining the history of California's petroleum industry.

The history of agriculture and of its sister industry, stock raising, is well represented in HEH manuscript holdings. The Stearns papers include much information on cattle raising and the trade in hides and tallow. Cattle also figure in the Couts papers after he became the owner of the Gaujome Rancho in San Diego County, and in the papers of the San Rafael Ranch Company, near present-day Pasadena, owned and managed by an English family. Details on California's wool trade in the late nineteenth century appear in the papers of Robert S. Baker.

Various papers in the Wilson Collection discuss California's wine industry, as do the papers of Shorb, Wilson's son-in-law and manager of the San Gabriel Winery, which Wilson and Shorb founded. Shorb's papers also describe the management of the San Marino Ranch and the development of California's citrus industry. Another Wilson son-in-law, George S. Patton, Sr., had important agricultural interests, including the citrus growing so common in southern California. Other collections worthy of note to students of California agriculture are the papers of Harriet Williams (Russell) Strong (1815-1939; 1,072 pieces), who introduced new techniques of flood control and business management as well as new types of crops when she took control of the family's property after her husband's death; Matthew Keller, founder of the Rising Sun and Los Angeles Vineyards winery; Matthew's son, Henry Keller, whose Thousand Acre Ranch in Colusa County conducted experiments in crop production, irrigation, and flood control; and David Jacks, the pioneer businessman in Monterey whose many interests in commerce and land included farming and stock raising. The development of the citrus industry, so crucial to the history of southern California, is traced by five sets of business records. The more important are the papers of the Duarte-Monrovia Fruit Exchange (1892-1937; 21,000 pieces) and the Pasadena Orange Growers' Association (1893-1938; 3,500 pieces) which document the establishment of organizations to centralize marketing of produce and the many aspects of their business operations.

Although their efforts produced no food for California's tables, a number of horticulturalists and botanists found the growing potential of California's landscape as intriguing as had the earliest cattle ranchers and farmers. They studied the native flora of the Golden State, experimented with the introduction of new species, and launched commercial nurseries. Among those were Charles R. Orcutt (1822-1899; 624 pieces); Jeanne C. Carr (1842-1903; 192 pieces); Charles F. Saunders (1859-1941; ca.1,500 pieces); Horatio Rust (1799-1906; 1,229 pieces); and Frank Weinberg (1901-1912; 56 pieces), who all discuss aspects of the nursery business and horticulture in southern California near the turn of the century. The most valuable source at the HEH for this topic, however, is the papers of William Hertrich (1904-1966; 2,687 pieces), who transformed the San Marino Ranch into the Huntington Botanical Gardens in the service of Henry E. Huntington.

California's hopes for economic growth and eventual prosperity, however, depended upon one indispensable natural resource: water. Many HEH manuscript collections focus upon this topic. Besides the Bishop, Catlin, and Morgan collections, mentioned earlier, other useful sources for information on early mining and water companies include the John Center Collection, which contains papers from the Center Company of Owens Valley in 1863, and the Joseph Pownall Collection, which contains the business papers of the Tuolumne County Water Company. Three other collections focus upon the question of irrigation. The Nathan Stowell Collection includes items about the Cucamonga region and the Imperial Valley. The papers of Charles Janin (1858-1937; 15,582 pieces), a major American mining engineer, contain correspondence, reports, and memoranda about the Santa Ynez Irrigation Project. Eugene C. LaRue's professional papers (1909-1949; 2,543 pieces) detailing a civil engineer's career, include maps, reports, and other documents about various water projects for California, such as the Colorado River–Los Angeles Gravity Flow Aqueduct and the Merced Irrigation District.

Several collections discuss the development of private or municipal systems to deliver drinking water and, later, hydroelectric power to the growing cities. Milo Hoadley's papers offer some details about the bitter struggle from 1852 to 1872 among various private companies to supply San Francisco with water. John Dockweiler, a consulting engineer for San Francisco and Oakland, takes up the same story through his field books in the decade after 1906. Among its many mining reports, surveys, and legal agreements from power and water companies in the Southwest, the Charles F. and Issac B. Potter Collection (1905-1940; ca.5,000 pieces) includes documents outlining the conflict between the Mono Power Company and the City of Los Angeles, 1905-1923, over Owens Valley water rights. Henry W. O'Melveny's personal and professional correspondence includes files that discuss efforts to acquire water rights and financing for many water and power companies, such as the Mentone Power Company, the Sierra Power Company, and the Pacific Power & Light Company. The Henry H. Sinclair Collection includes letters, notebooks, and diaries about various hydroelectric companies in southern California and about his trips to inspect power plants on the Kern River and elsewhere. Two very controversial episodes in the history of water use in southern California deserve special note. The disastrous failure on March 13, 1928, of the St. Francis Dam, designed to store water from the Owens Valley for the City of Los Angeles, is recounted in a series of documentary materials (1928-1930; ca.240 pieces) including engineering reports and investigative studies. The City of Los Angeles' lengthy struggle to exclude other communities from access to the San Fernando Valley's well water can be followed in the Los Angeles City Water Rights Collection (1874-1968; ca.115 pieces) which assembles court records and historical documentation about water rights and water usage as far back as the Spanish era.

Just as many of the HEH manuscript collections mirror the exploitation of California's natural resources for economic development throughout the nineteenth century, so others reflect the growing conservation movement that arose in opposition to unbridled commercial use of forests, rivers, and wild lands. John Muir, a founding father of modern conservation, is represented by a small but noteworthy collection (1902-1955; 86 pieces). Two other collections that fit very closely are the papers of Jeanne C. Carr and Theodore P. Lukens. The Lukens Collection (1869-1942; ca.3,600 pieces) includes eighty letters from his friend Muir. The William H. Thrall Collection (1873-1962; ca.3,500 pieces) focuses upon conservation and recreation in the San Gabriel Mountains through Thrall's career.

Economic development of any sort depended entirely upon reliable transportation to move passengers and freight within California and across the barriers of mountains and oceans that so thoroughly isolated the state. The papers of William Heath Davis, Jr., discuss, among other topics, shipping before and during the gold rush. The William Spencer and Henry L. Lowden Collection includes business correspondence and records of the Weaverville and Shasta Wagon Road Company and the Lewiston Turnpike Company. The enormous collection of the Pacific Mail Steamship Company (1851-1925; ca.190,000 pieces) focuses upon the line's business operations in coastal shipping and later in the trans-Pacific trade as well as the management of the Occidental and Oriental Steamship Company, a competitor founded in 1874 that merged with Pacific Mail in 1900. Another notable source for information about the shipping trade, although far smaller in bulk, is the papers of the American-Hawaiian Steamship Company (1901-1975; 278 pieces). The papers of the Banning Company and of George S. Patton, Sr., treat development of Wilmington, near San Pedro, as an entrepôt for shipping and freighting as well as the Banning Company's efforts to improve Los Angeles harbor.

The Banning Company papers also include records about another, and essential, form of transportation: railroads. Within HEH holdings are collections that deal with the great transcontinental lines, shorter-haul intrastate roads and many of the interurbans, especially in southern California, which were so important for urban growth.

The voluminous business records in the Huntington Collection, like the Banning Company's records, demonstrate not only the importance of such local lines, but also the complex ties that often bound them to the larger regional and transcontinental railroads. The Huntington Collection includes records from the Pacific Electric Railway and many other interurban lines, complementing several of the collections mentioned above. It also contains records of the Southern Pacific Railroad, one of many collections that refer to regional or national lines.

Other aspects of California's economic development can be traced through the many collections that discuss commerce and finance. Express companies, so important to gold rush California as freighters and bankers, are represented by several collections. Business papers of William A. Brown (1849-1855; 158 pieces) and Adams & Co. (ca.1855-1885; 750 pieces) detail the history of several early express companies, including the legal repercussions of Adams & Co.'s failure in 1855. The Wells, Fargo and Company Collection (1839-1911; 2,154 pieces) concentrates upon the late nineteenth-century operations of the firm and its relationship with its competitors. The Andrew Brown Collection (1856-1896; ca.2,756 pieces) views express companies from the perspective of a local agent.

Brown's papers also deal at considerable length with the various business enterprises, including a general store, that he ran in Kernville. This collection is only one of many describing the workings of businesses small and large in the second half of the nineteenth century: the papers of William R. Prince (1848-1854; 65 pieces); Foy Brothers' account books (1854-1925; 59 pieces); and the Selim E. Woodworth Collection (1834-1947; ca.1,600 pieces), for example. William Spalding's many careers, including citrus grower, newspaper executive, and Los Angeles civic leader, are encapsulated in his correspondence and business papers. The Banning Company records, beside the information they convey about railroads and harbor development, contain many letters, accounts, and ledgers relating to the business interests of the company and various members of the Banning family in real estate, freight handling, and petroleum. In the same vein, the Thomas Bard Collection (1866-1958; ca.50,000 pieces) describes Bard's involvement with the petroleum industry, especially as president of Union Oil Company, and with the development of Ventura County.

In their time, the express companies often had acted as bankers for the infant California economy; their records at the HEH document the early history of banking in the state. Beyond these collections, there are others that illuminate changes in the industry over time. The Bacon Collection includes information on banking in the 1850s; Price Collection discusses the business affairs of Ward & Price, a banking firm established in 1850 back East to serve as agents for California; Solon Chapman's letters and diaries (1859-1928; ca.600 pieces) portray his daily life as a businessman and banker for many years in the Napa Valley. Jackson Graves, one-time law partner of Henry O'Melveny in Los Angeles, also pursued a long career as a banker, which can be examined in his many letters about business and finance, especially with Isaias W. Hellman, Sr., president of the Farmers and Merchants Bank (Los Angeles), 1875-1920, and of Wells Fargo Nevada National Bank (San Francisco), 1890-1920. A very recent donation from the Santa Ana branch of Sanwa Bank brings the HEH collections on banking in southern California well into the twentieth century.

Lawyers and legal processes have been fundamental to the development of California since its acquisition by the United States. As we have seen, successful lawyers often moved easily between the law, business, finance, politics, and land development, and so many of those who have papers in the HEH will be or already have been mentioned in other contexts. However, their collections give valuable insight as well into the growth and conduct of the legal profession in California. Henry W. O'Melveny, for example, was for several decades one of the more prominent lawyers in Los Angeles, and his diaries and papers give a rich view of his life from law school at Berkeley to the year of his death. Jackson Graves was for a time senior partner of O'Melveny before becoming a banker, and his papers reflect in great detail both elements of his career. Another prominent Los Angeles lawyer whose business papers and correspondence are in the HEH is John D. Bicknell (1872-1911; ca.7,500 pieces). George S. Patton, Sr., perhaps better known for his other interests and, above all, for his famous son, was a successful lawyer. Finally, for the Santa Barbara area, there are the papers of lawyer Charles Fernald, who was also involved in petroleum and land development. More detailed information on the resources of the Huntington Library in this field can be found in Gordon M. Bakken, *Legal History at the Huntington Library* (San Marino, 1987).

The unfolding drama of politics and government in California since statehood can be studied through the HEH's large assortment of collections from players on the national, state, and local stages. Besides his many business ventures, Thomas Bard served as a United States senator for California, 1900-1905. References to national politics also appear in the letters of Orrin Peck, California artist, and of his sister Janet (1878-1948; ca.3,000 pieces) because of their close friendship with Phoebe Hearst and her son, the great newspaper magnate, William R. Hearst. Although the HEH does not possess a separate Herbert Hoover Collection, the political career of California's first president can be followed through the papers of Ralph Arnold, Clara Burdette, and Philip A. Stanton. These three collections, along with the papers of Marshall Stimson (1893-1951, 932 pieces), include details about Republican national politics and political events.

Both the Stanton and the Stimson collections address the involvement of these men in California politics during the turbulent first decades of this century. These collections are only two selections from the many at the HEH that deal with state politics and state government. Very useful for recreating the context of political affairs in California from statehood through the 1890s are the scrapbooks compiled by Winfield Davis (1849-1900; 40 pieces), a journalist, official court reporter of the City of Sacramento, and amateur historian. He carefully prepared album after album of newspaper clippings, keyed to a massive multivolume index. He also produced a five-volume handwritten history of the state from Spanish times to his own. Other details about political life later in the nineteenth century can be obtained from a number of sources. Henry H. Haight (1846-1885; 508 pieces), San Francisco lawyer, and Henry H.

Markham (1867-1899; ca.2,494 pieces), California mining entrepreneur, each served a term as governor, 1867-1871 and 1891-1895, respectively. Charles Maclay served in both the Assembly and the Senate as well as tending to his many business interests, and his papers discuss politics, 1860-1870. Mary E. Foy, pioneer resident of Los Angeles (1879-1957; ca.500 pieces) not only supported literary and historical societies in 1880s Los Angeles, but she also took part in the Women's Democratic League. The Shorb papers, of an influential Los Angeles businessman, include information about state politics in the late nineteenth century.

In regard to twentieth-century politics, both the Philip Stanton and the Marshall Stimson collections are revealing about state as well as national Republican politics. The papers of Thomas L. Woolwine, Los Angeles District Attorney. contain letters and documents about his campaigns for various offices, including his unsuccessful bids for the 1918 Democratic gubernatorial nomination and for the governorship in 1922. Reginaldo F. del Valle's papers discuss aspects of his long career in Democratic politics as an assemblyman, state senator, and member of many public service commissions for the City of Los Angeles.

On the local level, HEH collections reach back as far as the El Dorado County Archives (1850-1906) and various papers from the 1856 San Francisco Committee of Vigilance. The Vigilance Committee material (1853-1858; ca.3,750 pieces) contains information from individuals making charges or giving information about suspects or prisoners to the Vigilance Committee, applications for membership, lists of members and members of the executive committee, and financial documents. The El Dorado County Archives give a detailed if sometimes sporadic history of county administration as seen through court records, tax and assessment rolls, and school and land records. There are several other much smaller collections, as yet uncataloged, of documents from Santa Clara, Trinity, and Yuba counties. San Francisco politics, late in the nineteenth century, recur as a topic in the papers of Adolph Sutro, mining engineer and businessman, who served as mayor, 1894-1896. Santa Barbara County affairs appear in the papers of Charles Fernald. Myron Hunt (1815-1957; 4,156 pieces), although best known as a leading California architect, also became deeply involved in Pasadena politics. Two more recent political careers can be studied through the voluminous papers of Fletcher Bowron (1934-1970; ca.20,000 pieces), mayor of Los Angeles 1938-1953, and of John Anson Ford (1932-1971; ca.35,000 pieces), who sat on the County Board of Supervisors, 1934-1958. Both of these collections discuss politics and the enormous range of tasks required of twentieth-century municipal and county government.

Finally, although HEH manuscript holdings about politics center upon elected officials or civil servants, there are several collections that focus upon social and political reform. The Llano del Rio Colony, founded in the Antelope Valley by Los Angeles attorney Job Harriman, tried to create an agricultural utopia. The struggle for women's suffrage in California is a salient feature of the papers of Elizabeth Morrison (Boynton) Harbert (1863-1925; ca.4,400 pieces) and Alice Locke Park (1798-1953; 795 pieces), who labored long for the cause as well as for many other reform measures. Many papers from another prominent social reformer, Sara Bard Field, form a significant portion of the Charles Erskine Scott Wood Collection.

California's explosive growth after the gold rush and its subsequent economic development exerted enormous pressure upon the state's original inhabitants. The papers of Couts and Wilson contain much useful information about Indians in the southern portion of the state soon after the American conquest. Among many other topics, the scrapbooks of John G. Marvin, the state's first superintendent of public instruction, include his account of the Mariposa War in 1850-1851. Thomas W. Sweeney (1830-1944; 1,265 pieces) participated in the campaigns launched against the Yuma Indians from Fort Yuma in California, 1851-1853. From the end of the nineteenth century, when the Indians had become the objects more of curiosity or pity than of hatred, the papers of Horatio N. Rust and Charles F. Saunders discuss the contemporary circumstances of California's Indians. Grace Nicholson, prominent Pasadena art dealer, absorbed a vast array of details about Indian ways of life and collected thousands of artifacts from tribes all over the West. Her papers (1822-1951; ca.2,560 pieces) document her research into Indian cultures and the breadth of her collecting interests.

Fewer collections document the experience of other minority groups since statehood. The California File includes various letters about Chinese immigrants in the mines or the cities during the gold rush, while other collections contain references to Chinese communities in later decades. From our own century, several collections offer scholars information about the roles of different ethnic groups in the City and County of Los Angeles. The papers of Fletcher Bowron and of John Anson Ford discuss, among a multitude of other topics, the minority communities within greater Los Angeles and their often uneasy relationship with the dominant culture.

Beyond those collections that address economic and political matters, numerous others trace California's social and cultural development during the American period. Very shortly after statehood, for example, California's government began making provisions for public education while private citizens supported other institutions of general instruction and higher learning. The scrapbooks of John G. Marvin contain many of the reports and newspaper articles he wrote in support of a public school system. The papers of Charles Maclay document his involvement with the founding years of the University of Southern California. For the twentieth century, the Thompson Webb Collection (1798-1974; 20,740 pieces) reviews aspects of California education and in particular the Webb School in Claremont, which Webb's father founded and of which he served as headmaster until 1962. The papers of Clara (Bradley) Burdette (1843-1954; ca. 50,000 pieces), clubwoman and philanthropist, refer to her involvement with Mills College, California College in China, and the Southwest Museum.

Other manuscript collections discuss different phases in the history of leading cultural institutions. The Sutro Collection, besides its details about San Francisco business and politics, also illuminates the foundation of the California State Library's Sutro branch, whose cornerstone was Sutro's own library of rare volumes. The Charles F. Lummis Collection (1900-1925; 140 pieces) portrays his tenure as Librarian of the Los Angeles Public Library, 1905-1910. The Grace Nicholson Collection details her mounting fascination with Oriental art and her consequent establishment of Pasadena's Pacific-Asia Museum in 1929 to display her acquisitions. Huntington's papers and the correspondence of Max Farrand (1816-1947; 3,470 pieces), first director of the Huntington Library, shed light upon Huntington's collecting and upon the creation of the research library and the first art gallery.

Other prominent Californians took a very active part in philanthropic endeavors, charitable organizations, and the burgeoning women's club movement that arose in the late nineteenth century. The papers of Orrin Peck, California artist, for example, describe many of the good works pursued by his friend, Mrs. Phoebe (Apperson) Hearst. Students of late nineteenth- and early twentieth-century women's organizations in California will be especially interested in the papers of Caroline Maria (Seymour) Severance (1875-1919; 8,400 pieces) and Clara Burdette.

Scholars interested in the religious history of Los Angeles also could turn to the Burdette and Severance collections. Besides the Indian mission work discussed elsewhere, other manuscript collections that deal with religion in California touch upon missionary work in the gold fields and the early history of various Protestant denominations in postconquest California. Edward B. Walsworth's papers (1840-1889; 138 pieces) describe his activities on behalf of the Presbyterian Church in California (1852-1883). Manuscripts in both the Widney Family Collection and the Joseph Aram Collection (1835-1912; 90 pieces) discuss the Methodist Episcopal Church in California. The Aram Collection also includes the journal of Peter Y. Cool, early Methodist preacher, who toiled in the mining country during 1851-1852. Similarly, the George S. Phillips Collection (1840-1881; 205 pieces) includes details of his activities as an itinerant Methodist minister in northern California during the 1850s.

The social and cultural development of Los Angeles also meant the growth of an indigenous literature and the birth of local institutions to host the performing arts. Among its extensive literary holdings, the HEH possesses correspondence and manuscripts from a wide range of California authors including George Wharton James (1871-1921; 266 pieces), that tireless promoter of California and the desert Southwest; Helen Hunt Jackson (1850-1885; approx. 200 pieces), friend of the American Indian and author of *Ramona*; Margaret (Collier) Graham (1821-1934; 5,360 pieces), who displayed an acute sense of place in her many short stories set in southern California; Elwyn I. Hoffman (1893-1947; 393 pieces), a Sacramento journalist whose interests in poetry and literature led him to correspond with many California authors, including Jack London; Ina Coolbrith (1889-1932; 864 pieces), poet laureate of California from 1906 until her death in 1932; and Kate Rennie (Aitken) Archer, California poet and teacher (1932-1960; ca.400 pieces). Many of their manuscripts demonstrate how these authors drew upon California's climate, its landscape, or its heritage for inspiration, while some of their letters illuminate the relationships among these and other California writers. Equally revealing about such matters is the California Poetry File (2,100 pieces), which consists of poems, letters, and printed items written by and relating to Western writers and California poets in particular. The collection offers an interesting view of the California literary scene during the first half of the twentieth century, particularly in its concentration on many local and lesser-known writers. Finally, the HEH holds significant collections of letters and manuscripts from several major writers who had established a strong regional identity. The library's collections of George Sterling (1895-1927; 611 pieces), Mary Austin (1861-1950; ca. 11,000 pieces), and Jack London (1866-1977; ca.30,000 pieces), although far better known for their value to literary scholars or biographers, do contribute to an understanding of what Kevin Starr has called America's "California Dream."

In the realm of the performing arts, various collections document the history of music and theater in southern California. The Lynden E. Behymer Collection (1881-1948; ca.3,990 pieces) captures the efforts of this famous impresario to bring programs of opera, musical theater, and symphonic music to Los Angeles during the first half of this century. Correspondence and business papers for the Los Angeles Symphony, 1917-1920, supplement the Behymer with details about the operations of this one body. The business and personal correspondence of Dr. T. Perceval Gerson (1901, 1929-1938; 483 pieces), one of the founders of the Hollywood Bowl, and the records of Ojai Festivals, Lts. (1946-1953; ca.9,110 pieces), include correspondence with distinguished composers, conductors, and performers about the annual programs these two organizations produced.

Unfortunately, no listing can be absolutely comprehensive or fully up-to-date. Even this essay can only offer the briefest description of many collections and must omit many others entirely. The HEH continues to acquire new manuscript material on California history and to complete the cataloging of earlier acquisitions. Researchers seeking further details about any collection included in this essay or about new acquisitions are encouraged to consult several other sources of information. The HEH routinely submits collection descriptions to the *National Union Catalog of Manuscript Collections* and collaborates with the compilers of major topical bibliographies. Scholars interested in specific individuals or institutions or issues should refer to NUCMC or to subject guides such as *Women's History Sources*, ed. by Andrea Hinding (New York, 1979) or *North American Forest History*, ed. by Ronald Davis (New York, 1977). With the support of the National Endowment for the Humanities, the HEH itself has printed a series of manuscript guides, including a *Guide to American Historical Manuscripts in The Huntington Library* (San Marino, 1979) and a *Guide to Literary Manuscripts in the Huntington Library* (San Marino, 1979), which describe the bulk of the HEH's cataloged and uncataloged collections in far greater depth than is possible here. Significant new acquisitions in all fields are often described in the "Intramuralia" column of the *Huntington Library Quarterly*. Researchers who have found these various printed sources inadequate to their needs are invited to write directly to the HEH Manuscripts Department for further information.

Since the research library is not a public institution, access to the collections must be arranged by application in advance. In general, the HEH collections are made available to advanced graduate students, university faculty members, and responsible independent researchers engaged in detailed research requiring the use of primary sources. Interested persons should contact the Reader Services Librarian for applications and information about Library procedures. For those researchers who are unable to visit San Marino, the Photographic Services Department can supply photographic, xerox, or microfilm copies of materials that have been approved for duplication by the appropriate Curator and the Librarian. Although the limits of personnel and time preclude the Manuscripts Department from answering inquiries that require in-depth research, members of the staff will be happy to assist correspondents in identifying materials relevant to specific projects that can be reproduced. The HEH welcomes the opportunity to advance serious research into all phases of California's history.

17

CALIFORNIA COLLECTIONS AT UCLA

DAVID S. ZEIDBERG, ANNE CAIGER,
DAN LUCKENBILL, AND LILACE HATAYAMA

Street address:	Department of Special Collections
	University Research Library
	UCLA
	405 Hilgard Avenue
	Los Angeles, CA 90024
Mailing address:	Same
Telephone:	(213) 825-4879
Days and hours:	Monday–Saturday, 9:00 A.M. to 5:00 P.M.
	Closed: Sundays, New Year's Day, Fourth
	of July, Labor Day, Thanksgiving, Christmas

UCLA PURCHASED IN 1936 what remains today the core of its Californiana holdings—the second collection compiled by Robert Cowan. Of the 4,700 titles Cowan listed in his *Bibliography of the History of California, 1510–1930*, the Department of Special Collections (hereinafter cited DSC) holds more than 90 percent. Manuscripts, photographs, ephemera, and historical map collections are described at the collection level in the numbered collections catalog, which, like the rare book catalog, is a dictionary catalog combining name and subject entries and cross references. Most collection-level descriptions refer the reader to a finding aid to the collection with more specific information about the scope and content of materials in the collection. Collection-level descriptions of manuscript and photographic collections have been entered into ORION, the Library's on-line bibliographic system. The DSC's rare books are also on ORION.

UCLA holds several significant agricultural collections, the earliest being the papers of the Powell Family (1836– ; 16 ft.). The bulk of the papers are those of George Harold Powell, 1872–1922, who was general manager of the California Fruit Exchange from 1912 until his death. Two other important family papers are those of the Jones Family (1847–1946; 17 ft.) and the Gardner Family (1877–1960; 6 ft.). Jones was the founder of Santa Monica and served as U.S. Senator from Nevada, and Dian Rathburn Gardner, 1870–1960, and family were citrus growers in Orange County.

William M. Baird's Papers (1914–1930; 6 ft.) concern the development of water resources and farming in the San Bernardino valley. The papers of George P. Clements (1925–1945; 40 ft.) contain materials on twentieth-century agriculture, forestry, migrant labor, and soil and water conservation. James L. L. F. Warren (1837–1879; 2 ft.) was in the nursery business in the north, served as editor of *The California Farmer*, and worked toward the organization of the California State Agricultural Society. Theodosia B. Shepherd (ca.1900–1940; 1.5 ft.) was a pioneer of seed culture in California. The Department also has a Nursery Catalog collection (ca.1938–1960; 3.5 ft.) which contains catalogs of nursery stock, ornamental plants, and gardening.

The most comprehensive collection among the Department's architectural/urban planning holdings is the papers of international style architect Richard J. Neutra (to 1970; 190 ft.; 25 mapcase drawers). Many of Neutra's significant residential designs are in Los Angeles.

The bulk of the architectural holdings focuses upon southern California, including the papers of John C. W. Austin (1895–1963; 5 ft.); Albert R. Walker (unprocessed); Harold H. Martin (ca.1920s; 5 ft.), and Frederick Monhoff (ca.1922–1972; 15 ft.), whose papers focus primarily on work in Los Angeles. The Department recently received on deposit the papers of S. Charles Lee, the Los Angeles architect best known for his art deco designs of Los Angeles movie theatres.

Landscape architecture is one of the most active areas of collection development in the department. Selected papers of the American Institute of Landscape Architects (ca.1954–1977; 35 ft.) contain materials of the California Association of Landscape Architects and the California Council of Landscape Architects. Individual collections include the papers of Joseph Copp (1948–1978; 1800 drawings); Edward Huntsman-Trout (1922–1971; 36 ft.; 4 mapcase drawers); George A. Kern (ca.1925–1940; 3 ft.); and Warner L. Marsh (1927–1965; 13 ft.).

One cannot leave discussion of the architectural collections at UCLA without citing the papers of Harvey S. Perloff (40 ft.), the founding dean of UCLA's School of Architecture and Urban Planning. Perloff's tenure gave shape to the holdings at UCLA, and his scholarship in the field is as important as the primary resources in the collection.

The Department of Special Collections' holdings in fine arts include the corporate records of the Huntington Hartford Foundation, a Los Angeles foundation for the arts which flourished from 1948 to 1965 (37 ft.); approximately 100 manuscripts of Charles F. Lummis; and the papers of Los Angeles artist Myron C. Nutting (ca.1920–1971; 2 ft.).

On the performing arts side, the DSC holds the papers of Ruth St. Denis (ca. 1886-1968; 85 ft.), pioneer in modern and interpretive dance, who had a studio in Los Angeles and whose foundation in North Hollywood still conducts classes and seminars on the dance. The Oral History Program also conducted an interview with her shortly before her death. Two other collections in the dance are the records of the Southern California Folk Dance Federation (1945-1975; 15 ft.), and the Rudolphe Abel collection of ephemera relating to the dance in southern California (1920- ; 4 ft.).

Researchers will find a variety of materials relating to the theatre: for example, an extensive collection of theatre, movie, and concert programs (v.d.; 130 ft.), the bulk of which is from Los Angeles and southern California. The papers of Kenneth Macgowan (ca.1915-1970; 34 ft.) give a good overview of the theatre community in Los Angeles in particular. He was active in motion pictures and helped establish the Theater Arts program at UCLA.

Researchers should begin their inquiries about California music collections at the Music Library where the bulk of special collections in the field is housed. The Library holds notable California-related collections, including the Ernst Toch Archive, the Film and Television Music Archive, the Eric Zeisl Archive, the Popular American Music Archive, the Ethnomusicology Archive, and manuscript collections of many local composers.

Several collections in the DSC complement the Music Library holdings: a collection of music by Lionel Barrymore (v.d.; 7 ft.); the papers of Fannie Charles Dillon (1905-1942; 10 ft.); Sven Helga Reher (1918-1979; 7 ft.); and those of Elliot Griffis (1920-1965; 3 ft.), as well as two collections pertaining to the popular Monday Evening Concert Series in Los Angeles. The papers of music and theatre impresario Mary Bran (1938-1972; 1 ft.) include the typescript of her autobiography and memorabilia of her Los Angeles presentations. The papers of Bessie H. B. Frankel (ca.1905-1959; 3 ft.) provide materials on the California Federation of Music Clubs and the Los Angeles Philharmonic Association.

DSC's holdings pertaining to civil rights and civil liberties date from the 1930s. Among general collections is the Civil Rights Movement in the United States collection (1950- ; 6 ft.) with materials focusing on California activities.

The most extensive civil rights collection is the archive of the American Civil Liberties Union, Southern California (1935- ; 81 ft.), which adds materials annually. The archive includes records of the office and the major cases in which the organization has been involved. There are several other collections associated with the ACLU available as well.

Of interest in other civil rights areas are the papers of Everett T. Moore (1950-1975; 6 ft.) pertaining to the California Library Association's Intellectual Freedom Committee, and Stafford L. Warren (1917-1980; 181 ft.) concerning his role as the head of the medical team observing the Crossroads and Manhattan projects' nuclear testing.

The earliest holdings on California education are the papers of Edward Hyatt

(1880-1919; 3 ft.); the Boyton Teachers' Agency records (1908-1929; 18 ft.), an important resource for California county schools' annual directories; the papers of Edwin A. Lee (ca.1922-1965; 9 ft.), UCLA educator; and the collection compiled by Roy E. Simpson (1945-1958; 17 ft.), which documents the post-World War II developments while he was State Superintendent of Instruction. Holdings about education in the Los Angeles area begin with George W. McDill's collection (ca.1933-1937; 2 ft.) about the Los Angeles Board of Education, as does John R. Kelley's (1933-1945; 2 ft.). The papers of Frances R. Eisenberg (ca.1946-1968; 6 ft.) include materials about the California Teachers' Association and the Los Angeles Board of Education, while Paul Egly's papers (1977-1981; 75 ft.) document the *Mary Ellen Crawford* v. *Los Angeles Unified School District* desegregation, as do the papers of the Los Angeles School District Monitoring Committee (1978-1981; 120 ft.).

The Sierra Club and two book collections on mountaineering and national parks, respectively, form the core collection on the California environment. The DSC has three Sierra Club collections: printed materials (v.d.; 7 ft.); the records of the Club's Angeles Chapter, Los Angeles (1929- ; 11 ft.); and oral history interviews with prominent members.

Francis P. Farquhar's extensive book collection on mountaineering and Horace M. Albright's collection on national parks have significant California items. Albright also donated his papers (v.d.; 160 ft.).

Several other collections pertaining to the California environment are worth noting as well. Richard Richards's papers (ca.1954-1962; 24 ft.) relate to air pollution, particularly in the Los Angeles region, as do the papers of Willard Libby (1960s- ; 90 ft.). The records of the Federation of Hillside and Canyon Associations (1963-ca.1979; 12 ft.) detail its concern with almost all aspects of the environment in canyon residential areas.

One of the most significant groups of collections relating to the people of California is that assembled by the Japanese American Research Project (ca. 1899-1977; 400 ft.). The JARP guide gives an overview of the collection holdings. Another approach to the JARP collection is to consult Yuji Ichioka, *A Buried Past: An Annotated Bibliography of the Japanese American Research Project Collection* (Berkeley, 1974), although it does not reflect the arrangement of the collections the way the DSC's JARP register does. Supporting collections are the papers of Tetsuo Scott Miyakawa (1946-1981; 51 ft.), which document his life-long scholarship in Japanese-American history; Joe Masaoka (1927-1970; 5 ft.), JARP administrator, 1964-1970; and Frank F. Chuman (1900-1983; 50 ft.), documenting his legal history of the JACL and the JARP.

In addition, the DSC holds the archive of the Relocation Center at Manzanar, California (1942-1946; 57 ft.) and some of the correspondence of Ralph P. Merritt (ca.1940-1960; 1 ft.), who was the director. Portions of Shigeichi Kawano's papers (1940- ; 10 ft.) concern the Japanese evacuation from California, as do Charles Kikuchi's papers (1941-1979; 26 ft.), which also include materials about the U.S. Tanforan Assembly Center in San Bruno.

The black community in Los Angeles is represented by selected manuscripts from the Los Angeles Urban League (1944-1945; 200 items) and by the records of the Golden State Mutual Life Insurance Comapny (v.d.; 40 ft.), a prominent business which has flourished for most of the twentieth century. Two collections concern the Watts riots of 1967: the papers of Robert R. Kirsch (1967- ; 5 ft.), and those of Paul Bullock (1967-1972; 2 ft.).

Materials about the Mexican-American community are most fully represented by the papers of Carey McWilliams (v.d.; 17 ft.). Other McWilliams holdings include a second collection made up primarily of his correspondence (v.d., 28 ft.) and the papers of Eshref Shevsky (1945-1981; 4 ft.), which concern Mexicans in Los Angeles. Another important collection is that compiled by Alice Greenfield McGrath, the papers of the Sleepy Lagoon Defense Committee (1942-1945; 6 ft.), formed to aid young Mexican Americans tried and convicted en masse in a famous murder case.

The Mojave Indian tribe is documented by a lifetime of work by UCLA Professor Lorraine M. Sherer, whose papers and collected materials (ca.1700s-ca. 1975; 50 ft.) include manuscripts, ephemera, printed and research documents, and oral histories relating to the tribe.

The John R. Haynes and Dora Haynes Foundation's gift of books and manuscripts included several substantial collections relating to California history, notably the papers of Franklin Hichborn (1890-1940; 92 ft.), which cover political and social movements. Haynes also included his own papers (1890-1937; 170 ft.), which touch on many local and regional concerns.

Among nineteenth-century holdings, one of the most important collections is the papers of General William S. Rosecrans (1810-1920; 55 ft.). Another collection centered on mining is the papers of Henry Z. Osborne (1869-1947; 10 ft.). Smaller, but interesting, nineteenth-century collections include a portion of William Heath Davis's correspondence and papers (1840-1891; 1 ft.); the papers of Archibald H. Gillespie (1845-1860; 3 ft.); and a portion of the correspondence of Jonathan D. Stevenson (1840-1892; 1 ft.).

Historical holdings about the southern region of the state include three San Diego area collections: the papers of Victor B. Westfall (1897-1961; 2 ft.); Moses A. Luce and Edgar A. Luce, collected as Luce family papers (1861-1959; 2 ft.); and of Charles F. Stern (1909-1943; 4 ft.).

The Los Angeles area is represented by a variety of collections on its general history, its communities, and its important families. Readers wanting an overview can begin with two interesting oral history collections apart from the DSC's Oral History Program holdings. Former Los Angeles Mayor Fletcher Bowron, 1887-1968, conducted interviews as part of the Metropolitan Los Angeles History Project, documenting Los Angeles history (1900-1940), along with a substantial number of Bowron's letters in various collections. The second oral history collection consists of 115 interviews collected by David L. Clark and his students on a variety of Los Angeles subjects.

Among the papers of people who have written works about Los Angeles, the most comprehensive collection is the papers of W. W. Robinson (ca.1843-1972; 60 ft.). His knowledge of California land title controversies and the history they provide became the basis for his writing local history, culminating in *Land in California* (Berkeley, 1948), and a series of calendar booklets (1935-1961) on various Los Angeles and California communities. Another Los Angeles historian, John D. Weaver, has contributed an active collection of clippings and ephemera about the city (ca.1860- ; 50 ft.), a collection on the 1984 Olympic games, and has committed his own papers as a bequest. There are a number of supplemental collections as well.

Collections representing prominent Los Angeles families include the papers of the Griffith family (1845-1975; 14 ft., processed) and of the Wilshire family (1899-1955; 11 ft.). Dorothy Buffum Chandler recently contributed her papers relating to the development of the Music Center in Los Angeles (1955-1973; 11 ft.), although these papers remain restricted.

Researchers can find something about virtually every community in the Los Angeles area in the numbered collection catalog. As a sampling, there are the minutes of the Avalon City Council, Santa Catalina Island (1913-1942; 2 ft.), and the records of the Westwood Chamber of Commerce (1930- ; 13 ft.). The U.S. Works Projects Administration in California ran an Orange County historical project, O.P. no. 65-3-3885, WPA project no. 3105, in the 1930s, and a Southern California Writers' Project relating to a guide for California (90 ft., partly processed).

Major journalism collections provide almost as comprehensive resources for a wide variety of California subject interests as do the more substantial history collections described above. One collection of broader scope is the papers of Norman Cousins, formerly the editor of *Saturday Review* (ca.1940- ; 500 ft.). The rest of the holdings are almost all from the Los Angeles area, except for the papers of Chester Harvey Rowell (1898-1920; 2 ft.), who was editor of the Fresno *Republican*. Early twentieth-century Los Angeles journalists include George W. Savage, whose papers pertain to Owens Valley and San Bernardino County (4 ft.); a substantial number of collections of people associated with the Los Angeles *Times*, among them literary editor Paul J. Smith (ca.1909-1971; 25 ft.); and editor/reporter Edward M. Ainsworth (1945-1968; 37 ft.). Holdings among current writers include papers of columnist Jack C. Smith (1 ft.), and food editor Colman Andrews (1968- ; 6 ft.). The *Times* has also donated its photo archive (ca.1875- ; 2 million negatives, in process) which is supplemented each year.

Another major photographic resource is the photo morgue of the Los Angeles *Daily News* (1923-1954; 20,000 prints, 200,000 negatives). For access to these photographs, readers should consult Kayla Landesman, "Index. The Los Angeles *Daily News* Photograph Morgue" (UCLA, 1985).

In the field of labor, the papers of Pelham D. Glassford (1904-1959; 15 ft.) include materials relating to the Imperial Valley labor disputes of 1934; a selection of California Unemployment Labor Camps documents (ca.1932-1935; 1 ft.), which includes papers of Merritt B. Pratt and James Rolph; Philip M. Connelly's papers (ca.1942-1957; 3 ft.), which include materials on the Los Angeles CIO Industrial Union Council; and the papers of the United Office and Professional Workers of America (1937-1950; 14 ft.), which pertain to west coast union activities, among other holdings.

Collections pertaining to law in California begin with legal papers of Gregory Yale (1828-1871; 3 ft.); the correspondence and papers of Halleck, Peachy & Billings, San Francisco (ca.1842-1862; 4 ft.) concerning land titles in the Bay area; and the papers of Rodman M. Price (1847-1884; 1 ft.). Among other nineteenth-century holdings, the DSC also has selective legal documents of organizations and municipalities.

Holdings for the twentieth century include a collection of clippings, photographs, and memorabilia relating to the career of Judge Thomas P. White (ca. 1910-1961; 3 ft.); the papers of the first woman appointed Superior Court Judge in California, Georgia Philipps Morgan Bullock (ca.1922-1949; 6 ft.); Harold Garfinkle's papers (1959-1962; 75 ft.) concerning capital punishment and the case of Caryl Chessman, 1921-1960; and the papers of John Gilmore (1965- ; 4 ft.) containing materials relating to Bobby Beausoleil and Charles Manson.

A portion of the Shankland family papers (1846-1939; 4 ft.) offers a history of law in Los Angeles, while the papers of Joseph Le Compte Davis (1899-1957; 4 ft.) concern John J. McNamara and James B. McNamara, and the bombing of the Los Angeles *Times*. Other Los Angeles area law collections include the papers of Eugene W. Biscailuz (ca.1900- ; 17 ft.), which give a good overview of law enforcement in Los Angeles; and the papers of Léon R. Yankwich (1909-1959; 65 ft.) and Charles E. Haas (ca.1884-1957; 1 ft.), who served as judges in the Los Angeles County Superior Court. The papers of Judge Frederick F. Houser (ca.1940-1960; 8 ft.) include materials of his 1944 Senate campaign. The papers of Henry E. Carter (ca.1910-1940; 67 ft.) concern his Los Angeles law practice and his terms as a California State Senator. James H. Pope's papers (1920-1960; 2 ft.) include materials relating to the Los Angeles County Bar Association.

Although restricted and unavailable at present due to their confidential nature, the papers of Marcus E. Crahan (ca.1945-1977; 50 ft.) is a collection researchers will want to consult in the future. Dr. Crahan was the attending physician at the Los Angeles jail, and his papers include medical files used in Los Angeles County court cases.

One of the great strengths in the DSC is its holdings in nineteenth- and twentieth-century literature, both books and manuscripts. Among the important collections are the papers of Henry Miller (ca.1920-1980; 75 ft.), who lived his last years in Pacific Palisades. The papers of Anaïs Nin (1914-1977; 21 ft.) include her early diaries which are being published by Harcourt Brace Jovanovich and will be accessible after the series is completed. To get a sense of the Los Angeles *literati*, readers might begin with the papers of Bernadine S. Fritz (ca.1925-1974; 3 ft.), who settled in Los Angeles in 1939 and established a "Hollywood salon" in her home which served as a gathering place for the foremost literary and artistic personalities of the 1940s and 1950s.

Whether drawn by climate, the promise of screenwriting, or a more liberal atmosphere in which to write, many writers emigrated to Los Angeles. Among the German emigrés represented is Franz Werfel. The entire contents of his study—ephemera, pictures, objects, and books—were transferred to UCLA upon his death, along with his papers (ca.1900-1945; 20 ft.).

Among English emigrés, the Department has several single manuscripts and some correspondence, for example, of Christopher Isherwood, who makes his home in Santa Monica Canyon. The DSC also holds the papers of his friend and canyon neighbor Gerald Heard (ca.1935- ; 17 ft.), including manuscripts of his lectures, articles, and books, as well as some correspondence. The DSC acquired remaining papers (1925-1963; 6 ft.) of the English writer Aldous Huxley, who expatriated himself, including literary manuscripts, correspondence, and business correspondence with his publishers, Harper & Brothers.

Artist and poet Kenneth Rexroth lived in Santa Barbara, worked as a columnist for the San Francisco *Examiner* (1960-1968), and founded the San Francisco Poetry Center. His papers (ca.1920-1982; 32 ft.) include correspondence, manuscripts, and ephemera both by and about him. The papers of Lawrence Lipton (ca.1940-1975; 3 ft.) include his correspondence and drafts of his work *The Holy Barbarians*, which discusses Rexroth, Nin, and Miller, among many others.

Longtime Los Angeles writers include Guy Endore (ca.1925-1970; 19 ft.) and Robert R. Kirsch (6 ft.). The latter includes typescripts of his novels and short stories, some of which he wrote under the pseudonym Robert Dundee. The Los Angeles writer and novelist Carolyn See donated her literary papers (ca. 1950- ; 30 ft.). See also donated her extensive collection of Hollywood literature (6 ft.). Writers who emerged from detective writing and the pulps to create a part of that Hollywood literature include Horace McCoy (ca.1925- ; 3 ft.), and Raymond Chandler (ca.1930-1959; 12 ft.), a long-time resident of La Jolla.

Writers who have written actual history or historical fiction include Richard H. Dillon (ca.1957- ; 50 ft.); historical biographers Irving and Jean Stone (ca. 1925- ; 119 ft., restricted); Joseph Gaer (3 ft.); Paul I. Wellman (ca.1930-1966; 15 ft.); and historical novelist/poet Ruth Eleanor McKee (ca.1905-1972; 6 ft.). Regionalist writers represented include novelist Idwal Jones (1936-1950; 2 ft.); Lillian Bos Ross (ca.1940-1945; 2 ft.); and Edwin Corle (ca.1930-1956; 3 ft.).

Most of the medical and scientific collections pertaining to California are of the twentieth century. An early collection is the papers of Peter C. Remondino (1891-1917; 2 ft.) on medical climatology; Rhea Carolyn Ackerman (ca.1913-1969; 2 ft.) on the Los Angeles Children's Hospital and the Los Angeles County Juvenile Hall; and two collections from UCLA physicians, William P. Longmire, Jr., first chairman of the Department of Surgery at the UCLA School of Medicine (unprocessed; 41 ft.), and John M. Adams (1936-1970s; 11 ft.), who has done pioneer research on Sudden Infant Death Syndrome ("crib deaths"). The papers of Frederick Johnson (1948-1968; 5 ft.) concern his work with Willard Frank Libby on theories regarding the use of Carbon 14 as a dating process.

Los Angeles has had the good fortune to host two Olympics, in 1932 and 1984. The DSC has a collection of ephemera and memorabilia from the 1932 games (1 ft.). The 1984 Los Angeles Olympic Organizing Committee designated UCLA as the repository for its archive. Their records include papers from more than eighty offices in the organization; publications include posters, brochures, pamphlets, and booklets (1978- ; 312 ft.). Materials collected unofficially by Jeanne M. D'Amico form a separate collection (1979- ; 30 ft.).

Sheryl Conkelton's *University of California: Directory of Photographic Collections* (Riverside, 1985) is the first source for California-related photographs at UCLA, but readers should consult each repository on campus with substantial photographic holdings.

Political collections in the DSC are extensive and diverse. Corporate holdings include the records of the Socialist party [U.S.] (ca.1924-1946; 7 ft.); the John Birch Society papers (18 ft.); the California Republican Assembly (ca.1936- ; 35 ft.); and the papers of past CRA president Robert F. Craig (ca.1936-1974; 11 ft.). Recently acquired was the archive of the California Democratic Council (33 ft.; unprocessed).

The DSC also holds the papers of some prominent elected California representatives; among them the Cole family papers (1833-1943; 30 ft.) are primarily of Cornelius Cole who served as U.S. Senator, and Hugo Fisher's papers (1958-1962; 56 ft.) pertain to his California State Senate term representing San Diego county. Political holdings relating to the Los Angeles area include the papers of Joseph E. Shaw (1887-1963; 14 ft.); Clifford E. Clinton (ca.1934-1969; 7 ft.); Ernest R. Chamberlain (ca.1923-1972; 93 ft.); and Harold H. Story (1909-1963; 9 ft.), socialist and pacifist. Mayoral holdings include the personal papers of Norris Poulson (ca.1938-1965; 8 ft.) and Tom Bradley (1975-1977; 1 ft.).

The most comprehensive collection related to the Los Angeles City Council is the papers of Edward R. Roybal (1953-1962; 16 ft.), a U.S. congressman, who served as a councilman during the period covered by the bulk dates of his papers.

UCLA's collections again are strong resources for the study of the book world in California. Both the Department and the William Andrews Clark Memorial Library have extensive holdings of California printers. Ward Ritchie recently began to turn his papers over to the Clark; the first installment includes his own press materials and correspondence with Merle Armitage and Rockwell Kent concerning books they illustrated for Ritchie (1950-1985; 2 ft.).

The DSC's holdings in California printing include several composite collections: the Southern California Imprints, consisting of approximately 450 undated booklets and pamphlets and another 11,000 items dating from 1854 to the present, and a small collection of Los Angeles printing ephemera relating to art in printing and the printing trade (3 ft.). Jacob I. Zeitlin donated and augmented an important collection of graphic arts ephemera (twentieth century; 51 ft.), which concerns all aspects of book arts, printing, typography, and printing history with a substantial portion of the collection representing California.

Bookselling in the Los Angeles area is well represented. The DSC holds the personal papers of California collector, bookseller, and librarian Robert E. Cowan (1890-1942; 1 ft.); Olive Percival (ca.1880-1950; 17 ft.); and Dawson's Book Shop (ca.1905- ; 18 ft.) which includes the papers of the shop's founder Ernest Dawson, and his sons, Glen Dawson and Muir Dawson.

Jake Zeitlin has also given his papers (90 ft.). This collection includes not only records from his Los Angeles antiquarian bookshop but also personal papers which can be considered a microcosm of California collections at UCLA.

With regard to collections of California librarians, the papers of Lawrence Clark Powell rank with Jake Zeitlin's when documenting the book world of California (1914-1987; 35 ft.).

The DSC has a number of collections dealing with nineteenth-century and twentieth-century land development, the more important being the papers of Hobart J. Whitley (ca.1889-1946; 18 ft.); Fremont Ackerman (ca.1890-1945; 31 ft.); William G. McAdoo (1902-1938; 9 ft.); and Henry W. Keller (ca.1907-1938; 9 ft.).

UCLA's Department of Theater Arts runs one of the major academic programs in the country on the study of film, television, radio, and the performing arts. Readers should consult UCLA's printed guide to the holdings, *Film/TV/Radio: A Guide to Media Research Resources at UCLA*, for an overview of collections. Part of the Theater Arts Library's holdings have been described in *A Catalog of Books, Periodicals, Screenplays, Television Scripts, and Production Stills in the Theater Arts Library, UCLA* (Boston, 1974). The DSC holds more than 140 theatre arts collections, most of them again pertaining to film, television, and radio. These are described in Linda Mehr's *Motion Pictures, Television, and Radio: A Union Catalog of Manuscript and Special Collections in the Western United States* (Boston, 1977).

Besides important papers of individuals, there are also collections about the motion picture industry. George P. Johnson assembled a Negro Film collection (1916- ; 25 ft.; available on microfilm) containing correspondence, playbills, advertising materials, still photographs, posters, display cards, and clippings concerning blacks in motion pictures.

The major resource for the study of UCLA history is the University Archives [134 Powell Library, (213) 825-4068]. The University of California maintains its records in accordance with California acts passed regarding public records and information practices. Each campus has a Records Management Program functioning out of the Chancellor's Office, and a University Archives administered through the Library, DSC. Archives materials comprise 4,000 linear feet. Materials are accessible through a card catalog and unpublished finding aids.

Papers of distinguished faculty include those of economist Jacob Marschak (ca.1920s-1970s; 90 ft.); historian Waldemar Westergaard (ca.1910-1962;

109 ft.); political scientists Robert G. Neumann (ca.1920s- ; 64 ft.) and Bernard Brodie (1931-1978; 18 ft.); botanist Mildred Mathias (b. 1906- ; 1962-1965; 3 ft.); and zoologist Gordon H. Ball (1922-1979; 15 ft.).

The University of California has maintained a Water Resources Center Archives on both the Berkeley and UCLA campuses since 1957. G. K. Hall has published a *Dictionary Catalog of the Water Resources Center Archives, University of California* (Boston, 1970-) and supplements. The Water Resources Center Archives on UCLA's campus [2081 Engineering, (213) 825-7734] are regionally oriented and include a few manuscript and special collections holdings. Among them are the papers of Martin R. Huberty, the first director of the Center (48 ft.), a collection on Pillsbury-Coachella Valley (15 ft.), the Colorado River Board clippings files (63 ft.) arranged by subjects within single years, and the Blaney papers (1930s-1950s; 30 ft.) pertaining to citrus production and irrigation.

Water resources collections in DSC go back to the early nineteenth century, beginning with the Palmer family papers (1800-1960; 24 ft.), which relate to the Pomona Land and Water Company. Also from the eastern area of Los Angeles, the Monrovia city records (1886-1946; 30 ft.) primarily concern water supplies in southern California. A collection with strong ties to the Water Resources Center Archive is the papers of U.S. Congressman Philip David Swing (1890-1963; 75 ft.), which pertain to the Hoover Dam and the Colorado River.

UCLA collections are available to all postsecondary education researchers who have obtained a library card from the University Research Library's Circulation Department. A Reference Use card (free upon presentation of valid identification) is sufficient for use of DSC because materials do not circulate and must be used in the department's reading room. A limited amount of photocopying is allowed under the written provisions of the Department. Appointments are not necessary, although readers anticipating extended research in the department are advised to telephone or write in advance of their visit. Most of the department's manuscript collections are held in remote storage and must be paged. Materials requested in the early morning are available for use by 11:30 A.M.; requests after 11:30 A.M. are available by 3:30 P.M. that day; late afternoon requests are available by 11:30 A.M. the following day. There is no remote storage paging on Saturdays or on holidays when the department is open.

18

OTHER ARCHIVAL REPOSITORIES

GLORIA RICCI LOTHROP, LARRY E. BURGESS, AND
JOHN PORTER BLOOM

HISTORICAL SOCIETIES CONSTITUTE a little-known, much-neglected treasure for
the study of California history. The libraries, archives, manuscripts, and oral history collections of some large societies are fairly well utilized, but the resources
and great potential value of many small societies are often encumbered by problems, such as space, staff, and accessibility, that limit their exploitation, especially by researchers doing a quick study (whether by choice or by force of
circumstance).

California has an abundance of historical societies, some larger in respect to
their research holdings, but almost all having historical collections. Whether large
or small, however, this collective body of materials is a rich depository for the
study of California history.

Since it is not possible to list and describe all these depositories, the researcher
would be well advised to consult the annual "Roster and By-Laws" of the Conference of California Historical Societies (CCHS), distributed from the CCHS
office at the University of the Pacific, Stockton 95211, telephone (209) 946–
2169, which lists about 270 California historical societies.

Another important reference publication is a directory, *Archival and Manuscript Repositories in California*, published in 1984 by the Society of California
Archivists, compiled by the staff of the California Archives. It includes only
seventy-four historical societies, but for a typical entry, in addition to address
and phone number, it includes *major subjects* and *descriptions* of holdings,
volume in various media (manuscripts, public records, photographs, maps, tapes,
printed materials, newspapers, clippings, ephemera, etc.), *hours and days* open,
restrictions if any, and *copying* arrangements and cost. Equally useful is the
directory published at yearly intervals by the American Association for State

and Local History (AASLH), 172 Second Ave. N., Suite 102, Nashville, TN 37201.

In the nineteenth and early twentieth centuries, archival repositories in California were few in number and were private institutions or connected with a large university. Public libraries slowly moved into the archival scene. By the early 1970s, historical awareness and the archival pressures of regional and community historical consciousness caused an expansion of new programs. Since the late 1960s the number of archival repositories has nearly doubled, and new programs are being organized yearly. These archival depositories, both public and corporate, are listed in the 1984 *Archival and Manuscript Repositories in California*.

In addition, the researcher should note that each California State University has important archival material usually housed in its library's Department of Special Collection. These, too, are described in the aforementioned guide. Most of these institutions have listings and/or published guides to their respective holdings.

Researchers who are curious about the collections described below and others in repositories yet to be named can satisfy themselves best by personal inspection of the collections or, at least, of the guides (most often unpublished) to them; and to some degree by scrutiny of appropriate volumes of the *National Union Catalog of Manuscripts Collections* (Washington, D.C.: Library of Congress, annual volumes with indexes). This reference work is immensely valuable, but its limitations should be evaluated carefully. For thorough research it is an essential but merely a beginning step, a caveat that applies also to computer-assisted bibliographical searches such as are made with ARLIN (American Research Library Information Network) and similar computer services.

ACADEMY OF MOTION PICTURE ARTS AND SCIENCES MARGARET HERRICK LIBRARY

Street address:	8949 Wilshire Blvd.
	Beverly Hills, CA 90211
Mailing address:	Same
Telephone:	(213) 278-4313 Reference
	(213) 278-8990 General
Days and hours:	Monday, Tuesday, Thursday, and Friday,
	9:00 A.M. to 5:00 P.M.
	Special Collections by appointment only.

The history and development of motion picture art and industry are the subjects of the Academy's holdings, which include books, manuscripts, periodicals, pamphlets, microfilm, files of clippings, and photographs. Holdings also include Special Collections. The photograph holdings are extensive.

AMATEUR ATHLETIC FOUNDATION OF LOS ANGELES LIBRARY

Street address: 2141 West Adams
                       Los Angeles, CA 90018
Mailing address: Same
Telephone: (213) 730-9600
Days and hours: By appointment only.

This is the world's largest sports library, with publications dating back as early as the 1880s. The library answers letters and phone calls from around the world, and its Olympics collection is excellent. Holdings include biographical information on prominent California athletes.

THE AMERICAN FILM INSTITUTE

Street address: Louis B. Mayer Library
                       The American Film Institute
                       2021 N. Western Avenue
                       Los Angeles, CA 90027
Mailing address: P.O. Box 27994
Telephone: (213) 856-7660
Days and hours: Monday-Friday, 10:30 A.M. to 5:30 P.M.

The collection contains diverse motion picture and television materials. Scripts include published and unpublished shooting scripts from contemporary and classic American films, as well as early and current television shows. *The Defenders* Collection consists of over 115 shows. The George Byron Sage Story Analyst Collection focuses on Twentieth Century-Fox story sources. The Stewart Stern Collection consists of scripts and production workbooks for the films he wrote. The Directors Guild of America has deposited the papers of director/producer Robert Aldrich, 1918-1983.

ANAHEIM PUBLIC LIBRARY

Street address: Anaheim Public Library
                       Elizabeth J. Schultz Anaheim History Room
                       500 W. Broadway
                       Anaheim, CA 92805
Mailing address: Same
Telephone: (714) 999-1850 or 999-1880
Days and hours: Monday-Friday, 9:00 A.M. to 6:00 P.M

The collection documents Anaheim and much of Orange County history. An extensive postcard collection features Orange County cities and towns. Collections which contain information on southern California's wine, as well as on the business history of Orange and Los Angeles counties, include the Anaheim Chamber of Commerce Collection, 1895–present; the minutes of the Los Angeles Vineyard Society; Los Angeles County Assessment Records, 1856–1873; and a large citrus label collection. The Schultz Anaheim History Room is also a depository for Disney Company material, especially relating to Disneyland, 1953–present.

ASSOCIATION FOR NORTHERN CALIFORNIA RECORDS AND RESEARCH

Street address:	1st and Hazel Streets
	Chico, CA 95927
Mailing address:	P.O. Box 3024
	Chico, CA 95927
Telephone:	(916) 895-6144
Days and hours:	Access is through the Department of Special Collections, Meriam Library, CSU, Chico. Call (916) 895-5710 for hours or write for an appointment.

The ANCRR of Chico is included here not so much for its large membership or age, but because it is important and in some ways unique in helping preserve private and public records in Butte County and also in other nearby jurisdictions. ANCRR originated in the early 1970s when it became known that some Butte County records had been burned by county officials without being microfilmed, and more were marked for destruction because the county government lacked storage space. A group of citizens, including several faculty members from California State University, Chico, induced the university administration to take a role in preserving these records. Manuscripts and records preservation has been a joint activity since then, although campus storage space has been problematic and the collection has been moved several times. ANCRR now holds 1,500 ft. of manuscripts, 3,000 ft. of local government records, 20,000 photographs, 500 oral history tapes, etc. The collection also includes records of several kinds from nearby counties. There are a number of published guides and calendars to the ANCRR holdings which make the materials easily accessible for research.

CALIFORNIA HISTORICAL SOCIETY

Street address: CHS Library
                    2099 Pacific Street
                    San Francisco, CA 94109-2235
Mailing address: 2090 Jackson Street
                    San Francisco, CA 94109-2896
Telephone: (415) 567-1848
Days and hours: Tuesday–Saturday, 10:00 A.M. to 4:30 P.M.
                    Closed all holidays.

The CHS is a private organization which originated in 1871 in San Francisco and functions with its main base there. It has been designated as "the state historical society" by the legislature, but the designation carries no funding with it. In southern California a "History Center" has been opened in Los Angeles. The CHS's main library in San Francisco has been involved for several years in reconstruction and other improvements, mainly of the physical plant. Less-used materials have been kept in a storage annex in San Rafael, which has sometimes inconvenienced the many researchers who use this repository.

The CHS also maintains the Southern California Headquarters–History Center at 4201 Wilshire Blvd., 2nd floor, Los Angeles, CA 90010-3603, which houses an impressive photographic archive relating to southern California, the TICOR Collection, and the Los Angeles Area Chamber of Commerce Collection. It is open Tuesday–Friday, 1:00 P.M. to 4:00 P.M. Phone: (213) 937-1848. Prior contact is recommended for users.

CALIFORNIA STATE RAILROAD MUSEUM-LIBRARY

Street address: 111 I Street
                    Sacramento, CA 95814
Mailing address: Same
Telephone: (916) 445-7373
Days and hours: Tuesday–Saturday, 1:00 P.M. to 5:00 P.M.

This collection emphasizes operating companies in the Trans-Mississippi West in its railroad history holdings, which span from 1830 to the present, as well as North American railroad technology. Holdings include manuscripts, government records, photographs, maps, tapes, microfilm, books, pamphlets, ephemera, engineering records, and drawings.

CLAREMONT COLLEGES SPECIAL COLLECTIONS

Street address: Special Collections
                    Honnald Library
                    Claremont Colleges
                    Claremont, CA 91711
Mailing address: Same
Telephone: (714) 621–8000
Days and hours: Monday–Friday, 9:00 A.M. to 12:00 P.M.
                    and 2:00 P.M. to 5:00 P.M.
                    Additional hours during academic year:
                    Wednesday, 6:30 P.M. to 9:00 P.M.;
                    Sunday, 2:00 P.M. to 5:00 P.M.

Collections include volumes, papers, documents, scrapbooks, newspapers, photographs, original drawings, and paintings. Major subjects include California and local history, literature, music, politics, business, agriculture, water resources, and art. Of particular interest are the papers of former congressman Jerry Voorhis, Joaquin Miller, Orange County historian William McPhearson, Lincoln Honnald and other Claremont Colleges benefactors, original works by artist Edward Visher, papers documenting the history of the Congregational Church in southern California, and various music collections.

THE HAGGIN MUSEUM

Street address: 1201 N. Pershing Avenue
                    Stockton, CA 95203
Mailing address: Same
Telephone: (209) 462–4116
Days and hours: Tuesday, Thursday, and Saturday, 1:30 P.M.
                    to 5:00 P.M., by appointment only.

Holdings pertain to California history, especially that of San Joaquin and Stockton, and includes business records, letters, photographs, postcards, clippings, stereographs, drawings, cartoons, maps, books, and magazines. The subject areas include life and activities, cities and towns, architecture, scenics, transportation, business, industry, and automobiles.

THE HOLT-ATHERTON CENTER
FOR WESTERN STUDIES

Street address:	The Holt-Atherton Center for Western Studies
	University of the Pacific
	Stockton, CA 95211
Mailing address:	Same
Telephone:	(209) 946-2404
Days and hours:	Monday–Friday, 9:00 A.M. to 5:00 P.M.

Housing a significant collection of manuscripts, photographs, and pamphlet material relating to Stockton, northern and central California, the Holt-Atherton Center for Western Studies affords researchers insights into California's ethnic, mining, agrarian, and environmental history.

Crime and criminals are represented by a diverse collection containing information on Santa Cruz, San Joaquin, and San Luis Obispo counties. Included are mug books, registers, manuscripts, and criminal photograph books.

Ethnic history is represented in the Chinese collection (includes San Francisco records), Japanese (the Jacoby and Cook Collections) relocation records during World War II, and Jewish history in the West (the Astman Collection-Sacramento and the Rosenburg Collection-Stockton).

There are sixteen collections which relate to mining history and extensive photographic holdings (over 300,000 items, many relating to mining), including such collections as the Demarest Family Papers (1909-1967), which include an unpublished manuscript on the Mother Lode and miners in Calaveras and Tuolumne counties. The Hazelton Family Papers (1830-1904) also include mining history, 1849-1950.

The John Muir Collection (1856-1914) includes correspondence to and from Muir on a wide range of issues and topics, providing much insight into California's environmental, public, and private interests. Various governmental figures are represented in many collections. They range from city council officers to members of the assembly from the greater Stockton area. Oakland and San Francisco history may be found in such collections as the Stratton Family Papers (1900-1973), the Bendel Family Papers (1865-1965), and the Bolt Family Papers (1893-1973), with excellent photos, including the 1906 earthquake and fire.

INTERNATIONAL LONGSHOREMEN'S
& WAREHOUSEMEN'S UNION
ANNE RAND RESEARCH LIBRARY

Street address:	1188 Franklin Street
	San Francisco, CA 94109

Mailing address:	Same
Telephone:	(415) 775-0533
Days and hours:	Monday–Friday, 9:00 A.M. to 5:00 P.M.

Holdings include records of International Headquarters, case files from the trial to deport Harry Bridges, and records of the Maritime Unity, 1945-1946. The Union has members in many industries, include longshore, warehouse, sugar, chemical, and pineapple.

LABOR ARCHIVES AND RESEARCH CENTER

Street address:	Sutro Library
	San Francisco State University
	480 Winston Drive
	San Francisco, CA 94123
Mailing address:	Same
Telephone:	(415) 564-4010
Days and hours:	By appointment only.

Through the longtime efforts of the San Francisco Bay Area Labor Foundation this new center was dedicated in February 1986. It is a repository for the Foundation's documents, official records, oral histories, photographs, and other mementos of labor history of the working people of the Bay area. Among its other holdings are the records of the Bay Area Typographical Union, Local 21; the San Francisco Labor Council; the papers of the labor historian David F. Selvin; and those of labor lawyer Norman Leonard. The archival material is supported by a large collection of printed resources, including posters and broadsides, and a rich photographic collection.

LOS ANGELES COUNTY MUSEUM OF NATURAL HISTORY WESTERN HISTORY COLLECTION

Street address:	9000 Exposition Blvd.
	Los Angeles, CA 90007
Mailing address:	Same
Telephone:	(213) 744-3359
Days and hours:	Tuesday–Friday, 10:00 A.M. to 4:00 P.M.

The collection has valuable material on the Trans-Mississippi West, including accounts of voyages and expeditions to the New World, surveys of territories, and accounts of naturalists and scientists. Rich early California holdings include work of early printers, city, county, and Pacific Coast directories, as well as the *Great Register of Voters* for Los Angeles. The pre-1900 newspaper collection, including ethnic papers from throughout the state, is one of the finest.

In addition to tax assessment books, prints, maps, and iconographic collections, the manuscript collections, including the papers of Antonio F. Coronel and Ignacio Del Valle, accurately reflect the social and political life of nineteenth-century southern California.

Of the 200,000 photographs in the Seaver Center's collections, a large group is of images of southern California. Among the premier photographers represented are: Warren C. Dickerson, A. A. Forbes, Al Greene, Fred M. Maude, and Adam Clark Vroman. The California influence is well represented in the Antonio F. Coronel Collection (1817-1894); Del Valle family papers (1818-1920); Sepulved-Mott Collection (1849-1890); as well as in the Alcade Court Records of Los Angeles, 1830s and 1840s.

LOS ANGELES PUBLIC LIBRARY

Street address:	630 West 5th Street
	Los Angeles, CA 90017
Mailing address:	Same
Telephone:	(213) 612-3254
Days and hours:	Monday-Thursday, 10:00 A.M. to 8:00 P.M.;
	Friday and Saturday, 10:00 A.M. to 5:30 P.M.

The California collection is extensive, including accounts of seventeenth-century voyages of discovery. Overland narratives, settlers' diaries, and promotion literature are included along with local scrapbooks, travel guides, and mission materials collected by Charles Fletcher Lummis. The collection, particularly strong in architecture, theatre, religion, and ethnic history, includes city directories, publications of local historical societies, and several photo collections. Accessibility is enhanced by the several indices including the Comprehensive California Collection and a Biographical File. The Los Angeles *Star* is also available on microfilm. (Due to a disastrous fire, the collection will not be accessible until 1990(?).)

ONTARIO CITY LIBRARY

Street address:	Model Colony History Room
	Ontario City Library
	215 East C Street
	Ontario, CA 91764
Mailing address:	Same

Telephone: (714) 988–8481
Days and hours: Monday–Friday, 1:00 P.M. to 5:00 P.M.

Three manuscript collections will be of particular interest to researchers. The story of land and agricultural development in the 1880s is contained in the Chaffey Brothers' Collection, containing the papers of three Canadian developers who pioneered water and land use policies.

Business histories serving California and the nation as a whole are represented by the Armstrong Collection, 1890–1984, and by the Hotpoint/General Electric Iron Plant Collection. Armstrong Nurseries, a pioneering firm in horticultural research and direct-mail marketing, dominated segments of the American nursery industry for some eight decades. The country's largest flat iron plant, dating from 1904 to 1982, was owned by General Electric. Emphasis on plant operation in southern California is contained in the papers from 1915 to 1950.

PHOTOFILE

Street address: 2311 Kettner Blvd.
                    San Diego, CA 92101
Mailing address: Same
Telephone: (619) 234–4431
Days and hours: Monday–Friday, 9:00 A.M. to 5:00 P.M.,
                    by appointment only.

Holdings include color transparencies of international subject matter to be used as stock photography for publishers, periodicals, or for advertising and promotional use. All materials are original, and include such diverse subjects as California scenics, cities, people, sports, recreation, industry, vocations, agriculture, and plant life.

POMONA PUBLIC LIBRARY

Street address: Pomona Public Library
                    625 S. Garey Avenue
                    Pomona, CA 91769
Mailing address: P.O. Box 2271
                    Pomona, CA 91766
Telephone: (714) 620–2026
Days and hours: Monday–Tuesday, 10:00 A.M. to 9:00 P.M.;
                    Wednesday–Thursday, 10:00 A.M. to 6:00 P.M.
                    Friday, 10:00 A.M. to 5:00 P.M.; and
                    Saturday, 12:00 P.M. to 5:00 P.M.

The history of citrus in the Pomona Valley is well documented in the extensive collections of twenty-eight Pomona Valley citrus companies. The development of water resources is described in a collection representing sixteen private/mutual water companies.

Of cultural interest, and relevant to southern California's Mexican heritage, is the Padua Theatre collection dealing with the history of Padua Hills Theatre in Claremont.

The library's collection of more than 4,000 citrus labels is one of the largest in the state. The extensive postcard and wine label collections also number in the thousands.

SACRAMENTO HISTORY CENTER

Street address:	1930 J. Street
	Sacramento, CA 95814
Mailing address:	Same
Telephone:	(916) 447-2958
Days and hours:	Monday-Friday, 8:00 A.M. to 12:00 P.M.
	and 1:00 P.M. to 5:00 P.M.

Holdings include exceptionally large collections of photographs and television film, in addition to manuscripts, government records, maps, tapes, microforms, books, and pamphlets. Major subjects of the holdings include: Sacramento, city and county; the Sacramento Society of California Pioneers; business archives of California Almond Growers Exchange; Natomas Co. and Camelia Festival records; manuscripts of Sacramento Valley-related people and subjects; Californiana; the gold rush; a few railroad materials; and theatre and newspaper history. Other collections include the Eleanor McClatchey Collection of fine printing, T.V. newsfilm archives of NBC station KCRA, and photographs and negatives from the Sacramento *Bee*.

SAILOR'S UNION OF THE PACIFIC, AFL-CIO

Street address:	450 Harrison Street
	San Francisco, CA 94105
Mailing address:	Same
Telephone:	(415) 362-8363
Days and hours:	By appointment only.

Established 1885, holdings include books, serials, photographs, maps, ephemera, artifacts (banners, armbands, etc.); S.U.P. minutes (1885-1888/1907-present); minutes of other organizations (1880-1882/1913-present); correspondence files (1913-present); business papers (1934-present). There is an extensive card file covering diverse topics. Open to professional historians on approval by union officers.

SAN DIEGO HISTORICAL SOCIETY
RESEARCH ARCHIVES

Street address:	1649 El Prado
	San Diego, CA 92138
Mailing address:	P.O. Box 81825
	San Diego, CA 92138
Telephone:	(619) 297-3258
Days and hours:	Tuesday-Friday, 10:00 A.M. to 4:45 P.M.;
	Saturday, Noon to 4:45 P.M.

The Research Archives offers the possibility of research in scores of collections, not only of original materials but also of microfilm and other copies of records in other repositories in the United States and Mexico. Business records are a strength of these holdings, illuminating activities not only in San Diego but even internationally. The Ernst Benard Papers, for instance, came from a prominent nurseryman who dealt with nurseries throughout the world. The large collection of Thomas Whaley Papers (1823-1890) bear on the career of a Quartermaster Corps officer of the Civil War who was later a San Diego city official and a merchant with business involvements and a period of residence in Alaska. An important segment of the manuscript holdings is described in *A Guide to the San Diego Historical Society Public Records Collection* by Richard W. Crawford (San Diego, 1987); the others are in *A Guide to the Research Collections of the San Diego Historical Society* (San Diego, 1974).

Source material is indexed in 1,438 subject files, including manuscripts, diaries, letters, census records, directories, ledgers, books and periodicals, etc., documenting every facet of activity in San Diego from the earliest period of the Indians to current urban history. Also available are a large collection of city and county records, as well as more than 200,000 images covering 100 years of local history.

SAN DIEGO PUBLIC LIBRARY

Street address:	820 E. Street
	San Diego, CA 92101
Mailing address:	Same
Telephone:	(619) 236-5800

Days and hours: Monday and Wednesday, 10 A.M. to 9 P.M.;
                   Tuesday and Thursday, 10 A.M. to 5 P.M.; and
                   Friday and Saturday, 9:30 A.M. to 5:30 P.M.

This collection is strong in San Diego local history. It also includes materials on the gold rush and other California mining ventures. There are important materials on Father Serra and the missions, water, and the history of Imperial County. Visual materials include Sanborn maps, portraits and postcards, and a San Diego picture file. Of particular importance is the ongoing index of the San Diego *Union*, 1851–1903 and 1930 to the present.

SAN FRANCISCO PUBLIC LIBRARY
SAN FRANCISCO ROOM AND ARCHIVES

Street address: Civic Center
                   San Francisco, CA 94102
Mailing address: Same
Telephone: (415) 558-3949
Days and hours: Tuesday, Thursday, Friday, and Saturday,
                   10:00 A.M. to 6:00 P.M.;
                   Wednesday, 1:00 P.M. to 6:00 P.M.

The collections focus on California history, with major emphasis upon that of San Francisco. Holdings include books, letters, pamphlets, maps, sheet music, postcards, newspapers, periodicals, lithographs, and artifacts. Particularly large is the *News-Call Bulletin* morgue collection numbering over two million images.

SAN MATEO COUNTY HISTORICAL ASSOCIATION

Street address: 1700 West Hillsdale Blvd.
                   San Mateo, CA 94402
Mailing address: Same
Telephone: (415) 574-6441
Days and hours: Monday–Friday, 9:30 A.M. to 4:30 P.M.;
                   Sunday, 12:00 P.M. to 4:00 P.M.

This important society, which celebrated its fiftieth anniversary of founding in 1985, set forth three main goals: (1) preservation of historical places and sites; (2) getting written records of the pioneers; and (3) preserving historical records and relics. The association's collections include 326 ft. of manuscripts, 20,000 photographs, and other printed materials.

SANTA BARBARA HISTORICAL SOCIETY

Street address: 136 East De la Guerra Street
                    Santa Barbara, CA 93101
Mailing address: P.O. Box 578
                    Santa Barbara, CA 93102
Telephone: (805) 966-1601
Days and hours: Tuesday–Friday, 1:00 P.M. to 5:00 P.M.

This society, in addition to its museum displays, is a rich depository for the history of the city and county as well as of immediate adjacent areas, including the Channel Islands. It holds 400 ft. of manuscripts, over 12,000 photographs, some two dozen oral histories, a strong map collection, and is supported by over 4,000 ft. of books and pamphlets in the area of its historical focus.

SCREEN ACTORS GUILD

Street address: 7750 Sunset Blvd.
                    Los Angeles, CA 90046
Mailing address: Same
Telephone: (213) 876-3030
Days and hours: Monday–Friday, 9:00 A.M. to 5:00 P.M.;
                    appointment preferred.

The guild's holdings include photographs, oral history tapes, microforms, books and pamphlets, letters and minutes, all of which cover guild activities.

SEARLS HISTORICAL LIBRARY

Street address: 214 Church St.
                    Nevada City, CA 95959
Mailing address: Same
Telephone: (916) 265-9901
Days and hours: Monday–Saturday, 1:00 P.M. to 4:00 P.M.

Holdings include books, periodicals, pamphlets, documents, letters, newspaper clippings, maps and charts, tapes, photographs, and portraits pertaining to Nevada County history from 1849 to 1942.

SHERMAN FOUNDATION LIBRARY

Street address: 614 Dahlia Ave.
                     Corona del Mar, CA 92625
Mailing address: Same
Telephone: (714) 673-1880
Days and hours: Monday–Friday, 9:00 A.M. to 5:00 P.M.

The collection contains extensive materials on the Southwest, including maps, photographs, and personal papers of a number of business associates of Moses H. Sherman, electrical railroad pioneer and developer of portions of the Imperial and San Fernando valleys.

SIERRA NATIONAL FOREST

Street address: 1130 O Street
                     Fresno, CA 93721
Mailing address: Same
Telephone: (209) 487-5163
Days and hours: Monday–Friday, 8:00 A.M. to 4:30 P.M.;
                     by appointment only.

The information on the Sierra contained in the archives is extensive and diverse. A 40,000-plus card file has been developed with discrete classifications. A sample of the forest subjects includes: celebrations, cemeteries, earthquakes, explorers, history, Indians, place names, trappers, and wars.

A. K. SMILEY PUBLIC LIBRARY

Street address: Heritage Room
                     A. K. Smiley Public Library
                     125 W. Vine Street
                     Redlands, CA 92373
Mailing address: Same
Telephone: (714) 798-7632
Days and hours: Tuesday–Saturday, 9:00 A.M. to Noon;
                     1:00 P.M. to 5:00 P.M.

Water, the life-blood of southern California, is represented in the Bear Valley Mutual Water Company Collection. Much of the correspondence includes San Bernardino, Riverside, and Los Angeles County figures, all of whom were involved in the receivership of this company. In the Francis Cuttle Collection, the papers of the Tri-County Reforestation Committee (water and forest preserve interests in San Bernardino, Orange, and Riverside counties) contain a diverse correspondence between state, county, and local officials. Citrus packing houses in the navel orange belt make up the Citrus Packing House Collection; included is material on grower holdings, crop yields, and packing house affiliations of the Inland Empire.

The literary landscape is contained in the California Writer's Guild Collection, 1932-1971. A variety of southern California authors from Robert Nathan and Lee Shippey to Ray Bradbury and Remi Nadeau are represented. A diverse series of articles, manuscripts, and correspondence relating to southern California mining, transportation, water, exploration, and ghost towns is housed in the I. Burr Belden Collection, 1948-1970. The Mojave and Colorado deserts in southern California, particularly emphasizing mining, exploration, and transportation, are represented in the E. I. Edwards Collection.

SOCIETY OF CALIFORNIA PIONEERS

Street address: 456 McAlister Street
                     San Francisco, CA 94102
Mailing address: Same
Telephone: (415) 861-5278
Days and hours: Monday-Friday, 1:00 P.M. to 4:00 P.M.
                     (Closed July.)

The library's published and unpublished collections reflect the organization's focus on the gold rush and 1850s periods. Very valuable San Francisco Vigilance Committee papers can be seen here as well as the George W. Patterson Family Collection (ranch accounts, Alameda County, 1854-1898, are included), Cooper-Molera Papers (re Cooper-Molera Adobe, Monterey), a few papers of Thomas Starr King, Major Jacob Rink Snyder, Thomas Oliver Larkin and others, and the important Sherman Music Collection which spans a century, 1840-1940. This repository's most utilized resource, however, is the Charles B. Turrill Collection which includes not only books, manuscripts, and clippings but also more than 10,000 images, mostly photographic, mostly cataloged, 1776 to the 1920s, relating chiefly but not exclusively to the San Francisco Bay region.

SONS OF THE REVOLUTION LIBRARY
(FORMERLY HERITAGE LIBRARY)

Street address: 600 S. Central St.
                     Glendale, CA 91204
Mailing address: Same
Telephone: (818) 240-1775

Days and hours: Tuesday, Thursday, and Friday,
10:00 A.M. to 4:00 P.M.;
Wednesday, 10:00 A.M. to 9:00 P.M.; and
Saturday, 9:00 A.M. to 5:00 P.M.

Holdings include source material on early Californian pioneers, and family-tree-tracing assistance is available. This is one of the foremost sources for genealogical information in southern California.

SOUTHERN CALIFORNIA LIBRARY FOR SOCIAL STUDIES AND RESEARCH

Street address: 6120 S. Vermont Ave.
Los Angeles, CA 90044
Mailing address: Same
Telephone: (213) 759-6063
Days and hours: Tuesday-Saturday, 10:00 A.M. to 4:00 P.M.

This library houses literature on radical, progressive, labor, and minority movements dating back to the turn of the century. The library has some 25,000 volumes, 15,000 pamphlets, 2,000 audio tapes, and more than 150,000 clippings filed under 1,000 headings, many relating to California. It is also a superb source of recordings to listen to or to purchase.

SOUTHWEST MUSEUM LIBRARY

Street address: 234 Museum Dr.
Los Angeles, CA 90065
Mailing address: Same
Telephone: (213) 221-2163 or 221-2164
Days and hours: Tuesday-Friday, 1:00 P.M. to 4:45 P.M.

The library contains numerous manuscript collections as well as 100,000 items available to students and research workers interested in the history of the American Indian as well as the history of California and the Southwest.

STANFORD UNIVERSITY LIBRARIES

Street address: Special Collections
Stanford University Libraries
Stanford, CA 94305

Mailing address: Same
Telephone: (415) 497–4054
Days and hours: Monday–Friday, 8:00 A.M. to 5:00 P.M.;
                    Saturday, 9:00 A.M. to 12:00 P.M.

Much of the 8,000 ft. of material in Stanford's Special Collections concerns California. The David Jacks Collection contains the correspondence, documents, financial papers, and property transactions in Monterey, Carmel, and Salinas Valley. Typescripts of stories, poems, and folklore of the gold rush are contained in the Weston Gold Country Collection (1849-1944). Legal, mining, and business conditions, 1850-1853, are represented in the Dangerfield Family letters.

While the Pacific Slope Collection (1832-1953) covers Oregon, major California themes included in the manuscripts, notes, legal documents, and typescripts are the California mission system, 1890s California politics, and San Francisco reform movements.

The Californian and Western Manuscripts Collection contains miscellaneous items, diaries, letters, journals, and reports on California history, including the Spanish in California, the California election of 1884, and individuals such as Juan B. Alvarado, Franklin Hirschom, W. C. Jones, and Alfred Wheeler. Additional information on the Bear Flag Revolt, material pertaining to mining, and a manuscript by William B. Ide are contained in the Mary Sheldon Barnes Collection (1769-1898).

The Californio period is represented in the Paul Percy Parker Collection (1782-1936), which contains correspondence, manuscripts, narratives, and memoirs of the Monterey and Salinas valleys before 1900. Spanish and Mexican documents, and individuals such as José Figueroa (governor, 1833-1835) are included.

UNITED STATES DISTRICT COURT
NORTHERN DISTRICT OF CALIFORNIA

Street address: Archives, United States District Court for
                    the Northern District of California
                    450 Golden Gate Ave.
                    San Francisco, CA 94102
Mailing address: Same
Telephone: (415) 556–2790
Days and hours: Monday–Friday, 9:00 A.M. to 5:00 P.M.

While many of the holdings are presently uncataloged, a diverse collection includes docket books of the United States District Court for Northern California, which are available from 1851 to the present. For the U.S. Circuit Court, Ninth Circuit, the holdings are from 1863 to 1912. Manuscript collections include

U.S. District Court Judges Oliver Carter, George Harris, and Albert Wollenberg, as well as correspondence from the Clerk's Office for both the District Court and Ninth Circuit, 1871-1937.

UNIVERSITY OF CALIFORNIA, DAVIS
DEPARTMENT OF SPECIAL COLLECTIONS—
SHIELDS LIBRARY

Street address:	University of California, Davis
	Davis, CA 95616
Mailing address:	Same
Telephone:	(916) 752-1621
Days and hours:	Monday-Friday, 8:00 A.M. to 12:00 P.M.,
	and 1:00 P.M. to 5:00 P.M.

Approximately one million items (letters, photographs, diaries, sound recordings, and pamphlets) are held here pertaining to such subjects as the history and technology of agriculture, UCD campus history, dramatic arts, contemporary American literature, and California.

UNIVERSITY OF CALIFORNIA, IRVINE
SPECIAL COLLECTIONS AND
UNIVERSITY ARCHIVES

Street address:	University of California, Irvine
	General Library, Campus Dr.
	Irvine, CA 92717
Mailing address:	University of California
	P.O. Box 19557
	Irvine, CA 92713
Telephone:	(714) 833-7227
Days and hours:	Monday-Friday, 12:00 P.M. to 5:00 P.M.
	(summer and recess periods, 1:00 P.M.
	to 5:00 P.M.)

Holdings include manuscripts, photographs, maps, microforms, books, and pamphlets. Subject matter of holdings includes: UCI, regional California history, Orange County, Baja California, and California literature.

UNIVERSITY OF CALIFORNIA, RIVERSIDE
UNIVERSITY LIBRARY—SPECIAL COLLECTIONS

Street address: University Library
                    950 University Ave.
                    Riverside, CA 92517
Mailing address: University of California Library
                    P.O. Box 5900
                    Riverside, CA 92507
Telephone: (714) 787-3233
Days and hours: Monday-Friday, 8:00 A.M. to 4:30 P.M.;
                    weekends, by appointment

Holdings include letters, photographs, diaries, and sound recordings pertaining to such diverse subjects as UCR; Sadakichi Hartmann, 1867-1944; Heinrich Schenker, 1868-1935; and the Riverside Municipal Archives (1883-1953).

UNIVERSITY OF CALIFORNIA, SAN DIEGO
MANDEVILLE DEPARTMENT OF
SPECIAL COLLECTIONS

Street address: University of California, San Diego
                    Libraries, Torrey Pines Mesa
                    La Jolla, CA 92093
Mailing address: Mail Code C-075-G
Telephone: (619) 452-2533
Days and hours: Monday-Friday, 8:00 A.M. to 5:00 P.M.

Holdings include UCSD archival collections, faculty papers, serials, maps, photographs, manuscripts, and a couple of oral history tapes. Subject matter of holdings include history of California, and San Diego; modern poetry and contemporary music; the antinuclear movement; Pacific voyages; history of the sciences, and history of UCSD.

UNIVERSITY OF SOUTHERN CALIFORNIA

Street address: University Library
                    University of Southern California
                    Los Angeles, CA 90089-0182
Mailing address: Same
Telephone: (213) 743-6058
Days and hours: Monday-Friday, 9:00 A.M. to 5:00 P.M.

The library has extensive holdings of the papers of Los Angeles members of Congress, including Alphonso Bell (1973-1978; 170 ft.); Yvonne Burke (1966-1980; 452 ft.); Chet Holifield (1943-1974; 89 ft.); Craig Hosmer (1953-1974; 247 ft.); Gordon McDonough (1945-1963; 110 ft.); Thomas Rees (1960-1976; 117 ft.); and John Rousselot (1979-1982; 304 ft.). Assemblyman Frank Lanterman's papers cover the years 1950-1978 (45 ft.). The gubernatorial papers of Edmund G. "Jerry" Brown (1975-1983) are housed in Special Collections as well.

The development of aeronautics in California from 1920 to the 1950s represents an extensive collection, as do the files of the Warner Bros., Universal, and Hal Roach studios. The motion picture collection is augmented by extensive holdings on individual motion picture actors, producers, writers, and directors.

A long span of Los Angeles and southern California history is contained in two collections of the Hearst Los Angeles newspaper files, 1878 to 1960, and in an extensive clippings and photograph collection, 1920-1960s.

VENTURA COUNTY HISTORICAL SOCIETY

Street address:	100 East Main Street
	Ventura, CA 93001
Mailing address:	Same
Telephone:	(805) 653-0323
Days and hours:	Tuesday-Saturday, 10:00 A.M. to Noon,
	1:00 P.M. to 5:00 P.M. Prior contact suggested.

The Ventura County Historical Society owns and operates the Ventura County Historical Museum, established in 1913. It is now housed in a fine, modern building with the latest museum and library amenities. The holdings include a constantly growing number of documents, photographs, and publications based on the composite collections of the historical society, the Ventura County Archaeological Society, and the County History Collection of the Ventura County Library Services Agency. Included are 250 ft. of county records and some 9,000 photographs.

VISUAL COMMUNICATIONS OF
ASIAN AMERICANS STUDIES CENTRAL, INC.

Street address:	244 S. San Pedro St.
	Los Angeles, CA 90012
Mailing address:	309 S. San Pedro St.
	Los Angeles, CA 90012
Telephone:	(213) 680-4462

Days and hours:	Monday–Friday, 10:00 A.M. to 6:00 P.M., by appointment only.

Collection includes over 500,000 images of Asian Americans, mostly in southern California. Archive material is available for study. Prints may be purchased. Photo mural displays are available for rent or purchase.

WHITTIER COLLEGE–DEPARTMENT OF GEOLOGY FAIRCHILD AERIAL PHOTOGRAPHY COLLECTION

Street address:	Department of Geology
	Whittier College
	Whittier, CA 90608
Mailing address:	Same
Telephone:	(213) 693–0771, ext. 363
Days and hours:	Variable, advance appointment needed.

Collection contains aerial photographs, some 411,000 in number, taken mostly in California, and some taken in other states and countries. (Another 150,000 Fairchild photos are at UCSB, and a smaller number are at CSU, Northridge.)

WINE INSTITUTE

Street address:	165 Post St.
	San Francisco, CA 94108
Mailing address:	Same
Telephone:	(415) 986–0878
Days and hours:	Monday–Friday, 9:00 A.M. to 12:00 P.M.,
	1:00 P.M. to 5:00 P.M.,
	by pre-screened appointment only.

Holdings include books, clippings, articles, and brochures pertaining to enology, viticulture, wine, and wine industry.

19

ORAL HISTORY: A DIRECTORY

WILLA BAUM, SARAH SHARP, AND JAMES V. MINK

CALIFORNIA IS A REGION of transition, a magnet attracting people from every-where. It is also a dynamic laboratory for historical collecting, particularly of oral history, which depends on memories of people who were eyewitnesses to past events. Collecting began here at the dawn of modern American oral history—the term used by the late historian Louis M. Starr of Columbia University to describe the process of interviewing select individuals with an electromagnetic tape recorder to preserve their memories of the historical past for use of future scholars. Still, Starr's definition lacks comprehensiveness when describing the wide range of materials that have been collected as California oral history.

What has been collected and preserved can best be understood by considering the nature of oral history and how it is located and used. Many collections sur-veyed contain sound recordings of interviews, occasionally with transcripts; others are sound recordings of speeches, ceremonies, or other kinds of historical events. Some are a mixture of both. Some institutions cannot supply all of their oral history in an oral format because they have discarded the original sound recordings. The evidential integrity of the remaining transcripts is questionable. While a transcript may serve as a dependable interview content guide, only the original, unaltered sound recording reveals an interview's precise order and intrinsic form. It is the document of choice and should be consulted wherever available to determine the absolute value of the interview as historical evidence.

Many users accidentally discover oral history documents while searching repositories for traditional archival sources. Those who search directly for oral history are unlikely to find it under the term "oral history" in the computer or catalog of a large library. This entry is ordinarily used for holdings about the subject and its methodology. One exception is the entry *Oral History–Catalogues.*

This signals printed catalogs of interviews, frequently with subject indexes, which describe oral history collections that can be consulted. Try searching under names of individuals who may have been interviewed. If some names are found linked with the subdivision *Interviews*, oral history is probably in the library holdings. Also try searching under professions and vocations. Libraries holding multiple interviews often supply entries under such terms and subdivide them by locale: *Lawyers—California—Los Angeles—Interviews*.

Some programs have printed catalogs of their collections, but most interviews are located through the card catalog and unpublished content abstracts, indexes, and lists prepared by the library. These finding aids are prevalent in collections consisting exclusively of recorded interviews. Often collections are being built by volunteers. More than one visit may be required to make the correct contacts and gain access to a collection, and it might also be necessary to bring a tape recorder to use it.

Besides oral histories, libraries collect other kinds of sound recordings which are useful to the history researcher—for example, recordings of speeches, city council meetings, professional meetings, radio and TV broadcasts, folklore recordings, and historic "documents" like the Watergate tapes. These are sound recordings, not oral history, however, because they have not purposely been created for historical research and they have not been verified by the narrator.

Traditional bibliographic guides, while of limited help for oral history resources, are the place to begin. A somewhat outdated but useful guide is *Oral History Collections* (New York, 1975) by Alan M. Meckler and Ruth McMullin. The guide has a name and subject index, much better on names than on subjects, and a list of United States oral history centers by state. The California entry lists thirty-five centers with information about the focus of each. Users of *Oral History Collections* will find oral histories across the United States that deal with California topics; for example, under the subject "Mining Engineering," one finds a Columbia University collection with California mining leaders; under their names, oral histories with California's Governor Goodwin Knight and San Francisco *Chronicle* political editor Earl C. Behrens can be found in the Eisenhower Library in Kansas.

The Library of Congress' *National Union Catalog of Manuscript Collections* (NUCMC) has listed oral history collections since 1970, but these oral histories must be in transcript form. (Tape recordings are not included in their definition of manuscripts, although tapes may be listed if they are part of a collection of papers.) A special repository index which appears at the end of the index volume locates oral history collections and manuscript collections containing oral history transcripts and sound recordings.

Another guide, *Subject Collections* (New York, 1985), compiled by Lee Ash and William G. Miller, lists nine entries under "Oral History, California." The libraries therein are different from those submitting information to NUCMC, so both guides should be checked.

The two national data bases are OCLC (Online Computer Library Center) and

RLIN (Research Libraries Information Network). OLCL is oriented to title, author entry. It is good for searches for specific titles, but not good for subject searches. Searching place names as subjects may reveal some oral histories if there is a publication based on an oral history collection. RLIN uses the subject approach. With 16 million books and 43,000 manuscripts in the RLIN data base, and growing, there were 367 entries under oral history. Again, these were primarily published oral histories but these can include small publications, for example, local historical society paperbacks, which can lead the researcher to collections of oral histories. RLIN has a searchable genre field (field 655) for oral histories which will become useful as more individual oral histories are keyed into the data base.

MELVYL, the online data base for all of the University of California campuses and the State Library lists 289 entries under oral history. Some of these are individual oral history transcripts, some are bibliographies such as the Association for Northern California Records and Research's *Bibliography of the Oral History Collection at California State University, Chico,* and the *Catalogue of Oral History Holdings in San Luis Obispo County*.

The following list contains brief descriptions of oral history collections. More extensive descriptions of the northern California collections are available in the California Section, California State Library, Sacramento. Where possible the approximate number of tapes is indicated in parentheses.

Academy of Motion Picture Arts and Sciences, Los Angeles. The Academy's interviews have been collected among its archives and personal papers, although it does not have an oral history program. The Institute's library is the recipient of interviews produced by the American Film Institute's Fellowship Program, supported by the Louis B. Mayer Foundation (36).

Archives of American Art, Smithsonian Institution (Northern Regional Branch), M. H. de Young Memorial Museum, San Francisco. Tapes and transcripts of interviews with artists, collectors, curators, art dealers, and art historians focused on American art (+100). Printed catalog, 1984.

Archives of American Art of the Smithsonian Institution (Southern Regional Branch), Henry E. Huntington Library, San Marino. Collection includes interviews with regional artists specializing in architecture, photography, sculpture, decorative folk art, painting, and drawing. A further aspect of the program is interviews with private collectors, and museum and gallery administrators.

Bancroft Library, University of California, Berkeley, Donated Oral Histories Collection. Tapes and transcripts on diverse subjects such as agricultural labor, lumber business, Asian Americans, San Francisco neighborhoods, history of California State Civil Service, Yosemite Valley, care of mentally ill in California, Afro-American theatre in Bay Area and Los Angeles, working women, EPIC (1934 campaign for Upton Sinclair), army wives, cowboys of the high Sierra, Vietnamese refugees in the East Bay, others (1000). (*Also see* University of California, Berkeley.)

Berkeley Architectural Heritage Association, Berkeley. Tapes, most indexed, about Berkeley buildings and neighborhoods (+46).

Berkeley Historical Society, Berkeley. Tapes and some transcripts, dealing with history of the cooperative movement in Finland and the United States, especially at Berkeley, 1918–1985 (19); other aspects of Berkeley history. Copies also at Berkeley Public Library.

Berkeley Public Library, Berkeley. Transcripts relating to Berkeley persons, places, and issues produced by the Berkeley Historical Society or the Regional Oral History Office, UC Berkeley.

Beverly Hills Public Library, Beverly Hills. Collection consists of an oral-video history program documenting the lives of its prominent residents. The library also retains video tapes of interviews done for its "In Print" television program, featuring interviews with local authors.

Calaveras County Historical Society, San Andreas. Taped interviews and some transcripts of conversations with individuals 1950–present (40).

Calaveras County Museum and Archives, San Andreas. Taped interviews with early residents of Calaveras area (110).

California Historical Society, San Francisco. Tapes and transcripts of interviews with men and women in the American labor movement, 1920s–1980 (+30); other Californians notable in politics, business, agriculture (+30).

California History Center, Cupertino (De Anza Community College). Tapes and some transcripts of family histories (87); California wineries (17); historic places (37); ethnic groups in Santa Clara Valley (20); early aviation (7); early electronics (8).

California Institute of Technology, Pasadena. Caltech's documented history through the papers of the scientists who were its founders and faculty. Interviews with many of these academicians, astronomers, aeronautical engineers, chemists, biologists, and physicists, selectively conducted (63).

California State Archives, Sacramento. Copies of transcripts of oral histories from other organizations which relate to state government.

California State Capitol Museum, Sacramento. Tapes and transcripts from Restoration Project for the State Capitol: project's political origins, engineering and construction techniques, restoration technology and philosophy, project management, "Found" condition of building, capitol museum development, political history of the restoration, reminiscences of craftspeople, 1960–1981 (70).

California State Library, California Section, Sacramento. Copies of transcripts of oral histories from other organizations. California Oral History Bibliographic Center; a card catalog and collection of questionnaires listing agencies collecting oral history and lists of some interviews.

California State University, Bakersfield. Tapes conducted by the Kern County Historical Society focusing on the history of the Basque and Chinese communities, farm labor, country music, earthquakes, the California Land Company, and the communities of Glennville, Mojave, Lebec, Arvin, and Tehachipi. "California Odyssey Project" consisting of interviews with migrant Dust Bowl farm workers about their coming to the San Joaquin Valley (+225).

California State University, Chico, Library, Special Collections. Tapes and transcripts of all facets of northeastern California local history, including Chico State University history, cattle ranching, Maidu Indian Culture, local history of Glenn, Colusa, Tehama, Modoc, Shasta, and Butte counties (450). Printed *Bibliography of Oral Histories, Associations for Northern California Records and Research*, 1980.

California State University, Fresno, Chicano Latino Studies Department. Tapes and transcripts concerning growth of the Mexican American community in Fresno, 1919–1980 (50). Half of interviews are in Spanish. Publication, *Nuestras Raices: The Mexican Community of the Central San Joaquin Valley*, 1980.

California State University, Fullerton. The collection's catalog, Shirley E. Stephenson, ed., *Oral History Collection, California State University, Fullerton* (Fullerton, 1985), describes interviews focusing on its central research topic, the history of the Southwestern United States. Of interest to California historians will be the multiseries on Orange County community history, including subsections on Anaheim, Brea-Olinda, Buena Park, Fullerton, Huntington Beach, Irvine-El Toro, La Habra, Laguna Beach, Newport Beach, Orange, San Juan Capistrano, Santa Ana, Tustin, Yorba Linda. There is also a miscellaneous community history series covering: Chino, Crestline, Garden Grove, Glendora, Imperial Valley, Los Alamitos, Norco, Ontario-Upland, Pomona, Riverside, San Pedro, Santa Fe Springs, and South Gate. Regional ethnic history is investigated by series on Japanese Americans, blacks, native American urbanization, Jews, Chicanos, and Scandinavians. The program has also conducted interviews on the history of the university, and completed series on environmental studies, Orange County politics, the prepolitical years of Richard M. Nixon, and the science and technology of recent industrial development in the county (2000).

California State University, Long Beach. Oral interviews include institutional history and local history. A major research theme is women's studies. Many aspects of regional history are highlighted by studying the roles women have played in greater Long Beach and Southern California. The program's interviews are housed in the University Library's Oral History Archives and

Special Collections and located by its "Handbook and Finder's Guide to the Oral History Archive." Major projects include: Ethnic Studies (blacks, native Americans, Asian American and Long Beach women); Women in World War II, including the special project, "Rosie the Riveter Revisited;" Long Beach History; Southern California Arts; and the large Women's History Collection which is listed in University of Minnesota's *Women's History Sources Survey* (New York, 1979). Researchers should also be aware of the materials on local history, including Terminal Island, the Los Angeles harbor, the Bixby family, the great Depression, and the development of the petroleum industry (+1000).

California State University, Stanislaus, Turlock. Tapes covering local history and campus history. Printed list available.

Chapman College, Orange. Program in cooperation with the San Juan Capistrano Museum, has recorded local history, which includes archaeology and folk customs, mainly of the San Juan Capistrano region. The local history of the Orange County and the southern coastal region is well served and the subjects are familiar: agriculture, the citrus industry, labor, ethnic, and community history. Also there is some attention to more recent real estate development (50 audio, 15 video).

Claremont Graduate School Oral History Programs, Claremont. Transcripts are deposited in the Honnold Library and described in *Claremont Graduate School Oral History Program: A Bibliography* (Claremont, 1978), with an addendum. Listed is an extensive series of interviews with evangelical missionaries to China, many of them from California. In addition to the history of the Claremont Colleges and regional history of eastern Los Angeles County, there are special series on the history of the Atlantic Richfield Oil Company, the Bolsa Chica Gun Club, southern California booksellers, ethnic minorities: blacks and Chicanos, the citrus industry, Los Angeles' "Little Tokyo," aviation, and Parisian Expatriates (230).

Clarke Memorial Museum, Eureka. Tapes of interviews with northwestern California American Indian basketmakers from the Yurok, Hupa, Karuk, and Tolowa tribes (16); on history of the museum and Bank of Eureka building (12).

Coarsegold Historical Society, Coarsegold. Tapes and some transcripts on history of eastern Madera County, especially pioneer family history (75).

Columbia College, Library, Columbia. Tapes of interviews with pioneer family descendants and other local residents, covering history of Tuolumne County and Yosemite National Park (+75). Publication, *Mother Lode Bibliography*, 1980.

Craft and Folk Art Museum, Los Angeles. Museum has a strong archival collection that has been augmented with interviews covering sixteen different ethnic heritages with emphasis on the Japanese American, Mexican, and Ukrainian traditions (33 audio, 13 video).

Delta Chinese Cultural Project, San Francisco. Transcripts of interviews with residents of all-Chinese town in Sacramento—San Joaquin Delta, 1915–1986 (23).

Eastern California Museum, Independence. Tapes of interviews with early residents on eastern California history, descendants of pioneer families (41).

Ferndale Museum, Ferndale. Tapes covering Ferndale and Eel River Valley local history, 1960s to present (61).

Fremont Main Library, Fremont. Tapes of city, county, school, and water district officials on incorporation, city planning, and city problems in Fremont and Newark (33).

Fresno County Free Library, Fresno. Transcripts with Japanese Americans relocated during World War II (119); transcripts with various ethnic groups, Fresno County pioneers, and county and municipal officials (130). For details, consult the oral histories cataloged in *Bay Microfilm Catalog* (Palo Alto, 1985).

Hanna Collection, Hoover Institution, Stanford University, Stanford. Hanna Collection is accepting student-done oral histories covering aspects of California history, especially immigration.

Holocaust Library and Research Center of San Francisco, Holocaust Media Project, San Francisco. Tapes and transcripts of interviews with Holocaust survivors covering all facets of Holocaust experience and readjustment (200). Some in foreign languages (200).

Holt-Atherton Center for Western Studies, University of the Pacific, Stockton. Tapes covering life of John Steinbeck (2); history of the San Joaquin Delta (4); San Joaquin County history (1); Stockton, California history (5); California dredge mining (2); North American Indians (7); Vacaville, California 1932–1933 (3).

Institute of Industrial Relations, Library, University of California, Berkeley. Transcripts of interviews with California labor and management leaders (22).

Intertribal Friendship House, Oakland. Transcripts of interviews covering American Indian relocation to California (1953 to present), family relations, political and economic issues, and traditional and modern music of American Indians (+48). Photographic collection and news clipping and documents file augment oral history interviews.

Lake County Historical Society, Lakeport. Tapes of all facets of northern California history, especially family history, 1880–present (39).

Livermore Heritage Guild, Livermore. Tapes and some transcripts covering Livermore Valley history (the wineries, people of the valley, the mercantile, school teaching, cowboys) (23).

Long Beach Public Library, Long Beach. Local history collection supplemented with interviews concerning community development, city government, the World War II era, and the 1933 earthquake (90).

The Los Padres National Forest (U.S. Department of Agriculture, Forest Service, Goleta). Interviews reflecting changes in land management policy and relationships among the Forest Service, adjacent landowners, and other agencies. The James Blakely Archive covers forest history in Santa Barbara and Ventura counties, as well as the California Conservation Corps, mining, homesteading, hunting, and early forest use. Recordings include speeches and such events as Homesteader Days at Zaca Lake (130). A contents list is available.

Marin County Free Library, San Rafael. Tapes and transcripts covering lives of Marin County pioneers (267).

Mariposa County Historical Society, Mariposa. Tapes of interviews with residents, their memories, 1900–present (+50).

McHenry Museum, Modesto. Tapes of interviews with descendants of pioneer families in Stanislaus County (+50).

Mendocino County Museum, Willits. Tapes of interviews with county residents covering all facets of local history, 1870–present, including basketry, quiltmaking, business, politics, Indian songs, and family history (265).

Menlo Park Historical Association, Menlo Park. Tapes and many transcripts of interviews on all facets of local history, especially politics and community growth (23).

Mennonite Brethren Studies, Center for, Fresno. Tapes covering Mennonite Brethren history: local congregations, church planting, missionaries, Russia in 1905 Revolution (35). Some interviews are in German.

Monterey History and Art Association, Monterey. Tapes of interviews with local residents covering early family histories and reminiscences of life in Monterey, Salinas, Pacific Grove, and Carmel (19).

Moraga Historical Society, St. Mary's College, Moraga. Tapes and a few transcripts of interviews covering history of Moraga Rancho, Moraga family, and town of Moraga (54). List available.

Napa County Historical Society, Napa. Tapes covering local Napa County history and reflections of older local residents (62). Half are recorded talks given on some phase of county history.

National Maritime Museum, Golden Gate National Recreation Area, San Francisco. Tapes and a few transcripts covering maritime history, 1900–1940, especially Pacific coast and Pacific basin; Alcatraz as a prison and later (350).

Oakland Museum, History Division. Tapes with seventy longtime black residents of West Oakland, a middle-class railroad porters' community, prior to 1941 (100).

Oakland Public Library, Oakland History Room, Oakland. Tapes from Oakland Neighborhood Study of ethnic groups in Oakland, 1890-1950; churches, sports, fire department, effect of World War II (55).

Ohlone College, Fremont. Interviews with residents of Fremont, Newark, Niles, and Union City, covering local and family history (52).

Pacific Grove Public Library, Pacific Grove. Taped interviews with local residents on life in Pacific Grove 1890-1920 (26); interview with W. R. Holman, Pacific Grove businessman, 1900-1970s (10).

Pajaro Valley Historical Association, Watsonville. Tapes of interviews with area residents covering physical development of Watsonville, local business, political, agricultural, and social history, history of Japanese and Yugoslavian communities (35).

Pomona Public Library Special Collections, Pomona. Holdings include interviews and sound recordings on the history of the area (100).

Potrero Hill Archives Project, San Francisco Public Library, Potrero Hill Branch. Tapes, some transcripts, with the oldest residents of Potrero Hill, San Francisco. The working class neighborhood includes iron workers, shipbuilders, Russian Molokans who fled Tsarist Russia in the early 1900s for religious reasons; the impact of public housing on neighborhood (75).

Radical Elders Oral History Project, Berkeley. Tapes and some transcripts of sixteen radicals on labor history, Communist Party, IWW, Abraham Lincoln Brigade, anti-McCarthy, and anti-Loyalty Oath efforts (154).

Redwood City Public Library, Redwood City. Tapes and many transcripts of interviews covering history of Redwood City (26).

Sacramento City College, Library, Sacramento. Tapes of interviews with selected retiring faculty members, 1969-present (55).

Sacramento Museum and History Division, Sacramento. Tapes from Walerga Oral History Project, interviews with Japanese interned at Walerga Assembly Center during World War II (120); Sacramento Ethnic Communities Oral History Project, interviews with members of twenty-one ethnic groups living in Sacramento area (210); American Association of University Women, primarily interviews with charter members of Sacramento chapter (24); and miscellaneous interviews with area residents (16). Publication, catalog of interviews pertaining to public records of city and county of Sacramento.

Sacramento River Delta Historical Society, Walnut Grove. Tapes and some transcripts of interviews with local residents, focusing on social, economic, agricultural, other commercial and geographical reminiscences, 1880-1970 (24).

San Antonio Valley Historical Association, King City. Tapes covering history of San Antonio Valley and Monterey County, 1900-1920 (25).

San Diego Historical Society, San Diego. Collection, much of it indexed and transcribed, includes: a multitopic program with pioneers about life in "the back country" around the turn of the century; an oral history of the Theosophical Society, Point Loma; San Diego City and County in World War II; and the area's ethnic communities. The researcher uses the catalog to find the collection, but must realize the interviews are physically dispersed in a number of locations. Included are documents of a wide-ranging historical investigation: the fine arts, in most all aspects, philosophy and religion, science and technology, civil rights including women and the aging, journalism, sports and recreation, and ethnic minorities, particularly native Americans, blacks, Chicanos, and Asian Americans (500).

San Francisco African American Historical and Cultural Society, San Francisco. Transcripts of interviews with early black residents of San Francisco who were in the city before 1940 (25). Copies in San Francisco Public Library.

San Francisco Public Library, Archives, San Francisco. Transcripts of Afro-Americans in San Francisco before World War II (24), transcripts relating to San Francisco persons and issues produced by Regional Oral History Office, UC Berkeley. Some branches of the S. F. Public Library hold tapes about their neighborhoods.

San Francisco Study Center, San Francisco. Tapes and some transcripts of interviews with San Francisco residents, focused on life in the city's many neighborhoods (100). Black and white photos of each interviewee.

San Joaquin County Historical Museum, Lodi. Tapes of interviews with San Joaquin county residents, many descendants of pioneer families, on all facets of county and family history (52).

San Mateo County Historical Association, San Mateo. Tapes of interviews covering various aspects of county history, including the College of San Mateo (9), Half Moon Bay (1), San Mateo public schools (4), Volunteer Service Organization (1), Burlingame railroad station (2), Indian culture (1), Redwood City, fire warden (6), general county history (3); and tapes of various public programs and meetings, some given by the San Mateo County Historical Association (23).

Santa Barbara Historical Society, Santa Barbara. Collection includes county history and documents the period from 1900 to the present. Some interviews are transcribed (140).

Santa Clara University Archives, Santa Clara. Tapes covering SCU student life, 1906-1911 (1), 1915-1917 (1); 1928-1933 (5); women at SCU 1961-1970 (2); B. R. Hubbard, SJ, 1931 (2); City of Santa Clara 1940-1960 (2); presidents of SCU, 1957-1975 (2). Transcripts of interviews with Japanese-American farmers in Santa Clara Valley, 1895-1945 (22);

interviews with Japanese Americans during World War II, covering immigration and war experiences (14).

Sausalito Historical Society, Sausalito. Tapes and a few transcripts covering recollections of Sausalito (36).

Sequoia and Kings Canyon National Parks, Three Rivers. Tapes covering Three Rivers and Sequoia National Park history, local people, army and civilian administration of the parks, Kaweah Colony, Mt. Whitney Power Company, CCC, Mineral King mining history and logging history, all covering 1873-1973 time period (28); creation and expansion of Sequoia National Park, early park history and grazing history, covering time period 1900-1940 (4).

Shasta College Museum and Research Center, Redding. Tapes and transcripts covering life in Shasta, Tehama, and Trinity counties, Wintu Indian life; farming; mining; logging (115).

Sierra History Sites Association, Oakhurst. Tapes and some transcripts covering ranching, 1855-1920 (5); lumbering, 1850-1932 (13); railroading, 1872-1942 (3); mining, 1850-1914 (4); family history 1850-1920 (13); ethnic groups (Indian, Chinese, Mexican), 1850-1920 (8); Raymond granite quarry, late 1800s (1); John Muir and Frenchman trails, 1869 (2); schools, 1850-1920 (4); Eastern Madera County history (12).

Siskiyou County Library, Yreka. Taped interviews with longtime local residents, topics ranging from apple growing to mining and interviewees ranging from Indians to postmistress (25).

Sisters of Mercy, Burlingame. Tapes of interviews with Sisters of Mercy concerning their lives and work in California and Arizona, 1906-present (59).

Sisters of Notre Dame de Namur, California Province Archives, Belmont. Tapes of life history interviews with Sisters of Notre Dame de Namur (50).

A. K. Smiley Library, Redlands. This program, along with others in Ontario, Upland, and Riverside, has not only recorded the community history of the Inland Empire, but has also investigated certain natural regional phenomena such as the many disastrous fires, floods, and windstorms that frequently occur here; it is well adapted to oral history. Interviews have been conducted about the Kaiser Steel Corporation's Fontana plant and its influences on nearby communities. Water resources and irrigation, especially important to this area, have received attention, as have the decline of the citrus industry, the penetration of urbanization, and the concomitant problems of the coming of the freeways. Its local history program has included interviews with community leaders and reformers, as well as a study of the development of early telephone communication in the San Bernardino hinterlands (57).

Sourisseau Academy for State and Local History, San Jose State University. Tapes covering American-Scandinavian ethnic heritage; tapes and a few transcripts on early Sunnyvale industry, 1908–1956 (50).

South San Francisco History Room, Grand Avenue Branch, San Francisco Public Library. Taped interviews with early South San Francisco families, including information on families, work, schools, organizations, transportation, businesses, and houses (89); tapes of South San Francisco Historical Society tours and meetings (25); overview histories of banking, schools, newspapers, the post office in South San Francisco (4).

Stanford University Archives, Stanford. Tapes and many transcripts of Stanford University history, 1920–1985 (150); Women's Peace Oral History Project (30); Stanford University Archives Oral History collection, which includes tapes covering history of the *Aurora Collective* (campus feminist newspaper), or the California Center for International Studies, 1920–present, experiences of international students and faculty; and of Project South, 1965, experiences of civil rights activists (200). Cataloged in RLIN.

Stanislaus National Forest, Sonora. Tapes of interviews covering the history of Summit Ranger District, including information on railroad logging, forest service history, pioneer family history, ranger station history (24); tapes and many transcripts with many local residents (30).

University of California, Berkeley, Regional Oral History Offices, The Bancroft Library. Tapes and transcripts of oral histories with 900 prominent Californians in areas of agriculture, water resources, and land use; the arts; business and labor; conservation; law and politics; social history; University history, other topics (110,000 pages). In 1969, ROHO at UCB initiated the Earl Warren Era Project with the goal of interviewing individuals who were prominent in politics, state government administration, the legislature, and criminal justice during the period 1925–1953. By the time this project was completed in 1979, 145 people had been interviewed. Later projects on California political history have documented the gubernatorial eras of Goodwin J. Knight, Edmund G. "Pat" Brown, Sr., and Ronald Reagan. As part of this massive research and interviewing effort of more than 300 individuals active in state and national affairs, ROHO has collected significant papers, photographs, and memorabilia for deposit in The Bancroft Library to supplement the interview transcripts. These gubernatorial era projects, consolidated in the Government History Documentation Project (GHDP), have focused on persons in leadership positions around the state. The ROHO has also collected two volumes of interviews with persons involved in making and implementing the decision to relocate Japanese-American Californians during World War II, entitled *Decision and Exodus* (1976) and *The Internment* (1974). In addition, there are at least thirty-two tapes of interviews with Japanese Americans concerning the evacuation and relocation. Another collection, "Stockton Project," consists of sixty oral history interviews with women who emigrated to Stockton from Europe, Latin America, and Southeast Asia between 1920 and 1980. Excerpts have been published in *PH*, 26 (Summer 1986). The various ROHO collections are described in *Catalogue of the Regional Oral History Office*, The Bancroft Library, University of California (Berkeley, 1980).

University of California, San Francisco, Library, Special Collections, San Francisco. Tapes covering the history of practice of dentistry in the Bay Area, 1920-1968; history of the School of Nursing, UCSF, 1910-1960; history of the School of Medicine, 1900-1964; physician book collectors (65).

University of California, Santa Barbara, Library, Special Collections Department. Interviews on regional architecture; the Hope Ranch; Mission Santa Barbara; the local tile, marble, and petroleum industries; estates and gardening; the hotel business; and earthquakes (253).

University of California, Santa Cruz. Tapes and some transcripts covering Santa Cruz County history, 1900-1976 (101); UCSC history, 1961-present (81); astronomy and Lick Observatory, 1968-1983 (18); agriculture, 1964-1977 (53); lumbering, early 1900s (12); dairying, 1860-1930 (4); fishing, 1900-1972 (6); railroads, early 1900s (1); blacksmithing, ca. 1900 (10); U.S. history, 1900-1942 (27).

University of California, Los Angeles. Oral history collection housed in the University Research Library's Department of Special Collections is the product of a number of disparate collecting activities. Starting in 1950 the library generated interviews documenting California library history, the history of Inyo County, and the community of Duarte. In the 1960s the Oral History Program started building its collection and assembling copies of interviews of the UCB program through an interview exchange arrangement. In 1962 the Japanese American Research Project began interviewing Issei, Nisei, and others involved in wartime relocation (described in *Asian American Library Resources at UCLA* [Los Angeles, 1980], compiled by Kimberly Kanatani). Theater Arts faculty Professors Ralph Freud, Arthur B. Friedman, and Howard Suber developed interviewing projects on the local motion picture and television industries. Friedman also conducted a series of interviews, "Prison Record," on the prisons at Folsom, Chino, and San Quentin and their administration. In addition, the department received copies of interviews on forest history and conservation conducted by the San Francisco Sierra Club. While many of the interviews are in transcript form, with original sound recordings available, the Japanese American Research Project's interviews have not been transcribed. From its inception, the UCLA program has been library based and archivally oriented, articulating the University Library's collection development policies. Much of its documentation has been generated by the program staff and is frequently supplemented by video documentation and personal papers of those interviewed. The UCLA program is described in *The UCLA Oral History Program*, compiled by Constance C. Bullock with the assistance of Saundra Taylor (Los Angeles, 1982). Its major collecting strengths are the arts, including a special project on the greater Los Angeles Art Community; water resources and the Los Angeles Metropolitan Water District; social action and reform; printing and bookselling; and UCLA history. The catalog describes the individual interviews (over 250) and indicates those that are supplemented by personal papers and brief videotaped sessions. There is a special section listing contributed interviews which contain series on the Los Angeles International Airport, history of photography, the California Democratic Council, the black community of Allensworth, and miscellaneous regional history (1000).

University of California, Los Angeles Brain Research Institute, Los Angeles. The Institute has also collected the history of its own development, and of the progress of neuroscience in California. The interview transcripts and recordings are available at the Brain Research Institute, UCLA Center for Health Sciences (187 audio, 2 video).

University of Southern California, Los Angeles. USC oral history is retained in the Library's Special Collections Department and at a number of other campus locations. The Special Collections holds about thirty-seven interviews on California literature and politics. Regional motion picture history is a particular strength that includes nearly 1,000 interviews, the product of collecting by the aborted Hollywood (Motion Picture) Museum project and classroom projects supervised by Professor Arthur Knight. The Arnold Schoenberg Institute has conducted interviews to supplement its archival holdings of the personal and professional papers assembled on the musician and composer who was a longtime southern California resident. The School of Religion has interviewed nearly 100 Armenian Californians, mostly in regions outside of Fresno (1500).

Western Jewish History Center of the Judah L. Magnes Museum, Berkeley. Tapes and transcripts from primarily three projects: San Francisco Jews of European Origin, 1880–1940 (101); California Jewish Community Series (130); Bay Area Jews from Harbin, Manchuria (17). Printed catalog, *Western Jewish History Center: Archival and Oral History Collections*, 1986.

As this brief survey suggests, regional oral history's focus has been somewhat limited and sometimes repetitive. The citrus and motion picture industries are examples of considerable documentation. There are generous archival holdings of oral history interviews on oranges and film. There has also been a tendency, as elsewhere, to turn oral history loose on some recent trends of historical investigation that are contemporaries of the technique itself, for example, ethnic minorities, public, family, and women's history. Here it can shine, but the projects and programs often miss an opportunity to collect traditional source materials in the process.

Also, there are elusive oral history materials, hidden away and in danger of being lost to scholarship because not all of California's oral history has been collected by organized programs and preserved for future use. While increasing numbers of independent researchers have discovered the value of a tape recorder for the research, writing, and publication of regional history, after their work is in print, the residual by-products of tape-recorded interviews, notes, and other archival materials may simply languish away. Present tax laws do not encourage writers to donate their interviews to libraries or archives, but there are sound reasons for doing so. Evidence, oral or written, that forms the basis of historical research should be open to public scrutiny. Use of that evidence for a single work does not exhaust its value as a source for further research; the controlled environment of an archive to assure its preservation should take precedence over an attic, basement, or garage.

To bring more of California's oral history into view, the Southwest Oral History Association, a regional network within Southern California, Nevada, Arizona, and New Mexico, with support from the National Historical Publications and Records Commission and the California Council for the Humanities, is building at UCLA a computer database of Southwestern oral history. *Oral History Collections in the Southwest Region: A Directory and Subject Guide*, comp. by Cathryn A. Gallacher (Los Angeles, 1986), is the first product of this database. The 260-page publication consists of four sections listing collections, subjects, and two indices to oral history materials in the Southwest, with user instructions on accessing the database by computer. As it grows, many further hidden oral history resources will be identified and used. Their analysis will reveal subjects requiring further documentation. This cooperative approach to regional oral history will continue to broaden and deepen the contribution it can make to uncovering California's vibrant and diverse past.

Appendix I

CHRONOLOGY OF CALIFORNIA HISTORY

1510	First mention of a fictitious place called California in Montalvo's *Las Sergas de Esplandián.*
1533	Fortún Jiménez discovers Baja California.
1535	Hernando Cortés unsuccessfully colonizes Baja California.
1539	Francisco de Ulloa explores the coast of Baja California.
1540	Hernando de Alarcón reaches the Colorado River.
1542	Juan Rodríguez Cabrillo discovers San Diego Bay, the Channel Islands, Santa Monica Bay, and sails as far north as Monterey Bay.
1543	Cabrillo dies of injuries and is buried on one of the Channel Islands; second-in-command, Bartholomé Ferrelo, assumes command and sails as far north as the 42° parallel, California's northern border.
1565	Andrés de Urdaneta discovers a return route from the Philippines and inaugurates the Manila Galleon trade.
1579	Francis Drake careens his vessel, later named the *Golden Hind*, in a California bay and claims the land for Queen Elizabeth I.
1584	Francisco de Gali discovers the Japanese current which sweeps Manila galleons along the upper reaches of California's northern coast.
1587	Pedro de Unamuno enters Morro Bay.
1595	Sebastian Rodríguez Cermeno, commanding a Manila galleon, anchors in Drake's Bay where his ship, the *San Agustin*, is wrecked; he builds the *San Buenaventura*, a launch, and returns with seventy men to Navidad in New Spain (Mexico).

1602   Sebastian Vizcaíno, sailing from the west coast of Mexico, visits the bays of San Diego, San Pedro, and Monterey.

1613   Juan de Torquemada popularizes the view that California is an island in his book, *Monarquía Indiana*.

1628   The first account of California in English is published in *The World Encompassed by Sir Francis Drake*.

1697   Juan María Salvatierra, a Jesuit, founds the Pious Fund which makes possible the colonization of Baja California and the founding of the first mission at Loreto.

1701   The intrepid Jesuit missionary-explorer, Eusebio Francisco Kino, crosses the Colorado River into California, proving that Baja California is a peninsula and California not an island.

1757   Miguel Venegas publishes the first detailed account of the Californias in his *Noticas de la California*.

1765   José de Gálvez is appointed the first Visitor General to New Spain.

1768   While on a tour of inspection in Baja California, Gálvez decides on the colonization of Alta California to thwart a rumored southward thrust by the Russians out of Unalaska.

1769   The Sacred Expedition under the overall command of Gaspar de Portolá pushes north overland from Baja California, while two vessels approach by the sea; Father Junípero Serra, designated president of the Alta California missions, founds the first mission at San Diego; Portolá founds the first presidio.

1770   Serra founds Mission San Carlos at Monterey; Portolá designates the second presidio site; departs for New Spain leaving Pedro Fages as the military commandant.

1771   Missions San Antonio and San Gabriel are founded by Serra; Felipe de Bari is appointed governor of the Californias.

1774   Juan Bautista de Anza travels overland from Tubac, Sonora, to Mission San Gabriel; Fernando de Rivera y Moncada succeeds Fages as military commandant and Felipe de Neve assumes the governorship; Juan Perez sails northward from Monterey to about 55°, the northern extremity of Queen Charlotte's Island.

1775   Bruno Hecata and Juan Perez on a second expedition sail along the Pacific Slope as far north as 49° and discover the Columbia River and, in northern California, Trinidad Bay; Anza leads a second overland expedition of 240 colonists, 165 mules, 304 horses, and 302 cattle; Juan Manuel de Ayala, commanding the *San Carlos*, explores San Francisco Bay.

1776   Mission San Francisco de Asis (Dolores) and San Juan Capistrano are established; third presidio is founded at San Francisco; a trail is blazed overland from Santa Fe to the Colorado River by Padres Silvestre Escalante and Francisco Dominguez.

1777   Felipe de Neve designates Monterey the capital of the Californias; Mission Santa Clara is founded. On November 29 the first pueblo or town is established at San José de Guadalupe.

1779   Governor de Neve issues a *Reglamento*, a series of laws, which are approved two years later by the King of Spain.

1781   The Yuma Massacre closes overland contact to California until the late 1820s; a second pueblo is founded, La Reina de los Angeles.

1782   Mission San Buenaventura and the Santa Barbara presidio are founded; Pedro Fages becomes governor; Father Juan Crespí, companion to Fathers Serra and Francisco Palóu, California's first and most extensive diarist, dies and is buried at Mission San Carlos (Carmel).

1784   Junípero Serra dies at Mission San Carlos and is buried beside his friend Crespí; first three land grants are conferred by the Spanish government in southern California.

1785   Fermín Francisco de Lasuén succeeds as president of the Alta California missions.

1786   Mission Santa Barbara is founded; Jean François Galoup de la Pérouse, commanding the French frigates *Boussole* and *Astrolabe*, visits Monterey for ten days.

1787   Mission La Purísima Concepcíon is founded; Palóu's *Life of Serra* is published.

1790   Miguel Costansó's *Diario* of the Portolá expedition, published in Mexico in 1770, is published in London as *An Historical Journal of the Expeditions, by Sea and Land, to the North of California*, the first such eyewitness account.

1791   Missions Santa Cruz and Soledad are founded. José Antonio Roméu is appointed governor; the exploring expedition under command of Alejandro Malaspina visits Monterey.

1792   José Joaquín de Arrillaga assumes governorship on the death of Roméu; Capt. George Vancouver, commanding the *Discovery*, calls at San Francisco, his first of three California coastal visits, 1793–1794.

1794   Diego de Borica succeeds to the governorship, taking up residence in Loreto.

1809   Russian-American Fur Company establishes an outpost at Bodega Bay which leads to the building of Fort Ross in 1812.

1812   "The Year of the Earthquakes" greatly damages Missions San Juan Capistrano, San Gabriel, Santa Barbara, La Purísima, Santa Inés, San Buenaventura, and San Fernando.

1814   José Dario Argüello becomes interim governor on Arrillaga's death; John Gilroy becomes the first non-Hispanic settler.

1815   Pablo Vicente Solá becomes governor.

1816   Otto von Kotzebue, commanding the Russian expedition sailing on the *Rurik*, visits San Francisco; three members of the expedition subsequently write books of their experiences; a sailor, Thomas Doak, becomes first American settler.

1817   Luís Argüello explores the Sacramento and San Joaquin rivers; Mission San Rafael is established.

1818   A French privateer, Hypolyte Bouchard, commanding two frigates, captures and loots Monterey, followed by raids near Santa Barbara and at San Juan Capistrano.

1820   California's non-Indian population numbers about 3,300.

1821   Mexico gains independence from Spain; Luís Argüello explores the upper reaches of the Sacramento Valley.

1822   Iturbide becomes emperor of Mexico; California holds its first general election at Monterey; new provincial government is formed and the first legislature is elected and installed at Monterey.

1823   Luís Argüello, a native son, becomes California's first elected governor; Mission San Francisco Solano becomes the twenty-first and last of the missions to be founded by the Franciscans.

1824   Iturbide is replaced by a Mexican republic; a major Indian uprising takes place at Santa Inés, La Purísima, and Santa Barbara; Mexican Congress enacts a liberal land policy to encourage colonization both by Mexicans and foreigners.

1825   José María de Echeandía is appointed governor.

1826   Agustín Vicente Zamorano, using wood blocks, executes first printing; British expedition under command of Capt. Frederick W. Beechey, RN, on H.M.S. *Blossom*, explores and maps San Francisco Bay, later other coastal ports.

1827   Echeandía begins the secularization of the missions; Jedediah Smith leads the first American overland party of trappers into southern California.

1828   Smith returns overland with trapper party and travels back via the coastal route, a winter at Fort Vancouver before rejoining his fur-trade partners at the annual rendezvous in 1829; a trapper band under James Ohio Pattie arrives and spends two years, mostly in confinement.

1829   First California revolt, led by Joaquín Solís, fails.

1830   Manuel Victoria becomes governor only to be forced from office by a revolt led by three native sons, Pico, Bandini, and Castro.

1831   Echeandía becomes interim governor.

1833   José Figueroa becomes governor; Joseph R. Walker and Zenas Leonard lead first party of white men through the Sierra Nevada; the first party of Franciscan friars from the College of Zacatecas arrives from Mexico; secularization of the missions is ordered.

1834   Mission secularization is officially promulgated; first printing press is introduced by Zamorano; the Padrés and Híjar party of Mexican colonists, numbering some 200, including skilled artisans, arrives from Mexico.

1835   Figueroa issues his *Manifesto*; in death, he is succeeded briefly by José Castro; an Englishman, William A. Richardson, becomes first settler in Yerba Buena, the future San Francisco; Los Angeles is raised to the legal status of a *cuidad* (city).

1836   First vigilance committee formed in Los Angeles, which puts to death a man and woman for the murder of her husband; revolt led by Juan Bautista Alvarado and José Castro succeeds; Alvarado is made governor. Richard Henry Dana, a sailor on the *Pilgrim*, completes his California stay and returns to the east coast.

1839   Russians abandon Fort Ross; John Augustus Sutter, later to found New Helvetia (Sutter's Fort) at present-day Sacramento, immigrates.

1840   The non-Indian population reaches 6,000; Dana's classic, *Two Years Before the Mast*, is published; the Graham Affair leads to arrest of some three dozen Anglos; Garcia Diego y Moreno is consecrated first Catholic bishop of California.

1841   First parties of American overland pioneers arrive, the Bidwell-Bartleson party via the central route, the Workman-Rowland party via the Old Spanish Trail; the U.S. expedition under Lieut. Charles Wilkes, USN, calls at San Francisco with an overland party pushing south from Fort Vancouver (Portland).

1842   Gold is discovered in Placerita Canyon near Los Angeles; Manuel Micheltorena becomes governor; Mexico sequesters the Pious Fund; Com. Thomas Ap Catesby Jones, USN, occupies Monterey briefly.

1843   Thomas Oliver Larkin is appointed U.S. consul, assumes duties next year.

1844   The Stevens-Murphy party of overland pioneers arrives; Capt. John C. Frémont leads his first overland expedition into California.

1845   Revolt led by Alvarado and Castro overthrows Micheltorena and sends him and his troops back to Mexico; Pío Pico becomes governor; Frémont returns on second expedition.

1846   Juan María Flores becomes last governor under Mexican rule; Mexican War commences; Bear Flag Revolt is led by Americans under William B.

Ide, aided by Frémont; California is occupied by U.S. naval forces and the flag raised on July 6; Commodore Robert B. Stockton becomes military governor of occupied California; Sam Brannan arrives with Mormon colonists in San Francisco; Battle of San Pasqual sets back General Stephen W. Kearny's military contingent; first newspaper is published in Monterey, the *Californian*.

1847   A shortlived *Californio* insurgency is broken; Los Angeles is reoccupied; insurgents sign the articles of capitulation at Rancho Cahuenga (near present-day Hollywood Bowl); the New York Volunteers arrive by ship, the Mormon Battalion via the southern route.

1848   James W. Marshall discovers gold at Sutter's Miller at Coloma; nine days later Mexico signs the Treaty of Guadalupe Hidalgo, selling the Mexican Cession, including all of California, to the United States for $15 million; President James K. Polk authenticates the validity of the gold discovery.

1849   Gold seekers flock to the mines; non-Indian population mushrooms to over 100,000; General Bennet Riley, the last military governor, organizes a convention in Monterey; it swiftly moves to draft a constitution and seek statehood; state government is formed; San José is first capital.

1850   California admitted as the thirty-first state to the Union; first twenty-seven counties are formed; Yosemite is discovered; incorporation of cities begins; Peter H. Burnett is elected first state governor.

1851   San Francisco Vigilance Committee is formed; the universities of Santa Clara (Jesuit) and Pacific (Protestant) are established; Congress creates the U.S. Land Commission to adjudicate land claims; California Homestead Act is passed.

1852   Special state census tallies 255,000 population; Wells Fargo is founded; *Golden Era*, the first magazine, is published.

1854   Sacramento is made capital after various other sites served in the intervening years.

1856   Second San Francisco Vigilance Committee hangs Casey and Cora.

1857   State Normal School system is founded; Theodore P. Judah outlines plans for a transcontinental railroad.

1858   Butterfield Overland Stage begins operations.

1860   First rider for the Pony Express reaches San Francisco; at the end of year the city is connected to Los Angeles by telegraph; population rises to 380,000; Civil War crisis looms.

1862   San Francisco sees first Normal School; telegraph connects state to the east; first oil field is discovered at Ojai.

1863   Frederick F. Low becomes the state's first four-year governor after amendment of the constitution; construction begins on the first transcontinental railroad, the Central Pacific.

1864   State parks system is established.

1865   Southern Pacific Railroad is founded.

1868   The University of California, Berkeley, is established.

1869   First transcontinental railroad is completed at Promontory Point, Utah.

1870   Population totals 560,247.

1871   The Chinese massacre occurs in Los Angeles; California Historical Society is founded (revived in 1922).

1872   Modoc Indian War breaks out, last to be fought in California.

1877   Anti-Chinese movement is spearheaded by the Workingmen's party under Denis Kearney. First trainload of oranges is shipped to St. Louis.

1879   Second Constitutional Convention occurs; University of Southern California is founded.

1880   Population is 864,694.

1881   State Normal School, later UCLA, is founded in Los Angeles; Southern Pacific Railroad transcontinental link is completed.

1883   Historical Society of Southern California is chartered.

1885   Santa Fe Railroad reaches Los Angeles, third transcontinental link; first trainload of southern California oranges reaches eastern markets.

1886   Hubert H. Bancroft's *History of California* begins to be published (7 vols.; completed in 1890). Railroad competition brings some 200,000 new residents.

1888   First black mayor is elected in Wheatland, Edward P. Duplex.

1890   Population is 1,213,398; Yosemite and Sequoia National Parks are founded.

1891   Stanford University opens; Throop Institute, later California Institute of Technology, is established.

1892   Hydro-electric industry is founded in southern California.

1895   California establishes a Bureau of Highways.

1900   Population reaches 1,485,052.

1902   Laying of a Pacific cable begins.

1903   Los Angeles adopts the initiative, referendum, and recall petitions in new city charter.

1905   California Fruit Growers Association (Sunkist) is organized.

1906   Occurrence of the disastrous San Francisco earthquake and fire.

1907   San Francisco graft trials begin; construction on the Owens Valley

Aqueduct begins; Lincoln-Roosevelt League is formed to reform state government.

1908   First motion picture is made in Los Angeles. Glenn L. Martin starts aircraft manufacturing in Santa Ana.

1909   Direct primary is adopted, ending the reign of boss control by the Southern Pacific Railroad.

1910   Population reaches 2,377,549; first community (junior) college opens; infamous bombing of the Los Angeles *Times* occurs; Dominguez Air Race, the first public air meet, is held.

1911   Hiram Johnson is inaugurated as a reform governor; state adopts the use of initiative, referendum, and recall petitions; woman's suffrage is approved; first studio in Hollywood opens.

1912   Governor Johnson runs as vice president on Bull Moose ticket.

1913   California Land Act is passed, aimed at Japanese ownership of land; Los Angeles Aqueduct opens.

1915   Panama-Pacific International Exposition opens; Panama-California Expedition occurs; first transcontinental telephone call is made.

1916   Preparedness Day Parade bombing occurs in San Francisco; talking pictures are patented and demonstrated in Hollywood.

1917   Hiram Johnson is elected to U.S. Senate.

1920   Population is 3,426,861; Los Angeles becomes largest city in the state, surpassing San Francisco; shift in population base to southern California leads to long political struggle over reapportionment.

1921   Beginning with Signal Hill near Long Beach, numerous rich oil fields are brought in during the 1920s in southern California; prohibition is enacted.

1923   Colorado River Compact is approved.

1924   First airmail is flown from San Francisco to New York; first circumnavigation of the globe by airplane from Santa Monica, takes six months.

1927   Philo T. Farnsworth transmits first television picture; the first talking picture, "The Jazz Singer," is produced in Hollywood; by constitutional amendment, state adopts the federal plan to end reapportionment stalemate; California is ranked first in petroleum production.

1928   St. Francis Dam collapses, resulting in over 400 deaths; daily passenger airflights between San Francisco and Los Angeles begin.

1930   Population reaches 5,677,102; Los Angeles soars to 1.2 million.

1931   Voters approve the Metropolitan Water District bond issue.

1932   Los Angeles hosts the Tenth Olympiad.

1933   Long Beach earthquake occurs; Townsend Plan is proclaimed; construction on Colorado River Aqueduct begins; sales tax is enacted.

1934   Upton Sinclair mounts the EPIC campaign for governorship; Frank Merriam is elected; San Francisco General Strike occurs.

1935   Transpacific airmail service begins, followed by passenger flights to Honolulu the next year; Boulder Dam (now Hoover) is completed.

1936   San Francisco–Oakland Bay Bridge opens.

1937   Golden Gate Bridge opens.

1938   Ham 'n Eggs plan becomes focal point of political debate.

1939   Culbert L. Olson, first Democratic governor since 1899, is elected; brings New Deal to California.

1940   Population reaches 6,907,387.

1942   Japanese residents are relocated as a World War II measure.

1943   Earl Warren is elected governor; becomes the first in that office to be re-elected for two additional terms; All American Canal is completed.

1945   United Nations is founded in San Francisco.

1946   Richard M. Nixon is elected to Congress.

1947   The ordeal of the Hollywood Ten launches the national Communist (Red) scare; Los Angeles County Air Pollution Control District organized.

1949   Loyalty Oath controversy in the University of California system occurs.

1950   Population reaches 10.6 million; Los Angeles, 1,970,358; Levering Act is passed; Nixon is elected to U.S. Senate.

1952   Nixon, running with Eisenhower, is elected vice president.

1953   Warren is appointed Chief Justice of the U.S. (serves to 1969); Goodwin J. Knight succeeds as governor.

1956   Cross-filing in primary elections is abolished.

1958   Edmund G. Brown, Sr., is elected governor; San Francisco Giants and Los Angeles Dodgers bring major league baseball to the state.

1960   Population, 15,717,204; Los Angeles, 2.5 million; Master Plan for Higher Education is introduced; Nixon is defeated for presidency; California Aqueduct is begun.

1962   California becomes the most populous state in the Union; Nixon loses gubernatorial race to incumbent Brown.

1963   Rumford Fair Housing Act is passed.

1964   Free Speech Movement begins on the UC Berkeley campus.

1965   The Watts Riots erupt.

1966   United Farm Workers movement begins under Cesar Chavez; Ronald W. Reagan is elected governor.

1967   Levering Act (loyalty oath) is declared unconstitutional.

1968   Robert F. Kennedy is assassinated in Los Angeles; Nixon is elected president; first nuclear powered generating plant opens at San Onofre.

1970   Population, 19,953,134; Los Angeles, 2.8 million.

1974   Edmund G. Brown, Jr., is elected governor; March Fong Eu becomes first woman and Asian elected to statewide office.

1976   Brown and former Governor Reagan vie unsuccessfully for the presidential nomination of the Democratic and Republican parties respectively.

1977   California Agricultural Relations Act is adopted.

1978   Proposition 13, limiting property tax, is approved by voters.

1980   Population totals 23,667,947; Reagan is elected president.

1982   George Deukmejian is elected governor over Tom Bradley, the black mayor of Los Angeles.

1984   Reagan is re-elected president; Twenty-first Olympiad hosted by Los Angeles.

1986   Three State Supreme Court justices, including Chief Justice Elizabeth Rose Bird, fail voter confirmation; Deukmejian is re-elected governor, again defeating Tom Bradley.

1987   California's total merchandise export reaches $28 billion.

Appendix II

REFERENCES TO LISTS OF ORGANIZATIONS WITH SPECIAL INTEREST IN CALIFORNIA HISTORY

The American Association for State and Local History sponsors the publication of a *Directory of Historical Societies and Agencies in the United States and Canada* (Nashville, 1987). The current volume, the thirteenth edition, compiled and edited by Betty Pease Smith, lists California societies and agencies, alphabetically arranged by place of city locations for each entry. This invaluable reference is periodically updated by the AASLH. Each entry provides information as to address, phone, hours, holdings, staff, and usually names of the presidents or directors. The latter are usually continuously out-of-date, so this is not a reliable reference for personal contact. It is always best to write ahead to any such society/agency to check on public service hours and/or the need for a specific appointment. A letter directed to either the director or librarian will usually do the trick. Copies of the directory are available from the AASLH, 172 Second Avenue North, Suite 102, Nashville, TN 37201. Since it is expensive, try your local large library reference desk.

Annually, the California Conference of Historical Societies publishes a current and up-to-date list. The list provides addresses, phone numbers, and usually a contact person. Any current list can be had for a nominal charge by placing your request to the CCHS, University of the Pacific, Stockton, CA 95211. Telephone: (209) 946-2169.

A third helpful list is published occasionally by CCHS, which lists in alphabetical order a *Directory of California Genealogical Societies and Family Organizations*, compiled by Marie E. Northrop. The present list, published in 1983, can be obtained from the CCHS for a modest cost.

INDEX

ABOUT THE
CONTRIBUTORS

MICHAEL ANDERSON received a B.A. from the University of North Carolina at Chapel Hill and attended graduate school at George Mason University in Fairfax, Virginia. He began his career with the National Archives in 1974; became an archivist at the National Archives–Los Angeles Branch in 1979; served as director of the National Archives–San Francisco Branch, 1983-1986; and is currently with the National Archives Office of Federal Records Center, Washington, D.C.

FRANCISCO E. BALDERRAMA is associate professor of Chicano Studies and History at California State University (CSU), Los Angeles, where he also serves as chairperson for the Department of Chicano Studies. He received advanced degrees in history at UCLA and has conducted extensive research in Mexico. He has written *In Defense of La Raza: the Los Angeles Mexican Consulate and Mexican Community, 1929-1936* (Tucson, 1982) and has contributed various articles to scholarly publications.

GUNTHER BARTH studied at the University of Cologne, University of Oregon, and Harvard University, where he received his Ph.D. in 1962. He teaches cultural history at the University of California, Berkeley (UCB). Among his publications are: *Bitter Strength: A History of Chinese in the United States, 1850-1870* (Cambridge, Mass., 1964); *Instant Cities: Urbanization and the Rise of San Francisco and Denver* (New York, 1975); and *City People: The Rise of Modern City Culture in Nineteenth Century America* (New York, 1980).

WILLA BAUM directs the Regional Oral History Office at UCB. She played a major role in developing the technique of oral history with *Oral History for the*

Local Historical Society (Nashville, 1971) and *Transcribing and Editing Oral History* (Nashville, 1977), both published by the American Association for State and Local History. She is co-editor of *Oral History: An Interdisciplinary Anthology* (Nashville, 1984).

JOHN E. BAUR received his Ph.D. from UCLA in 1951. He has taught at CSU, Northridge, since 1964. In addition to over forty articles, he has published four books on Western American history, including *The Health Seekers* (San Marino, 1959).

PETER J. BLODGETT has been an assistant curator of Western Historical Manuscripts at the Huntington Library since August 1985. Before joining the staff, he was a graduate student in Western history at Yale University, where he received his M.A. and M.Phil. degrees.

JOHN PORTER BLOOM has taught at universities in New Mexico, Oregon, Washington, D.C., Georgia, and Texas. He has also worked as a museum planner and editor of a number of studies, including two volumes of *The Territorial Papers of the United States* (Washington, D.C., 1971) and *The American Territorial System* (Columbus, 1973). From 1981 to 1984 he was director, Holt-Atherton Center for Western Studies, University of the Pacific, and editor, *The Pacific Historian*.

PAUL BULLOCK was for many years research economist with the Institute of Industrial Relations at UCLA. He authored many articles and books, among them a biography of Jerry Voorhis, former southern California congressman, as well as studies of minority youth in the labor market. He served as a consultant to numerous commissions, notably the 1965 McCone Commission and the 1967 Kerner Commission in California. Shortly after retirement, he died in 1986.

LARRY E. BURGESS received his B.A. from the University of Redlands and a Ph.D. in history from the Claremont Graduate School. Since 1972 he has served as archivist and head of special collections for the A. K. Smiley Public Library in Redlands. He also serves as adjunct associate professor in the Graduate Program in Historical Resources Management at UC, Riverside. He has published a number of articles, reviews, and books on California and the history of the West.

ANNE CAIGER is Manuscripts Librarian at UCLA. She holds a B.A. in history, a diploma in Archive Administration from the University of London, and worked as an archivist in England, Jamaica, and Canada before she became an assistant curator (English Manuscripts) at the Huntington Library in 1970. Since 1975, she has served as Historical Manuscripts Librarian and University Archivist at UCLA, before appointment to her present position in 1985.

LAWRENCE B. DE GRAAF is professor of history at CSU, Fullerton. He is the author of several articles on Western black history appearing in the *Pacific Historical Review*, as well as a number of pieces on public history appearing in *The Public Historian*. He has written numerous reviews and contributed to surveys and anthologies in black and public history.

IRIS H. W. ENGSTRAND received her B.A., M.A., and Ph.D. in history from USC. She is professor and chair of the Department of History, University of San Diego. She is author of numerous articles, reviews, and monographs including *Spanish Scientists in the New World: The Eighteenth Century Expeditions* (Seattle, 1981).

WILLIAM P. FRANK has been at the Huntington Library since July 1983 as assistant curator of Hispanic and Western Historical Manuscripts. He has taught at UCLA, Kansas State University, and CSU, Northridge, and was an editor for the UCLA Latin American Center. He completed his Ph.D. in Spanish history at UCLA in 1981.

DONALD TERUO HATA, JR., is professor of history at CSU, Dominguez Hills, and vice president of the California Historical Society.

NADINE ISHITANI HATA is dean of the Division of Behavioral and Social Sciences, professor of history at El Camino College, and former chair of the California State Historical Resources Commission.

Don and Nadine Hata received their doctorates in history at USC. Their numerous co-authored publications include *Japanese Americans and World War II* (St. Charles, Mo., 1974; 5th printing, 1981) and "Asian and Pacific Americans: Still Strangers in Their Own Land," *American History and Culture: A Reader*, Joseph Collier, ed. (Los Alamitos, Calif., 1977).

LILACE HATAYAMA holds a B.A. and an M.A. in history from UCLA. Since 1974 she has worked in the UCLA Department of Special Collections as exhibits coordinator and assistant with literary and historical manuscripts. She has published numerous articles on literary collections and related exhibits in UCLA Library publications.

GARY F. KURUTZ, director, Special Collections Branch, California State Library, has also served as Sutro Librarian, director of the California Historical Society Library, and curator of Rare Books and Photography at the Huntington Library. His publications include numerous articles on library collections and California history as well as a biography on Benjamin C. Truman.

DAN LUCKENBILL holds a B.A. in English from UCLA. He has worked at UCLA Library since 1970, for many years as senior manuscripts (primarily historical) and archives assistant. He has researched and mounted exhibits and written, edited, or contributed to numerous library publications on topics in literature, university history, California art, etc.

JAMES V. MINK, a specialist in California and Western American history, received his graduate degrees at UCLA and American University, Washington, D.C. He has served at the Bancroft Library and in the UCLA Library's Department of Special Collections, where he served as historical manuscripts librarian, department head, university archivist, and director of the oral history program. He has published research guides, articles, and reviews as well as serving as the first president of the Society of Southern California Archivists and the founding chairman of the national Oral History Association.

DIANE S. NIXON received her B.S. in political science from CSU, Fullerton, and M.S. in Library Science from USC. She has served as head of the Acquisitions Department, Naval Post-graduate School, Monterey; as serials acquisitions librarian, UC, Santa Barbara; and chief of the appraisal and disposition section of the Los Angeles Records Center. Since 1984 she has been director of the National Archives–Los Angeles Branch.

KENNETH N. OWENS has degrees from Lewis and Clark College and the University of Minnesota. Since 1968 he has been at CSU, Sacramento, where he is professor of history and coordinator of the public history graduate program. He has recently contributed a chapter on the preservation and management of California's historic resources to a volume entitled *Cultural Resources Management* (Melbourne, Fla., 1986).

JACKSON K. PUTNAM received his Ph.D. from Stanford University (1964). He is a professor of history at CSU, Fullerton. His publications include *Old-Age Politics in California: From Richardson to Reagan* (Palo Alto, 1970) and *Modern California Politics* (2nd ed.; San Francisco, 1984).

JAMES J. RAWLS received a B.A. from Stanford University and a Ph.D. from UCB. Since 1975, he has been an instructor of history at Diablo Valley College, Pleasant Hill. He is the author of *Indians of California: The Changing Image* (Norman, 1984) and co-author of *California: An Interpretive History* (5th ed.; New York, 1988).

WILLIAM M. ROBERTS received his B.A. from CSU, San Jose, the M.A. and M.L.S. degrees from UCB. He has been associated in a variety of capacities with the Bancroft Library since 1966. Since 1984 he has served as university archivist for UCB.

SARAH SHARP is assistant professor of U.S. history and co-chair of a graduate program in public history at Bowling Green State University in Ohio. She received her B.A., M.A., and Ph.D. at UC, San Diego. Between 1978 and 1986 she was an interviewer-editor with the Regional Oral History Office at UCB.

DAVID L. SNYDER received his B.A. and M.A. in history from UC, Davis. Since 1964 he has been associated with the California State Archives, where he currently serves as Archivist II in charge of the Processing Section.

DANIEL TYLER graduated from Harvard College. He received his M.A. from Colorado State University and Ph.D. from the University of New Mexico. Since 1970 he has taught at CSU, San Diego. His most recent publication is *Sources for New Mexican History, 1821–1848* (Albuquerque, 1984).

DAVID S. ZEIDBERG is head of Special Collections at UCLA. He holds a M.S. in Library and Information Science and a M.A. in Medieval English Studies from Syracuse University, where he taught English literature and served as Rare Books Librarian from 1969 to 1975. In 1975 he became curator of Special Collections at George Washington University, Washington, D.C., where he served until coming to UCLA in 1984.

ABOUT THE EDITORS

DOYCE B. NUNIS, JR., is professor of history at USC. A prolific scholar in the history of California and the American West, he has authored and edited some three dozen books and numerous articles. Since 1962 he has been the editor of the *Southern California Quarterly*, the publication of the Historical Society of Southern California.

GLORIA RICCI LOTHROP is professor of history at CSU Polytechnic, Pomona. In addition to numerous articles and reviews, her publications include *Recollections of the Flathead Mission* (Glendale, 1978). She is co-author of *California Women: A History* (San Francisco, 1987) and *Pomona, A Centennial History* (Northridge, Calif., 1988).